The Battle of Adwa

THE BATTLE OF ADWA

REFLECTIONS ON ETHIOPIA'S HISTORIC VICTORY AGAINST EUROPEAN COLONIALISM

Edited by
Paulos Milkias
&
Getachew Metaferia

Contributors
Richard Pankhurst
Zewde Gabra-Selassie
Negussay Ayele
Harold Marcus
Theodore M. Vestal
Paulos Milkias
Getachew Metaferia
Maimire Mennasemay
Mesfin Araya

Algora Publishing
New York

www.algora.com

ISBN: 0-87586-413-9 (softcover)
ISBN: 0-87586-414-7 (hardcover)
ISBN: 0-87586-415-5 (ebook)

Library of Congress Cataloging-in-Publication Data —

The Battle of Adwa: reflections on Ethiopia's historic victory against European colonialism / edited by Paulos Milkias, Getachew Metaferia.

p. cm.

Includes bibliographical references and index.

ISBN 0-87586-413-9 (trade paper: alk. paper) — ISBN 0-87586-414-7 (hard cover: alk. paper) — ISBN 0-87586-415-5 (ebook)

1. Adwa, Battle of, Adwa, Ethiopia, 1896. I. Milkias, Paulos. II. Metaferia, Getachew.

DT387.3.B39 2005
963'.043—dc22

2005013845

Front Cover:

Printed in the United States

This book is dedicated to all peoples of the world who have stood up to colonial subjugation and courageously sacrificed their lives for the love of freedom and liberty

ETHIOPIA - 1890'S
Italian Claims
International Boundaries
Provincial Boundaries
Major Towns
AFRICA
ARABIA
RED SEA
YEMEN
ADEN
INDIAN OCEAN
SUDAN
ERITREA
MASAWA
DOGALI
KUFIT
ASMARA
GURA
GUNDET
AXUM
ADWA
DANKALIA
BEGEMDIR
METEMMA
GONDAR
MAQALE
ASAB
WALLO
MEQDELA
DESE
DJIBOUTI
BAHIR DAR
GOJAM
DEBRE MARQOS
DEBRE BERHAN
WALLAGA
SHOA
DIRE DAWA
HARAMAYA
AMBO
ADDIS ABABA
NAQAMTE
QELLEM
Dambi Dollo
HARAR
ARBA GUGU
JIJIGA
SOMALIA
Gambela
GORE
ILUBABOR
ASALA
ARSI
HARARGE
JIMMA
AGARO
KAFA
AWASA
GOBA
WALWAL
GAMU GOFA
BALE
SIDAMO
UGANDA
KENYA
SOMALIA
©2005 Paulos Milkias

Ethiopian Titles

Afe-Nigus — ("Mouthpiece of the Emperor") equivalent to the U.S. "Chief Justice."

Asiraleqa — ("Commander of 10") Corporal, as a military title.

Atse — Emperor.

BalambaRas — ("Commander of the Citadel") Commander, as a military title, and "Chevalier" as a civilian title.

Bejrond — An official responsible for state finance; equivalent to the British "Chancellor of the Exchequer" or the U.S. "Treasury Secretary."

Bitwoded — ("Beloved by the king") the highest non-royal title, ranks after "Ras" in precedence.

Dejazmach — ("Field commander") field commander, as a military title and "Earl" as a civilian title. This is just below "Bitwoded."

Fitawrarri — ("Commander of the Vanguard") As a military title, this is equivalent to "Chief of Staff of the Armed Forces" and in rank it is equivalent to "Ras." However, as a civilian title, it is equivalent to the British "Count" and is just next in importance to "Dejazmach."

Grazmatch — ("Commander of the Left Flank") A military title, equivalent to "Baron" as a civilian title, it follows "Kegnazmach" in importance.

Hamsaleqa — ("Commander of 50") Sergeant, as a military title.

Itege — Empress.

Kegnazmach — ("Commander of the Right Flank") A military title; "Marquess" as a civilian title, ranking next to "Fitawurari."

Leul — Prince.

Lielt — Princess.

Lij — ("Child") This title is reserved only for children of the nobility. For example, the Ethiopian Emperor preceding Haile Selassie (Iyasu) is historically referred to as "Lij Iyasu," because he was never crowned as "King of Kings."

Merid-Azmach — Commander, in the military sense, but in recent times this title was used exclusively by the princes. For example, Emperor Haile Selassie's eldest son Prince Asfa Wossen, who was the crown prince, was referred to as "Merid Azmach Asfa Wossen."

Mesfina — "Duke of..." As, for example, the title of Haile Selassie's second son, Prince Makonnen, who was referred to as "Mesfina Harar Makonnen" (meaning "Makonnen, Prince of Harar")

Metoaleqa — ("Commander of 100") This is equivalent to the military title of "Lieutenant."

Nigist — Queen

Nigus — King

Niguse Negest — King of Kings

Ras — ("Head") Equivalent to the British "Duke"

Shaleqa — ("Commander of 1000") A military title is equivalent to "Major."

Shambel — A military title equivalent to "Captain."

Woizero — Traditionally, this referred to an aristocratic lady; now, it is equivalent to Mrs.

Table of Contents

Preface

The Scramble in which the Europeans of the 19th century willfully subdivided Africa among themselves has not allowed the continent to follow its own natural course of cultural and political evolution. However, the speed of European conquest, the depth of its penetration and the magnitude of its control were not always dictated by the outsiders who were vying to exploit its resources. Through resistance, dramatically symbolized by the Battle of Adwa, Africa has also affected the politics of Europe and North America. This book is a starting point to reflect on that neglected fact. Africa was not simply a "dark continent" out there to be colonized, nor was it simply a necessary link in the inhuman triangular trade, with slavery at one end. It was — and is — also a land of defiance, victory, and pride. Our thanks to the many who share our view in this regard and who have encouraged us to publish this book.

Summary

The Adwa victory over European imperialism is an important event in the shared memory of the entire African population. Indeed, it is the only secular episode in the whole history of Africa that has been celebrated for more than a century with unabated popular enthusiasm.

A phenomenon such as Adwa is a complex nexus of various historical processes with wide-ranging but as yet not fully explored meanings. The contributors to this collection show that Adwa not only reflects its time but transcends it, and that the aspirations and meanings that flow from it have been a powerful constitutive force in the rise and evolution of modern Africa. Indeed, it is an event that awakened the hope for emancipation and fired the struggle against colonialism and racism among Africans in the colonies and in the diaspora.

In an effort to elucidate the diverse implications of this unique victory over colonialism, the texts assembled here analyze Adwa from various perspectives — diplomatic, historical, normative, cultural, political, and theoretical — and consider critically the event's significance to the understanding and the resolution of the grave problems that confront contemporary Africa.

The monograph charts new avenues of exploration of this momentous historical landmark and opens up new dimensions of investigation of the significance of Adwa for the present and the future of Ethiopia, Africa, and the African diaspora.

INTRODUCTION

If Adwa holds a significant place in Africa's history, it is because its meanings overflow the social and political conditions that made it possible and go beyond any relevance to its initial circumstances. The success at Adwa throws light on the normative dimensions of Ethiopian civilization; it challenges the demeaning Western conception of African cultures; it demonstrates that being targeted for colonization is not a prelude to fatality and that colonialism can be defeated; and, to Africans, it poses new political questions and sets novel historical tasks.

Interpreting such a momentous event inevitably raises formidable questions, both methodological and theoretical. However, the examination of these questions is not the primary objective of this collection. Rather, the texts assembled here explore the significance of the meanings that transcend Adwa and make it the watershed that marks Africa's, and particularly traditional Ethiopia's, entrance into the modern age.

Adwa is incontestably a complex nexus of events and narrations. It is said that each age writes its own history, not so much as to understand the past (though this certainly is an important objective) but to understand also how and why — of all the possible futures that the past could have given rise to — a particular future has become the concrete present we now inhabit. Contemporary Africa is dominated by ethnic politics and our quest to understand Adwa arises from a profound uneasiness with this present condition.

Ethiopians in particular are now embroiled in ethnic politics more than a century after a victory that was seen by many as the conclusive proof of the existence of an Ethiopian nation free from the kind of ethnic conflicts that characterize the Balkans and some other countries in the South. This emergence of ethnic politics is a challenge to our understanding of the present and of that event, Adwa, in which the present was incubated. Politics is in a very important way a mirror in which society sees itself and becomes conscious of itself. The current practice of ethnic politics reflects back an image incongruent with the national self-image that generations of Ethiopians have grown up with. It is thus imperative that we step back from the Adwa we have taken for granted and reexamine it in order to see in what sense and to what extent it could throw light on the contradictions between the historical consciousness of all Ethiopians and their current self-image as ethnic beings conveyed by the politics of the present regime.

To paraphrase an Ethiopian saying, a person who cannot draw sustenance from history is like a tree in a dry soil, which has to be watered every day. Such a person's fate is to live from day to day, blind to the past and to the future. This is a life emptied of humanity and dignity. To choose and build a future that is free from ethnicism and its transgressions of humanity and dignity, all Ethiopians and indeed all Africans need to know their past, not because the past determines the future, but rather because it can disclose the various options for the future that it points toward; and thus it awakens them to the possibilities of emancipation that gestate within it. To draw from history is not to make the future a prisoner of the past. Rather, it is to open the future to new possibilities of a better society; it is also to make possible an immanent critique of the present from the standpoint of a possible better future; it is to rediscover the present and future generations as subjects who make history — as the ones who can make these new possibilities come true. It is with the conviction that Ethiopian history is pregnant with and is thus open to the possibilities of building a free and just society that we are reexamining the momentous historical event of Adwa.

The text by Theodore Vestal introduces Adwa to those who are not familiar with its genesis and its implications for today, Paulos Milkias discuss the origins and outcomes of the battle. Dejazmach Zewde Gabre-Selassie explains the local, regional and international imperatives that impelled Menelik to confront a mighty European power. Then Negussay Ayele conducts a normative assessment of the behaviors of the adversaries. Getachew Metaferia examines the impact of Ethiopia's victory over colonialism on Africans both at home and in the diaspora; Richard Pankhurst considers the British reaction to the defeat of a European army by "a native force"; and Harold Marcus scrutinizes

European racist discourse about Ethiopia before and after Adwa. Mesfin Araya looks at contemporary Ethiopia in the context of the Battle of Adwa; and Maimire Mennasemay proposes that we rethink the significance of Adwa in the Third Millennium.

Theodore Vestal's introductory chapter, "Reflections on the Battle of Adwa and Its Significance for Today," is written for those who want to know what Adwa was and is and underscores the importance of the battle not only for the recognition of the sovereignty of Ethiopia but also for the preservation and extension of ancient Ethiopia, with the important exception of Eritrea. He argues that, as a meaningful negation of the colonial domination of Africa, Adwa procured for Ethiopia diplomatic and economic benefits and, for Ethiopians, a sense of national pride that was lost to other Africans.

Vestal evaluates then the present ethnic-based political system in light of the unity Ethiopians have historically achieved, and finds it wanting. He contends that the present regime's organization of the country on an ethnic basis is an implementation of the ethnic divide-and-rule policy designed by Italy to weaken Ethiopia in order to carry out her colonial project. The ethnic policy followed by the present ruling party — the Ethiopian People's Revolutionary Democratic Front (EPRDF), he argues, is detrimental to Ethiopia's progress, and he calls for the revival of the spirit of Adwa to defeat this new threat of ethnic disintegration.

Paulos Milkias' chapter scrutinizes the internal conditions in Italy which led her to covet Ethiopia as a colony. He notes that Italy was made up of mini-sovereign states until the Risorgimento, the unification of the Italian state, was achieved. By 1872, the reunified state, he argues, faced tremendous economic and social problems — lack of investment outlets, massive unemployment, poverty, and demographic pressures — and, the Italian ruling class embarked on colonial expansion as a solution to Italy's multiple crises. In this context, Italy's claim that Ethiopia was within her sphere of influence found receptive ears at the 1885 Berlin Conference.

The chapter examines the background to the Wuchalé Treaty, the machinations regarding the translation of Article 17, and how Count Antonelli willfully misled Menelik into believing that the Amharic and the Italian versions were identical. Milkias compares the original versions and points out the radical inconsistency between the two regarding the sovereignty of Ethiopia. He scrutinizes the various steps taken by the Negus to resolve the issue peacefully and shows how Menelik was forced to abrogate the Treaty in light of Italy's refusal to recognize the independence of Ethiopia as stipulated in the Amharic version. He then describes Italy's belligerent response to the abrogation of the Treaty, Menelik's preparation for war, the overall structure of the Ethiopian armed forces, and the armament available to them. He complements this with a discussion of the conduct and outcome of the battle.

Of additional interest are his reflections on the lessons of Adwa for contemporary Ethiopians. His analysis brings out Menelik's magnanimity in victory, which has to be put in the wider context of the Emperor's patient, open-minded and future-oriented way of dealing with his opponents, be they Ethiopians or foreigners. Paulos Milkias examines how steadfastly Menelik knitted a network of loyalties and allies by patiently creating areas of consent between rivals such as Ras Mengesha, Dejazmach Araya, and Ras Aregawi. The Emperor's ability as a consensus-builder, he argues, permitted him to defeat the crude Italian attempts to turn the usually truculent nobles against him. Thus, he shows how the Emperor avoided the pitfalls of division and demonstrated the virtues of unity for prosperity.

This text draws our attention to some facts that are often not sufficiently recognized — that the soldiers at Adwa came from every nationality and that peasants and women played very important roles in making the victory of Adwa possible. In other words, his chapter shows that Adwa was, in every sense of the word, a "national" struggle against Italy's design to colonize Ethiopia.

Dejazmach Zewde's text, "Continuity and Discontinuity in Menelik's Foreign Relations 1865-1896" which is based on empirical data, is intended for scholars who are curious about Menelik, the shadowy figure who emerged from the mountain fastness of Showa and put Ethiopia and himself on the world stage. It discusses the meanderings of Menelik's foreign policy by placing it within a triangular context: national, regional and international. He shows how the European scramble for Africa, the opening of the Suez Canal and the ensuing importance of the Red Sea as a seaway to India and beyond, and the increasing intervention of Britain, France, and Italy in the internal affairs of Ethiopia, shaped Menelik's foreign policy. He articulates this international context with the internal conditions that kept Menelik busy fending off rivals, expanding his territory, and patiently pursuing his ultimate objective to become the emperor of Ethiopia.

This articulation of national, regional and international dimensions leads Dejazmach Zewde to identify three phases in Menelik's foreign policy. In the first phase, extending from 1865 to 1878, Menelik was more interested, he argues, in consolidating his rule over Showa and the surrounding areas, and in the second phase, 1878 to 1889, in managing his relations with Emperor Yohannes while biding his time for the crown. These two phases are characterized by a continuity of foreign policy the main purpose of which was the garnering of external support for his aspiration to become the Emperor of Ethiopia.

Dejazmach Zewde argues that the third phase, from 1889 to 1896, introduces a discontinuity in Menelik's foreign policy. During this last phase, the main purpose of the Emperor was to defend his enlarged empire. To this end, he acquired arms and ammunition and the necessary financial resources by seeking loans from abroad and expanding trade.

Dejazmach Zewde explores meticulously the triangular relations between Yohannes, Italy, and Menelik. He discusses the beginnings of close relations between Menelik and Italy in 1876 and the intensification of these relations with the arrival of Count Pietro Antonelli in 1882. He explores the issue of the demarcation of the frontier between Italy and Ethiopia in the North and the signing of the Wuchalé Treaty in 1889, considers Menelik's diplomatic relations with other powers, and examines the interpretation of the Treaty whose disputed Article 17 was the match that set the guns firing at Adwa. From Dejazmach Zewde's analysis emerges the picture of an emperor whose capacity for political maneuvering in foreign affairs is seldom equaled in the annals of Ethiopian history.

The next three chapters in Part II widen the horizon of discussion about Adwa. Negussay's text, "Adwa 1896: Who was Civilized and Who was Savage?" is, as the title suggests, an examination of the consistency of the actions of the adversaries with the values each professes to uphold. It does this through a study of the interactions between Ethiopia and Italy before, during, and after the war.

Negussay points out that moral and religious beliefs influenced the actions of the Emperor. Menelik repeatedly told his Italian interlocutors that it is wrong for Christians to spill each other's blood and acted consistently with his beliefs. Though the colonial myth paints Ethiopians as savages, argues Negussay, it was in fact the Ethiopians who in practice followed civilized precepts: they acted on the premises that peace is more honorable than war, that respect is the foundation of friendship, and that honesty and trust are the cement of treaties. The Italians, on the other hand, despite their claims to be Christians and civilized, were endlessly engaged, writes Negussay, in "chicanery, cheating, cunning, duplicity, immorality, illegality, and forging or doctoring or eliminating materials" during negotiations with Ethiopians.

Many were the Ethiopian leaders who became victims of this kind of "savage" demeanor, and indeed, in one of those cruel ironies of history, victims of their own civilized behavior. Emperor Yohannes, Negussay contends, could have routed the Italians in 1888 at Sahati but he preferred to abort his campaign against the Italians, citing Christ as the maker of peace, and to march westward against the Moslem expansionist force — the Mahdist Ansar movement. Negussay maintains that if Yohannes had been as perfidious as the Italians were, he could have ousted the Italians from "Mereb Melash," and then perhaps Adwa might not have happened. The retreat, he points out, weakened Yohannes's authority and whetted Italy's colonial appetite for more territory.

Negussay puts the events surrounding Adwa in the context of Europe's colonization of Africa — a process of wanton destruction and inhumanity. It is in this context that the road from Wuchalé to Adwa, the confrontation at Adwa, and Menelik's magnanimity in victory, gain significance not only as a political struggle between two powers but also as a struggle between civilization and barbarism. Negussay discusses the striking example of the Emperor giving permission to the Italian garrison at Mekele, rendered completely helpless by a siege that deprived them of their water supplies, to leave the fort with their armament and their honor intact. This civilized behavior was lost on Italy, he argues.

The text raises the thorny question of why Menelik did not pursue the defeated Italian army and cross the Mereb. After examining some of the possible reasons, he argues that Menelik's decision not to cross the Mereb cannot be regarded as the only cause of the loss of "Mereb Melash." He concludes his chapter with a discussion of what he calls the "soft" and "hard" legacies of Adwa, all of which are pertinent to the understanding of some of the important questions that Ethiopians are now facing.

Getachew Metafaria's chapter, "Ethiopia: A Bulwark Against European Colonialism and Its Role in the Pan-African Movement," brings out the African repercussions of Adwa. Getachew argues that the Ethiopian victory at Adwa had profound impact among the colonized, particularly in Africa and in the African diaspora. The victory of Adwa, he shows, was a flood of light welcomed with joy by Black people living in the darkness of racism and colonialism. It was received as a symbol of their dignity, as a message of liberation, and as a promise of African unity and self-sufficiency. He discusses how this new horizon opened up by the victory of Adwa led to the rise of Ethiopianism and Pan-Africanism.

The text explores how Ethiopianism found various forms of expression — religious, ideological, literary, political, and even economic — and how one of these, Pan-Africanism, made a profound political impact in Africa and in the African diaspora. At the heart of these movements was the core belief that the independence of Ethiopia was indispensable for the emancipation of Black people. Thus, Getachew shows that the Fascist invasion of Ethiopia was experienced by Africans in the diaspora and at home as a racial war, as an aggression against Ethiopianism and Pan-Africanism. He also considers the links between Ethiopianism and the demands by Africans for political independence and equal rights in the post-World War II period. The crowning of the Ethiopianist and Pan-Africanist movements, he observes, was the creation of the Organization of African Unity in 1963 in the very country that conferred on Black people all over the world the honor of the Adwa victory, which in turn endowed them with unyielding self respect.

Getachew then reflects on the post Adwa developments and argues that the rise of African socialism as an alternative ideology, the overthrow of Emperor Haile Selassie, and the political and economic crises confronted by Blacks everywhere, eroded the significance of Ethiopianism. He maintains that the erosion of the ideas and beliefs associated with the unity and uniqueness of Ethiopia is a process that is also taking place within Ethiopia itself. He considers how the imposition of ethnic identity as the organizing principle of politics and civil society by the group that came to power in 1991 has eroded the central elements of Ethiopianism: Ethiopian unity and identity.

The next text, Richard Pankhurst's "Reactions to the Battle of Adwa as Illustrated by The Times Newspaper for 1896," considers Britain's reactions to the Italian defeat at Adwa. Pankhurst introduces his chapter with a consideration of European thinking prior to the war and moves on to the analysis of British reactions to Italy's military disaster at Adwa. It shows that prior to the battle of Adwa, the *Times*, the voice of the British establishment, was not opposed to Italy's colonial objectives in Ethiopia, which it described as a country of "ill-armed savages."

The *Times*, points out Pankhurst, continued its pro-Italian stance even after Adwa, describing Ethiopians as "the enemy," misrepresenting the Ethiopian army as "the Showans," expressing its deep regret that a European army has been defeated by a "native" force. Though it now grudgingly admitted that Ethiopia was a "civilized power," The *Times* did not condemn the aggression but rather, argues Pankhurst, it proffered advice as to how Italy could maintain its colonial foothold in Ethiopia.

British sympathy for Italian aggression, he argues, had its own objectives which were, among others, the desire to prevent unrest in the British colonies triggered by the demonstration effect of an African victory over a colonial power and to use Italy as an obstacle to France's ambition in the area. Through his study of British reactions, as mediated by the *Times*, Pankhurst shows the impact Adwa had on the foreign policy of European powers.

The chapter by our late colleague, Harold Marcus, which is entitled "Racist Discourse About Ethiopia and Ethiopians Before and After the Battle of Adwa," scrutinizes German, French, British, and Italian writings on Ethiopia, shows that the European perception of Ethiopia was a complex mélange of fascination with and denigration of Ethiopian civilization, of admiration and admonition of Ethiopian Christianity, of recognition and denial of the diplomatic talents of the Negus and the military prowess of his soldiers, all colored by the racist lens through which Europeans saw the peoples they projected to colonize.

Marcus organizes these views into two kinds of discourse: one which is openly racist, and the other — an alternate discourse — which presents Ethiopia in a positive light. He compares the pre-Adwa with the post-Adwa writings on Ethiopia and finds that the victory of Adwa forced Europeans to abandon their openly racist discourse of the pre-Adwa period and to rationalize the defeat of Italy by presenting Ethiopia, her civilization, her soldiers, and the Negus in a positive light. But, argues Marcus, this alternate discourse was still informed by a racist sub-text which eventually came out into the open and reached its apogee in 1935–36. Marcus's chapter thus traces the filiations of European racist discourse on Ethiopia from the pre-Adwa period to the Fascist invasion of Ethiopia.

The chapters in Part III are reflections on the significance of Adwa for contemporary Ethiopians. The first text considers Adwa from a political perspective while the third chapter considers the kind of theorizing needed to confront the questions raised by Adwa.

Mesfin Araya's "Contemporary Ethiopia in the Context of the Battle of Adwa, 1896" discusses Adwa as a "people's war," characterized by the internal unity of the ruling class, partly the result of the shared history that Ethiopians identify with and partly the result of the consensus building skills of Emperor Menelik. The author argues that Adwa, a great victory against colonialism, was at the same time a disaster for highland Eritreans insofar as Menelik did not pursue his campaign to liberate them from Italian occupation. Indeed, he continues, despite the achievements of Menelik, the historical circumstances of

Adwa not only led to victory but also spawned their own internal contradictions that still weigh heavily on contemporary Ethiopia.

Nevertheless, the present ruling elites' politics of ethnic and regional divisions, Mesfin argues, do not reflect the historical experience of Ethiopians. The divisive politics pursued presently, he contends, negates the historically founded Ethiopian unity and reflects the weakness and internal divisions of the ruling elite rather than that of Ethiopians. This divisiveness and weakness, argues Mesfin, opens the door for foreign meddling in the internal affairs of Ethiopia and makes her a pliant client of neo-colonialism.

The concluding chapter, Maimire Mennasemay's "Ethiopian History and Critical Theory: The Case of Adwa," proposes that we rethink Adwa more in terms of its internal aspects, as the progenitor of Ethiopia's modernity and its contradictions, rather than as a military and diplomatic victory of Ethiopia over Italy. From this perspective, he argues, what is surprising is the fact that Ethiopians who united to defeat the threat of external oppression have failed to show the same unity and resolve to defeat internal oppression. He traces this to the absence of an internal critical theory capable of eliciting the emancipatory themes that inform the various peasant revolts in Ethiopia and to the failure of linking these themes with the ideals of freedom, equality and justice which were sown in the resistance against external oppression.

Maimire's chapter thus revolves around the issue of the absence of an "intellectual Adwa" in Ethiopia. Resistance to foreign political and military domination was not matched by resistance to foreign interpretations of Ethiopia's political and social problems. He discusses how the uncritical borrowing and mechanical application of social and political theories generated a systematically distorted understanding of Ethiopians, of their society, and of their problems; and points out how such an approach relegated Ethiopia, the nation that entered the contemporary epoch with the glorious victory at Adwa, to the level of one of the most "wretched nations" on the planet.

Maimire argues that Adwa is, from the internal perspective, a battle not yet finished, and that to complete this battle with an internal victory for freedom, equality and justice, Ethiopians need to throw a new light on their modern history through an immanent critique of Adwa and its aftermath. He discusses some of the major obstacles for developing a critical and reflexive theory in the Ethiopian context and offers a preliminary critique of "Adwa the unfinished battle."

In the past, the study of Adwa has been generally dominated by the state perspective, and not surprisingly, its diplomatic and military aspects have attracted the attention of historians. But as the texts in this collection demonstrate, Adwa is constituted by a multiplicity of complex circumstances, actions, aspirations, events, and consequences, sometimes converging with each other, sometimes contradicting each other. Adwa's meanings and significance to the modern conditions of Ethiopia cannot be exhausted by its military and diplomatic aspects. Adwa has still secrets to disclose. Its consequences have overflowed into the present but their meanings and implications are not yet fully elucidated. The editors of this monograph believe that in a modest way, the collection that has been thematically put together here contributes to the opening up of new avenues of exploration of Adwa's significance for the present and the future of oppressed people all over the World.

Prologue

A fuller grasp of the events surrounding the battle of Adwa as described in detail herein requires a brief background to Ethiopian history leading to the conflict between Ethiopia and Italy in 1896, albeit not for Africanist pundits but for the casual reader of the book. It is safe to start to describe this from the time of Ezana, commencing in AD 330, when detailed written records were left to posterity.

After the fall of the Christian Axumite Empire of Ethiopia, whose power reached its zenith in the 4th century AD, an amalgamated Christian state of Zagwe led by the Agaws of the north central region appeared at the end of the first millennium. In the late 13th century, the Zagwes in turn gave way to a dynasty that claimed descent from King Solomon and the Queen of Sheba, a genealogy providing the legitimacy and continuity so honored in Ethiopia's subsequent national saga.

The Solomonian Empire extending south and east of the country conducted an international trade, which was dominated by its citizens who followed the Moslem religion through Massawa (Mitsiwa) in Eritrea and Zeila (Seylac) on the northern Somali shoreline. The Ethiopian rulers of the period permitted those on the coast to carry out their business and self administration independently as long as they pledged submission and paid taxes to the central government. Starting in 1332, however, the Moslems of Yifat, who controlled Zeila, rebelled and carried out a jihad against the sovereignty of the central Christian empire; but the uprising was quelled by the armies of Emperor Amda Tsion.

By the 15th century, owing to succession problems and the sheer complexity of governing a large empire, the Solomonian state begun to decay. This was followed by a challenge from another Moslem vassal; the Adal Sultanate of the Harar region refused to pay tribute and a percentage of its trading profits to the central government of Ethiopia. In 1527, the Adal leader, Ahmad ibn Ibrahim al-Ghazi, known in Ethiopian history as Ahmad Gragn ("Ahmad the Left-handed"), who was equipped with firearms and was aided by the Ottoman Turks, ravaged the Christian empire that still depended on outmoded weapons of war. By 1535, Gragn lorded over a vast Islamic empire stretching from Zeila (Seylac) in Somaliland to Massawa (Mitsiwa) in present day Eritrea. He also controlled much of the interior of Ethiopia except for a few staunchly Christian enclaves remaining in the mostly inaccessible mountain fastnesses of Amhara and Tigray. With the help of the Portuguese Christians, who came with firearms to aid the Ethiopian Christians of what they called "the land of Prester John," Gragn's forces were routed by Emperor Galawdewos in 1543.

It was during this period that Oromo Ethiopians from Ganale, Bale and Borana regions who were neither Moslems nor Christians found an opportunity to expand militarily into much of the Christian highlands. Soon, the Oromos were to a large extent converted either to Islam or Christianity. This was followed by a period of feudal anarchy known as the Zemene Masafent ("Age of the Princes"), where figurehead Solomonian monarchs were put on the throne by Oromo generals while the country was, in reality, ruled by independent feudal lords. Zemene Masafent lasted for 150 years until the accession to the throne of Kassa, from Amhara Gondar, who was crowned emperor under the throne name Tewodros II of Ethiopia in 1855.

Tewodros died at Maqdala in a battle against the Napier expedition that was sent to free British and other European prisoners of the Emperor, and Kassa Hailu of Tigray aided the British in trouncing Tewodros when they agreed to leave the country once their mission was accomplished. As a tribute for his service, the British general gave Kassa plenty of modern arms, which he used with devastating effect to crush his rivals. Kassa then fought his way to the Solomonian throne on January 21, 1872, adopting the crown name Yohannes IV. By this time, the northernmost Oromos, particularly those of Wallo, had been to a large extent assimilated into the Amhara-Tigre culture and Ethiopia's national unity had been re-established again after a long hiatus of feudal anarchy.

It should be clear that Ethiopian history is replete with bloody wars waged due to the strong rivalry for the Solomonian crown between the kings of Tigray and Amhara. In the second half of the nineteenth century, this struggle was conducted between Yohannes IV of Tigray and King Menelik of Showa. In the initial scuffle, Yohannes forced the submission of all of Ethiopia's princes. But he also had other external challengers, among whom was the Ottoman viceroy in Egypt, khedive Isma'il Pasha, who was an unabashed expansionist. By the mid-1870s, the Egyptian Khedive had encroached on some vital Ethiopian territories located to the east and south, but Ethiopian forces, in what verged on an anti-Muslim crusade, won crucial victories in the mountainous country of the north in 1875 and 1876. Then came Italy, the next aggressor. With the tacit approval of the British, the Italian colonialists usurped the formerly Turkish and Egyptian occupied Ethiopian sea port of Massawa in 1885 and named territories covering the lowlands as well as the Hamasen plateau, straddling the Christian highlands of the Tigrigna-speaking peoples of the north, Eritrea. They then embarked on an aggressive expansion campaign further onto the highlands, only to be decisively defeated by Emperor Yohannes in 1887. In the same year, the Messianic Islamists of Sudan, known as the Mahdists, encroached on Ethiopian territory. After defeating King Tekle Haimanot, the regional King of Gojam, they devastated the old Ethiopian capital of Gondar. In retaliation, Yohannes moved in full force against the Sudan.

Yohannes's main Amhara rival to aspire for the Solomonian crown was Menelik of Showa, who did not recognize Yohannes as emperor until 1878–79, when he faced a military defeat. Menelik's eclipse was, however, only temporary, for in 1882 a dynastic marriage was arranged between Menelik's daughter (the future Empress, princess Zewditu) and Yohannes's son (Ras Araya Selassie) and it was agreed that Menelik would be Yohannes's successor as Emperor. Yohannes on his part recognized Menelik's unchallenged rule over the south, and the separate spheres of influence of the two rival monarchs were carefully defined.

The ambitious King Menelik II of Showa now began a re-conquest of Ethiopia's southern and eastern prefectures. Throughout the next decade, Menelik engineered Ethiopia's return into the southern and Western regions that had been abandoned in the 17th century when the kingdoms of Dawaro, Fatagar and Damot were swept away by the swift tide of Oromo warrior age groups known as Lubas. By waging numerous wars with the new weapons he acquired from Europe, he succeeded in incorporating within his domain all major Oromo confederacies and sovereign territories, including those of Arusi, Harar, Jimma, Limu and Wallaga and several other kingdoms and states of southern Ethiopia such as Kafa, Walayta, Sidama and Janjaro. In their conquest of the south, Menelik and his followers were inspired by the idea that they were regaining lands that had once been part of the Christian empire. For them, it was a holy crusade to restore Ethiopia to its historic grandeur.

It was from the rich territories of the south that Menelik procured commodities to sell for the weapons and ammunition he required in his fight for the Solomonian crown. As time passed, new hostilities emerged between Yohannes and Showa's strongman. This was caused by the fact that Menelik, fearing that Yohannes's son Mengasha (supported by the famous imperial army general Ras Alula) might try to follow his father to the throne, made an agreement with the Italians in 1888 in exchange for arms supplied to his Showan kingdom. By the time of Yohannes's invasion and military success in the Sudan, which was unfortunately marred by his own death on the battlefield of Matama in 1889, Menelik had emerged as the strongest man in Ethiopia; thus, he assumed the Solomonian throne for which he had aspired for many decades.

As a diplomat, the new Ethiopian Emperor made a great impression on the European envoys who visited his court. The Italian plenipotentiary, Count Pietro Antonelli, provided Menelik with sizable amounts of ammunition, weapons and loans. With such assistance, the monarch was able to conquer even more territories and import more firearms, the better to supply his armies and to furnish the garrisons and settlers who came in their wake. Furthermore, Menelik mobilized Italian and French speculators, scientists and missionaries who organized Showan caravans to convey to the coast the monarch's gold, ivory, hides, coffee, civet, spices and furs, all appropriated from the newly conquered south. From these, substantial revenues enabled him to purchase still more firearms. Both before and after Yohannes's death, when Menelik and his followers were engaged in the aggressive expansion to the south with their fabulous wealth, they seemed to be pre-empting Europe's "scramble for Africa," which had been consecrated at the Treaty of Berlin in 1884-85 and was slowly but surely advancing towards greater Ethiopia.

In the late 1890s, the economy of the Red Sea region was stimulated by the opening of the Suez Canal, by the establishment of a British military base in Aden, and by the founding of a French coaling station at Obock on the Somali-Afar coast. The United Kingdom sought to seal off the Nile Valley from its colonial rival, France, by facilitating Italy's colonial objectives in the Horn, the latter having perennially complained that it did not have a great enough share in Africa. Thus, after 1885, Italy assumed control of major ports in Ethiopia and southern Somalia. This, fulfilling the British objective, restricted the French to their mini-colony of Djibouti and left the United Kingdom in possession of ports in northern Somalia from where foodstuffs were exported to their new colony of Aden.

During the period of Menelik's rivalry with Emperor Yohannes IV and the latter's son, Mengasha, the Showan monarch appeared to create amicable relations with the Italians, but an intractable squabble soon emerged. The Italians interpreted Article XVII of the Treaty of Wuchalé (Uccialli) concluded in 1889 by the Italians and Menelik as giving Italy a protectorate status over Ethiopia. Indeed, it is quite inconceivable that Menelik would have agreed to his historic country becoming a protectorate of Italy or any other power. But, when he learned that the Italian interpretation which was concocted by Antonelli was slowly gaining ground in Europe, the Emperor at once rebuffed the Ethiopian-Italian protocol of friendship and in 1893, unilaterally abrogated the treaty itself.

After much intrigue and several minor military clashes, the Italian colonialists who by 1890 had established themselves along the Red Sea coast (which they had named the colony of Eritrea) risked a major confrontation. But they were soundly defeated by a hastily mobilized Ethiopian peasant army in one of the greatest battles in the history of the world — the Battle of Adwa, of March 1, 1896.

Adwa was the greatest military operation between Africans and Europeans since the time of Hannibal. For the victors it was the most deceive, for the vanquished, the most catastrophic, given that the Italian colonialist soldiers were crushed totally and in every way. Indeed, their defeat was extraordinary in scale: their casualty figure was 70%; all their artillery pieces were captured; one out of four of their generals were taken prisoner and two of the remaining as well as almost half of their staff officers were killed on the battlefield. *The Battle of Adwa — Reflections on the Historic Victory of Ethiopia against European Colonialism* elucidates and scrutinizes this event with the hindsight of over one hundred years.

Chapter 1. Reflections on the Battle of Adwa and Its Significance for Today

Theodore M. Vestal, Ph.D.
Professor of Political Science
Oklahoma State University

In 1896, Italy, a late-comer to the family of nations and a slow-footed scrambler for colonial spoils in Africa, made her move to conquer Ethiopia, the only remaining prize on the continent unclaimed by Europeans. Expansionist leaders of the recently unified Kingdom of Italy dreamed of a second Roman Empire, stretching from the Alps to the Equator, and it was assumed that a show of military would quickly bring "barbarian" lands and riches into an Africa Orientale Italiana. The Italian dream was turned into a nightmare, however, in the mountain passes and valleys near the northern Ethiopian city of Adwa by the knockout punch by the mailed fist of a unified Greater Ethiopia. The Italians retreated, humiliated. On the other hand, the battle put Ethiopia on the map of the modern world and had ramifications that are still being felt today by her own populace and by other African people everywhere. The preparation of a book to commemorate the Battle of Adwa provides an appropriate time to reflect upon the significance of the victory and to attempt to discern any lessons from that auspicious event that might be of value to present day Ethiopia and by extension, to Africa and the entire Third World.

A detailed analysis and interpretation of the 1896 episode and its aftermath would require many books. This section is only a "thumbnail" picture of Adwa, past and present. The details of the political machinations in Ethiopia and in Europe and the description of the war itself will be covered in the next two chapters.

PRELUDE TO THE BATTLE

Italy entered the Horn of Africa through a window of commercial opportunity. Following the opening of the Suez Canal in 1869, an Italian steamship company, Rubattino, leased the Port of Assab on the Red Sea from the Sultan of Raheita as a refueling station. During the next year, Rubattino purchased the port for $9,440 (a bargain for such a hot property). Rubattino hoped to make money by controlling the traffic in slavery and arms smuggling.

Meanwhile, in Europe, the parliament of the newly united Kingdom of Italy met in Rome for the first time in November 1871. The new government was ambitious and sought ways to prove its bona fides in the eyes of the world. Colonization of lands unclaimed by other European powers was viewed as one path to national prestige. Although Italy coveted African lands across the Mediterranean, it failed in attempts to occupy Tunisia and Egypt in 1881–1882. Considerations of prestige were thought to demand expansion somewhere, and imperialists of the time proclaimed that the "key to the Mediterranean was in the Red Sea" (where incidentally, there would be less chance of Italy's clashing with other European interests).[1] Thus, in 1882, the Italian government bought Assab from Rubattino for $43,200, thereby providing the steamship company a handsome profit on its investment and unofficially establishing the first Italian colony in Africa since the days of the Caesars.[2]

Emboldened by its real estate acquisition on the Red Sea, Italy participated in the Conference of Berlin in 1884-1885 that "divided up" what was left of Africa after the initial wave of European colonialism. At the conference, Italy was "awarded" Ethiopia, and all that remained was for her troops to occupy the prize. This would take time, and cautious expansion from Assab.

To ensure the safety of its new port, Italy moved to the surrounding interior. From its Assab base the Italians, through the good office of Britain, occupied the nearby Red Sea port of Massawa (replacing the Khedive of Egypt, who had decided he could no longer keep a garrison there) and adjoining lands in 1885. At that time, the Ethiopian emperor, Yohannes, was distracted by wars in the highlands and against Sudanese Mahdists who were also battling the British in the Sudan. After the Mahdi defeated General Charles "Chinese"

1. Dennis Mack Smith, *Modern Italy, A Political History* (Ann Arbor, University of Michigan Press, 1997), 164.
2. Getachew Mekasha, "The Battle of Adwa Remembered," *Ethiopian Review*, March 1995, p. 18.

Gordon at Khartoum in 1885, the Italians were left as the only Europeans in what they perceived as a hostile land. The Italian government felt compelled to increase the military support of its commercial stations.[3]

Emboldened by their easy occupation of the coastal areas, the Italian army and local conscripts invaded the highlands in the late 1880s. Italian government leaders probably overestimated the possible gains in commerce and prestige from this move. The reputation of Ethiopians as spirited fighters, evidenced in battle against the Egyptians in the 1870s and against the Mahdists in the 1880s,[4] apparently was not taken seriously by the Italians. That attitude soon changed when Ethiopian mettle was tested in the rough terrain of Tigray. After the Italians provoked some "incidents" on the frontier, their soldiers encountered an Ethiopian force of 10,000 led by Ras Alula Engeda, Emperor Yohannes's governor of the Mereb-Melash, the territory north of the Mereb River and stretching to the Red Sea — in other words, the land the Italians were occupying. At Dogali, some 500 Italians were trapped and massacred in battle by Alula's men.

Their pride wounded, the Italian government moved aggressively in retaliation. Parliament voted 332 to 40 to increase military appropriations, raised a force of 5,000 men to reinforce existing troops, and attempted to blockade Ethiopia.

To ease his "Italian problem," Emperor Yohannes sought the diplomatic help of Great Britain. As part of the peace diplomacy, Yohannes agreed to give compensation to the Italians for Dogali and to use Massawa as a trading post.[5] By this time the French had started building a railroad from Addis Ababa to Djibouti. This would give Ethiopia a trading outlet on the Red Sea outside Italian influence. Italian leaders, nursing a sense of shame and a thirst for revenge, decided something had to be done.[6]

The man to do it was Francesco Crispi, the prominent leader of the democratic or radical left wing of the Italian government and the most striking political personality produced by the new Italy.[7] Eloquent, forcible, and dominating in Parliament, the Sicilian Crispi served as Prime Minister from 1887-1891

---

3. Smith, 164.
4. Donald N. Levine, *Greater Ethiopia: The Evolution of a Multiethnic Society* (Chicago: University of Chicago Press, 1974), 12.
5. Bahru Zewde, *A History of Modern Ethiopia 1855-1974* (London: James Currey, 1991), 57.
6. Martin Clark, *Modern Italy, 1871-1982* (New York: Longman, 1984), 99-100.
7. Salvatore Saladino, "Parliamentary Politics in the Liberal Era 1861-1914," in Edward R. Tannenbaum and Emiliana p. Noether, eds., *Modern Italy: A Topical History Since 1861* (New York: New York University Press, 1974), 40.

and again from 1893–1896. A super-patriot, Crispi longed to see his country, that he always called "my Italy," strong and flourishing.[8] He envisioned Italy as a great colonial empire, and Crispi's impulsive hubris would play a vital role in shaping the events that would unfold in the region. Following the debacle at Dogali, Crispi told German Chancellor Otto von Bismarck that "duty" would compel him to revenge. "We cannot stay inactive when the name of Italy is besmirched," Crispi asserted. Bismarck is purported to have replied that Italy had a large appetite but poor teeth.[9]

With their military momentum stalled and the bluster of their milites gloriosi punctured, the Italians, led by Crispi, resorted to guile and diplomacy to promote their expansionist aims. Taking a page from the British book of colonial domination, the Italians pursued a policy of divide and conquer. They provided arms to Ras Mengesha of Tigray and all other chiefs who were hostile to the Emperor. During his internecine rivalry with Yohannes, even the Negus of Showa, Menelik, sought closer collaboration with the Italians. Menelik allegedly welcomed the Italians as allies in a common Christian front against the Mahdists.

When the Emperor Yohannes was killed in battle against the Madhists at Metemma in March 1889, the Italians sensed an opportune moment to solidify their foothold in the country through negotiation. Count Pietro Antonelli headed a mission to pay homage to the new Emperor, Menelik II, and to negotiate a treaty with him. The Treaty of Wuchalé (Uccialli, in Italian), signed in Italian and Amharic versions in May 1889, ultimately was to provide the raison d'être for the Battle of Adwa.

Under the treaty, the Italians were given title to considerable real estate in the north in exchange for a loan to Ethiopia of $800,000, half of which was to be in arms and ammunition. The pièce de resistance for the Italians, however, was Article XVII, which according to the Italian version bound Menelik to make all foreign contacts through the agency of Italy. The Amharic version made such service by the Italians optional.[10]

Proudly displaying the Roman rendition of the treaty in Europe, the Italians proclaimed Ethiopia to be her protectorate. Crispi ordered the occupation of Asmara, and in January 1890 he announced the existence of Italy's first official colony, "Eritrea." To bolster Italy's colonial policy, on April 15, 1892,

8. Arthur J.B. Whyte, *The Evolution of Modern Italy* (Oxford: B. Blackwell, 1959), 195, 201.
9. Smith, 165.
10. Bahru, 75.

Great Britain recognized the whole of Ethiopia as a sphere of Italian interest. Italian Prime Minister Giovanni Giolitti (whose eighteen-month premiership interrupted Crispi's tenure in the office) affirmed that "Ethiopia would remain within the orbit of Italian influence and that an external protectorate would be maintained over Menelik."[11] The Ethiopians were not too concerned with such Italian braggadocio until 1893, when Menelik denounced the Wuchalé treaty and all foreign claims to his dominions and attempted to make treaties with Russia, Germany, and Turkey. In a display of integrity rare among belligerent nations, Menelik paid back the loan incurred under the treaty with three times the stipulated interest. He kept the military equipment, however, and sought to rally the nation against a foreign invader.[12]

The Italians railed at this insubordination by a "Black African barbarian chieftain," and prepared to go to war to teach the Ethiopians a lesson in obedience. Having claimed a protectorate, Italy could not back down without losing face.[13] Crispi, under fire at home from both conservatives and the extreme left bloc of Parliament for his "megalomania," may have seen victory in Africa as his last chance for political success.[14] From his perspective, a colonial war would be good for Italy's (and his) prestige, and Crispi envisioned a protectorate over all of Ethiopia. General Antonio Baldissera, the military commander at Massawa, had a more modest goal — the permanent occupation of Tigray. The Italian Deputies would have been content with a peaceful commercial colony. With such occluded aims, the African campaign suffered generally from a lack of will among Italians in the homeland.[15]

While the Italians massed arms and men in their Colonia Eritrea, their agents sought to subvert Ethiopian Rases and other regional leaders against the Emperor. What the Italians did not realize was that they were entering into the Ethiopian national pastime: the tradition of personal advancement through intrigue.[16] Menelik, master of the sport, trumped the Italians' efforts by persuading the provincial rulers that the outsiders' threat was of such serious nature that they had to combine against it and not seek to exploit it to their own ends. The Emperor called his countrymen's attention to the fate of other African

11. Glen St. John Barclay, The Rise and Fall of the New Roman Empire: Italy's Bid for World Power, 1890-1943 (New York: St. Martin's Press, 1973), 33.
12. Getachew, p. 19.
13. Smith, 166.
14. Saladino, 40.
15. Smith, 166-67.
16. Richard Greenfield, *Ethiopia: A New Political History* (London: Pall Mall Press, 1965), 120.

nations that had fallen under the yoke of colonialism. The magic of Menelik worked. Whatever seeds of discord the Italians had planted sprouted as shoots of accord on the other side.

Meanwhile, Italy carried out further intrusions into Ethiopia. On December 20, 1893, Italian forces drove 10,000 Mahdists from Agordat in the first decisive victory ever won by Europeans over the Sudanese revolutionaries and "the first victory of any kind yet won by an army of the Kingdom of Italy against anybody."[17] Flushed with success on the battlefield, the Italian populace embraced new national heroes, the Bersagliere, soldiers of the crack corps of the Italian army. The Bersagliere, depicted in the press wearing "a pith helmet adorned with black plumes, facing a savage enemy on an exotic terrain," appealed to the passionate patriotism of the masses and to the romantic adventurism of young men. Enthusiastic conscripts responded to the call to the colors.[18]

The belligerent Italians soon mounted the strongest colonial expeditionary force that Africa had known up to that time. The Governor of Eritrea, General Oreste Baratieri, had about 30,000 Italian troops and 15,000 native Askaris under his command (Great Britain would surpass that number a few years later when 250,000 troops would be sent to South Africa during the Boer War). Secure in his new military strength, Baratieri again went after the Mahdists. On July 12, 1894, his forces drove the Dervishes from Kassala, killing 2,600 while losing only 28 Italian dead — the most one-sided victory won by Europeans over the Mahdists.

The Italians were not doing so well on the diplomatic front, however. In July 1894, Russia had denounced the Treaty of Wuchalé. An Ethiopian mission was received in St. Petersburg "with honors more lavish than those accorded any previous foreign visitors in Russian history." To add injury to diplomatic insult, Tsar Nicholas sent Ethiopia more rifles and ammunition.[19]

In 1895, Baratieri followed up his victory over the Dervishes with another successful offence at Debre Aila against an Ethiopian force larger than his own, under the command of Ras Mengesha. The Italians drove out the ruler of Tigray and prepared for a permanent occupation of his land. Other minor military actions of the Italians in 1895 fuelled the anger of the Ethiopian masses and leaders alike, who viewed the invasion as a threat to their nation's sovereignty.

17. Barclay, 33.
18. Barclay, 34.
19. Ibid.

Emperor Menelik's reforms had transformed the economy and improved the tax base of the country enabling him, as never before, to raise and equip armies.[20] In the highlands, Menelik massed his troops and marched north to meet the Italian aggressors. In December, an Ethiopian army of 30,000 trapped 2,450 Italian troops at Amba Alaghe, the southernmost point of Italian penetration. In the ensuing battle, 1,320 Italians were killed or taken prisoner. At the same time, Ethiopians laid seize to a formidable Italian fort at Mekele. Menelik, perhaps still hoping to settle his conflict with the Italians peacefully, negotiated a settlement whereby the besieged were evacuated and allowed to join their compatriots.[21]

These events infuriated Crispi, who taunted his commanders for their incapacity and cowardice. He called the Ethiopians "rebels" who somehow owed allegiance to Italy. Although the opposition in parliament led by Giolitti criticized the government for providing inadequate food, clothing, medical supplies, and arms to the troops, Crispi was able to garner additional military appropriations by claiming that the troop movements were purely defensive. He assured parliament that the war in Ethiopia would be a profitable investment.[22]

THE BATTLE OF ADWA

By late February 1896, the Italian army was entrenched around Mount Enticho in Tigray. Led by General Baratieri, who was just back from Rome (where he had been awarded the "Order of the Red Eagle"),[23] the 20,000 Italians and Italian-officered native auxiliaries had waited for the Ethiopians to attack their fortified positions as they had done in previous battles. When such an attack did not occur, Baratieri ordered what he hoped would be a surprise attack on the Ethiopians assembled near Adwa. Defeat was unthinkable for a modern European army of such size with its disciplined and well-equipped formations. A decisive victory over the upstart natives would win a vast new empire for Italy.[24] Unfortunately for Baratieri, he was maneuvering over unfamiliar terrain

20. "Adwa's Impact on Current Ethiopian Attitudes," *Defense & Foreign Afairs Strategic Policy*, (2, 1999), 6-7.
21. Bahru, 77.
22. Smith, 168.
23. *New York Times*, 4 March 1896, 1.
24. Anthony Mockler, Haile Selassie's War: The Italian-Ethiopian Campaign, 1935-1941 (New York: Random House, 1984), xxxix.

without accurate maps, relying upon ineffective intelligence, and leading troops garbed in uniforms designed for European winters — a disastrous combination of ingredients.[25]

Awaiting the Italians was a massive Ethiopian army, 100,000 men strong, with contingents from almost every region and ethnic group of the country. They were commanded by an all-star team of warriors amassed by Menelik in "an eloquent demonstration of national unity." [26] About two-thirds of the troops raised as part of national mobilization were recruited under the Gibir-Maderia system, a non-monetarized form of payment of land grants and food and drink to the soldiers from tenants working the land. The Emperor and Empress mobilized about 41,000 troops while the governors-general and regional princes raised most of the others.[27]

When the Italian troops made a three-column advance against Ethiopian positions on March 1, St. George's Day, the combined forces of Greater Ethiopia were primed for a fight. The Ethiopians surrounded the Italian units and in fierce combat, closed with and destroyed many of the enemy in the bloodiest of all colonial battles. Peasant troops fought ruthlessly and a large number of Ethiopian women, following the example of the "Warrior Queen," Empress Taytu, were on the battlefield. They served as a water brigade for the fighting men, paramedics, and guards of prisoners.[28]

The Italians inflicted heavy casualties upon their attackers. The artillery crews were especially noteworthy in firing their cannons as long as they could and defending their positions until they were all killed. But the main Italian force and its supplies were caught in Menelik's strategic trap and were hammered by Ethiopian infantry and artillery in a place of their choosing.

At the end of the day, the Italians had suffered one of the greatest single disasters in European colonial history (the British lost more men in Afghanistan; the Spanish were to leave 12,000 dead on the field in Morocco in 1921).[29] There were 11,000 dead from both sides, including 4,000 Italian soldiers. In one day nearly as many Italians lost their lives as in all wars of Risorgimento put

25. Smith, 168; Barclay, 34.
26. Bahru, 77.
27. "Adwa's Impact on Current Ethiopian Attitudes," *Defense & Foreign airsAffairs Strategic Policy*, (2, 1999), 6-7.
28. Chris Prouty, *Empress Taytu and Menilek I: Ethiopia 1883-1910* (Trenton, NJ: Red Sea Press, 1986), 155-161.
29. Barclay, 35; John Keegan, *Fields of Battle: The Wars for North America* (New York: Knopf, 1996), 313.

together.[30] Remnants of the Italian army retreated northward, leaving behind 1,900 Italian and 1,000 Eritrean askari prisoners of war. In addition, the Ethiopians captured four million cartridges and fifty-six cannon.[31]

Menelik chose not to pursue the routed army. With the battle over, he held a religious service of thanksgiving and proclaimed a three-day period of national mourning. The victory celebration of the jubilant Ethiopians was muted because the Emperor saw no cause to rejoice over the death of so many Christian men.[32]

The military advantage won by Menelik was not followed up politically. Why he did not press his advantage and drive the foreigners from his country remains a puzzle. The Emperor may have been concerned about consolidating his territorial interests in the south and may have been afraid of over-extending his resources.[33] At the time, the kingdom was beset with famine and internecine quarrels. Whatever his reasons, Menelik allowed the Italians to remain in their colonial foothold in Eritrea, creating what was to be a continuous source of problems for Ethiopia ever since. He also missed a golden opportunity to guarantee Ethiopia an outlet to the sea. What Menelik had demonstrated, however, was that he had the power to defy any European imperialists.

The defeat at Adwa brought Italy its greatest humiliation since unification and genuinely demoralized the Italian public. Their string of relatively easy colonial victories, the first their army had attained, came to an abrupt and shocking end. Political leaders had not prepared the populace for defeat in Africa, let alone a total disaster.[34] "All is saved except honor" proclaimed the Tribuna.[35] Stunned crowds outside of Parliament shouted, cheered, cursed, hissed, howled, and groaned.[36] Some were heard to cry, "Long live Menelik!"[37] All available Italian transport steamers were ordered to assemble at Naples "to take troops to Massawa." It was rumored that Baratieri planned a military coup to rehabilitate his reputation, before Baldissera superseded him.[38] Church

30. Smith, 168.
31. Getachew, p. 21. Numbers of combatants engaged, killed, wounded, and captured, as well as accounts of spoils, vary in different accounts of the battle.
32. Mockler, xxxxii.
33. Greenfield, 123.
34. Barclay, 35.
35. 14 March 1896. Quoted in William C. Askew, "Italy and the Great Powers Before the First World War," in Tannenbaum and Noether, eds., *Modern Italy: A Topical History Since 1861*, 316.
36. *New York Times*, 6 March 1896, 1.
37. Ibid., 7 March 1896, 1.

fathers were described as being delighted at the failure of the "Satanic" Italian armies that had paid the wages of a divine vendetta at Adwa.[39] The Pope was so disturbed by the news that he cancelled a Te Deum and a diplomatic banquet in celebration of the anniversary of his coronation.[40] A shameful scar had been inflicted on the nation — one that would fester for forty years[41] until Mussolini would pour his snake oil over it.

Crispi's political career was shattered as was the nation's colonial ambition that he had come to personify.[42] Hailed as the greatest parliamentary statesman of Italy, the seventy-seven year old Prime Minister was recognized as one of the chief political figures of Europe.[43] Crispi was acclaimed as the most important Italian and was the only Premier who really captured the nation's imagination. His impulsiveness marred his career, and his actions all too often were "neither informed by knowledge nor controlled by sound judgment." His ideas were grandiose beyond the resources of the country.[44] As the New York Times editorialized, "his greatest mistake [was] in supposing the attention of the Italian people could be successfully diverted from domestic scandals by foreign embroilments."[45]

In June, General Baratieri was brought to trial and, although he was acquitted, it was "in terms that branded him with incapacity."[46] With all Italian troops withdrawn from Tigray and reassembled in Eritrea, General Baldissera defended the colony and drove the Dervishes away from Mount Mocram a month after Adwa. The Italians killed 800 of the invading force of 5,000 and in short order won a brisk series of skirmishes with the Mahdists.[47] In 1897, Kassala was ceded to Great Britain, and during the following year, forces under the British general Horatio Kitchener defeated the Mahdists in a decisive battle at Omdurman.

In the United States, newspaper reporting generally was not sympathetic to the Italian cause. The New York Times ran front-page stories with consec-

38. Ibid., 4 March 1896, 1.
39. R.J.B. Bosworth, Italy, the Least of the Great Powers: Italian Foreign Policy Before the First World War (London: Cambridge University Press, 1979), 24.
40. *New York Times*, 4 March 1896, 1.
41. Barclay, 36.
42. Saladino, 40.
43. "The Fall of Crispi," Editorial, *New York Times*, 6 March 1896, 5.
44. Whyte, 195, 201.
45. "The Fall of Crispi," Editorial, *New York Times*, 6 March 1896, 5.
46. Smith, 170; *New York Times*, 5 June 1896, 5; 13 June 1896, 5.
47. Barclay, 36.

utive day headlines heralding "Italy's Terrible Defeat," "Italy is Awe-Struck," "Italy Like Pandemonium," and "Italy's Wrathful Mobs."[48] An editorial on March 5, 1896, opined, "The Italian invasion of Abyssinia...was a mere piece of piracy...an enterprise unrighteous. In truth, the Italian 'colonial expansion'...is not founded on fact or reason, and has nothing to say for itself in the form of morals and of civilization. It is no more businesslike than it is moral...It is not on business but for glory that they go to war."[49]

The Significance of the Battle

For the victor, the rewards were immediate and long lasting. In the negotiated peace following the battle, the Treaty of Wuchalé was annulled, ending Italy's self-proclaimed "protectorate" over Ethiopia. The settlement acknowledged the full sovereignty and independence of Ethiopia. The Italians paid an indemnity of $5 million in gold; but they were allowed to remain in Eritrea. The price paid by Italy for its belated quest for empire was extravagant in terms of money, lives, arms, and prestige at home and abroad. Eritrea, instead of paying for itself, devoured money. The Red Sea evidently was not a key to the Mediterranean,[50] and the Italians' zest for empire had disappeared for the moment.[51] It would not be until 1911-1912 that Italian agents of imperialism would again venture into Africa in the Libyan War and begin the colonial activity described as "the collecting of deserts."[52]

By winning the battle, Menelik had preserved and extended the territories of ancient Ethiopia — with the important exception of Eritrea. By uniting most of the leaders from almost all parts of the country against a common foe, the Emperor began to implement the idea of a central government that might supplant the Ethiopian Orthodox Church as the symbol of national unity.[53] Thus, the battle gave momentum to the creation of the modern Ethiopian empire-state, and the future of Ethiopia diverged from that of the rest of Africa.[54]

---

48. *New York Times*, 4,5,6,7 March 1896, 1.
49. "The Italian Disaster," Editorial, *New York Times*, 5 March 1896, 5.
50. Smith, 169.
51. Askew, 316.
52. Smith, 169.
53. Greenfield, 119.
54. Bahru, 84, 229.

Internationally, Ethiopia supplied the most meaningful negation to the sweeping tide of colonial domination of Africa. Egged on by Italy's defeat, European nations rushed to conclude treaties with Menelik's government. Indeed, 1896 became the "year of the ferenj" in Ethiopia. Expatriate traders flocked in and spearheaded the acceleration of economic activities. In record numbers, European governments set up consulates throughout the country and aided foreign merchants and investors in seeking concessions and royalties. Menelik's retaining the defeated Italians as good neighbors had positive results: "aspirations of the peaceful penetration school of imperialism and of the more narrowly based small traders on the Red Sea were a major factor in influencing the nature and direction of Italian imperialism that served both as a counterweight and an alternative to the designs of more militant expansionists."[55] A major benefit also accruing to Ethiopia at that time was the introduction of European medical practices.[56] Shortly after the battle, Menelik applied for Ethiopia's admission into the Red Cross Society, another sign of acceptance into the family of nations.[57]

In addition to material changes, the Battle of Adwa produced psychic rewards. Ethiopians basked in national pride and a sense of independence, some say even superiority, that was lost to other Africans mired in the abasement of colonialism.[58] This post-Adwa spirit of Ethiopia, instilled in successive generations, gave Ethiopians a confidence and a unique Weltanschauung.

The image of independent Ethiopia, the nation that successfully stood up against the Europeans, gave inspiration and hope to Africans and African-Americans fettered by racial discrimination and apartheid in whatever guise. Ethiopia provided a model of independence and dignity for people everywhere seeking independence from colonial servitude.[59]

---

55. Robert L. Hess, "Italian Imperialism in Its Ethiopian Context," *International Journal of African Historical Studies* 6 (1973): 108-109.
56. Prouty, 181-183.
57. *New York Times*, 6 March 1896, 1.
58. Teshale Tibebu, "Ethiopia: The 'Anomaly' and 'Paradox' of Africa," 26 *Journal of Black Studies* (March, 1996), 419.
59. Levine, 12-14.

Lessons from the Battle

One hundred plus years after the Battle of Adwa, Ethiopia faces an internal threat to its people's dignity from a government dominated by Marxist-Leninist ideology intent on dividing the nation along ethnic lines. There is little danger from external sources, although it can be argued cogently that the EPRDF-led government remains in power only by being propped up by developmental financial assistance from donor nations.

As in 1896, the danger to Ethiopia originates in the mountain passes and valleys of Tigray and Eritrea. Although the artificial administrative border drawn between Eritrea and Tigray by the Italians is now proclaimed to be the boundary of sovereign nations, it remains an artificial creation, for the people on both sides of the frontier are one in race and civilization.[60] Both are indeed part of Greater Ethiopia. In a similar fashion, the boundaries of the EPRDF administrative region drawn along ethnic lines ignore historic ties between areas that transcend linguistics and lineage. Both the EPRDF and the EPLF (now PFDJ)[61] should ponder an episode of the battle of Adwa: as a result of faulty map reading (or a faulty map), an Italian brigade found itself isolated and the target of the combined fury of the Ethiopian troops.[62] Cartographic misjudgments may haunt their makers.

That is exactly what happened in May 1998, when Eritreans, using faulty maps, threw down the gauntlet before Ethiopia in the Badme triangle. The ensuing slaughter and human suffering in the two-year war that followed was a curse upon both nations.[63] The ruling Ethiopian party, whose leaders had denigrated the history of the Battle of Adwa and its uniting of the people of Greater Ethiopia, suddenly recovered its memory and sent young volunteers off to fight the invading Eritreans with songs and dances recalling that defining moment in the nation's past.

By June 2000, the Ethiopians had won the war, and the two nations signed a ceasefire agreement which provided for a UN observer force to monitor the truce. This was followed in December by Ethiopia and Eritrea signing the

---

60. Edward Ullendorff, *The Ethiopians: An Introduction to Country and People* (London: Oxford University Press, 1960), 37.
61. People's Front for Democracy and Justice
62. Bahru, 79.
63. Theodore M. Vestal, *Ethiopia: A Post-Cold War African State* (Westport, CT: Praeger, 1999), 192-94.

Algeria Peace Agreement, formally ending the conflict. The agreement established the Eritrea-Ethiopia Boundary Commission (EEBC) to delineate the disputed border. The boundary commission's decisions were supposed to be binding on both sides. In April 2002, however, the EEBC ruled that the disputed town of Badme was in Eritrea, and Ethiopia found the ruling unacceptable. Once again, cartography ignited hostilities in the Horn, and the armies of the two neighbors glared menacingly at each other across a twenty-five kilometer-wide UN-monitored buffer zone.

The right of "nationalities" to secede from Ethiopia (proclaimed in Article 39 of the Constitution of the FDRE) may be a paraphrase of European rhetoric, but the roots of the problem of secession have their origins in the creation of the Italian colony in the late nineteenth century. One can only speculate about the different course Ethiopian history might have taken had Emperor Menelik dispelled the Italians from the land of the Habesha.

Like the Italians under Baratieri, the present government seeks to divide and conquer its opposition. Some leaders of the political opposition have taken the bait and succumbed to the old national pastime of seeking personal advancement through intrigue. Although the TPLF and EPRDF applaud their efforts, most Ethiopians who want real democracy in their country have grown tired of demagogues' games. In the May 2005 elections, opposition leaders agreed to combine forces to oppose the divisive ethnic politics and the deficits of democracy of the EPRDF regime. This was a significant event, but missing from the election fray was a Menelik of today to ignite a national flame uniting peasants and metropolitans from every background and from every part of the country against a common foe and for the good of Ethiopia. Present in 2005, however, were today's Taytus, "warrior queens," exhorting the opposition to strive for victory. The legacy of the Battle of Adwa is a powerful beacon for the inheritors of an independent and proud Ethiopia. Can its light lead all Ethiopians to come together to bring the blessings of democracy to their homeland?

In 1896, increased Italian military action steadily aroused the nationalism of Ethiopia and the chances of exploiting her feudalism and dividing her nobles was correspondingly diminished.[64] Today, one sees signs that heavy-handed government repressions have steadily aroused Ethiopians' spirit of nationalism and the chances of exploiting ethnicity and dividing the country will correspondingly be diminished.

---

64. Greenfield, 119.

Perhaps Emperor Menelik captured best the spirit that might motivate all freedom loving Ethiopians to get involved in efforts to bring democracy to their homeland by peaceful means. In a wax- and gold-laden statement, just as pertinent now as it was over a century ago, said Menelik: "If powers at a distance come forward to partition Ethiopia between them, I do not intend to be an indifferent spectator."[65] Ethiopians are no longer limited to their highland fortress on the Horn of Africa; they are part and parcel of a globalized world that recognizes sovereignty — a value for which the heroes of Adwa sacrificed their lives.

65. Quoted in Greenfield, 118.

CHAPTER 2. THE BATTLE OF ADWA: THE HISTORIC VICTORY OF ETHIOPIA OVER EUROPEAN COLONIALISM

Paulos Milkias, Ph.D.
Professor of Humanities and Political Science Marianopolis College/Concordia University

"Many died...[and] no one knows their names...but their names are written in Heaven, in the book of life...for they became martyrs..." The Mannawe Manuscript [66]

The battle of Adwa is rightfully considered one of the most important events in history, not because finer battles have not been fought or greater heroism displayed, but rather because it was the first major reversal for the European colonialists who, without consulting the people of Africa, were carving up the continent for themselves. Its cardinal import, however, lies in the fact that it is a victory for the underdog, a victory for right over wrong.

THE RISORGIMENTO AND THE SCRAMBLE FOR AFRICA

To understand the historical impact of Adwa it is imperative to investigate the proximate and immediate causes of Italy's interest in Ethiopia and its fateful road to war far from the hills of Rome. Indeed, the annals of Italy's obsession with the conquest of Ethiopia and its humiliating defeat at Adwa cannot be complete without a proper documentation of the history of that country in the mid-nineteenth century. Until the 1850s, Italy was, like the Ethiopia of the Zemene Mesafint, fractionalized into mini sovereign states. Following the first Napo-

66. [Quoted in H. Ehrlich, *Ras Alula*]

leonic campaign, a sense of nationalism was created throughout Italy. Support came from the intellectuals and the middle-classes; and many secret patriotic associations such as the "Young Italy" of Giuseppe Mazzini actively agitated for unity.[67] Garibaldi was one of the first to initiate a bold bid for the reunification of the independent Italian principalities. Then appeared Count Camillo Benso Cavour in the government of Piedmont, with his almost religious dedication to raising the standard of the royal house of Savoy among Europe's established dynasties. Cavour cultivated good relations with the imperialistic European powers and his tiny country was involved in the Crimean War, thus entering the game, first though reunification of the separate states and then through an aggressive policy of colonial conquest.

Italian nationalists reached their first goal in the year 1859, when Vittorio Emanuele II of Piedmont, in a speech from the throne, openly supported Cavour's dream of reunification. From here on, the events in the region changed very rapidly. Austria, after failing to have Piedmont disarmed, declared war on the Kingdom of Sardinia. This enabled Cavour to openly agitate for the political unity of the disparate Italian states. The conflict triggered a chain reaction of revolutionary situations that Cavour was waiting for. When France intervened in the insurrections and regional conflicts in the region, the accord of Villafranca was signed and ultimately led to the cession of Lombardy.

In the meantime, the people of central Italy and Romagna rebelled and overthrew the old parochial regimes. A plebiscite held in 1860 favored the annexation of the existing independent principalities to Piedmont, thus leading to reunification in March 1861, together with the territory of Southern Italy that had been taken by Garibaldi's expedition of "The Thousands of the United Kingdom of Italy."[68] Venice joined the union in 1866, and Rome was taken by conquest in 1870. The Risorgimento, as the Italian reunification was called, thus settled the problem of the territorial unity of the Italian nation.

Before long, the nationalists who were riding on the euphoria of the Risorgimento were calling for rearmament. Their parliamentary leader, Crispi, proclaimed in 1872 that Italy must "arm, arm and always arm herself."[69] This was music to the ears of Italian arms manufacturers, merchants and speculators of all kinds because the Italian economy was still too small and too fragile to promise

67. E.E.Y., Hales, Mazzini and the Secret Societies, London: 1956.
68. George M. Trevelyan, *Garibaldi and the Making of Italy*, London: 1911; Garibaldi and the Thousands, London: 1909.
69. F. Crispi, Government of Italy *Discorsi Parlamentari i*, Rome, 1915, pp. 136-137.

them new wealth. Although the idea of a colonial adventure was not universally approved in Italy and was actually opposed by the industrially developed Lombardian bourgeoisie who wanted to consolidate their gains, the Ligurian capitalist entrepreneurs supported expansionism abroad.

Even though the nationalists were filled with euphoria, the reunified new state of Italy soon faced numerous and complex problems. There was an immediate need to bring uniformity to a territory that was far from being politically and economically homogeneous. The wholesale application of fiscal, judicial and administrative structures of the old Piedmont exposed a rift between the Mezzogiorno — the structurally weaker Southern sector of Italy — and the more industrially developed Northern and Central regions of the country. Southern Italy's aristocrats and latifundisti (big landowners) were afraid of agrarian reform and wished for a colonial expansion that would reduce the demand for land. This region was actually so economically depressed that, as one observer puts it: "the hungry and illiterate masses of South Italian peasants...dreamed of a colony as their salvation: they were fascinated by the myth of a terra facile, an 'easily acquired land.'"[70]

A mass migration of peasants and the poorest classes to the two Americas occurred, and ultimately millions of Italians left their country to look for a better life elsewhere. The financial dynamos of Italy, such as the Orlando Brothers, who controlled the Genovese Bank and the rich Banco di Roma, were looking for areas where they could invest their capital. The parliamentarian Crispi was quick to promise them:

> Without a single drop of bloodshed, an immense space is being offered to our industry and our trade where they can invest their money safely and to their great advantage.[71]

King Umberto of Italy often spoke of "Italy's glorious mission" in Africa. Colonial expansion was thus touted as a way to address the problem of investment markets, poverty, unemployment and demographic pressure in Italy. Armed with aggressive nationalism, colonial conquest was promoted as providing lebensraum for the newly amalgamated European entity. And this became a prelude to Italy's colonial adventure in Ethiopia, which was ultimately settled at Adwa.[72]

---

70. R. Ciasca, Storia Coloniale dell'Italia Contemporanea, Milan, 1940, pp. 39-40.
71. G. Agnese, *l'Africa Italiana al Parlamento Nationale*, 1882-1905, Rome, 1907, pp. 188-307.
72. A Plebano, *Storia dela Fianza Italiana* III, Turin, 1902, pp. 445-450.

The connection between the Risorgimento and Italian colonial designs on Ethiopia was very clear. It is not surprising that General Baratieri, who was sent to carry out colonial expansion in Ethiopia, was Garibaldi's and Crispi's political companion in the 1860 expedition of "One Thousand." Baratieri always addressed Crispi as "My Honored and Beloved Duce." When he won the battle of Agordat against Ras Mengesha's poorly armed and hopelessly small peasant army, in 1894, he wrote: "I feel my Garibaldian blood circulating in my veins."[73]

As for the European environment of the period, it was characterized by unbridled expansionism. The 1885 Treaty of Berlin, by which the European powers subdivided Africa, demarcated Ethiopia as being under the sphere of influence of Italy.[74] By 1890, all the leading European powers had political dependencies in Africa and many European entrepreneurs encouraged their governments' role in the opening up of what was then called "the Dark Continent," with its abundant riches.

In the case of Italy, Magnate Rubattino, the Genovese ship-owner, had bought the small port of Assab, near the southern entrance of the Red Sea, from a local sultan whose predecessors traditionally paid annual tribute to the Emperor of Ethiopia, in March 1870, in order to use it, as he claimed then, as a provisioning station for his ships. The importance of Assab to the Italian merchant marine was enhanced by the opening of the Suez Canal. After he took over more land in 1879 and 1880, Rubattino's acquisition was bought out by the Italian government, thus putting the port of Assab under the direct control of the Italian state.

It should be pointed out at this juncture that Rubattino's transactions had a colonial mission from the beginning. This company and Flori (another merchant marine) had actually encouraged Italian colonization in the region and they established the Societa di Navigazione Generale, which donated to the Italian government sixteen steamships in Assab to be utilized for colonization.[75] The aim was to pass Assab to the Italian state so that it would be used as a staging ground to expand into the hinterland of Ethiopia and thus open up potential agriculture and mineral resources for exploitation by Italian entrepreneurs, which would in the long run bring enormous profits for their shipping industry.

---

73. See R. Battaglia, *la Prima Guerra d'Africa*, Turin, 1958,, pp. 574-599.
74. J. Gallagher, "The Partition of Africa,"in *New Cambridge Modern History*, vol. xi, Cambridge, 1962, pp. 601-602.
75. R. Battaglia, *La Prima Guerra d'Africa*, pp. 303-32.

Aware that Ethiopia had problems of distribution of political power between the regional princes and the emperor in the center, and finding that Menelik of Showa and Emperor Yohannes IV saw each other as rivals for the Solomonian crown, the Italian politicians of the period made contact with the Showan Negus in an aggressive pursuit of the policy of divide and conquer. They promised Menelik large arms shipments if he would agree to attack Yohannes from the south, as they expanded from the north.[76] And as the Italian nationalist of the period, A. Oriani, openly admitted in 1889, the "Italian national revolution was being continued in Africa" and the conquest of an empire in Ethiopia was "a raison d'être for the Risorgimento."[77] What this meant was, in a sense, "we have built our unity; let us destroy yours."

As regards Italian ambitions and the relations among the European powers, Italy was suspicious of France which had an insatiable desire to expand its colonies from the French Congo on the Atlantic Ocean to the Horn of Africa where it already controlled Obock, in an area that (like Assab) had traditionally paid tribute to the Ethiopian emperor. The region soon became French Somaliland, with Djibouti as its capital. Crispi, the architect of the Adwa conflict, howled in parliament: "France will kill us! Africa will escape us!"[78]

Germany was another rival because it had, by April 1884, occupied South West Africa (present day Namibia); but, since Berlin wanted to keep Italy from allying itself with France, it acceded to Italy's ambition in Ethiopia. Britain also had aspirations to control Ethiopian territories adjacent to the Bahr El Gazal swamps, so that it would be able to build a railway line from the Cape of Good Hope at the Southern edge of Africa to the city of Cairo in the extreme North, and also to control the headwaters of the Nile, to which river Ethiopia supplied not only almost all the silt that had made Egypt exceedingly fertile for millennia, but also contributed 86% of its waters. Nevertheless, the leaders of the United Kingdom had slowly come to the conclusion that they could not afford to face a protracted war in a heavily armed and war-like "Abyssinia," and in the vacuum, they preferred having Italy on their borders rather than their greatest rival, France, so close to their East African colonies.

It was in 1882 that Count Pietro Antonelli was dispatched to the court of Showa in order to improve Italy's relations with Menelik who was only a

76. Carlo Zachi, Crispi i Menelich nel Diario Indedito del Conte Augusto Salimbeni, Turin, 1956, p. 231.
77. A. Oriani, *Fino a Dogali*, Bologna: 1889 (second edition), 1923) pp.357-361.
78. F. Crispi, Government of Italy, *Discorsi Parlamentari, ii, pp.* 693-695.

regional king but was nevertheless in control of the richest part of Ethiopia to the South. The Italians were aware that there was an intractable rivalry between Menelik who showed overt signs of yearning to ascend the Solomonian throne and Yohannes IV of Tigray from the North who was the Emperor of Ethiopia - equally determined to maintain his sovereign control. Rome obviously sought to exploit the situation.

After Antonelli made the initial contact, other missions followed, but both Emperor Yohannes and King Menelik became suspicious of Italian designs when with the tacit agreement of Britain, the Italians occupied Massawa from the Egyptians. Massawa, it should be pointed out, was historically an Ethiopian port and its major outlet to the sea but was lost during the Islamic expansion on the Red Sea coast and was at that time in the hands of the Egyptians. The Italian occupation of Massawa with the implicit approval of Britain was highly resented by Menelik and Yohannes because, by the treaty concluded with the British and an Egyptian mission under Admiral Hewett and Mason Pasha in 1884, free transit of goods was to be guaranteed through the port and both leaders needed to import arms for the defense of their country.[79]

In two years, the Italians had inched up the highlands, and matters came to a head in January 1887, when Emperor Yohannes asked General Gene (who had camped with Italian troops further inland from Massawa) to withdraw from the region. The Italian general refused to comply, and a detachment of Italians encamped at Dogali was annihilated by the armies of Emperor Yohannes, commanded by Ras Alula, the governor of Baher-Mellash province (which the Italians later named Eritrea). Of the 500 Italian invaders, 400 died on the battlefield and 21 out of their 24 officers were also killed; the remaining three were captured.[80]

The Italians, enraged at the Dogali defeat, sent a fresh expeditionary force from Italy under the command of General San Marzano. The latter fortified his position and stayed camped, refusing to give battle to Emperor Yohannes. The emperor, unable to flush the Italians out of their embankment and finding it hard to keep his soldiers too long in the hot environment of the Eritrean lowlands, moved his army temporarily to deal with the Mahdists because, while Yohannes

79. The occupation of Massawa by the Italians was strongly opposed not only by Emperor Yohannes IV but also by Negus Menelik. This can be seen in the latter's letter to King Umberto II, written on Miazia 3, 1877 [Julian calendar] April 10, 1885 in Government of Italy, *Documenti Diplomatici*, 1885-1890, xv, p. 191.

80. Roberto Battaglia, *la Prima Guerra d'Africa*, Turin, 1958, pp.225-242.

was awaiting an opportunity to forcibly evict the Italians from Mereb-Mellash, the Dervishes who had now come to power in the Sudan had occupied the Ethiopian town of Kassala.

Earlier, Ras Alula, Yohannes' chief general, had succeeded to inflict a costly defeat on the Mahdist leader, Osman Digna at Kufit in September 1885.[81] but after the Italians moved into the highlands and started to occupy Yohannes' attention, the Sudanese Moslem leaders got bold and tried to take over Ethiopian territories on their borders. Yohannes who was hitherto preoccupied with the Italian colonialists saw no other choice but to turn his attention to the Eastern part of his empire; he had to curb the encroachment of his aggressive neighbors first.

The war between the Dervishes and the Ethiopians escalated rapidly. In August 1887, the dervishes penetrated deeper into the heartland of the Amhara region. They soon invaded and sacked the old Ethiopian capital at Gondar. Emperor Yohannes now took the field in force against the Moslem invaders. A major battle ensued at Gallabat, in which the dervishes, under Zeki Tumal, were badly beaten. But a stray bullet struck the Emperor, and the Ethiopian fighters retired. The Emperor died during the night of March 9, 1889, and his body fell into the hands of the Dervishes.[82] This hiatus gave a breathing space to the Italians and enabled them to continue to occupy more and more land on the highlands of Eritrea. Rome had now to deal only with one ruler; and the treaty of Wuchalé, which was drafted before the death of Yohannes, was rammed through by the Italian envoys to be signed by the new Ethiopian emperor who was crowned as Menelik II, Elect of God, Conquering Lion of the Tribe of Judah, King of Kings of Ethiopia.

The Wuchalé Doublecross

It was at a time when Emperor Yohannes and King Menelik of Showa were bracing for a showdown that the Italian plenipotentiary, Count Antonelli, came to the Showan court to gain for Italy through diplomacy what it could not seize through intimidation and war. The future emperor was duped by Antonelli's

81. Haggai Erlich, Ethiopia and Eritrea during the Scramble for Africa: A Political Biography of Ras Alula, 1875-1897, pp. 68.
82. Richard Gulk, "Yohannes IV, the Mahdists and the Colonial Partition of North East Africa," *TransAfrican Journal of History*, I, 2, (1971) pp. 22-42.

subtle wiles and allowed him free access to the court. Later, the Italian diplomat became so close to Menelik and so influential that he even started to advise him on internal matters. Aleqa Atsme, who was close to the imperial court, starting from Ankober, states that Antonelli was advising Menelik not to sign agreements with the French and the other European governments, "because, if you do," he used to tell him, "you will open your country to them and since they are powerful, they will usurp your throne. Italy, on the other hand, is small and weak and cannot even fight with you." Antonelli then started playing on the weakness of the power structure in Ethiopia, namely the rivalry between Menelik and Yohannes for the Solomonian throne, and as Atsme discloses, Antonelli was impressing it "upon the Showan King how Italy would: 'provide [Menelik] with weapons so that [he would] be stronger than Emperor Yohannes.'"[83] Antonelli succeeded to win the trust of Menelik and as soon as the latter acceded to the Imperial throne, the "treaty" of Wuchalé (which will go down in history as one of the greatest infamies in international relations) was signed. In return for signing it, Italy promised to give the new emperor 10,000 rifles. The treaty, drafted in Amharic and (as the emperor assumed) then translated into Italian, was signed in Addis Ababa on May 2, 1889. In one of its paragraphs, it stipulated that for interpretation, the two texts, the Amharic as well as the Italian, would carry equal authority.[84]

Paragraph XIX of the Amharic text states: "This treaty will be accurately translated in Amharic and Italian and [both would] become a final authority in interpretation." What this meant was that neither the Italian nor the Ethiopian version ought to have priority if problems in interpretation emerged. The interpretation had to totally correspond. The Italian version even stressed the need for accuracy in translation and subsequent interpretation. While stating that the treaty written in both languages would have the same authority, it left no doubt about the similarities between the two and the fact that there should be no place for discrepancy. It specified: "le due versioni concordando perfettamente fra loro" (the two versions being perfectly in concordance with each other).[85]

In December of that year, Ras Makonnen, Emperor Haile Selassie's father, signed an additional convention in Rome.[86] Aleqa Atsme, who knew about the

83. Atsme Giorgis, Aleqa, *Yegala Tarik*, Dire Dawa: 1913 p.76.
84. Sven Rubenson, *Wichale, an Attempt to Establish a Protectorate over Ethiopia.* Addis Ababa: Haile Selassie I University Department of History Historical Studies, No. 1. 1964.
85. Ibid, Appendix, See also 34; Conti Rosini, Italia ed Etiopia dal tratato di Ucciali alla. battaglia di Adua, Rome, 1925, pp. 67-68.

dangers of the pact, points out that the Emperor kept the new treaty secret. He wrote:

> 'No one among Showan dignitaries nor the entire Ethiopian population knew what was being said and done. Only Antonelli, the emperor and the translator knew what was being drafted and signed." But the dabtara (Church scholar) who had a chance to read the treaty warned Menelik of the trickery particularly in paragraph XVII; Atsme warned Menelik with his letter: "[Concerning] the treaty to be sent to Italy:... the idea is fine but re-examine paragraph XVII, its weight today may be no more than a dime; a year later however it will be heavier than a thousand tons...of lead."

After receiving the letter, Menelik had the Amharic version read to him to see if there were problems. When none was found, he ordered Atsme to be jailed and his property confiscated. He was later released after paying fines. When the warning came true, years later, Menelik offered him a position in government — which the former declined, having been mistreated and insulted.[87]

The treaty of Wuchalé was not openly discussed in court, much less in public, presumably for two reasons. One was Menelik's apparent need to keep his acquisition of so many firearms secret from his internal enemies and contenders for power. But second and more important was the explosive nature of Paragraph III, particularly in the Tigrigna-speaking areas of the north, which it divided up.[88]

It was by invoking paragraph III of the treaty of Wuchalé that the Italians occupied areas in Baher-Mellash including Halai, Saganeiti, Adi Nefas and Adi Yohannes. Although Menelik did not acquiesce to it, the Italians later moved further inland and incorporated areas bounded by the Mereb-Belesa line. First, they occupied the strategic city of Keren and a month later took over Asmara, the capital of Mereb-Mellash. Then, by a royal decree of 1890, the Italians christened their new colony in Baher-Mellash "Eritrea" (a name derived from the Roman Marus Erythraeum, or Red Sea), thus separating Hamasen, Akele Guzay and Seraye from Tigray.

Even though Paragraph III was the most important from the point of view of Ethiopian sovereignty, for Menelik it was not the most momentous; he had acquiesced to it due to the exigencies of the era. The immediate problem for him

---

86. Battaglia, La Prima Guerra d Africa, p. 384.
87. Atsme Giorgis, *Yegala Tarik*, p.79.
88. Tesfa Tsion Medhane, *Eritrea, Dynamics of a National Question*, Amsterdam: Gruner, 1986, p. 7.

was Paragraph XVII. The trick of this paragraph, concocted by Count Antonelli and approved by Prime Minister Crispi, read, in the Italian version:

> S.M. il Re dei Re d'Etiopia consente di servirsi del Governo di S.M. il Re d'Italia per tutte le trattazioni di afari che avese con le potenze o Governi.[89] [His Majesty, the King of Kings of Ethiopia, consents to avail himself of the government of his Majesty the King of Italy for all negotiations in affairs which he may have with other Powers or Governments.][90]

The Amharic version, which was supposed to be the original, however, read:

> His Majesty, the King of Kings of Ethiopia, may, if he so desires, avail himself of the Italian government for any negotiations he may enter into with other Powers and Governments.

The difference is fundamental. In the Ethiopian version, paragraph XVII clearly means that Menelik was under no obligation to use Italy's good offices to communicate with other powers. Yichalachewal means "may, if he desires to." In the Amharic version, Ethiopia's sovereignty and independence was not questioned. The Italian version obliges him to use the good offices of Italy; this makes Ethiopia an Italian protectorate.

Interestingly, the translator of the treaty of Wuchalé, Grazmach Yosef Negussie, spoke only Amharic and French; he did not understand Italian and therefore could not translate the Amharic text into Italian. One should therefore conclude that the Italians had already drafted it in Rome and made Grazmach Yosef Negussie pretend that he translated it. It was known that Grazmach Yosef was in Italian pay at the time though he also worked for the Ethiopian Imperial palace. It cannot be mere coincidence that the Italian copy read exactly like the rough copy written earlier by Antonelli and approved by Crispi before he came to negotiate with Menelik. This was supposed to be a working draft but it became the actual document that eventually led to war.[91]

Sven Rubenson has no doubt that Wuchalé was prewritten in Italy and brought to Menelik for assent. He states: "What is absolutely sure is that Article XVII was conceived and drafted in its final Italian wording by the Italian government before Antonelli left for Ethiopia."[92]

---

89. Rubenson, *Wichale*, Appendix.
90. Ibid.
91. Ibid.
92. Ibid. p. 32.

Even though he does not mention Wuchalé by name, Menelik's Minister of Pen, who was by Ethiopian court tradition the scribe for such matters, comments:

> Antonelli mischievously wrote [the treaty of Wuchalé and informed] foreign governments that Ethiopia had become an Italian protectorate.

Wuchalé was undoubtedly contrived to trick Menelik into signing a treaty which the Italian government hoped might ultimately receive de facto acceptance by the Ethiopian side.[93] Furthermore, because the Italian officials had no doubt that they would be able to conquer Ethiopia soon by force, if not by diplomacy, they surmised the discrepancy in translation would be discovered too late and would be irrelevant after occupation.

The emperor found about Antonelli's doublecross second hand. Not thinking that his signing of the treaty of friendship with Italy had any effect on his relationships with other nations, Menelik wrote letters to European powers asking them to lift an embargo they had imposed on Ethiopian arms shipments.[94] But, to his astonishment, the replies of the European heads of state came in with shocking and similar results. The Kaiser of Germany (who humiliatingly referred to Menelik as "Your Highness" instead of the traditional "Emperor") and Queen Victoria of Britain informed him that, henceforth, he should communicate with them through Italy and not directly. In politely refusing to deal with Menelik directly, Queen Victoria's letter stated:

> [The] Italian government have notified us that by a Treaty concluded on the 2nd of May, ...[1889] between Italy and Ethiopia, it is provided that his Majesty the King of Ethiopia consents to avail himself of the government of His Majesty the King of Italy for the conduct of all matters which he may have with other powers or Governments.[95]

The idea that Ethiopia should become a protectorate was an insult for Menelik. As Afework Gabre Yesus, Menelik's biographer, explains, the Emperor angrily told Count Salimbieri, the Italian envoy who came to his court:

> I have never even dreamt of Ethiopia being an Italian protectorate.[96]

---

93. Gabre-Selassie, *Tarik Zedagmawi Menelik* Neguse *Negest Ze -Etiopia*, Addis Ababa: Artistic Printing Press, 1959 [Eth. Cal.) p. 233.
94. Menelik's letters to Queen Victoria of Britain, King Wilhelm II of Germany and to French President, Carnot were written on Tahsas 6, 1882 [Ethiopian calendar], December 14, 1890. See a copy of this letter in: Government of Britain, Public Records Office, London:*Foreign Office Records*, 95/750.
95. A letter by Queen Victoria to Emperor Menelik, February 20, 1890, Ibid. 95/751.
96. See Afework Gabre Iyesus, *Dagmawi Ate Menelik*, Rome: 1901, p. 73.

The emperor persistently explained his belief that, just as all men are equal before the law, all nations are also equal in the international arena. In a letter to King Umberto, Menelik protested vehemently:

> When I made that treaty of friendship with Italy, in order that our secrets be guarded, and our undertaking should not be spoiled, I said that because of friendship, our affairs in Europe might be carried on with the aid of the Sovereign of Italy, but I have not made any treaty which obliges me to do so, and today, I am not the man to accept it. That one independent power does not seek the aid of another to carry on its affairs, your Majesty understands very well.[97]

Menelik sent similar letters to Europe's great powers, imploring them to ignore the Italian communication asserting that Ethiopia was their protectorate; and stating that, indeed, it was not, and that the Amharic version of the treaty, which was binding and which had been signed by both parties, was clear on the subject. Immediately after sending the letter, Menelik stopped using the 4,000,000 Lire of loan promised when Ras Makonnen signed a convention contracted with the National Bank of Italy under the guarantee of the Italian state. He even paid back the portion of the loan he had already taken.[98]

The dispute over the interpretation continued and by 1890, Ethiopia and Italy were not only quarrelling about the content of the Treaty of Wuchalé, they were in utter disagreement over the boundary dividing the Ethiopian province of Tigray and the Italian colony of Eritrea. The Italians brought every pressure to bear on Menelik to accept the Italian version, but Menelik was adamant in not accepting it.

On February 12, 1893, Menelik unilaterally abrogated the Treaty of Wuchalé as well as the additional convention signed by Ras Makonnen, and notified King Umberto of his resolve to declare the Treaty of Wuchalé null and void. He followed it up by a letter to the European powers, stating that Italy was "trying, under the mask of friendship, to take possession of this country...My county is strong enough to maintain its independence, and it does not care for any protectorate."[99] Quoting from the Bible, he concluded: "Ethiopia stretches her hands to God." Crispi's arrogant answer to the Emperor's communications to the European powers was to warn them to have nothing to do with Ethiopia — sarcastically adding, "Ethiopia stretches her hands to us!"[100]

---

97. A letter by Emperor Menelik to King Umberto of Italy, Nehassie, 19, 1882 (Ethiopian calendar): Government of Italy, *Documenti Diplomatici*, 1890-1891, XVII p. 10.
98. See letter written by Salimbeni to General Baratieri, November 15, 1890, Government of Italy, Documenti Diplomatici, 36/12.
99. Comite de l'Afrique Francaise, *Buletin, No. de* Juillet, 1893, p. 8.

Even after showing this unshakable resolve, Menelik was still trying to be conciliatory. When Ras Makonnen under the instructions of the emperor asked for a way out of the impasse with Italy, the Italian reply on January 18, 1896 suggested a treaty which was even more sweeping than that of Wuchalé. The proposed treaty sought to impose the following terms:

The entire province of Tigray would be ceded to Italy. The rest of Ethiopia would be an Italian protectorate whereby Italy would represent Ethiopia with all other powers. A residing Italian general in Ethiopia would decide on matters dealing with other nations and Ethiopia. Italian diplomats and consular officials would represent Ethiopian citizens abroad. The number of the Ethiopian Emperor's and his officials' soldiers would be decided by Italy. Ethiopia was not to give any agricultural, mineral, commercial and industrial concessions to foreign countries and their companies without the approval of Italy. Italy would have an ambassador at the court of the Emperor and that of his vassals. The ambassador as well as his assistants would be allowed to keep an army of their own. The appointment of the Rases and provincial governors would have to be approved by Italy. Italy could decide whether any foreigner was to be expelled from Ethiopia. The customs and tariffs of Ethiopia would be under the sole jurisdiction of Italy. All foreigners residing in Ethiopia would be governed by the penal jurisdiction of Italy. No loans could be taken by the Emperor and his Rases without the approval of Italy. Ethiopian money could be minted only in Italy. Italy would not be responsible for the debts already incurred by Ethiopia. Italians could own any non-movable property in Ethiopia. If the Italian colony of Eritrea were attacked, all Ethiopians would have the obligation to come to its defense with everything including the deployment of their troops. Italy would take the responsibility for Ethiopian telegraph, commerce, agriculture, education, and the tariff and taxation systems. The Italian government would have to be informed of all disputes between the Emperor and his Rases and between the Rases and the provincial heads and the "petty officers." In cases of armed combat, the Italian colonial army in Eritrean would be called upon to settle the dispute and the expense would be paid by the party that called for help. The final clause [clause 18], then adds: "The Italian government assures to Emperor x and his successors, the throne...."[101] [Note that the name of Menelik, was avoided suggesting that they could chose some one else in his place].

100. Francisco Crispi, Government of Italy, *Scritti e Discousi Politici*, Rome, 1890, pp. 704-706.
101. Government of Italy, *Documenti Diplomatici*, No. XXIII, Document 202.

The conditions enumerated in this draft treaty appear to have been drawn up by Antonelli and Crispi with the express intention of having it rejected. It was clearly a call for war.

Crispi then instructed General Baratieri, the governor of Eritrea, to try once more to sell the Wuchalé Treaty in case the shock effect of the new proposal had intimidated Menelik. He still wanted to get him agree to the new Italian occupation of Tigray. Menelik, however, replied that Italy had no right to occupy Ethiopian territory and that he was to evacuate from there immediately. After moving his army further inland into Tigray and camping at Enticho, on February 13, 1996, Baratieri wrote to Menelik that it was "impossible to accept" the terms set by the government of Ethiopia and that he "would not discuss the matter further." The General added: "The negotiations must be considered ended and each of us remains free in his action."[102] By this, he had thrown down the gauntlet, and Menelik demonstrated his readiness to take it up.

Crispi's Call for War

In their bid for the acquisition of colonies, the Italians were moving fast in the north. They now had over 20,000 soldiers in Eritrea. A Dervish threat on the Western part of the colony of Eritrea was settled when on December 21, 1893, Colonel Arimondi occupied Agordat for Italy and on July 17, 1894, Baratieri occupied Kassala. But their attempt to move south to occupy Tigray was frustrated; they were defeated first at Amba Alaghe and then at Mekele. The Italian Prime Minister was impatient with Baratieri for not concluding the Ethiopian war on the southern front. Brushing off Italian losses in these two places as inconsequential reverses, Crispi wrote Baratieri on February 25, 1896:

> This is a military phthisis [lung consumption], not war...a waste of heroism, without any corresponding success....It is clear that there is no fundamental plan in this campaign and I should like one to be formulated. We are ready for any sacrifice in order to save the honor of the army and the prestige of the Monarchy.[103]

It was by then clear to Menelik that a military confrontation with Italy was inevitable. Thus, after a national mobilization was put into place, he ordered Showan fighters to move to Wara Ilu and the armies of Gojam, Dembia Quarra,

102. Ibid., Document 275 p. 126.
103. Jana Mrazkova, "The Colonial War in Ethiopia, 1885-1895, *Archiv Orientalni*, 46, 1980, p. 207.

Begemder from Checheho north, to move to Ashengie. Those from Simien, Wolqayit and Tegene were told to move to Mekele. The rest marched with Menelik and camped at Edaga Hamus. And just before war broke out, the Ethiopian army moved from Edaga Hamus to Abba Garima, near Adwa. However, as Gabre-Selassie points out, Menelik did not mean to stay at Adwa for long, as the emperor was planning to march north to Adigrat and Hamasen in order to reconquer Eritrea.[104]

But Baratieri did not want Menelik to cut him off from Eritrea; that could have created a logistics nightmare. By the beginning of 1896, he was in dire straits because the fortification at Sauria was being harassed. The Tigrayan army of Ras Sebhat and Dejazmach Hagos, who had defected to the Ethiopian side, had already denied the Baratieri army the opportunity to replenish its supplies through Asmara. They systematically disrupted communications to Eritrea by destroying the telegraph lines. If his antagonists cut off vital supplies to the Italian army for too long, he might face the humiliation of having to surrender without a fight. His most logical option was therefore to make a surprise attack and dislodge the Ethiopian forces from Tigray and ultimately from the rest of the country. By the end of February, 1896, Baratieri had provisions for only four days. This happened to coincide with an important Ethiopian Orthodox Tewahdo holiday, during which time one-third of the Ethiopian fighters were attending religious services at Axum-Tsion and other churches far from the scene of military confrontation. He thus proposed to his general staff a choice between retreating to Asmara and taking the opportunity to give battle to Menelik's army; all four of his Generals chose the latter, and were confident of winning the battle.

Afework Gabre Yesus explains that Baratieri was not only confident that he would defeat the Ethiopian army by using superior Italian artillery, he was under the impression that many of Menelik's regional commanders including Ras Makonnen, Negus Tekle Haimanot and Negus Wolde Mikael would defect to the Italian side. The latter princes were actually communicating with Baratieri to confirm his wishes. Afework adds that this was a strategy devised by Menelik to mislead the Italians concerning the strength of the Ethiopian forces. Why did he decide to attack at that particular time? Because, as Afework Gabre Yesus explains:

104. See Gabre-Selassie, *Tarik Ze-dagmawi Menelik*, Neguse *Negest Ze -Ethiopia*, Addis Ababa: Artistic Printing Press, p. 257.

> The Italian military commander [Baratieri] was receiving secret letters written by Ras Makonnen, King Tekle Haimanot and Ras Mikael that they were going to defect from Menelik to [the Italians] when the battle starts; but there was nothing hidden from emperor Menelik.[105]

THE ITALIANS OCCUPY STRATEGIC POSITIONS FOR ATTACK

Baratieri commanded a well-trained modern army of 17,700, of whom 10, 500 were Italian soldiers and the rest were native-born Eritreans raised and trained for the invasion. Nine hundred Eritreans not included in the above figures were also in the advance column leading the mules that carried the ration, ammunition, and hospital supplies. An additional 1,415 Italian soldiers accompanied by 1,600 Eritrean recruits were left behind to guard the main Italian camp at the rear.

After learning that Menelik had made camp at Abba Gerima, near Adwa, Baratieri wanted to make a barrier between his army and that of Menelik by occupying a line formed by the hills of Belah, Rebbi-Arienni and Kidane-Mihret. The general gave his orders to his commanders and his columns started to march to battle on a fateful leap year day of February 29, 1896, at 9:00 P.M. On the morning of March 1, they were deployed at their chosen site, hidden behind Mounts Rebbi-Arienni and Raio, only seven and a half miles from the Ethiopian army encampment.

Baratieri's intentions in taking these strategic positions were several. He figured that his line of defense would be safe for it afforded him a line of retreat with strong defensive posture, each flank covering the other's communication lines. They could march back to Sauria, if need be, without being harassed by the Ethiopian forces on the other side. The path presented no insurmountable escarpments path by which his antagonists could cut him off from his base. Most importantly, he could easily shell the Ethiopian army at Adwa from Mariam Shawitu on his right flank.

As General Albertone was ordered to move to his line of formation, two place names were confused on the map made for the occasion: the mountains of Kidane-Mehret and Enda Kidane-Mehret. Baratieri aimed to march following three paths at night hidden behind the mountains with the intention of deploying his army and occupying a strong defensive position on the front

105. See Afework Gabre Yesus, *Yedagmawi Ate Menelik* Tarik, pp. 92-93.

slopes. Thus he ordered Gen. Dabormida to occupy the spur of Mount Belah on the right flank and General Arimondi stationed in the center to occupy Mount Belah itself. And, most fatefully, due to deliberate misinformation by the Ethiopian peasants, General Albertone initially occupied a hill several miles away from the intended Mount Kidane-Mehret. This was corrected after a loss of some time. General Ellena was to stay behind at Rebbi-Ariani as a reserve.

Baratieri had no doubt that, in such a position, he would repulse the Ethiopian army if it moved into attack. In actual fact, he suspected that the Ethiopian army might even withdraw when it realized the strength of the Italian forces and their topographic advantage, and thought that he might be able to march into Adwa as a modern day Roman conqueror. He also aimed to raise the morale of his wavering officers who thought that the unimaginable idea of being defeated by an African army might bring about their demise. In all this, Baratieri had not only underestimated the determination of the Ethiopian army, he also seems to have underestimated the difficulty of negotiating the natural barriers of the country that forced his European soldiers to march through narrow paths up and down precipices.

The Ethiopian Fighters Take Their Position for Defense

The Ethiopian fighters from all parts of the country rallied to the cause, but they were not as disorganized as some European military strategists suggest. Even though formal drills were unheard of, each individual commander and each fighter knew what was expected of him. They chose the most strategic positions possible on their mountains and hills, though they rarely built European-style forts and trenches for defense. They encamped in a formation that allowed them to come to the aid of one another during combat operations.

At Adwa, Negus Tekle Haimanot's Gojam Amhara infantry and cavalry were camped on a high, slightly asymmetrical amba or plateau, with its southern side resting safely against cliffs. Winding between these cliffs were narrow footpaths, hard to negotiate by a heavily armed and orderly European army. The Gojam Amhara cavalry spread through the lower ground below the mountains among the meadows where the horses could graze while the fighters awaited a call to action. Next, came a mélange of Amhara, Oromo and Gurage armies from Harar, commanded by Ras Makonnen and encamped at the town of Adwa and the high ground in its vicinity. The Gojam and Harar infantry were sheltered by the rocks and broken ground on the mountaintops. To meet them, an advancing foe would have to move up the gradually rising mountain position, and if he did, he would be open to attack from above. The Wallo cavalry (commanded by Ras Mikael), most of whom were armed with rifles, were encamped at the southern and southwestern gradients of Mt. Selado. Ras Mengesha's Tigray army commanded the ground to the north of the Wallo army position. Ras Alula's Tigray army stood guard at Mt. Adi Abuna on the extreme left. Menelik's Mehal-Sefari, mostly Amhara, Oromo and Gurage and Taytu Betoul's Yejju fighters were encamped in the center near the crumbling walls of the 16th-century Portuguese monastery of Fremona, which afforded a good defensive position with broken ground, deep riverbeds and rows of hills yielding an opportunity for combat maneuvers. The Mehal-Sefari fighters were stationed at a position from which they could rally to the support of the Wallo, Tigray and Harar armies if need be. The Gondar Amhara armies of Ras Wolle and Wagshum Gwangul's Agaw, Amhara and Tigre fighters were also encamped behind Harar's and Gojam's armed forces that could be reinforced quickly during combat operations. Dejazmach Bashir's army attached to the Emperor's Mehal-Sefari was strategically camped in reserve at the foot of the mountains overlooking Adwa from where it could reinforce the center. The Oromo cavalry from Wallaga were encamped near the meadows some distance from the center from where they could gallop at top speed to the central as well as the southern, the eastern and Western flanks during combat.

The Overall Structure of the Ethiopian Formation

The Ethiopian formation near Adwa resembled a cross. This was to enable it to respond in the same manner no matter from which side the enemy's attack came. Even though the Fitawrari's army (in this case, Fitawrari Gebeyehu Gora's) was normally the leader of the advance guard, the Qegnazmach or the Grazmach (leaders of the Right and Left flanks respectively) took the duties of the Fitawrari. There was no name for the leader at the back of the formation, but this was also put under the command of one of the Azmachs or senior operation officers.

The Ethiopian army commanders had made sure that no harm should come to the Emperor and the Empress, lest the tragedy of Metemma (where an Ethiopian victory against the Dervishes turned to a rout) be repeated. Initially, therefore, Emperor Menelik and Empress Taytu, the kings and Rases were carefully stationed at the Church of Ide-Gerima from were they could see with binoculars the whole theater of war. Although they ventured out on several occasions to encourage the fighters and the commanders, and this was particularly true of Taytu Betoul and Menelik, the strategy had always been that the head of state and his Rases encamp safely in the center or the rear from where they could give orders for the overall conduct of the war. Once a combat was underway, each commander knew what to do and changed strategies as the battle developed.

ARMAMENT

Of the estimated 90,000 people who rallied to the call of their motherland, 20,000 Ethiopians had no guns:[106] they carried only their animal skin shields, spears, traditional swords, and knives. In terms of modern weapons, the armies of Emperor Menelik had 40 cannons versus 56 for the Italians encamped near Adwa. The Ethiopian fighters also had some 70,000 rifles. But whereas Italians had modern and very efficient rifles, the Ethiopians were armed with a melange of old European weapons ranging from Remingtons to Martini-Henrys, Fusil Gras, Berdans, Mousers, Lebels, and Wetterlis. Except for the fighters of Ras Sebhat and Dejazmach Hagos, numbering about 2,000, who were armed by the Italians before they defected to the side of their countrymen, the Ethiopian fighters (who did not manufacture their own rifles and produced very little of their powder), employed the weapons they had previously acquired through purchase and treaty negotiations. What they had, they employed extremely efficiently. Augustus Wylde (who interviewed the Ethiopian commanders, including Emperor Menelik himself), describes Ethiopian strategy in employing the weapons in combat as follows:

> With [European made] weapons, the Abyssinians make good practice up to about four hundred to six hundred yards, and at a short distance they are as good shots as any men in Africa, the Transvaal Boers not excepted, as they never throw a cartridge away if they can help it, and never shoot in a hurry. They know nothing whatsoever about fire discipline nor any European drill, their one object being when an enemy is in their country, to attack him at the most favorable moment to themselves as possible. When the word of command is given to advance, they can tell from the position they are in what their duties are, and they know the general

106. Berkeley, *The Battle of Adowa*, London, p. 270.

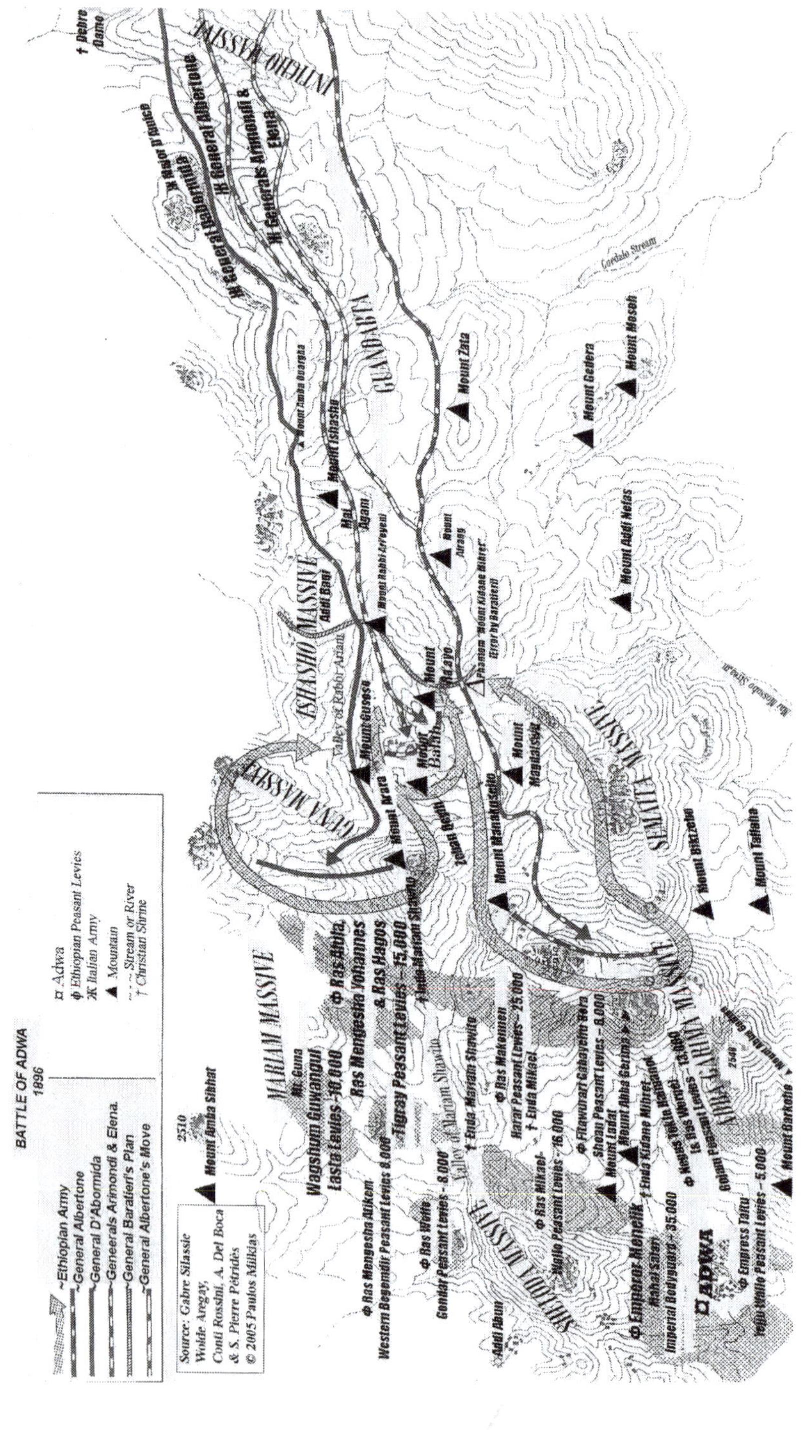
BATTLE OF ADWA
1896
Ethiopian Army
General Albertone
General D'Abormida
Generals Arimondi & Elena.
General Baratieri's Plan
General Albertone's Move
Adwa
Ethiopian Peasant Levies
Italian Army
Mountain
Stream or River
Christian Shrine
Source: Gabre Silassie
Wolde Aregay,
Conti Rossini, A. Del Boca
& S. Pierre Pétridès
© 2005 Paulos Milkias
ADWA
MARIAM MASSIVE
ESHASHO MASSIVE
SEMAYATA MASSIVE
GUANDAPTA

> plan of battle, namely, to surround their enemy as quickly as possible, and when the circle is complete, to make use of every possible bit of cover on their advance to the center where their enemy is situated. When they arrive well within musket range, they commence firing, not before, and as their invaders have always fought in close formation, the target offered has been a large one. The Abyssinian with his light load and unbooted foot can move with ease at a sort of jog-trot, at a ratio of at least four to one as compared to the European, and as he need never fight an engagement unless he wishes, and as a rule can fight at a time he chooses, and not when his enemy would like him to, he always has an immense advantage.[107]

Beginning and End of Battle

The Albertone brigade that had moved to occupy Mount Kidane-Mehret and the Ethiopian forces started exchanging shots at 5:00 A.M. The first group to engage with Albertone was the Tigray army under the command of Ras Mengesha and Ras Alula. This was immediately joined by Ras Mikael's Wallo army.

As the engagement started, the Italians trained their artillery on Ethiopian troops that were ranged in close formation. The first artillery blasts wreaked havoc in Ethiopian formations but they swiftly scattered, to attack in smaller groups. Soon the scene on Enda Kidane-Mehret Mountain started to change. One of the Eritrean units, the First Battalion, strayed and was mowed down by the Ethiopian forces that had already surrounded it.

In the combat with Albertone and soon with the other generals, the Ethiopians followed their own strategy, tested and proved successful in their different wars with the Egyptians, the Ottomans, the Dervishes and the Italians themselves. When they encountered a battalion or a large body of an invading army, they employed afena, the poor man's blitzkrieg. In afena, the Ethiopian fighters surrounded the enemy and advanced towards the center, using whatever cover was available to them. Encirclement was conducted with the Fitawrari's troops dividing into two and making a detour around the flanks of the invaders. The army would then go to direct attack from every side. The center and the reserve formation at the rear continued to push towards the mid section of the enemy's forces. Skirmishers moved in from every direction to confuse and demoralize the enemy. They continued their steady trot towards the center even if they sustained heavy loses in the process. It was considered a necessary sacrifice if the battle were to be won. As they put up a sacrifice and arrived at close range, they

107. Augustus Wylde, *Modern Abyssinia,* London, 1901, p.203. p.203.

discarded their rifles and drew their shields and swords, which every fighter carried. The swordsmen went immediately into hand-to-hand combat and either hacked the heads of their enemies or, if they had helmets, mercilessly cut their throats while the mounted infantry came from behind and hurled their spears over the heads of their comrades towards the Italian invaders until they shattered the defense in front of them.[108]

As the intense rifle fire, the hurling of spears and hand-to-hand combat raged in the left flank of the Italian army, other Ethiopians led by the hero of Adwa, Dejazmach Balcha Abba Nefso, deployed their quick-firing Hotchkiss guns on the lower side of Mt. Abba Gerima. At this point, Albertone's advantage in artillery fire was removed and his guns were silenced as his gunners were slaughtered as well as the mules they were mounted on. The few who remained soon ran short of ammunition. Many Italian soldiers, knowing full well that they had no way to escape, continued to fight with whatever weapons were available to them but some saw the futility and gave themselves up at the first opportunity.

As both of Albertone's flanks were being mauled, Ethiopian sharpshooters climbed the heights behind his position and started to score devastating shots at his army's rear position. The fighting continued for a while even though it was clear that the Italians could reverse the tide only with a miracle. Albertone then realized that to persist would be madness; it would only mean the death of all his remaining troops. Thus, at 11:00, after five hours of stubborn resistance, General Albertone surrendered to the Ethiopian forces with a few of his remaining Italian officers.[109]

As Albertone's battalions were being annihilated, danger was looming over the remaining Italian forces at Mts. Raio and Kidane-Mehret. Here, the Italian center (commanded by Generals Arimondi and Ellena) were kept in reserve, crouched in close formation and in a fixed position. Then, masses of armies came against them from a deep ravine near the Spur of Belah: the armies from Harar, Tigray, Wallo, Gondar, and Lasta, which had just cut communications between Albertone's and Dabormida's armies. When they came running towards the front, the close formation of the Italians afforded an easy target for Ethiopian rifle power. While that combat was raging, other Ethiopian contingents moved to attack the reserve regiments at the rear. The aim of the Ethiopian forces was

108. Ibid, p.221-223.
109. Achille Bizzoni, "Ricerche impressioni Delusioni di un Giornalista,"V *Eritrea nel passato e nel presente*, Milan, Societa Editrice Sonzogno, 1897.

clear. They intended to block the Memash Pass so that the Italians would not use the escape route to Enticho, Adigrat and Akele Guzay.

Soon, the Italian army at the center was cut in two and eventually they were surrounded. The encirclement was so complete that Baratieri now had no hope of communicating with General Dabormida's army (which he thought was still intact). Baratieri deployed General Arimondi's and Galliano's battalions and four batteries (two of them from General Ellena's reserve brigade) between Mts. Raio and Belah. With the confusion of Albertone's retreating army in their way, the Italian batteries on Mt. Raio had no choice but to shoot at the fugitives in order to check the pursuing Ethiopians. Nevertheless, the Ethiopians succeeded to penetrate the Italian defense by creeping up the mountain; they reached the top, and lined up menacingly overlooking the Italian columns. The better Ethiopian marksmen sniped at the enemy and hand-to-hand fighters rushed forward to capture the battery but were repulsed by a reinforcement of Galliano's reserve battalion. Colonel Stevani's daring attempt to retake the heights now occupied by the Ethiopians led only to the annihilation of his regiment.

When the Italian forces, attacked on the hills and Mt. Belah, started to scatter, Baratieri failed to rally them to stand their ground. He could not send in the reserve to bolster their position because the reserve itself was surrounded and was fighting desperately for survival. The Eritrean-manned Galliano battalion (numbering 1,200 men) broke its flank and fled and Galliano himself died of wounds he sustained in the first twenty minutes. General Arimondi and almost all his officers were cut down by Ethiopian swordsmen.

While Albertone's battalions were being annihilated by the Ethiopian fighters near Mount Kidane-Mehret, the Italian command at the rear and center was in utter confusion. Communication was lost not only with the unfortunate Albertone battalions that had to take the brunt of the first engagement, but also with General Dabormida, originally assigned to guard the right flank. The latter had advanced farther away, exposing himself to the Ethiopian fighters who smelled victory and withdrawing beyond the point from which he could come to the rescue of Albertone. Baratieri, sensing the looming disaster, tried desperately to call back the remaining forces of Albertone and the still intact Dabormida forces to occupy their original positions. But communication was either not delivered on time, was distorted, or never arrived at the intended destinations.[110] In the rapid advance of the Ethiopian freedom fighters, the Italian army's left as

110. Berkeley, *The Battle of Adwa*, p. 297.

well as its right (which were kept apart by the loss of Mt. Guosso to the Harar fighters) were no where to be found. Baratieri now realized that he had no choice but to concede defeat and make a hasty retreat. He gave orders to fall back in an orderly fashion — but it became a far from orderly rout.

The only reserves remaining, the 16th battalion and two companies of the Alpini fighters, were kept behind to cover the retreat, but they could not stem the tide. They were overwhelmed in minutes and were cut to pieces. Leaving the disaster behind him, Baratieri abandoned General Ellena's forces to fend for itself and chose to escape with some close associates to Eritrea at about 11:00 A.M. Baratieri arrived at Adi Qeyih on March 3, 1896 together with his chief of staff General Valenzano, and General Ellena, who was wounded.

Later, Baratieri blamed Albertone for the error, claiming that the latter had marched alone, knowing full well that more than 10,000 Ethiopian fighters were encamped in the vicinity of the areas he initially occupied, that he had the obligation to keep in touch with the column on his right and that once he suspected that communication had been cut off, he should have sent guides to ask for help. Failing to do that, he prevented himself from getting relief from other brigades.[111] But, of course, that was after the fact.

The last holdout was General Dabormida, who occupied two heights and a valley in the Belah, Rebbi-Arienni and Kidane-Mehret mountain ranges. His aim was to outflank the Ethiopian left formation, from where he could negotiate the high ground around Mt. Soludo to the north in order to have free access to the open valley overlooking Adi Abuna and Adwa. As the initial engagement with Ras Alula's Tigrayan forces got underway, the two armies were engaged in intensive combat. Then Dabormida saw Ethiopian horsemen galloping toward his army. Under the General's orders, part of the Italian army quickly climbed the heights to deny access to their adversaries. But that was to no avail. Despite sustaining heavy losses from Dabormida's square formation, the Oromo and Amhara cavalry from Showa, Wallaga and Wallo pushed forward, falling upon their foes and cutting them down.

After fighting furiously to keep the heights, four of Dabormida's companies were overwhelmed by the Ethiopian lances and riflemen creeping up the hill. The Italians soon fell back to their original position between the heights, where they intended to make a last stand. This also proved futile. Even after receiving artillery reinforcements from two White regiments commanded by Colonels

---

111. Wylde, Modern Abyssinia, p. 207.

Arighi and Ragni, they could not hold their ground for long. In twelve minutes of engagement, the Italians lost twelve of their fourteen White officers to the barrage of fire and hand-to-hand combat with the Ethiopians. One of the remaining two was captured.

Colonels Ragni and Arighi, with over 2,500 of their troops, tried to make a stand on the hills but they were stampeded by the retreating Italian army. Even though they could not stop the soldiers running to save their lives, Colonel Ragni gave orders to his troops to charge forward. They succeeded to check the pursuing Ethiopian forces for a while but the latter came charging again. The Italian officers made a new defense with artillery batteries deployed near a huge sycamore tree that provided shelter to the commanders, at least, who made quick decisions under rapidly changing circumstances in this fast-moving battle.

The Ethiopian fighters as usual tried to employ afena in a daring encirclement of Dabormida's army, as they had done to Albertone's; but they were prevented from doing so by Arimondi's brigade that had taken a defensive position inside an old wall on a hill at the rear of the Italian columns. But taking cover in the tall grass in front of them, an Ethiopian cavalry shouting a battle cry fell and upon them.[112] The Italians poured artillery and riffle fire against them. The Ethiopian cavalry were stunned by the volley of fire and large numbers of their men were cut down. The few that remained galloped back to their camp to regroup. This gave Dabormida's army a chance to prepare for an offensive. But it was short lived. The cavalry came charging back, and those who succeeded to get through the volley of fire shot the Italian officers at close range or used swords and lances.

At one stage, in a desperate attempt to bring the fight to an end, Colonel Arighi charged against the Ethiopian position and briefly succeeded to repulse them. Dabormida lost most of his officers in the charges and counter charges, but the lull brought a moment of cheer and high morale to the Italian soldiers. This too, however, was short lived. Within minutes, the Ethiopian fighters who had just defeated Generals Arimondi's and Arena's armies were swarming in their direction, on foot and on horseback, and with mounted artillery. They moved to encircle the Italians from the rear, thus threatening to cut them off from De Amice's strategic embankment. Rayneri's and De Amice's troops fought desperately to prevent this, but to no avail.

112. Ibid. p. 209.

Dabormida was still unaware that the other Italian troops had been annihilated. He had not received any communication from Baratieri, who had abandoned the battlefield and was headed towards Eritrea with the handful of Italian officers who had survived the carnage. The Italians under Dabormida now had only one choice, to concede defeat, break out of the encirclement and make a hasty retreat north. But Dabormida was killed while trying to lead his retreating army in a break out in the direction of Hausen and Adi Qhuala. The Ethiopian fighters pursued Dabormida's retreating men relentlessly and rendered impossible an orderly flight. As Berkeley records, from eyewitness accounts, "the Abyssinians, wild with enthusiasm, redoubled their fire, and then rushed in upon them, reckless of losses or death."

The last battalion to retreat was that of De Amice. This last Italian contingent had been well entrenched within walls and embankments, but as soon as it left its trenches to retreat, it was wiped out by the Ethiopian forces who were already confident of victory at Adwa. The fate of this last battalion that had checked the Ethiopian afena (encirclement) for so long and thus had caused the death of many an Ethiopian fighter was described by Berkeley as follows:

> Hardly had they got clear of the trenches than the [Ethiopians] dashed forward with furious yells, and butchered every one of them with swords and lances.[113]

The Scene after the Victory

What did the battlefield look like after the combat was concluded, giving total victory for Ethiopia? A Russian visitor who witnessed the scene immediately after the battle's conclusion described the scene as follows:

> The dead lay in heaps....Streams of blood turned into rivers...and the enormous field of killing looked like some horrible chessboard where fate with a merciless hand had interfered in a terrible endgame....The Abyssinians set fire to the grass and as the flame spread, in their fiery glow could be seen in outline shadows rising from the earth. These were unfortunate Italians, some wounded, some lying as if dead to avoid capture. They were compelled into resurrection to save themselves from being burned alive. They were seized and led to the emperor with the triumphant cry: "Sing, Black vultures, sing...Here is human flesh for you to eat."[114]

113. Berkeley, *The Battle of Adwa*, p. 341.
114. Yu Elets, [Leontiev], Emperor Menelik and His War with Italy, St. Petersburg, 1898, C. 16.

One Italian prisoner of war described the scene when he was captured by Ethiopian forces and led to the Emperor's campsite:

> [The camp] was a city without end... an inferno of drums beating, deafening screams...agonizing weeping and continuous firing of guns into the air. My tenuous grip on reality snapped and I lost track of how long it took before I was tied down to a cot. Men jumped up and down hysterically around me....I was covered with a Black cape...and fell into a nightmarish sleep.[115]

The Rout

It is known that the Ethiopian soldiers pursued their fleeing enemy for more than nine miles. But what was the fate of the Italian soldiers who somehow survived this fierce and bloody battle and fled towards Eritrea? In places, some Italian units stopped and tried to exchange fire to give cover to their fleeing comrades. But they were cut down. As Augustus Wylde explains:

> On these human barriers, the Abyssinians came like the spates in their own mountain rivers, sweeping all before them. As the rout continued, fatigue and thirst were taking their toll.

Berkeley explains:

> One can picture the miserable column of men who had been marching all night and bungled all day, who were trudging onward down that fatal valley of Yeha. So stupefied by weariness, disaster and thirst that they cared little even when the Ethiopian horsemen halted to take deliberate aim at them within a short range.[116]

General Baratieri reported the engagement and the final debacle in a coded top secret message to his government:

> The enemy,...with great boldness, were mounting upwards to our position and were penetrating our files, firing almost point blank at our officers. Then all was at an end and no orderly retirement could be organized. The officers sought in vain to hold the troops at one of the successive positions; because enemy eruptions and a few [Ethiopian] horsemen below discouragingly sufficed to throw everything into a state of confusion. Then our true losses commenced; [Italian] soldiers like madmen threw away rifles and ammunition because they thought that if they were captured unarmed, they would not be castrated, and almost all of them were abandoning their rations and cloaks....[117]

---

115. G. Tedone, Angera: I Recordi du an Prigionero di Menelik dopo il Disastro di Adwa, Rome, 1915, pp. 29-31.
116. See another version of a translation of this report by General Baratieri in Berkeley, *The Battle of Adowa, p. 309.*
117. Ibid. p. 311.

Four days after the Adwa battle, Menelik started to march his army on the way to Asmara. He arrived at Enticho (now liberated from the Italians) and sent scouts to study the condition of the road to Asmara. But an Italian envoy, Salsa, came and begged Menelik to refrain from crossing the Mereb into Eritrea. He told the Emperor that the Italian King was interested in signing a peace treaty with Ethiopia on Menelik's terms. Menelik demanded the immediate removal of the Italians hauled up at the fort in Adigrat. Salsa agreed. According to Gabre-Selassie, "since the road to Hamasen was not conducive to the march of a large army," Menelik decided not to pursue them to the sea. But one can surmise that the emperor must have had other reasons not to pursue the Italians to Massawa.

On October 26, 1889, Italy was forced to sign a document that stated, inter alia:

> The treaty of Wuchalé ... is and will remain definitely annulled, with its annexes....[and Italy] recognizes absolutely and without reserve the independence of the Ethiopian Empire.[118]

This time, the treaty was in Amharic and French, not in Italian. Obviously, Menelik did not want to allow another opportunity for foul play by the likes of Antonelli.

Repercussions in Italy

The Italian public, having been fed false information about a series of Italian successes in Ethiopia, was stunned when it heard the news of the disaster in Adwa. Anti-government demonstrations were held in most major cities.[119]

The universities and hospitals in Rome were closed down due to public disturbances. In Pavia, protesters built barricades across rail tracks to prevent the transportation of army troops. And in Naples, police could not handle the riots and troops had to be called in. Italy's King Umberto II, who had been referring to the campaign as "an action by civilized people against barbarians," designated his birthday, March 14, a national day of mourning.[120]

General Baratieri was the first casualty of this enormous Italian military disaster. He was deposed from the governorship of Eritrea and was court mar-

118. Gabre-Selassie, Tsehafe Te'ezaz Gabre-Selassie, Tarik Zemen Ze -Dagmawi Minilik Neguse Negest Ze -Etiopia, p.271.
119. Chris Prouty, Empress Taytu and Emperor Menelik I, Ethiopia, 1883-1910, p. 159.
120. Ibid.

shaled for abandoning his command from 12:30 P.M. on March 1 to 9:00 A.M. March 3, 1896.

As crowds shouted "Long live Menelik!," Crispi, a symbol of the humiliating adventure at Adwa, faced the wrath of his people. The Prime Minister's office became a target and the police had great difficulty to disperse rock throwers. This storm of protest led to the fall of Crispi's government on March 14, 1896, following which a new government was created under the Prime Ministership of di Rudini.[121]

The Lessons of Adwa

Magnanimity

The rightwing Italian press of the period singled out one case concerning the fate of some Bashbazuks (Eritrean-born recruits) in order to malign Menelik and confirm the repeated charge that the Ethiopians were "barbarians." It is true that a group of Eritrean fighters, who sided with the Italians in the war against Ras Mengesha, were brought before the traditional court by the Ras himself and were punished with amputation. Menelik listened to Ras Mengesha's unrelenting call for the most severe retribution to be meted out to the 406 Tigrayans from Eritrea for siding with an invading foreign force and fighting against their county and their kith and kin — a treasonous act, in any nation. Considering the dire repercussions that might follow if he took the matter into his own hands, the emperor referred the case to the Church to decide; and it was the Egyptian Archbishop, Abune Matewos, head of the Ethiopian Orthodox Church, who, quoting the Fetha-Negest (Laws of the Kings), also of Egyptian origin, passed the sentence.[122] It was not impossible for Menelik to violate the decision of the Abuna but, by tradition, it would have been very difficult: he had the right to excommunicate him if he found him spiritually insubordinate. Ultimately, the emperor deliberated on the matter and let the sentence stand.

Many Ethiopians, including biographer Afework Gabre Yesus, felt that the Emperor should have commuted the sentence no matter the decision of the Abun. However, the anger among the Tigrayan population against those who sided with the enemy was extremely severe. Leontiev, the contemporary Russian

121. See *Die Grosse Politik*, Vol. XI No. 2769 p.234.
122. Yu Elets, [Leontiev], Emperor Menelik and His War with Italy, Op. Cit. C. 16.

visitor, reported from Tigray: "feelings against these turncoats was such that no one would give them water and no one would bind their wounds."[123] A conservative church presented Menelik with what he considered Divine command. The people of Tigray and their leader wanted to exact retribution, and the emperor erred in giving in to them. But this unfortunate event should not be allowed to tarnish Menelik's image entirely.

It should not be surprising that more than a millennium before, Mohammed's biographer, Ibn Hisham, referred to the ancient Axumites as the "righteous Ethiopians." In keeping with this tradition, except in the isolated Bashbazuk incident mentioned above, Menelik was magnanimous throughout the struggle for the protection of the independence of Ethiopia. His treatment of the Italians who were flushed out of the walls of Mekele after the spring from where they drew their drinking water was occupied, and his humanity in allowing them to leave with their weapons, and the fact that he provided them with escorts and 500 mules to carry their baggage is, to say the least, legendary. Not to be misunderstood, Tsehafe-Te'ezaz Gabre-Selassie points out that Menelik told the Italian national who negotiated the relief of the Mekele garrison:

> The fact that I let these helpless people who are surrounded and are suffering from thirst go free with their weapons should not be looked at as an act of foolishness. Mark that I did so out of respect for my kingdom. Now, if you are looking for peace, excellent, but if you still want war, bring your army together with these ones and try it![124]

Menelik also gave strict instructions to his troops that they should never kill or mistreat those who gave themselves up. As an English encyclopedia of the period wrote, "the... prisoners taken by were exceedingly well treated by him, and...he behaved throughout the struggle with Italy with the greatest humanity and dignity."[125] Though stubborn in guarding their independence, therefore, the evidence shows that the Ethiopian rulers of the period were fundamentally magnanimous to everybody, including a vanquished foe.

---

123. Ibid.
124. See Gabre-Selassie, Tsehafe Te'ezaz, Tarik Zemen Zedagmawi Menelik, Neguse Negest the Ethiopia p.250; Also Government of Italy, Atti Parliamentari, XIX Legislatura, Prima Sessione 1895-1896, No. XXIII, 1896, No. 206.
125. See "Ethiopia," *The Guttenberg Project, Encyclopedia* (original publication 1909), London, p. 201.

The Pitfalls of Division

If the Italians had followed any one policy consistently throughout their attempt to colonize Ethiopia, it was the policy of divide et impera (divide and conquer), which had been refined by their Roman ancestors thousands of years ago. It should not be surprising that Italian officials had declared openly, early during the struggle, that divide et impera ought to be the principal element of their policy and that it ought to be the motto of their colonial venture. Unfortunately, many Ethiopian leaders played into their hands.

Despite the remarkable achievements of the nationalistic leaders of Ethiopia who guarded their country's independence, they did err on many an occasion. Take the case of Dejazmach Kassa Mircha of Tigray, who supported the British in their expedition against Tewodros and allowed them to penetrate Ethiopia as far as Maqdala, in return for which he received arms from Napier, which enabled him to defeat or intimidate his rivals and become the Emperor of Ethiopia.[126] The British, who knew that they would get into a military quagmire, did not stay; they left, as they promised they would do. But one may rightly wonder at the risk, should they have broken their promise and decided to stay.

Another major point that figures prominently in recent Ethiopian history is how Mereb-Mellash (later renamed Eritrea, by the Italian colonialists) was lopped off from its mother country. It should be made clear from the outset that the loss of Eritrea had nothing to do with the bulk of the Eritrean population. The responsibility for the dismemberment of Eritrea lies squarely in the ranks of the Ethiopian ruling classes, who were more interested in securing their own political power base than the future of their country.

There had long been an intractable rivalry between the three lineage's of Tigray: that of Ras Mikael Sehul (such as Ras Mengesha of Tembien); that of Ras Wolde Selassie (the great grandfather of Dejazmach Debeb Araya); and that of the house of Dejazmach Sebagadis of Agame, headed in the late 1880s and 1890s by Ras Sebhat Aregawi.[127] The latter, it should be remembered, gave his loyalties to the Italians and did not return to the Ethiopian fold until the Battle of Amba Alaghe, a decisive battle that was a prelude to Adwa. The reasons for his defection are connected with his rivalry with Ras Mengesha Yohannes.

---

126. Sven Rubenson, *The Survival of Ethiopian Independence*, Heinman: London, 1964, pp. 258-259.
127. Carlo Conti-Rosini, *India ed Etiopia*, Rome, 1935, p. 26.

As the Ethiopian ruling classes fought for political supremacy, the Italians only encouraged and exploited the existing rivalries and rarely intervened directly. In fact, General Baldissera had a plan that "no action should be taken by the [Italian] colonial force until the strength of the conflicting parties [in northern Ethiopia] was entirely exhausted."[128]

The division in the Ethiopian ranks started early when Ras Wolde Mikael Solomon, who was the hereditary ruler of Hamasen and who was contemptuous of the supremacy of Mircha Kassa (Emperor Yohannes), started to look for foreign collaborators to weaken his rival in the north. Augustus Wylde, in a book written in 1888, remarks that as early as 1868 Ras Wolde Mikael was encouraging foreign powers to invade the country.[129] By the 1870s, his relations with Egypt (which was already occupying part of Mereb-Mellash) were so warm that he sent his son Dejazmach Mesfin to Cairo.[130] When Ras Wolde Mikael openly rebelled against Yohannes and killed Dejazmach Hailu, the Emperor's appointed ruler of the province, he marched against him but the rebel prince escaped to Bogos, where he was bolstered by his foreign allies, the Egyptians.[131] Yohannes appointed Turk-Basha Alula of Inderta (now raised to the rank of Ras) as the governor of Hamasen. In time, Ras Wolde Mikael was captured and imprisoned at Amba Salama with his children. This made the rupture between the ruling houses of Tigray and Hamasen complete. Wolde Mikael's son-in-law with his father-in-law's encouragement soon joined Italian ranks.[132] Another rival of Alula, Dejazmach Bahta Hagos, was armed by the Egyptians and worked hard to undermine Ethiopian control over Mereb-Mellash. But the most notorious turncoat among the northern aristocrats was Dejazmach Debeb Araya, son of Ras Araya Demissew and brother-in-law of Ras Alula, who at one time appealed to the British to support his claim to the throne of Ethiopia.[133] In the meantime, he shifted his loyalties from Yohannes to the Egyptians and then to the Italians, simply because he did not get the title of Ras from Emperor Yohannes.[134] During the time when Alula was on a national mission to

128. B Baldissera, *Realizione*, 1889, LVXVI, 1, 9.
129. Augustus Wylde (83-86), *in the Soudan*, London, 1888, Vol. I, pp. 324-326.
130. Government of Britain, *Foreign Office Documents*, Gordon's Memo, September 15, 1879.
131. Mohammed Rif Bek, *Jabral-kaser fial-khilas min al-asr*, Cairo, Kolmolin, No. 251.
132. Haggai Erlich, Ethiopia and Eritrea during the Scramble for Africa: A Political Biography of Ras Alula, 1875-1897, 1982, p.25.
133. See Conti Rossini, *Italia ed Etiopia*, Rome, 1935, pp. 154-155. See also, *Eritrea Report*, Government of Britain, War Office, 33/55.
134. A letter by Debeb to Baldissera, Government of Italy, Archivo Sstorico del Soppresso Ministero dell' Africa Italiana, Rome; February 10, 1889.

Metemma, Debeb found a power vacuum. He conferred with the Italian commanders in the area, General Baldissera and Major Plano, and with their blessing marched his 2,000 troops into Segeneiti.[135] Then he engaged in battle with Yohannes loyalists, killed Dejazmach Haile Selassie (who was the emperor's appointee), and occupied Asmara on February 2, 1889.[136] During the same week, Dejazmach Kifle Iyesus — urged by his father-in-law, Ras Wolde Mikael Solomon of Hamasen, marched into Keren with the Italian expeditionary force.[137] With the cooperation of these two individuals, the Italians officially took over both Keren and Asmara and raised the Italian flag.[138] The same was true in the Moslem areas of Baher-Mellash, where loyalties shifted between the Egyptians and Yohannes and later, due to a religious dispute with Alula, the chiefs of Beni Amer openly sided with the Italian invaders.[139] Ras Mengesha himself had allied with the Italians and was even at one time writing the British to help him against Menelik, in return for which he was prepared to make territorial concessions. In his letter to Queen Victoria, Mengesha pointed out that he was deserting Menelik together with King Tekle Haimanot of Gojam; but the Queen counseled him to work closely with Italy, described as the United Kingdom's "friend and ally."[140] Even Ras Alula, the great nationalist warrior (who once remarked with reference to the Egyptian occupation of Massawa that "he will not return until his horse has drunk from the Red Sea") had approached the Italians and promised them more than even the Treaty of Wuchalé provided — "the whole of Mereb-Mellash" — in return for Italian support for the autonomy of Tigray from the control of Emperor Menelik.

Despite his admirable diplomatic and military achievements, Menelik himself was partly responsible for the loss of Eritrea. In the beginning, the Showan Negus was very cautious in questions involving the unity and territorial integrity of the Ethiopian nation. But as his struggle for the Solomonian crown intensified, he started to compromise his stand. After he fell for the bait proffered by Antonelli, Menelik agreed not to come to the aid of Yohannes if the Italians attacked him from the north. For this neutrality, Italy agreed to provide

135. Government of Italy, Ministero della Guerra, *Storia militaire dela colonia Eritrea*, Rome 1935, p. 195.
136. Government of Britain, War Office, *Eritrea Report*, 33/55.
137. Ibid.
138. Ibid.
139. A letter from Kennedy to Salisbury, Government of Britain, *Foreign Office Documents*, June 19, 1887, 403/89.
140. Mercatelli, "Nel Paese,"*Corriere di Napoli*, 13-14 May, 1891.

the Showan ruler with 5,000 Remington rifles. But at this stage, Menelik was not contemplating Italian occupation of any Ethiopian territory. On Menelik's instructions, the agreement he signed with the Italians stated very clearly: "The Italian [government] is obliged not to annex any Ethiopian territory." So, at least in the beginning, Menelik was not ready to sacrifice parts or all of Baher-Mellash.[141]

Menelik's decision to agree to the treaty of Wuchalé was bolstered by the attitude of Yohannes, who considered the Showan Negus a threat to his imperial throne. It is not surprising that, just before advancing towards the Sudan to engage the Mahdists, the Neguse-Negest marched in the direction of Showa to assail Menelik's army; he changed his mind after the Ethiopian Orthodox Church's mediation and decided to first tackle the Dervishes before dealing with his rival. In the meantime, Menelik, who was ambitious, was desperately looking for a situation that would strengthen him against Yohannes.

The Italians obviously found in this development a golden opportunity. On account of the immediate danger he faced from Yohannes, Menelik agreed not to oppose Italy's occupation of certain territories adjacent to Massawa and straddling the cooler mountainous areas of in Mereb-Mellash in return for their tying up Yohannes's army in the north as well as providing him with 10,000 rifles and 400,000 cartridges.

After the death of Yohannes in Metemma, Ras Alula pressed Ras Mengesha to crown himself emperor. Menelik's pragmatic decision was therefore to get more weapons from the Italians, prepare himself for any threats to his ambition to secure the Solomonian crown, and in the meantime to be able to expand his empire to southern Ethiopia unhindered. The Negus also wanted the Italians to deny arms shipments to Tigrayan and Baher-Mellash rebels in the north. Crispi and Antonelli were gleeful because they had been looking for such a division between Ethiopia's rulers all along. Antonelli thus wrote Crispi: "the unity of Ethiopia is on the verge of being shattered." He was not wrong. As Sven Rubenson puts it, in his article quoted previously: "Menelik was a supplicant and the team Antonelli-Crispi prepared to reap the fruits of the situation."

The Treaty of Wuchalé provided a de jure status to the Italian occupation of a territory they were later to name Eritrea. The Negus recognized Italian control of Mereb-Mellash from Massawa and Arfali on the Red Sea coast to the highlands, which included Keren in Bogos and Asmara in Hamasen.[142] In a letter

141. Sven Rubenson, *Wichale I*, Op. Cit.

to Crispi, Antonelli calls Paragraph III of the Treaty of Wuchalé (by which Italian control of Ethiopian territory in Mereb-Mellash was legitimized) "il piu importante (the most important)." In other words, it was a coup for the Italians.[143]

Menelik himself must have appreciated the gravity of his actions in accepting Paragraph III.[144] He considered it so important that he made Antonelli swear that in agreeing to allow them territory in Bogos and Hamasen, and in confiding to him his aspiration for the Solomonian throne, Antonelli would be highly discreet with the secrets confided to the Italian envoy.[145] As if that was not enough, at one time Menelik had even gone as far as urging the Italians to bring their troops to Massawa in order to weaken the position of his Tigrayan rivals. His perceived rivals included Ras Mengesha Yohannes and the other ambitious rulers of the north, such as Dejazmach Debeb Araya , whom he referred to as "Shiftas." In a letter to King Umberto of Italy Menelik wrote:

> The Tigrayans have informed me that the Italians have failed to come through Massawa and have thus betrayed us. It would not be a bad idea if your [Italian] army shows up through there.[146]

It is universally agreed by historians that, after Adwa, Menelik had the military capability to drive the Italians into the sea. The Italians were almost annihilated because they had sustained heavy (70%) casualties — 7,500 Italian soldiers of European origin and an additional 7,100 Eritrean-born recruits were killed, altogether numbering almost 15,000. Furthermore, 1,428 Italian soldiers were wounded and 1,865 became prisoners of war. The Italian army at the conclusion of the Adwa battle had, therefore, for all practical purposes, ceased to be a viable fighting force.[147]

The Ethiopian casualties were heavy particularly because of the age-old tradition of hand to hand combat. They lost about 7,000 dead and 10,000

---

142. Government of Italy, Ministero deli Affari Esteri, *Archivo Storico del Sopresso del'Afrcia Italiana*, Rome, 3614-41.
143. The success of the Italians in getting Menelik sign Article III of the Wuchalé treaty was considered a coup by Antonelli who wrote Prime Minister Crispi: "It is the first time that a king of Ethiopia cedes part of his territory by accord,"21 March, 1890, *Documenti Diplomatici Riservatissima Etiopia 1, No.* 1 69.
144. Government of Italy, *Documenti Diplomatici*, 1889-1890, XV, p. 427.
145. Government of Italy, Ministero degli Affari Esteri, Archivo *Storico del Sopresso del'Africa Italiana*, Rome 3615-47.
146. A letter dated Yekatit 14, 1881 [Ethiopian calendar], written by king Menelik of Showa to king Umberto of Italy, Government of Italy, Ministero degli Affari Esteri, *Archivo Storico del Sopresso del'Africa Italiana*, Rome 3616-53.

wounded, but that was a small fraction of the 100,000 army still at Menelik's command. The Ethiopian military force was also bolstered by the 56 artillery pieces and more than 10,000 rifles captured from the Italian army.

In hindsight, it is indeed surprising that in the treaty of Addis Ababa, signed after the Adwa victory, the Mereb-Belesa-Mai-Muna line was de facto recognized by Menelik even going over the provisions of Wuchalé thus being clearly unfavorable to Ethiopia. Menelik asked for a minimum, such as the evacuation of the garrison at Adigrat and the abrogation of the Wuchalé Treaty. With the fulfillment of these conditions, he decided not to challenge the Italians beyond the Mereb.

The assertion of Menelik's Tsehafe-Teizaz (Minister of the Pen), Gabre-Selassie, that the Emperor decided to return to Addis Ababa because the road to Hamasen was not conducive to marching a large army may be apocryphal. One may ask whether Menelik, having come north from Addis Ababa with such a large army, could not have finished the job if he wanted to, especially considering the fact that there was a huge peasant insurrection in Eritrea against the Italian invaders.

Some Ethiopian historians mention the fact that the new Italian governor of Eritrea, Baldissera, had an army of some 16,700 and that Menelik did not want to taint his Adwa victory with an inconclusive battle or even worse. The Italian general's forces were demoralized by the Adwa debacle, but the next fight might not have been an easy one. The Italians might have not offered an open war as in Adwa but rather a frustrating campaign based upon forces holed up in fortifications and trenches in places such as Udi Ugri, Arkiko, Ginda and Sa'ati. If that became a reality, it would have had a disastrous effect on the Ethiopian armed forces. It was a déjà vu repetition of Yohannes's dilemma in failing to engage the Italian army that dug trenches and stayed secure in fixed locations, constantly frustrating the Emperor's military commanders. Under the circumstances, Menelik might have believed that Seraye, Akele Guzay and Hamasen were too poor agriculturally to feed his large army of 100,000 for an extended period of time and that the best course was therefore to stop at Mereb.[148]

---

147. Total Italian loss is 70%. See Harold Marcus, *The Life and Times of Menelik I, 1844-1913*, Oxford: Clarendon Press, 1975, p. 173; for a slightly different figure, see Berkeley, *The Battle of Adowa, p.* 346. An Italian diplomat told Baron Kerchov in 1935, "Mussolini n'a jamais oublié Adwa"; See Anthony Mockler, *Haile Selassie's War*: the Italian-Ethiopian Campaign, 1935-1941, New York: Random House, 1984, p. 48.
148. Ibid. *pp.* 177-181, 113.

One may also conjecture that the Emperor's decision came after weighing the loyalties of Mengesha, his able general Alula and the other ruling houses of Tigray, Seraye, Hamasen and Akele Guzay, and finding that he could not be sure of them. So as to fend off any viable challenge to his imperial power, he still wanted his rivals in the north to stay weak. If Menelik's personal plan was to divide the Tigrigna-speaking rulers of the north to assure himself that the Solomonian crown would remain secure for him, he had succeeded in his aims; even if, in this struggle, Ethiopia lost Eritrea.

It is true that Menelik must have calculated other odds, involving matters beyond the problem of the loyalty of the Tigrayan ruling families. First, the Italians (who were determined to carve out a colony covering all or at least part of the Ethiopian empire) were going to be engaged in a major war with Ethiopian rulers one way or another. That being the case, he might have thought that the best option was to arm himself. His fixation on armaments was also predicated on his immediate mission — to bring into the fold of the central government the hitherto independent kingdoms of southern Ethiopia, with their abundant riches in minerals, livestock and agricultural products.[149]

It could not be hard for Menelik to figure out that if he did not centralize the southern areas stretching from Harar to Wallaga, Kafa, Walaitta, Sidama and Benishangul, small, weak and disunited as they were, these kingdoms might fall first to the Egyptians or the Dervishes and then be swept under the onslaught of the European scramble for Africa. Already, France had her eyes on Harar and Britain on Gondar, Gojam and Wallaga and the other territories adjacent to its East African colony of Kenya.[150]

If the scenario above had been played out, the history of contemporary Ethiopia would have been radically different. Maybe even the success in Adwa could not have been achieved without the riches of southern Ethiopia, which had given Menelik the confidence to refuse to use the loan the Italians had offered him in connection with the treaty of Wuchalé.

Menelik might have also thought that, even if he refused to sign away Mereb-Mellash to the Italians, his rival royalists from the north, such as Ras Wolde Mikael Solomon of Hamasen, were already doing so. That being the case, he might have decided to simply legitimize their deeds — only, in the process, arming himself.

149. See Gabre Selassie, *Op. Cit.*
150. See Sven Rubenson, *The Survival of Ethiopian Independence, pp.* 165-166,188,269,408;297-8,349-50,277,175-7,222-31.

Indeed, all these possibilities cannot justify Menelik's legitimization of foreign occupation of Ethiopian territory and he could not have been oblivious to the judgment of history. But one thing is clear. Menelik was a pragmatic person and as such he might have calculated that the ultimate judgment of history would have to balance that loss against even a partial success in fending off colonialism, remarkable as it was during that trying and difficult period of European expansion. In hindsight, one can even say that Menelik had at least partly vindicated himself through his resolve not to accept paragraph XVII of the infamous Treaty of Wuchalé and by winning a celebrated victory against the Italians at Adwa.

The saga of the loss of Mereb-Mellash did not end there; forty years later, Mussolini used Eritrea as a staging ground to amass an army of half a million soldiers equipped with hundreds of tanks, planes and poison gas to invade Ethiopia, avenging the Italian defeat at Adwa. The 30-year civil war which led to the independence of Eritrea in 1993 is also rooted in this historical fact because the separatists' justification, whether acceptable or not, was that the Eritrean case had to be treated like all other cases of African nations gaining independence from colonialism. One would be hard put to accept the idea that the U.N.-sanctioned 1952 federation between Eritrea and Ethiopia and even the former's unitary status within the sovereignty of the Ethiopian nation state, as engineered by Haile Selassie in 1962, portended a colonial relationship because Eritrea was historically the cradle of the Ethiopian nation state itself. Even though for many this argument has become simply academic after Eritrea's independence in 1993, many Ethiopians still think that history may ultimately play itself out as it did in Germany and reverse the Woyane-Shabiya or Tigray People's Liberation Front, [TPLF] and Eritrean People's liberation Front [EPLF] cabal's plot to create a wedge between these two artificially divided brotherly peoples.

The Virtues of Unity

It was not only armed men who succeeded in this famous battle. Adwa was a common effort between fighters and noncombatant personnel. The civilian population supporting the war came from every corner of the country. The Gindebel unit, numbering 7,000 to 8,000, looked after the rations and the camping equipment of the warriors. The Chagn and the Quami units followed the army altogether with some 600-mule loads of ration specifically reserved for the military commanders. The Desta unit carried axes, scythes, chain saws and the like and pitched the main tents, including that of the Emperor and the Empress. The Wore Genu unit looked after hundreds of cattle slated for slaughter. The civilians responsible for logistics worked day and night in shifts to cook food, to store and to clean up the camp. When the Gibir (the general luncheon) was to be served, specified numbers of workers "carried the food in their hands all day long." The Satin Chagn unit from Dejazmach Joté Tullu's Leqa Sayo and Benishangul Wallaga administrative region with some 4,000 well trained and fully armed personnel led 4,00 mules loaded with boxes of rations. Abba Jifar of Jimma's contingent supplied tarps and draperies that were installed in the camp. Altogether, numerous tents were pitched with the emperor's and the empress' tent at an epicenter, the soldiers resting around them. Tsehafe Te'ezaz Gabre-Selassie points out that this was a tradition set by Ethiopian monarchs going back to Emperor Libne Dingil and was not a new system created by Emperor Menelik.[151]

Adwa was a continuation of the traditional Ethiopian zemecha. It knew no class, no boundaries, no religious denomination, no age group. Even adolescents were involved. This was a struggle the nation would either win or lose together. That was why, after being informed that the battle of Amba Alaghe was concluded in Ethiopia's favor, those galloping towards the site dismounted their horses with anger and grief and those walking on foot sat down and cried because they had been denied the opportunity to participate in the action.[152]

According to Gabre-Selassie:

> There were numerous monks, priests and nuns on the battlefield. Some covered themselves with sheepskin coats. Others donned hats made of straw. All were involved in strengthening the combatants, and invoking the name of God to urge those who were tired never to shirk their duties until they achieved victory.[153]

Translated literally, Adwa was a Zemecha, a "campaign" or "war". However, the Amharic connotation of the term is much deeper. For an Ethiopian, Zemecha is a way of proving one's communion with one's countrymen; it is a way of purging the possibility of failing to fulfill one's national duty. It is a catharsis that the heroes of Adwa had to undergo, even if subconsciously.

---

151. See Gabre-Selassie, Tsehafe Tẹ'ezaz, Tarik Zemen Ze-dagmawi Menelik, Neguse Negest Ze-Ethiopia, p. 230.
152. Ibid. p. 230.
153. See Ibid. for Gabre-Selassie's statements, p. 239; For Berkeley's description see, *The Battle of Adwa, p.* 280.

What unity can yield was seen when on May 15, 2005 election a peaceful revolution played itself out in this ancient land; Ethiopia that has few records of effecting a peaceful transition in the past, saw the dawn of true democracy on the horizon. There were open debates, profound and wide scale political participation, huge rallies that dwarf even those in countries where democracy is entrenched. There was an enormous voter turnout on election day to caste a ballot either for the ruling EPRDF or the opposition Qinijit [Coalition] and Hibret [Unity] or other smaller parties. When they heard the debates in the election and were urged to vote for the party of their choice, the people of Ethiopia, regardless of ethnic and linguistic affiliations, came freely forward. They rallied in millions in the capital and in the major towns. They stood in long queues sometimes for 24 hours peacefully waiting to caste their votes. When the disputed election results were announced, the opposition won almost two hundred out of the 500 seats in parliament. Interestingly, the pan-Ethiopian opposition party Qinijit swept not only the capital Addis Ababa but also all the major towns (regardless of their location in the country's ethnically divided Kilils, which the EPRDF instituted). This is indeed a landmark in Ethiopia's long history. The people of Ethiopia have indicated clearly that no force can divide them; they have shown a preference for a democratic governance based on the rule of the majority and the protection of the minority. This is indeed a spin-off from the victory in Adwa because if a country is not free from foreign domination, then democracy, liberty and the pursuit of happiness surely remain unattainable luxuries.

Vigilance

The battle of Adwa was won because of the vigilance of the Ethiopian people, who were not oblivious to the dangers of a surprise attack. The Italian commanders charged, and Ethiopian veterans of the period agree, that General Albertone's army was fed wrong information by his Ethiopian guides, thus giving the Ethiopians time to prepare for battle.[154]

Perhaps more importantly, the informers of the Ethiopian hero, Ras Alula, were watching every Italian move, and had observed the unexpected abandonment of the fortified Italian position at Sauria and the march towards Adwa, obviously to offer battle to the Ethiopians whom they derided. This vigilance

154. See Afework Gabre Yesus, *Dagmawi Ate Menelik, p.* 92.

that saved the lives of thousands of Ethiopians who could have been slaughtered while still at camp.

"Applied" Nationalities

Adwa's fighters represented every Ethiopian nationality. As Berkeley, who was a witness to the Adwa of 1896, points out: "Every tukul and Village in every far off glen of Ethiopia was sending out its warrior in answer to the war drum."[155] For the combatants of Adwa, Ethiopianness was never an artificial bond or primordial ligature but a collective identity and an enduring shared desire of living with freedom and dignity. Indeed, despite their manifest diversity of language, religion and culture, all Ethiopians stood together to fight against a common enemy.

No nationality and no religious group has a monopoly on the colossal achievement at Adwa. What is particularly striking about the Adwa zemecha was that the civilian as well as the armed response was not limited to Showa, Gojam, Gonder, Tigray, and Wallo (the traditional Abyssinia, known to the Europeans of the period). Fighters came, according to Gabre-Selassie, from other parts of Ethiopia also: Dejazmach Moroda Bakare from Wallaga Leqa, Abba Jifar from Jimma; Dejazmach Joté Tullu from Qelem, Sayo and Benishangul; Kao Tona from Walaitta — all rallied with their fighters. Ras Wolde Giorgis of Kulo Konta, Limu, and Kafa and Dejazmach Tessema of Ilubabor were all mobilizing to march north when Menelik instructed them to stay behind because of the intense rainy season that created seasonal floods and because of the distance involved. He also sent back most of the regional kings mentioned above who rallied to the cause so that they could guard the country against the Mahdists and other enemies that might take advantage of the mobilization against the Italian threat

As regards the makeup of the army, the Mehal-Sefari or central Ethiopian fighting unit was mainly drawn from Showa Amhara infantry from Menz, Tegulet, Wogda, Moret, Insaro, Washa, Merha-Bete, Yifat, Qewet, Gidim, Gishe, Efrata Anstokia and Ankober, and Oromo cavalry from the Machaa-Tulamaa of Salalé, Ada'a, Ambo, Jaldu, Gudar and others. The Mehal-Sefari had always to accompany the emperor. Ras Makonnen's troops were mainly composed of Showan Amhara and Gurage infantry and Oromo cavalry. Fitawrari Tekle led the Wallaga Oromo infantry and Cavalry. Ras Wolle's army was composed of

155. See Berkeley, *The Battle of Adwa*, p. 126.

Amharas from Quara, Begemder, Semien and Dembia. Ras Wolle Betoul's was comprised of Moslem and Christian cavalry mostly from Yejju and Borana Wallo. Ras Mikael commanded mostly Wallo Moslem and Christian cavalry. Empress Taytu led her own Simien Amhara and Yejju fighters. Ras Alula and Ras Mengesha Yohannes, son of the former Emperor Yohannes IV, were mainly with Tigray but also significant numbers of Azabo Rayya Oromo infantry bolstered by the defectors from the Italian side, Ras Sebhat and Dejazmach Hagos of Agame, Tigray. Wag-Shum Gwangul led Agaw and Amhara infantry from Wag and Lasta. Negus Tekle Haimanot commanded Gojam Amhara infantry and cavalry. The Ethiopian army at Adwa was, therefore, a mosaic of scores of nationalities that marched north ready to shed their blood together for a common cause.

The Peasantry

In discussing Adwa, one cardinal fact that is neglected by most historians is the role of the peasantry. But the Ethiopian peasant bore the brunt of the war.

It was the Ethiopian peasants that fed an army of one hundred thousand. Their cows, sheep and goats were slaughtered to feed the soldiers. Gabre-Selassie is candid when he says that Menelik hastened to march north before the peasants removed the harvest from the fields.[156] On the return to Addis, also, the riches of the Azabo and Rayya district kept the soldiers well fed.[157] Furthermore, many Ethiopian peasants such as Ato Aw'alom served as scouts and informers for the national cause.[158]

More on the Eritrean Factor

After the defeat, the Crispi government sacked Baratieri and appointed General Baldissera as the governor of Eritrea. But the situation in Eritrea following Adwa was unenviable. Anticipating an Ethiopian advance against Eritrea, General Baldissera burnt Italian provisions at Adi Qeyih and retreated to Asmara where he desperately tried to regroup the remnants of Baratieri's defeated army. Altogether, he managed to collect 3,260 Italian and 3,041 Eritrean

156. Gabre Selassie *Tarik Zemen Ze-Dagmawi Menelik*, Addis Ababa: Artistic Printing Press, 1959, [Ethiopian calendar]. 238; 266-268.
157. Ibid. 270.
158. Bizzoni points out that the Ethiopians had a "magnificent network of intelligent and loyal informers .... [The Italians] on the other hand ...[depended] solely on the news brought by ... Abyssinian spies generously paid by us." See Achille Bizzonni, '*Eritrea nel passato e nel presente, p.2.*

survivors to form four battalions to defend Eritrea, hoping to ultimately create an army of 18,000 with fresh supplies of troops and arms from Italy.[159]

At this juncture, it should be pointed out that those who castigate the Eritreans for being on the side of the enemy during Adwa should bear in mind that their part of the country had already been signed over to Italy and that therefore they could not be accused of treason against their mother country, Ethiopia. Mark that the Eritrean masses never gave up thinking that they would once again unite with their mother country. Thus, when Emperor Menelik decided to return back to Addis Ababa after Adwa instead of driving the Italians into the sea, they felt betrayed. The Eritreans nevertheless went on harassing the enemy with the hope that Menelik might change his mind and evict the invader from Baher-Mellash.

The Italian agricultural colonists on the Hamasen Plateau fled to Asmara and then to Massawa. Italians in Keren, Asmara and other villages in the new Italian colony all ran to the coast for protection. The Italians were secure only in the forts they created in places such as Adi Ugri, Adi Qeyih. All other areas were hostile, since there was a general uprising against the Italians.[160] As Berkeley recorded:

> The Italian stragglers returning to their...sanctuary were constant targets of Eritreans who sympathized with the Ethiopian victory at Adwa....The whole of the newly conquered provinces had risen; almost every ridge on the sixty or seventy miles between Sauria and Adi Qeyih was defended by armed peasants. The detached groups of survivors spent days and nights wandering without guides or food, struggling against superior numbers, sometimes firing on each other in the dark, and often deceived by the enemy into marching peacefully up the hostile camp fire — finally reaching a post on the lines of communication only to meet the bitter disappointment of finding it evacuated and destroyed.[161]

The Eritrean masses were so jubilant at the defeat of the invader that they kept on harassing the retreating colonial army, to such an extent that the Italian command in Eritrea was forced to ask that an emergency fleet be prepared to transport the Italians out of Eritrea if the situation deteriorated and Menelik decided to cross the Mereb. Indeed, the Eritreans were good Ethiopians, as patriotic as any of the 80-odd nationalities of the country who found themselves in a situation not of their own choosing and over which they had no control.

---

159. Baldissera's total force scattered throughout Eritrea was 16,717, most of Eritrean origin and all encamped within fortresses and demoralized by the disaster their army encountered at Adwa. See Berkeley, *The Battle of Adwa, pp.* 353; 362.
160. Ibid. 270.
161. Berkeley, *The Battle of Adwa,* pp. 262-360.

Unless one is cynical enough to believe that history is nothing more than accepted fiction, one has to try to set the record straight vis-à-vis the prevalent concept regarding the Eritreans of the 1890s and the battle of Adwa. Despite what some rabidly chauvinistic intellectuals who are reacting to Woyane's and Shabiya's divisiveness claim, the Eritrean public and the other linguistic groups there and in Tigray were not traitors during the Adwa struggle. If the reactionary elements in Ethiopia fail to debunk this dangerous idea, not only are they failing to maintain the dignity of history — their action is, to say the least, worrisome for the future of Ethiopia since many of this ancient country's enemies would rejoice as it sinks into the abyss of tribalism and Balkanization prepared for it by its enemies. The cabal that emerged on the country's political scene starting in 1991 only fosters that miserable attempt.

The Anonymous Ethiopian

The history of Ethiopia has so far been treated as the biography of great men. Numerous articles and books have been written concerning the achievements of Emiye Menelik and his Rases, Dejazmachs and Fitawraries. But one has to keep in mind that Adwa involved the effort of many an Ethiopian martyr whose name is no longer known. Adwa and all other Ethiopian victories were won by thousands of nameless freedom fighters.

The Role of Women

Just like their men-folk, Ethiopian women were ready to sacrifice themselves to prevent colonialism from creeping into their country, thus forcing their children to live in servitude. Their slogan was "freedom or death." Taytu is clearly a symbol of all these patriotic qualities. Considering Menelik's trust in others, Taytu was extremely watchful of foreigners. For example, when she saw that Antonelli was becoming so influential with the Emperor, it started to worry her. As a watchdog, she then ordered:

> In future, no treaties should be signed without my participation.

Atsme adds:

> [Henceforth, after Wuchalé] nothing could be done without the Empress being informed.[162]

---

162. Aleqa Atsme Giorgis, *Yegala Tarik*, p. 80

When Count Antonelli insisted that Italy could not notify the other European powers that they had erred in informing them of the protectorate status of Ethiopia, because it had to maintain its "dignity," the Empress replied:

> We also have made known to the Powers that the said Article, as it is Written in our language, has another meaning. Just like you, we also have our dignity to protect. You wish to have Ethiopia represented before the other powers as if it is your protectorate, but that will never be.[163]

Once, in what seems to be a work of the Empress with the collaboration of the Emperor, Menelik succeeded in getting Count Antonelli to sign a new treaty wherein, unbeknownst to the Italian envoy, the troublesome paragraph XVII of the Wuchalé treaty was abrogated. When the Italian envoy belatedly discovered that he had signed something that he did not intend to, he stormed back to the court of Menelik and told him in the presence of the Empress that he did not know that he was signing a treaty which abrogated paragraph XVII. Antonelli then asked why it had been abrogated. Menelik replied, "You and I agreed and you 'consented' to the words included when you signed; nothing new has been added since then. Why are you posing a question now? Did you have a change of heart?" Menelik asked sarcastically.

Antonelli denied that he had agreed to abrogate the paragraph, saying he had only suggested, "let us leave" the question of paragraph XVII until the five-year period elapsed, during which time the treaty remained in force. Menelik told him, "our conversation through the translator was that you had agreed to the abrogation of the paragraph."[164] Antonelli at this stage turned to the translator, Gabriel Gobana, and remarked: "you contrived it: you are the cause of this entire problem, how treacherous of you!"[165]

The empress reminded Antonelli that he was breaching protocol in speaking so harshly to the attendant of the Ethiopian court. She added:

> In the first place, the treaty of Wuchalé that both of us signed never stipulated that Ethiopia would be Italy's protectorate. And if you deny this, show us where it stated otherwise to justify your allegation. As you claimed a while ago, yes you did say, 'let us leave' the question of paragraph XVII; and that was precisely what we did. We 'left' the question of Paragraph XVII. You may have your regrets but His majesty's [emperor Menelik's] words have never changed from beginning to end.[166]

---

163. Government of Italy, *Docomenti Diplomatici, No. XVII* (1890-1891) Part 3, Document IV, p. 71.
164. Afework Gabre Yesus, Yedagmawi Ate Menelik Tarik, pp. 76-79.
165. Ibid.
166. Ibid.

When Antonelli demanded that the [Italian] version be checked, the empress replied, "we do not know [Italian] but since you know our language, check the Amharic version for yourself."[167] The empress, who seems to have cunningly engineered this strategy, relaxed, with an air of meek triumph, but Antonelli angrily tore the treaty to pieces and threw it to the floor. He then threatened that Italy would go to war with Ethiopia and started to storm out of the court. Empress Taytu caught Antonelli's attention for one last moment, gave a sardonic laugh and told the Italian Count defiantly:

> Go ahead with your threat, do it even in a week's time. No one here is afraid of your threats. We will slaughter those who come to invade us. There is no Ethiopian who will not plant his feet in the sand and face death to save his country. To shed one's blood and lose one's life for the motherland is not death, it is an honor!...Do not even waste your time here. Go on with your war. We will wait you eagerly![168]

Afework, who was at the court, describes Antonelli's condition immediately thereafter. "The Ferenj's [White man's] hands and feet started to tremble and his face turned red. Shaking with anger, he stormed out without proper salutations."[169]

As she was frank, Taytu was steadfast in character. And she was not prepared to tolerate any softness amid her ranks. At one time, she turned to her wavering brother who was counseling diplomacy rather than war, and told him to rise to the occasion and fight the Italians, and if he did not, she taunted: "here, take my skirt and I will wear your trousers!"[170]

Taytu was not only a diplomat and stateswoman with resolve. She was an ingenious commandant versed in the art of war — a tactician par excellence. The queen's part in defeating the Italians at Mekele, which was a prelude to Adwa, was legendary.

The Italians had barricaded themselves in a thickly constructed Church embankment. When repeated charges failed to dislodge the enemy, Taytu instructed the soldiers to see if it might be possible to capture the source of the water the Italians were using. When she was informed by one of the military commanders, Liqe-Mequas Abate, that the water source was only about a hundred meters from the Italian camp, she immediately instructed that some

---

167. Ibid.
168. Ibid.
169. Ibid.
170. Quoted in Prouty, Op. Cit., p. 71.

1,000 of her special guard take control of it; they crawled up, at night, while the enemy was diverted by other forces that used artillery fire from the main gate.

When the Italians discovered that the stream flowing near their fortification had been captured, they used artillery and rifle fire in an attempt to regain it. Every time the Italians came out to evict them, the Ethiopian solders commanded by Taytu fought, in the words of Gabre-Selassie, like "angered tigers."[171] As they run short of water, the Italians attempted again and again to "liberate" the spring but were repeatedly driven back. Many were trampled to death by others trying to return to the embankment. This went on for fifteen days, until the Italians started to suffer from thirst and asked to be relieved. An appeal was made by the Italian command on their behalf and the fort was consequently evacuated. This victory was engineered by Ethiopia's ingenious empress, as recognized by friends and foe.[172]

At Adwa, the queen was supposed to be sheltered within the compound of the Church of Abba Gerima. But as Tsehafe-Teizaz Gabre-Selassie points out:

> Taytu, leaving her femininity behind, surrounded herself by her riflemen, both on the left and on the right and directed combat like an army commander. Her artillery pieces were responsible for breaking and putting to flight the Italian advance guard that was attempting to penetrate the Ethiopian formation. And she walked among the combatants far a-field, chastising them: "Courage! come on! victory is ours! cut down the enemy![173]

Taytu was not limited to combat operations. Nor was she the only woman carrying out her patriotic duties at Adwa. Here is another report from a veteran of Adwa:

> Her Majesty [Empress Taytu] went with the emperor to the outer limits of the camp and organized the defense perimeter with the 5,000 men of her personal army. What happened then would have made Europeans laugh. The empress collected the ten or twelve thousand women in the camp and issued water jugs to all of them. This army of another kind filled their jugs at the river and were ready to carry water to those who fought, wherever they stood. Hundreds of women remained in camp prepared to care for the wounded.[174]

As Gabre-Selassie commented: "In the battle of Adwa, we cannot but venerate and revere the contribution of Empress Taytu and the women with her."[175]

171. Gabre-Selassie, Tsehafe Te'ezaz, TarikZemen Zedagmawi Menelik, NeguseNegest Ze-Ethiopia, p. 246.
172. Ibid. p. 262.
173. Ibid.
174. Ibid.
175. Ibid. p. 265

On another front, peasant Tigray women took part in harassing the Italian fort camped at Adigrat. They cut telegraph wires by rubbing them between two stones.[176] The Italian engineer Dr. Ambrogetti, who was trying to repair the telegraph lines destroyed by the armies of Ras Sebhat and Dejazmach Hagos, admitted that he had seen with his own eyes "a woman firing a rifle" at them. The role of Ethiopian women in the Adwa battle and elsewhere is emblematic of women's courage and contribution in the Third World.

Valor

The heroes of Adwa simply joined other Ethiopian martyrs of yesteryear who fearlessly sacrificed themselves so that their children would live in freedom and not in servitude. Documented in these pages are only a small sample — a small fraction of what history has recorded and not recorded. One can include, for example, an account of the heroes of Gura, Gundet, Dogali, Gallabat, the patriots who in the last sixty years showed exemplary courage in Amba Aradom, Maitchew, Korea, Katanga, Jijiga, among others. But let us for now only concentrate on Adwa and the confrontations that preceded it.

The battle of Amba Alaghe, a prelude to Adwa, was one of those many heroic combats that testify to the valor of the Ethiopian people. As the armies of Emperor Menelik were marching northward, the Italians were encamped in the most inaccessible mountain sanctuary with forts and trenches. Fitawrari Gebeyehu's army stumbled upon units of this Italian force on December 7, 1895 and a battle ensued. Gebeyehu was sick but even though he could not carry his weapon, he held a cane and gave directives to his soldiers to fight to the end and told them that if they exhausted their bullets, they must use their swords, kill the enemy and die in honor. The Ethiopians, although outnumbered and at a great disadvantage, fought gallantly against well-armed soldiers sheltered by a mountain fortification.

Other Ethiopians wanted to rally to their compatriots' aid but Shum-Agame Tesfaye of Tigray, who knew the difficulty of giving battle in such an inaccessible place, warned that it would be suicidal. He pointed out that, let alone fighting an entrenched European army with modern weapons including cannons and rifles, their position was so secure it could be defended with nothing but a collection of stones as weapons. He counseled that they save the soldiers for the major confrontation with Baratieri, instead of sacrificing so many

176. Prouty, Empress Taytu and Menelik II, p. 153.

brave men in a fight at great odds. Other Ethiopian fighters however refused to leave Gebeyehu and his army to be slaughtered without support.

Even though the mountain of Amba Alaghe was inaccessible to horses and mules and was almost as difficult for humans to negotiate, no one could stop the Ethiopian fighters rallying to the help of their comrades. One would first climb the cliff and then pull another up. Weapons were passed from soldier to soldier up the precipice. The Italians, who never expected such a daring attack, used everything they had at hand — artillery and showers of bullets — but failed to turn the tide. The enemy together with their leader Major Toselli were annihilated; two thousand Italian soldiers lay dead and the first round to Adwa was won decisively.[177]

Tsehafe-Te'ezaz Gabre-Selassie, who was with Menelik, at Adwa wrote:

> At the start of battle, fighters and their commanders moved in every direction. [Everyone] was running towards his rifle and his cannon. The soldiers were never perturbed by the possibility that they could be cut down by a cannon fire or that they could be felled by a bullet. Anger had set their minds singularly on protecting the sovereignty of their motherland. Their valor was at its peak. Instead of being distracted by the plight of his fallen commander, or even that of his brother, the soldier just went on fighting on his own. The wounded prodded on and even chastised in the name of God those engaged in combat to continue their fight and not to try to save their lives. Those who had exhausted their bullets took more from the waists of their fallen comrades and pursued their enemy and mercilessly slaughtered him.[178]

As the Adwa battle was coming to a conclusion, Captain Franzini marched 15 miles to rescue the Italians in trouble and positioned his battery behind his retreating comrades, but the tumult of the Ethiopian advance was so bold and so swift that he and his men were cut down before they could shoot their artillery a second time. The boldness of the Ethiopian fighters was met with bewilderment and awe by those who saw the fight or interviewed the survivors. General Baratieri, the commander of the Italian forces, commented that his Ethiopian foes "dashed themselves into the middle of [the Italians], leaping as if possessed by a madness to kill or to be killed."[179]

Berkeley, who consistently calls the Ethiopians "barbarian hordes" and "the enemy," explains this feat as follows:

> When [the Ethiopians}]...were beginning to press back the formidable White men, then their enthusiasm rose to madness. It was then that they began to dash up

177. Gabre-Selassie, Tsehafe Te'ezaz, Tarik Zemen Zedagmawi Menelik, Neguse-Negest the Ethiopia, p. 238-242.
178. Roberto Battaglia, La Prima Guerra d'Africa, pp. 635-676.
179. Berkeley, *The Battle of Adwa*, p. 305.

> to within ten or fifteen yards of their enemy before firing, so that no bullet should be wasted. The sentiment appears to me to explain with some vividness the scene described by General Baratieri.[180]

"Madness" or courage, the Ethiopians won the battle through this type of sacrifice.

In another case, the Ethiopian fighters tried to surround Dabormida's army as they had Albertone's, but were prevented from doing so by Arimondi's brigade that had taken a defensive position inside an old wall on a hill at the rear of the Italian columns. But taking the cover of the tall grass in front of them, the Oromo cavalry, shouting a battle cry, fell upon them with war frenzy. Menarini, one of the Italian officers who saw this charge, described it with awe:

> How fine, how superb was that charge of the Gallas [Oromos] with their strange and rich trappings glancing in the sunlight, bending low over the small horses that dashed headlong forward, and coming stoically onward to be massacred by our guns![181]

The Italians poured artillery and rifle fire against their "frenzied" foes but the cavalry charge continued until masses of Ethiopians had fallen, but ultimately they succeeded to annihilate the enemy. Indeed, it is through this type of determination and fearless sacrifice that Ethiopia's independence was guarded for thousands of years.

Adwa and its International Dimension

Right from its inception, the battle of Adwa had racial overtones, through attitudes that were projected at Ethiopians and all Africans in that period. Italian nationalists fired up by the Risorgimento were already pointing the way to Fascism. One such zealot who wanted Italy to conquer Ethiopia remarked that colonization "is a gleam of the chivalrous spirit of our race."[182]

While Italy was preparing its invasion of Ethiopia, King Umberto of Italy was so contemptuous of Africa and the Africans that his speeches were filled with acrid and racist remarks, commenting on "Italy's glorious mission on the Black Continent" and Italy's duty to conquer Ethiopia as "the great victories of civilization over barbarity."[183] And the President of the Italian Senate, in

180. Ibid.
181. Ibid.
182. Menarini, La Brigata Dabormida a la Battaglia d'Adwa, Rome, 1896, p.20.
183. *La Tribuna*, Rome, 9/5/1896.

response to opposition in some quarters in Italy after the defeat in Mekele, addressed the parliament with the comment: "It is the first time that a civilized nation has trembled over the outcome of its action against barbarians."[184] But whether they liked it or not, at Adwa, as the British periodical, the Spectator, reported in its March 7, 1896 edition: "The Italians suffered a great disaster...greater than has ever occurred in modern times to White men in Africa."[185]

Even those who came to Ethiopia as friends to record this historic battle could not get out of this racist frame of mind. Both Augustus Wylde and Berkeley, who were treated with respect by Emperor Menelik and by all Ethiopians, referred to the heroes of Adwa as "barbarian hordes and half savages." Wylde even admitted that the reason why he wrote a book on Adwa was to prevent another failure by European people in invading Ethiopia.[186] Even though they were not Italians but rather of British descent, both consistently referred to Ethiopia as "the enemy,"[187] And the Ethiopian people of the period were not unaware of all this. The refrain in the song of the heroes of Adwa was:

> If you are bitten by a black snake, you can be cured by an antidote;
>
> But be vigilant for life's sake, that white snakes will strike you not!

Beyond the racial divide that the Europeans of the period imposed on the African people, the colonialists had no doubt that they would win a war against any underdeveloped country. They were extraordinarily overconfident in their colonial venture in Ethiopia. In was with this spirit that Travaesi (who was stationed at Addis Ababa as an Italian envoy) wrote: "This Empire [Ethiopia] looks like a colossus, but in reality it has no solid foundations. Woe to it, if we wanted to defeat it one day, it would not require, on our part, much time, effort or sacrifice."[188] It is not surprising therefore that Italian colonialists were dumbfounded when faced with defeat at Adwa.

It is now universally recognized by political historians that the Battle of Adwa marked the turning point in the scramble for Africa and set the stage for the struggle against colonialism and imperialism. Even though the Ethiopians

---

184. Government of Italy, L Africa Italiana al Parlamento Nationale, 1882-1905, 120-121
185. *The Spectator*, March 7, 1896.
186. Augustus Wylde, *Modern Abyssinia, pp.* 197-198.
187. See Berkeley, *The Battle of Adwa, pp.* 24-360 and Augustus Wylde, *Modern Abyssinia, pp.* 196-225
188. Quoted in Chris Prouty, *Empress Taytu and Menelik l;* See also, Augosto Salimbeni, *Tre Ani di Lavoro nel Gojam,*" Rome, 1896.

sustained enormous loss of life, they decisively defeated an invading European army and forced the architects of the Berlin Conference (who had carved up Africa among themselves, like a birthday cake) to formally acknowledge the sovereignty and territorial integrity of Ethiopia.

The battle of Adwa closed the chapter of two adversaries standing with equal determination, one to colonize and dominate, the other equally resolute never to give in. It was the combat of David vs. Goliath. And as in the biblical stories, the bully lost and the underdog won. But the Adwa victory transcends the perimeters of Ethiopia. It is the victory of all Africans, the victory of all the oppressed masses of the Third World.

Every year that the Adwa victory is celebrated, the anniversary points towards both the birth of and the culmination of the struggle for freedom of the peoples of the Third World. It also marks the beginning of a new era of endeavoring to forge nationhood and to strive to promote economic and political development without colonial and neo-colonial domination. Adwa sent out the message that, for self-respecting human beings, it is infinitely better to die on one's feet than to live on one's knees.

Chapter 3. Continuity and Discontinuity in Menelik's Foreign Policy

Dejazmach Zewde Gabre-Selassie M.A., D. Phil. (Oxon.)
Former Minister of Foreign Affairs, H.I.M. Haile Selassie's Government

To fully comprehend the genesis of the battle of Adwa, one needs to clearly grasp the nature of the triangular relations between Emperor Yohannes IV, whose political base was Tigray, the government of Italy (which had an insatiable desire to colonize Ethiopia), and King Menelik of Showa, who aspired to be the inheritor of the Solomonian crown and whose impressive maneuvers had secured a special status for Ethiopia, thus earning for him the epithet of strategist par excellence during the period of the Scramble for Africa. After a brief comment on the general characteristics of the period, we will explore the policies of the countries with which Menelik, who later became Emperor of Ethiopia and confronted the Italian colonialists at the battle of Adwa, had to deal with during the period from 1865-1896.[189]

The scramble for African territories among the European powers was at its height during the latter half of the nineteenth century. The opening of the Suez Canal in 1869 reduced the voyage from London to Bombay by 44 percent; even while it was in the process of being built, the Canal had attracted the colonial powers eager to establish coaling stations bordering the Red Sea and Indian Ocean.

---

189. Based on the discourse given at the Institute of Ethiopian Studies in the University of Addis Ababa on October 17, 1995, and a public lecture I delivered at the National Library on January 16, 1996, as a prelude to the commemoration of the Centennial Celebration of the Victory of Adwa.

Britain was the only one that had established itself in the area prior to the middle of the nineteenth century. She acquired Aden as early as 1839, and took British Somaliland in 1885. By 1862, France was in possession of Obock and subsequently Tadjoura, which later came to be known as the Côte Française des Somalis or French Protectorate of Djibouti. Father Giuseppe Sapeto, an Italian missionary, acquired a plot of land from the Sultan of Raheita in 1869 for the sum of 8,100 Maria Theresa thalers on behalf of Rubattino shipping company. The company used it as a coaling station for twelve years, after which it sold it to the Italian Government. On June 26, 1882, the Italian Government proclaimed Assab as its possession.

The other neighboring nation was Egypt, which had occupied the Sudan since the 1820s and was in those days the country which supplied the head of the Ethiopian Orthodox Tewahdo (Monophysite) Church. Moreover, Egypt under Mohammed Ali's dynasty had virtually usurped the authority of the Sublime Porte over this part of the world. A Firman was granted by the Sultan of Turkey delegating his authority over Massawa to the Khedive of Egypt in 1865.

We may add to this list of neighboring countries the Mahdist State of the Sudan, which existed during the period extending from the fall of Khartoum to the Dervishes in January 26, 1885 up to the fall of Khartoum to the Anglo-Egyptian forces in September 22, 1898, when it was absorbed into the Anglo-Egyptian condominium.

The foreign relations of Menelik, therefore, revolved mostly with the powers close by, although he also approached both Russia and Germany (sparingly, before 1896), and other nations afterwards.

During the period extending from 1865 to 1896, Menelik played different roles:

- First, as ruler of Showa and the adjacent territories over which he extended his control, he was virtually detached from the central government. During this period, he assumed the title of King of Showa and the Galla (Oromo) and at times in his correspondence with foreign powers (as in his letter to Queen Victoria, written in 1867), he referred to himself as Emperor of Ethiopia.
- Second, as King of Showa, a vassal of Yohannes.
- Finally, as Emperor of Ethiopia.

Accordingly, Menelik's foreign relations during this period can be discussed in three phases:

- The first phase, from June 1865 to March 1878.
- The second phase, from April 1878 to March 1889.

- The third phase, covering the years of his reign after he proclaimed his accession to the throne as Emperor of Ethiopia on the death of Yohannes in 1889. Although his reign extended up to December 1913, we will deal in this study only up to 1896.

During the first and second phase, from his assumption of the control of the government of Showa after his escape from Magdalla in 1865, up to his accession to the throne of Ethiopia in 1889, the dominant factor in his foreign relation was his aspiration to gain the imperial crown.

The difference in his foreign relations during the first and second phases is only a difference in style, not in substance.

During the first phase, he acted more overtly as he was virtually detached from the central government, whereas during the second phase, his correspondence with foreign powers was shrouded with secrecy and skilful diplomacy: appearing faithful to his sovereign while actually pursuing his aspiration to attain the supreme power and the imperial crown.

During the third phase, there was a discontinuation in the foreign policy which he had pursued hitherto. From 1889 onwards, the dominant factor was to defend his enlarged empire by taking any measures necessary; this, in effect, was a continuation of the policy pursued by his predecessors.

Constant features in all three phases were the acquisition of arms and ammunition through gift, credit or purchase, and acquiring the necessary finance by seeking loans and by expanding trade. Clearly, Menelik realized that without acquiring adequate arms and ammunition, he could neither maintain Showan independence nor reach his goal of possessing the supreme power over the whole empire.

I.

Menelik, arbitrarily assuming the title of Emperor of Ethiopia in Tewodros's time, first approached the British by sending his envoy Ato Mekbib to the British Resident at Aden in 1867. The British were making preparations for their expedition to Magdalla when they received his letter addressed to Queen Victoria, announcing his accession, hinting for assistance in arms and expressing his willingness to establish friendly relations between the two countries.[190] For logistical reasons, however, the British preferred landing at Zula, near Massawa, and taking the short route to the highlands through Senafe-Addigrat-Magdalla

190. Public Records Office, London: F.O. 1/20 folio 215: undated received August 6, 1867. Menelik to Victoria.

instead of the arduous, long, desert route Zeila-Aussa-Magdalla. Menelik's attempt to free the British citizens detained by Emperor Tewodros on his own, shortly before the arrival of the British force, did not materialize. According to Menelik's own account, as explained in his subsequent letter to Queen Victoria, "his army dispersed as they were not accustomed to spend Easter away from Home."[191] So, while Kassa (later Yohannes) and to a lesser extent Gobeze (later Tekle Giorgis) benefited by receiving arms from the British, Menelik did not get any.

In 1874, Menelik approached Khedive Ismail of Egypt when the latter was planning his fateful wars against Yohannes. Menelik sent two emissaries, Aleqa Birru (whom he refers to in his letter as Ras Birru) and Giorgis Negussie, a brother of his interpreter Yossef Negussie.

In a letter written by Menelik to Ismail, from Woreilu, on 24 Megabit, 1867 (April 1, 1875), the objective of the mission is stated as follows:

> You [Ismail] have written to me stating that Egypt and Ethiopia have a common boundary and should thus establish good relations. This delighted me. I have therefore instructed Ras Birru, whom I trust and like, to go to Munziger Pasha, in order to conclude a treaty between us, so that there should not be friction and to avoid hardship to the common man. [192]

In a subsequent letter to Ismail, written after the departure of his envoy Birru from Woreilu, on 15 Ginbot, 1867 (May22, 1875), Menelik stated:

> My friendship for you remains for always true and can only be affected by death. After sending Ras Birru, who was empowered to conclude a treaty, I heard that a Patriarch has been elected in your country. Our religion is the same as that of Egypt [the Copt]... we wish you would order the Patriarch to send us a Bishop. [193]

The whole thing ended in a fiasco when Egyptian forces of 400 men led by Werner Munzinger, the governor of Massawa and Eastern Sudan, accompanied by Menelik's envoys, were virtually wiped out by Mohammed Hanfari at Aussa, on November 14, 1875, by order of Yohannes. Furthermore, the repeated defeats of the Egyptian forces at Guda Gudi and Gurae, in Seraie and Akele Guzai, on November 7, 1875 and March 7, 1876 respectively; and the Egyptian occupation of

---

191. Public Records Office, London: F.O. 95/728 Doc. No. 191: March 4, 1869, Menelik to Victoria – carried by Menelik's emissary, Abba Merze, to the British Resident at Aden.
192. Egyptian Government Abdin Archive, Cairo, Doc. No. 5/2/1: Woreilu, 24 Megabit, 1867, (Aprill, 1875) Menelik to Ismail.
193. Egyptian Government Abdin Archive, Cairo Doc. No. 5/2/2: Woreilu, 15 Ginbot, 1867 (May 22, 1875) Menelik to Ismail.

Zeila and Harar, which obstructed the flow of trade from that port to Showa, disrupted the cordial relation between Menelik and Ismail.

In a letter to Ismail from Litche, dated 10 Sene, 1868 (June 16, 1876), Menelik stated:

> I have instructed my envoy, Pierre Arnoux, a French Merchant, to discuss with you matters pertaining to our respective governments [Ethiopia and Egypt] and trade and to conclude an agreement of friendship which will increase the welfare of our people... Now I am in the process of introducing into my country proper administration, technology, and trade, in view of which I wish to arrive at an agreement of friendship and cooperation with my neighbors and the European powers. This can only be performed by opening up the route to the coast. Your government seems to be blocking my objectives.
>
> Your troops which came to make war on my neighbors [northern Ethiopia] have also fought in the southern part of Ethiopia. Even now they have not stopped fighting. They have captured Tagure [Tadjura] and Awash, with its salt mine. Adal [the Afar territory] and Hararghe, which were paying tribute to the Showan government: and the Galla [Oromo] country, have fallen into the hands of your troops.
>
> Your army has advanced near us. We have been told that a third column of your army has proceeded up the White Nile and has been seen in the Galla [Oromo] country. We have been told that the army which has marched through Hararghe and Zeila shall meet in Guraghe with the army from the north. This is no secret, and Guraghe is my country.
>
> Today the ports on the Eritrean sea as well as those of the Indian Ocean have hindered the entrance of all goods except textiles; guns and ammunition required for our defense have been deliberately blocked. Egyptian soldiers, having surrounded the whole region, will shortly enter my own territory as far as Awash. Should this occur, my worst fears will have been realized. This I must make known to you. [194]

Subsequently, following the advice of Mgr. Gugliemo Massaja (who had been in Showa since 1868), Menelik approached the Italian and French governments by sending envoys such as Abba Mikael and Pierre Arnoux, a French merchant. While Arnoux's mission failed for different reasons, Abba Mikael's mission from June to December 1872 succeeded in reaching Rome where Mikael was granted an audience by King Umberto. There, he also met with the founders of Italian Geographical Society who were interested at the time in sending a scientific exploration mission to Central African lakes. Although the request for arms was not acceded to at the time, it paved the way for the scientific exploration mission of the Reale Societa Geografica Italiana to come to Showa.

---

194. Egyptian Government Abdin Archive, Cairo. Doc No. 5/2/7: Litche, 10 Sene, 1868, (June 7, 1876) Menelik to Ismail.

The mission was headed by the Marchese Orazio Antinori, one of the prominent founders of the Society. Antinori arrived at Ankober on August 28, 1876, with letters from the Italian government and gifts from Umberto to Menelik. The mission was given a cordial reception and a grant of land at Let Marefia by Menelik to enable them to build their station.

Thus Fikre Gimb (where the Catholic Mission led by Mgr. Massaja from 1868 until his expulsion in June 1879) was established, and Let Marefia (under Antinori) were the forerunners who opened the gate, establishing the intimate relation between Showa and Italy which lasted up to 1889.

Soon after the arrival of Antinori, one of the men who came with the scientific mission, Sebastiano Martini, was sent as Menelik's envoy to acquire arms from Italy in 1877, but he returned unsuccessful in November 1879. This rebuff, however, did not deter Menelik from his persistent quest for arms.

The second phase of Menelik's foreign Relations began at a time when Emperor Yohannes, having heard that Menelik had campaigned the Begemder and Gojam earlier in 1877, and strengthened by the arms and ammunition captured at Guda Gudi and Gurae in his successive victories over the Egyptians, came to Begemder and camped in Debre Tabor in order to assert his control over the central provinces.

During Menelik's absence from Showa, a series of revolts erupted in his home province. The first one, led by his uncle Mered Azmatch Haile Mikael (commonly known as Haile), son of King Sahle Selassie, was crushed by Dejazmach Guermame Wolde Hawariat, who was left as Menelik's deputy during his campaign. This incident was followed by a more serious one led by Menelik's consort Woizero Bafena, who returned from the campaign and liberated Menelik's closely guarded political rivals, Meshesha Seifu, son of Abeto Seifu Sahle Selassie, Menelik's uncle, and Imam Abba Wattew, one of the claimants to the lordship of Wallo, who were detained at Enewari.

Bafena moved with the liberated captives to Tammo, the fortress at her home region in Merabete. Subsequently, Bafena collaborated with her son-in-law Imam Mohammed Ali (later known as Ras Mikael), who rebelled in Wallo and had Menelik's residence at Woreilu burnt. Thus, when Menelik hurriedly returned to Showa, he found himself embroiled in a complicated situation which was exacerbated by the news that Yohannes would be coming to Showa from Debre Tabor.

While at Debre Tabor, Yohannes received urgent appeals from three sources urging him to come to Showa:

1. Meshesha Seifu, who was liberated by Bafena, had sent Ato Semu Negus, the son of Dejazmach Guermame asking Yohannes to come to Showa by the shortest route through Amara Saint.

2. The Showan clergy of the Tewahdo (Unitarian) sect appealed to Yohannes to come and save the traditional creed of the Ethiopian Orthodox Church since Menelik, in their view, had espoused an alien creed favoring the three-Birth sect and had brought Abba (Mgr) Massaja as his bishop.

3. All those who had collaborated in the rebellions instigated by Merid-Azmatch Haile and subsequently by Woizero Bafena had also appealed to Yohannes to save their lives by coming to Showa. [195]

Thus Yohannes came to Showa in January 1878. Menelik made his full submission. Yohannes confirmed Menelik's authority over Showa and the territories under his control and crowned him as King of Showa.

Mgr. Massaja was ordered by Yohannes to leave Showa, but the Italian scientific mission was allowed to continue its work. Antinori persistently encouraged Menelik to maintain his independence. The Marchese was elevated to be the official political representative of the Italian government in 1881, a year before his accidental death. Antinori was succeeded by the young and ambitious Count Pietro Antonelli, a nephew of Cardinal Giacomo Antonelli, who remained as the representative of the Italian government in Showa from 1882 up to the beginning of 1890. Thus, in his dual capacity as the official representative of the Italian government and confidant of Menelik, Antonelli was the intermediary between the Showan Negus and the Italian government during these crucial years.

Antonelli concluded two secret agreements of Conventions in May 25, 1883, and October 20, 1887, respectively; and the Treaty of Wuchalé on May 2, 1889.

The First (secret) Treaty of Friendship and Commerce, which was signed in Ankober on May 25, 1883, established the exchange of diplomatic representative between Italy and Showa; full reciprocal freedom of transit for people and goods; exemption from customs duty for Showan goods transported via Assab; 5 per cent ad valorem duty to be paid on Italian goods upon exit or entry; consular jurisdiction over all Italian affairs and those of diplomatically unrepresented foreigners given to the Italians.

---

195. Hervy Wolde-Sellassie: Unfinished, *History of Ethiopia*, undated, (circa 1935) Addis Ababa, p.9.

The second secret Treaty of Friendship and Alliance was concluded at Entoto on 10 Tiqimt, 1880, which corresponds to October 20, 1887, with the main object of securing Menelik's neutrality in case of war between Italy and the Emperor, by offering him 5,000 Remington rifles. In a separate contract between Menelik and Antonelli it was specified that 5,000 Remington rifles with 200 cartridges for each rifle, at a cost of 28 Maria Theresa thalers, would be provided by Antonelli each year for a period of ten years, which would add up to 50,000 rifles. Menelik in turn had agreed not to use the guns against Italy.

The third agreement was The Treaty of Wuchalé, signed at Wuchalé, on May 2, 1889, two months after the death of Yohannes, with the main objectives of (1) securing the recognition of Menelik's accession as Emperor of Ethiopia; (2) granting concession of territory to enable the Italian in Massawa area to move up to the highland; and (3) allowing Italy to represent Ethiopia in international relations.

Not long after Antonelli concluded the first secret treaty in 1883, Italy proceeded to occupy Beilul, followed by the occupation of Massawa on February 5, 1885. Menelik was attempting to steer a middle course between his attachment to the Italians and loyalty to Yohannes. He wrote to King Umberto, on 2 Miazia, 1877 (April 10, 1885):

> It is just for Beilul to belong to Italy because it was there that the Italian blood was spilt [referring to the incident in which an Italian commercial explorer Gustavo Bianchi and his two companions, Diana and Monari, were assassinated by the Afars]. As regards Massawa, however, it would have been better to come to an agreement with the Emperor before occupying this place.[196]

The Italians did not just remain in Massawa. They began to encroach from the coast inland towards Uaa and Sahati. This led to the Dogali incident, in January 1887, when the Italian column of 500 men led by Lt. Col. De Cristoforis attempted to encroach from Massawa into the highlands and was virtually wiped out by Ras Alula, the commander of the Imperial army and governor of Hamasen and Seraie.

Reaction in Italy to the incident at Dogali was immediate. In the Italian Parliament, a credit of 5,000,000 lire was at once voted and was supplemented by 20,000,000 lire on June 2, 1887, to strengthen the military force at Massawa and its vicinity: troops began to leave Italy with large quantities of ammunition and supplies.

---

196. *Libro Verde* XV, Etiopia, Doc. No. 89: Entoto, 2 Miazia, 1877 (April 10, 1885), Menelik to Umberto.

It appeared as though, in revenge, there would be a limited war with an Italian advance as far as Sahati and Ghindae most likely. Ferdinando Martini, who later became governor of Eritrea, summed up the possibilities that were open for further Italian action: "A large-scale war would be extremely unwise. A limited war — with an advance as far as Sahati or Ghindae was likely to be unsuccessful, and even humiliating." For the Italians to remain in Massawa, Martini felt it was "pointless, in view of the Ethiopians' expressed desire for an outlet to the sea and the complete breakdown in relations between the two countries." In his view: "it would be wiser to abandon the Eritrean coast, withdrawing the military forces gradually, so as not to lose face." [197]

In May 1887, Italy blockaded Ethiopia, and Italy's actions appeared increasingly war like. A British attempt to mediate by sending a mission led by Sir Gerald Portal to Yohannes failed to attain its objective of making the Emperor agree to allow the Italians to possess Sahati and Uaa and to make Ghindae the frontier town of Ethiopia.

Yohannes's answer was:

> If your wish were to make peace between us it should be when they are in their country and I in mine. But now on both sides the horses are bridled and the swords are drawn...the Italians desire war, but the strength is in Jesus Christ.[198]

Yohannes summoned Abune Matteows, the bishop of Showa, to join him at Debre Tabor, in September of 1887. In his letter, Yohannes informed him of his intention to march against the Italians in Sahati. Menelik, caught between the camp of the Emperor and that of the Italians, was most concerned lest Yohannes should discover the extent to which he was involved with Italy. Antonelli was at his court and the negotiations for the entente, which was concluded a month later, had already begun. The fact that Yohannes had not sent him a letter concerning the planned move against Italy in the north led Menelik to suspect that Yohannes doubted his loyalty. To allay suspicion, Menelik sent Dejazmach Meshesha Worqe and Bejirond Atnafe to Yohannes with a considerable amount of tribute and a letter.

The letter, however, contained an inherent contradiction. Menelik asked to be allowed to join the Sahati campaign [199] while at the same time offering to

197. Martini, Gerdinando: *Cose Africane*, Milan, 1896, pp. 5-20.
198. Public Records office, (PRO), London - FO. 95/748 No. 209: Ashenghe, 24 Hidar, 1880 (December 2, 1887) Yohannes to Victoria, reproduced in Portal, Sir Geral H: *My Mission to Abyssinia*, London, 1892. pp. 172-174.

mediate between Yohannes and the Italians. His first proposal was, of course, in complete contradiction to his negotiations with Antonelli.

Menelik found himself in a dilemma. He had to consider carefully the amount of support within Showa for closer co-operation with Italy. It is clear from Antonelli's accounts that most of the influential opinion in the Showan court supported a close alliance with the Emperor; but Menelik did not want to alienate the Italians, from whom he was expecting to receive valuable support to further his ambitions.[200]

The extent and enthusiasm of the Dogali victory celebrations in Showa indicated the strength of Showan feeling against close relations with the Italians. Menelik himself had had to take an official part in the rejoicing.[201] The celebrations were described by a usually reliable source as "delirious."[202] Count Carlo di Robilant, the Foreign Minister, immediately after the Dogali incident, asked Antonelli for a frank assessment of Menelik's position.[203] Antonelli replied that the Italians could expect no active assistance: procrastination and delay were the best that could be hoped for from Menelik, if Yohannes asked for his assistance.[204]

Thus the aim of Italian policy shifted from seeking to gain Menelik's active assistance to merely ensuring his neutrality. At this point, Menelik tried to act as a mediator between the Italians and the Emperor.[205]

Yohannes's reply to his overture was distinctly favorable. Yohannes said:

> For my part, if the Italian government does not come to take possession of my country and allows the free passage of goods at Massawa, I am disposed to make peace and come to an agreement.[206]

---

199. Heruy Wolde Sellassie: Heruy Wolde Sellassie: *Etiopia ena Metemma*, Addis Adeba, 1929, p. 77.
200. *Libro Verde* XV, Etiopia, Doc. No. 119, enclosure, in Ministry of War to Ministry of Foreign Affairs, 6 July 1887: Antonelli to Saletta, Entoto, April 2, 1887.
201. *Libro Verde* XV, Etiopia, Doc. No. 120: 10 July 1887, Antonelli to Acting Minister of Foreign Affairs.
202. *Bolettino della societa geografica Italiana* (BSGI) Vol. 24, No 87, p.498: Entoto, 22 March, 1887, Traversi to Vedova.
203. *Libro Verde* XV, Etiopia, Doc. No. 116: March 1887, Ministry of Foreign Affairs to Commander at Massawa.
204. *Libro Verde* XV, Etiopia, Doc. No. 120, Attachment in code: 22 March, 1887, Antonelli, to Acting Minister of Foreign Affairs.
205. *Verde* XV, Etiopia, Doc. No. 124: Entoto 9 Oct. 1887, Antonelli to Acting Minister of Foreign Affairs.
206. *Libro Verde* XV, Etiopia, Doc. No 129: 21 Nov. 1887 Yohannes to Menelik: also Rossetti, C.: *Storia diplomatica del' Etiopia*, Torino, 1901, p.48.

The response from the Italian government, on the other hand, was distinctly a refusal.[207] The second secret Treaty of Friendship and Alliance of October 20, 1887, focused simply on securing Menelik's neutrality by offering him 5,000 Remingtons. Menelik in turn agreed not to use the guns against the Italians. [208]

Menelik then wrote to the King of Italy on 15 Tiqimt, 1880 (October 25, 1887), which was sent with Dr. Vincenzo Ragazzi stating:

> I love Italy — on the other hand, either out of love or for other reasons, which this is not the place to go into, I am bound to the Emperor by an oath of friendship and loyalty — I wish to have permission from the King of Italy and from the Emperor to act as peace maker — If either rejects peace... I will never give my aid to any one who wishes for war.[209]

Although there was no immediate response to this letter from Umberto, his Prime Minister Francesco Crispi notified Antonelli that:

> Menelik's offer for intervention is refused. He [Menelik] could, however, render a great service if he advised the Emperor to sue for peace.[210]

Crispi also wrote to Menelik on 5 February 1888, stating that:

> Ragazzi was to purchase the arms according to the Convention concluded with Antonelli [referring to the 5,000 Remington rifles]. These are offered to you as gifts by the King of Italy. Over and above these Dr. Ragazzi will make a gift to you of 1,000 Remington guns with the necessary ammunition: these will help to destroy your enemies and the enemies of my country.[211]

In this statement, Crispi is obviously referring to Yohannes.

In January, 1888, Menelik with 110,000 to 120,000 followers had departed to Wallo from Debre Birhan by the order of the Emperor given in November, 1887. Antonelli reported:

> Menelik [before his departure] granted me an audience and informed me that he had tried to be an intermediary for peace and he had not succeeded...the Italian government has reason to make itself respected and vindicate the blood of its sol-

---

207. *Libro Verde* XV, Etiopia, Doc. No. 135L: 27 Nov. 1887, Acting Minister of Foreign Affairs to Consul-General, Aden.
208. Archivio Storico del Ministero dell' Africa Italiana (A.S.M.A.I.) 36/4-40, the Amharic original of treaty concluded between Menelik and Antonelli, 10 Tiqimt 1880 (20 Oct.1887). See, also, Rubenson, Sven: 'Wichale XVII,' *Journal of African History*, 512 (1964), where the treaty is analyzed.
209. *Libro Verde* XV, Etiopia, Doc. No. 126: Addis Ababa 15 Tiqmt, 1880 (October 25, 1887), Menelik to Umberto-enclosed in Antonelli to Crispi, Addis Ababa, October 25, 1887.
210. *Libro Verde* XV, Etiopia, Doc. No. 125: Rome, November 27, 1887, Crispi to ConsulGeneral in Aden for Antonelli.
211. *Libro Verde* XV, Etiopia, Doc. No. 132: February 5, 1888 Crispii to Menelik.

> diers... [referring to Dogali] write to your government and when you have received the reply come to me to Boru Mieda.[212]

In this statement Menelik is acquiescing that the Italians should fight Yohannes.

After relaying Menelik's view, Antonelli commented:

> I believe that Menelik holds these sentiments but the Tigre element is too powerful at the Showan court to allow him to act energetically: the only thing that he can do would be to gain time and to take a decision when he knows what has happened.[213]

After the Sahati campaign, which took place in March 1888, Antonelli reported to Crispi from Ankober, on May 16, 1888:

> I am convinced that Menelik is with us at heart, but he cannot show these feelings openly because he lacks...the moral strength. The Showan court is surrounded by the Tigre elements and the weight of the army is, by blood or by reasons of personal friendship, with the Emperor [Yohannes].[214]

And a week later, on May 22, Antonelli wrote to Crispi:

> I have no doubt of the real feeling of Menelik...he wanted an absolute Italian victory over the Emperor so that he could present himself to the people as the savior of Ethiopia, signing a peace treaty with Italy and thus realizing his longstanding plan of being supreme head of the empire. But what gives rise to my misgivings is that the court which surrounds him is all devoted to the Emperor Yohannes, as is a part of the army and a great number of generals.[215]

Antonelli, feeling uncertain of Menelik's behavior, advised the arms to be detained in Assab.

When Tekle Haimanot was defeated by the Dervishes, Menelik moved to Begemder by the order of the Emperor. From there, Antonelli received two letters from Menelik. The first one from the encampment of Dembia, dated April 24, 1888, stated that: "the Dervishes have fled and he [Menelik] will be returning soon to Showa." The second letter dated 10 Ginbot, 1880 (May 17, 1888), from Amba Tchara stated: "I have very important business for which I shall have to send you to Italy as soon as I reach Entoto."[216]

On July 2, 1888, Antonelli had an audience with Menelik and he reported:

---

212. *Libro Verde* XV, Etiopia, Doc. No. 136: Let Maretia, January 18, 1888, Antonelli to Crispi.
213. Ibid.
214. *Libro Verde* XV, Etiopia, Doc. No. 145, and A.S.M.A.I. 36/5-46: Ankober May 16, 1888, Antonelli to Crispi.
215. *Libro Verde* XV, Etiopia, Doc. No. 147 and A.S.M.A.I. 36/5 - 46 Let Maretia, May 22, 1888, Antonelli to Crispi.

> Menelik assured me that he was ready to help Italy instead of Yohannes and asked the King of Italy to advance him the amount necessary to buy 10,000 Remington guns and 400,000 Wetterly cartridges — when he had all this, Italy must not think of spending so many millions to avenge the dead of Dogali... He also wished the caravans of arms to be escorted by 500 or 1,000 Italian soldiers...King Tekle Haimanot is with him and he has sent Dejazmach Wolde to persuade Ras Mikael to join him.[217]

Antonelli's report was confirmed by Menelik's letter to Umberto of 30 Sene, 1880 (July 6, 1888), in which he said: "I can revenge the Italians who have died at Dogali," and demanded "no less than 10,000 Remington guns which will not be used to harm Italians." Menelik concluded his letter by saying, "I have confided to Antonelli many things that I cannot write which he should tell you.[218]

In a letter addressed to Prime Minister Francesco Crispi, dated Entoto, 26 Sene, 1880 (2 July, 1888), Menelik raises the question of Zeila. He stated: "If Zeila is in your hands, the commerce will open from Zeila to Harar and from Harar to Kafa."

The reference to Zeila is omitted in the Libro Verde, probably to avoid offending British feelings. Menelik concluded his letter to Crispi, stating:

> The time has come for me to show my strength and love to the Italian government, and for the Italian government to manifest its love and its strength to me. I beg you, therefore, to pay attention to my request [for arms] most promptly.[219]

Antonelli, writing to Crispi on August 11, 1888, said: "Menelik hopes for our military action [in the vicinity of Massawa] and that we will provide him with arms to avenge the dead of Dogali."[220]

After hearing the message brought by Antonelli, Umberto wrote to Menelik from Torino, on September 12, 1888, stating:

> Antonelli has been given the task of submitting for approval a pact of friendship and trade such as will make peace in all Ethiopia sure and lasting [i.e. the draft of the Treaty of Wuchalé]. After you have signed this pact you will allow Antonelli to

216. *Libro Verde* XV, Etiopia, Doc. No. 147 and 152: Let Maretia, May 22, 1888, Antonelli to Crispi — reporting two letters received from Menelik dispatched from dembia, Miazia 15,1880 (April 22, 1888) and Amba Tchara, 10 Ginbot, 1880 (May 17, 1888) respectively.
217. *Libro Verde* XV, Etiopia, Doc. No. 152: Aden, August 8, 1888, Antonelli to Crispi.
218. *Libro Verde* XV, Etiopia, Doc. No. 152: Enclosure in Antonelli to Crispi dated August 8, 1888 and original in A.S.M.A.I. Doc. No. 36/5-45 – 30 Sene 1880 (July 6, 1888), Menelik to Umberto.
219. *Libro Verde* XV, Etiopia, Doc No. 152: Enclosure No. 2, Entoto, 26 Sene 1880 (July 2, 1888), Menelik to Crispi. The original letter in A.S.M.A.I. Doc. No. 36/5-45.
220. *Libro Verde* XV, Etiopia, Doc. No. 153: Massawa, August 11, 1888, Antonelli to Crispi.

> return to Italy with the envoy that you have many times promised to send. This envoy could be empowered to ratify the said pact. From the side of Massawa our troops will occupy in strength those parts where the Italian soldiers were killed.[221]

Bertole-Viale, the Italian Minister of War, also wrote to Menelik, on September 12, 1888, stating:

> the dispatch of arms was held up because of the difficulty of finding means of transport through the Danakil regions and that it could not be done with the secrecy you desired...Antonelli is returning to Showa...you can take with him all necessary measures to assure a way for the passage of our officers and our soldiers that you wish to have as an escort for the future. [222]

In the meantime, Ragazzi, who had been sent to Italy with the Treaty of Friendship and Alliance concluded on October 20, 1887, returned to Showa on October 22, 1888, with 1,000 Remington guns sent as gift by Umberto to Menelik.

The following day, after the arrival of Dr. Ragazzi, Menelik wrote to Crispi, complying with the request made by Italy and announcing that he would send Dejazmach Makonnen and Aleqa Yosef on a mission to Rome. He also stated that Yohannes and his army were in Gojam and that they were laying it waste. If Yohannes crossed the Abbai (Blue Nile) and came to Showa, he would fight him at the frontier. And he concluded by saying:

> I have learnt that the Emperor Yohannes has offered you some territory in order to make peace and that you have refused on account of your friendship with me, and for that I thank you. [223]

This last statement is difficult to understand since no offer of territory was made by Yohannes to the Italians; and it was a contradiction of Menelik's former overture to act as mediator in order to pacify the two parties, namely Yohannes and Italy. One can only surmise that Menelik must have been told, probably by Ragazzi, that Italy had declined to accept Yohannes's alleged offer for the sake of its friendship with Menelik.

Three months later, in February of 1889, Antonelli returned with 4,700 Remington guns and 220,000 bullets sent as gifts to Menelik loaded on 580 camels. In a letter to Umberto dated 14 Yekatit, 1881 (20 February, 1889), Menelik reassured Umberto, saying: "with deeds rather than words I will show

---

221. *Libro Verde* XV, Etiopia, Doc. No. 157: Torino, September 12, 1888, Umberto to Menelik.
222. Ibid.
223. *Libro Verde* XV, Etiopia, Doc. No . 193, 4th Enclosure: Entoto, 14 Tiqimt, 1881 (October 23, 1888), Menelik to Crispi.

my gratitude to Italy for the rich presents that you [Umberto] sent and also for the arms and munitions." [224]

Referring to the draft treaty which Antonelli presented to him, Menelik said: "The treaty that you have sent me I have examined very carefully and I am happy to say that up till now, I have not found anything that is not to my full satisfaction." [225]

Regarding the territorial cessation, he said: "The way in which you intend to stabilize the part round Massawa has my approval and if one day providence permits that it shall belong to me, you may be sure that no difficulty will arise to disturb our full accord and our sincere friendship." [226]

II.

The second phase of Menelik's foreign relations covers the period from his submission to Yohannes in March 1878 up to his announcement of his accession to the throne on the death of Yohannes in March, 1889. Menelik's dealings with the Italians were very much at variance with the Emperor's policy. As mentioned earlier, he was unable to press too far for fear of public opinion even in Showa, especially after the incident at Dogali in January, 1887.

Antonelli in his reports to the Italian government repeatedly refers to the "Tigrayan Elements" or "Pro-Tigrayan Party" at the Showan court as a stumbling block impeding Menelik's wish to act energetically in favor of Italy.

It would be appropriate to question who Antonelli could possibly be referring to when he said, "the Tigrayan elements who are tied to Yohannes by blood or loyalty" were infesting the Showan court. The only close blood relation to Yohannes in the Showan court at that time was Dejazmach Seyum Gabre Kedan, son of the Emperor's sister, Itege Dinqinesh, whom Menelik brought from Gojam in 1888, where he had been banished by Yohannes. Seyum was completely devoted to Menelik, as he was a renegade from his uncle the Emperor.

If Antonelli was referring to the non-Showan elements in Menelik's court, there were large numbers who had come to join Menelik since his escape from Magdalla. Among the well known were persons such as Wolle Betoul (later Ras), Mengesha Atikem (later Ras Bitwoded), Meshesha Worqe (later

---

224. Ibid.
225. Ibid.
226. *Libro Verde* XV, Etiopia, Doc. No. 218, Enclosure No. 2 and original in A.S.M.A.I. 36/6-53: Addis Ababa, 14 Yekatit, 1881 (February 20, 1889) Menelik to Umberto.

Dejazmach) and many others who joined him afterwards. But all these were most devoted to Menelik and their loyalty cannot be questioned.

He must be referring indiscriminately to the region from which they came, including Showa, notably the clergy and those who tacitly resented or openly rebelled against Menelik, mostly to advance their respective political ambitions (such as his own previous consort, Bafena, his cousin Meshesha Seifu, or even his second consort, Taytu, and the older statesmen in Menelik's court, such as Dejazmach Guermame, Ras Gobana, Dejazmach Wolde Gabriel Abba Seitan) and even Menelik's loyal uncle, Ras Darge, who did not appear to be actively involved in the entente cordiale with the Italians and had shown dislike of foreign meddling in internal affairs.

Thus, in reality there were no Tigrayans in large number tied in blood or loyalty to Yohannes as Antonelli's report leads us to believe. The so-called "Tigrayan Elements" or "Pro-Tigrayan Party" were simply those who did not collaborate with the Italians and who entertained patriotic or nationalistic sentiments.

When the Italians encroached onto the highlands in March 1888, no engagement took place at Sahati. The Italians had a trap prepared and wanted the Ethiopians to attack. Yohannes would not be lured and kept on demanding that the Italians return to Massawa and that they abandon the blockade in accordance with the Hewett Treaty. Yohannes stayed for over a month at the desert area near the coast, where food and water were scarce. This affected the morale of his troops and compelled him to move to the Gondar region to confront the Mahdist threat from Metemma, feeling secure that there was no immediate threat from the Italians.

The latter, for their part, were extremely worried about the climate and attempted to arrange for most of their troops to move with Bismarck's assistance either to Cyprus or Aden, leaving 7,000 men at Massawa. [227]

When the death of Yohannes occurred in the following year at Metemma, the Italians took advantage of this situation to reap the benefits of over a decade of hard labor in building cordial relations with Menelik.

---

227. German Government Archive: (Bonn) A.A.A. *Italianisches Besitzungen in Afrika* (IbiA) Bd. 4: Berlin April 2, 1885, Bismarck to Solms: IbiA, Bd, 4: London, April 2, 1888, Hatzfeldt to Salisbury, and PRO (London) F.O. 403/91 Enclosure No. 129: Rome, March 4, 1888, Slade to Savile.

A non-partisan objective assessment of Menelik's foreign relation during the period 1878 to 1889 is given by Hakim Worqneh Eshete, commonly known outside Ethiopia as Dr. Charles W. Martin.

He was unique in many ways among Ethiopians of his time. Apart from being one of the very few foreign-educated and certainly the only medical doctor, he also had a profound knowledge of European colonial policy of the period, having served as a British medical officer and district administrator for decades in India and Burma. During his first two consecutive visits to his country of birth, he had the opportunity to meet Emperor Menelik in person and even served as one of his medical doctors for a while during his prolonged illness. Hakim Worqneh, after he finally came to settle in Ethiopia around 1920, had served his country as a pioneer in various fields. As educator, modernizer, administrator, and diplomat, he was an accomplished statesman and a great patriot.

His assessment of Menelik's foreign relations before his accession to the throne is given in the book entitled Haile Selassie, by Princess Asfa Yilma, as follows:

> After Theodore's death in 1868 it was the Emperor John [Yohannes] who succeeded him as Emperor of Ethiopia. It was during his reign that Menelik, who first ruled under him as King of the Showa Province, began to conceive great ambitions. It was also at this time that the Italians had been given Massawa, an Egyptian-occupied Ethiopian port [referring to British acquiescence]...having obtained a footing on the coast, immediately began to penetrate inland, and thus came constantly in contact with the Emperor John [Yohannes], whose trusted general Ras Alula fought them in a dozen minor engagements and always drove them back. Finding it impossible to make headway in the north, the Italians began their Machiavellian tricks in the south, their victim being King Menelek [sic] of Showa. Finding him young and ambitious to secure the Imperial crown they promised to supply him with arms so that he might defeat his suzerain and become Emperor. Being unacquainted with European diplomacy he accepted their protestations of friendship at their face value. The Emperor John [Yohannes], hearing of this intrigue and of Menelik's increasing friendship with the Italian Government, wrote and told him that he would grievously regret placing any trust in these foreigners whose only aim was to steal. But Menelik, grossly enthralled by ambition, continued his course of action, and when at length the valiant and farseeing Emperor John [Yohannes] was killed in battle with the Dervishes, Menelik, with Italian aid, became Emperor. In gratitude for the Italian help he handed over the northern province of Hamasen to his wily friends.[228]

228. Contained in Asfa Yilma (Princess): *Haile Selassie*, with an introduction and historical commentary by Azaj Worqneh C. Martin. London, 1936, pp. 95-96.

It would be appropriate to conclude this section with a prophetic remark allegedly made by Yohannes when he repeatedly heard of secret treaties being concluded between Menelik and Italy:

> King Menelik perhaps believes that he would harm me by doing so [concluding treaties of friendship and assistance with the declared national enemy]: in actual fact, the fire that he [Menelik] had kindled will probably consume him eventually.[229]

III.

The watershed which divides the second and the third phase of Menelik's foreign policy is the death of Emperor Yohannes in March, 1889. Although Yohannes on his deathbed nominated his son Mengesha to succeed him, Menelik, at this time, had no rival. He was cautious, however, of any possible mishaps.

When news of the Emperor's death at Metemma reached Menelik, camping at Ghidim, he sent the following letter to "His great and mighty friend, Umberto I, King of Italy," on 18th Megabit, 1881 (March 26, 1889). After announcing the death of Yohannes at Metemma, Menelik said:

On May 2, 1889, Menelik signed the Treaty of Wuchalé with Antonelli, the draft of which had been presented to him three months earlier in February. The Italians occupied Asmara on August 3, 1889.I would beg your majesty [Umberto] to give orders to all the generals in Massawa not to listen to the words of the rebels who are to be found in some parts of Tigray and to forbid the passage of arms. After this news[230] all will want to make believe that they have a right to the throne of Ethiopia. I would like the soldiers of your Majesty to occupy Asmara and make sure that this route is well guarded and defended.

Dejazmach Makonnen and Aleqa Yossef, the interpreter, were designated by Menelik to go to Italy with Antonelli. They left Harar on July 20, and disembarked at Naples on August 21, 1889. Dejazmach Makonnen was received with great pomp and was granted an audience at the Quirinale on August 28, 1889. Every effort was made to impress him with the military might of Italy.

---

229. Quoted by Heruv Wolde Sellassie: Unfinished, *History of Ethiopia*, n.d. (circa 1935), p.66.
230. The original in A.S.M.A.I. 36/6-53: Ghidim, 18 Megabit, 1881 (March 26, 1889) Menelik to Umberto-contained as Enclosure in Antonelli to Crispi, Ghidim, March 26, 1889.

After the Treaty of Wuchalé was ratified by the Italian government, Makonnen signed the Additional Convention to the Treaty of Wuchalé with Crispi in Naples on October 1, 1889. This Additional Convention modified Article III of the Treaty, which refers to territorial boundaries, by stating that:

> in virtue of the proceeding articles [referring to Article III of the Treaty of Wuchalé], a ratification of the two territories will be made, taking as a basis the actual possession de facto. [231]

Makonnen at this time was not aware that the Italian authorities in Eritrea had not confined themselves to Asmara, Keren and other territory ceded in the Treaty of Wuchalé, but had seized a large portion of Akele Guzai and Seraie, and were in the process of preparing themselves for a great advance even beyond the Mereb river to Adwa and Axum. The "possession de facto" clause was thus bound to cause a serious conflict. Furthermore, based on Article XVII of the Treaty of Wuchalé, the Italian government communicated to all the European powers, in a formal manner on October 11, the establishment of a protectorate over Ethiopia. Both the territorial issues became the basis for demolishing the hitherto ongoing cordial relations between Menelik and Italy.

By the Additional Convention, Menelik was also to be allowed to borrow four million lire from an Italian bank, the government agreeing to guarantee the loan. In case of failure to pay the interest of slightly above five percent, the customs of Harar would pass into the hands of Italy. It was stipulated that half of it should be paid in silver; the other half, which amounted to two million lire, was to remain in the Italian treasury to be used as payment for purchases, chiefly in the form of rifles and cartridges. On December 4, 1889, after a three-month stay, the Ethiopian mission left Italy and returned to Ethiopia.

Meanwhile, the coronation of Menelik as Emperor of Ethiopia took place at Entoto on the 25th of Tiqimt 1882 (Ethiopian calendar), which corresponds to November 3, 1889. Menelik left Entoto on December 1, in a campaign to Tigray to obtain the submission of Ras Mengesha Yohannes.

While he was in Tigray, the mission led by Dejazmach Makonnen, accompanied by Count Antonelli, arrived at Menelik's camp at Hauzen in February 1890. At this time Menelik made the following appointments: Dejazmach Seyum Gabre Kidan was given command over Agame, although he was removed after a while for being turbulent and was imprisoned in Harar. Ras Mengesha Yohannes was appointed as governor over a large part of Tigray.

---

231. Ibid.

The Italians anticipated that Menelik most probably would appoint as governor of Tigray Seyum Gabre Kidan, whom he had sent after the death of Yohannes and who had been waging successive wars on his behalf against Mengesha and Alula; or else another among his trusted men. They were utterly surprised by the appointment of Mengesha, after his submission. They induced Menelik, however, to give them assurances that Ras Alula, who, as Haggai Erlich puts it, was "the most offensive culprit in the Italians' eyes, [would] be excluded from any command in Tigray." [232]

During his stay at Menelik's camp in February 1890, Antonelli may have influenced the Emperor to appoint his close friend Dejazmach Meshesha Worqe as governor of the region adjacent to the colony. Antonelli dispatched the following telegraphic message to the Italian Ministry of Foreign Affairs from Hauzen, on March 21, 1890:

> *Fu posto governatore di Adua, Mesciecia Uorche,*
> *Ottimo elemento per noi.*
> *Risiedera presso nostri confini.*[233]

Which translates: "Meshesha Worqe has been posted as governor of Adwa, the best one for us. He will be residing near our border."

Leopoldo Traversi, who is normally reliable in his account of the events during this period, also wrote that Meshesha was "appointed as governor of the provinces of Akele Guzai, Seraie, Adwa and Axum." [234]

In actual fact, Meshesha was appointed as governor of Seraie, Akele Guzai and whatever was left of Hamassen which had not been incorporated to the Italian colony: and was to reside in Adwa with the additional responsibility of ensuring a peaceful coexistence between the two enemies, namely the Italians and the Tigrayans, as well as between Mengesha and Seyum Gabre Kidan.

Menelik was enraged by the audacity of General Orero, the Italian governor of Eritrea, who had advanced as far as Axum while Menelik was approaching Tigray in January, 1890. Orero retreated after a strong protest made by the Emperor Antonelli who, as usual, tried to appease the Emperor by stating that it was an unauthorized blunder on the part of the governor and arranged, with the Emperor's consent, that a rectification of boundary should be made by a joint commission chosen respectively by the two governments.

---

232. Erlich, Haggai. Ethiopia and Eritrea during the Scramble for Africa: A Political Biography of Ras Alula, 1875-1897, Michigan, 1992. p.152.
233. Traversi, Leopoldo: *Let Maretia*, Milan, 1931. pp.387-388.
234. Ibid.

But discussions regarding the demarcation of the frontier were broken off between Dejazmach Meshesha Worqe, who was delegated by Menelik, and Major Pietro Toselli, who was appointed by the Italian authorities. The latter insisted on the Mereb-Belesa-Muna line, while the former clung to the original line indicated in Article III of the Wuchalé Treaty, which would leave Akele Guzai and Seraie on the Ethiopian side.

Menelik's attempt to settle the dispute by offering additional territory beyond what was ceded in Article II of the Wuchalé Treaty, as far as Shiket, about twenty kilometers south of Asmara, was turned down by the Italian government. Italy remained in possession of the territory as far south as the Mereb-Belesa-Muna line. [235]

Furthermore, Antonelli convinced the Emperor that in order to avoid the restriction on arms importation to Ethiopia it would be to his advantage to delegate the Italian government to represent Ethiopia at the ensuing conference at Brussels on March 4, 1890, where the questions of the Commerce in Arms and Alcohol with "Backward Nations" and also the Slave Trade would be discussed.

Antonelli's hidden motive, however, was to make Article XVII of the Treaty of Wuchalé effective; he was less concerned about the adverse effect that an arms restriction might have produced on Ethiopia. Though full of suspicion about Antonelli's recommendation, in order to help smooth future relations with Italy, Menelik authorized Rome to represent Ethiopia at the Brussels conference. To his pleasant surprise, Ethiopia's participation by proxy did not pose any danger. It actually produced an unintended spin off: it categorically entitled Menelik to import arms.

Having accomplished his mission, Antonelli returned to Italy to become Under Secretary in the Ministry of Foreign Affairs, and his former post in Addis Ababa was filled by Count Augusto Salimbeni, who had been familiar with the country and people since 1883.

During 1890, Menelik received the response to his letters to the European powers announcing his coronation and requesting their recognition. Notably, Britain and Germany responded that according to Article XVII of the Treaty concluded with Italy, Menelik's communication ought to have been made through Italy. Angered by this response, Menelik at once wrote to Umberto on Meskerem 17, 1883, or September 26, 1890, denouncing Article XVII of the Treaty

235. Battaglia, Roberto, *La Prima Guerra d'Africa*, Torino, 1958. Pp. 420-426.

of Wuchalé, pointing out that he had only agreed that if he so desired — not that he would be obliged — to employ Italy in his foreign relations and negotiations.

Antonelli was then sent to Ethiopia and arrived in Addis Ababa on December 17, 1890, with instructions to give way on the question of the frontiers, provided that he could secure the maintenance of the protectorate. Fruitless negotiation continued. Menelik remaining adamant that he would not entertain placing himself under obligatory protection of another nation. The Empress Taytu, Menelik's consort who had taken part in the deliberation, reprimanded Antonelli when he lost his temper. Finally, Antonelli was obliged to leave with Salimbeni on February 11, 1891, without accomplishing his mission.

Menelik wrote to Umberto complaining of the rude behavior of his envoy (Antonelli) and sent a circular to all the European Powers on Miazia 14, 1883, i.e., April 21, 1891, describing the boundaries of his Empire and concluded by saying:

> I have no intention of being an indifferent spectator while far distant powers make their appearance with the intention of carving out their respective empires in Africa, Ethiopia having been for fourteen centuries an island of Christians amongst a sea of pagans. As the Almighty has protected Ethiopia to this day, I am confident that he will protect and increase her in the future. I have no doubt that he will not let her be divided under the subjection of other governments. [236]

This circular is very similar to the letter written to the European Powers by Menelik's predecessor Yohannes, dated Samera, (a place near Debre Tabor), 11 Yakatit, 1873 i.e., 17 February, 1881, outlining the extent of Ethiopia's territorial claims. [237]

Antonelli on his way back to Italy apparently passed through Eritrea. According to Meshesha (in his letter to Ras Makonnen, written from Asmara on 25 Megabit, 1883, which corresponds to April 2, 1891), Antonelli came to Asmara especially to meet with him and discuss "pertinent issues," presumably related to Italo-Ethiopian relations. In the same letter Meshesha expressed his view the "the Italians have never done any ill to us [Ethiopia], any one who speaks ill of them is their and our enemy." [238] Then, referring to Antonelli's last mission to

236. PRO-FO 95/751 Doc. No. 100: Miazia 14, 1883(April 21, 1891) Menelik to Queen Victoria: Archives diplomatiques (AED) (reserved) du Ministere des Affaires Etrangeres, Paris, Protocole C 41: April 21, 1891, Menelik to President Carnot; Politisches Archives des Auswartigen Amts [A.A.A.], Bonn, A. Italienisches Protektorat uber Abessinien 4: April 21, 2891, Menelik to Kaiser Wilhelm II: A.S.M.A.I. 36/13-109: April 21, 1891 Menelik to Umberto I.

237. German Government Archive, Bonn: A.A.A. IB 9 (ABESSINIEN) Bd 2: Samera (a place near Debr Tabor), 11 Yekatit, 1873, which corresponds to February 17, 1881, Yohannes IV to Kaiser Wilhelm I.

Ethiopia when he came to persuade Menelik to accept the protectorate clause of the Wuchalé Treaty, Meshesha expressed his regret, saying that "after all Count Antonelli had done for us and sustained much suffering for the sake of our friendship he should be treated in such a way."[239] He expressed his fervent wish that on his return (to Addis Ababa) both he (Meshesha) and Ras Makonnen would rectify matters. Meshesha also wrote to Antonelli and Gandolfi, the governor of Eritrea, on April 12, 1891, saying:

> The friendship and accord between Italy and Ethiopia have been ruined for something of no account, I hope to remedy the situation and re-establish the state of relation ship as had existed earlier. [240]

This last statement is rather surprising, especially from a person like Dejazmach Meshesha, who was regarded as one of the most enlightened among Menelik's entourage. Article XVII of the Wuchalé Treaty could scarcely be considered as inconsequential or insignificant.

The Italian response was indecisive and ambivalent. Up to then the government in Rome supported Antonelli's view that they should continue to support Menelik with the objective of gaining the protectorate over all the Ethiopian Empire. In protest against this policy, Baldissera and his successor Orero resigned from the governorship of the Eritrean Colony, since, in their view, the only true course for Italy to pursue was one of "Divide et Impera," namely, to play off the Tigrayan against the Showan and increase the territory of the colony. Now, in desperation, the green light was given to the new governor Giuseppe Gandolfi, who replaced General Orero in June, 1891. Dr. Cesare Nerazzani and Dr. Angelo de Martino were sent to join Tennente Benedetto Mulazzani who was resident in Adwa, on October 23, 1891, with a letter from Umberto to convince Ras Mengesha that he should meet General Gandolfi.

The principal motive of the Italian government in allowing Gandolfi to conclude the so-called "Mereb Convention" undoubtedly was to exert pressure on Menelik by alienating Mengesha from him and creating hostility between them in the hope of inducing Menelik to accept the protectorate clause of the Wuchalé Treaty.

The colonial authorities in Eritrea, on the other hand, may have regarded the new policy as a prelude for the expansion of the Italian colony and for estab-

238. Ibid.
239. Ibid.
240. The text of Meshesha's letters to Makonnen, Antonelli and Gandolfi are reproduced in Traversi, Leopoldo, *Let Marefia*, Milan, 1931, pp. 389-390.

lishing a paramount influence or even hegemony over the rest of Tigray, rather than the effect it would have on the protectorate issue.

The new policy, for whatever motive, was a clear departure from the policy pursued by Italy since 1889, which regarded Mengesha and Alula as arch enemies and were persistent in supplying arms ammunition and finance to their principal adversaries, Dejazmach Seyum Gabre Kidan, Dejazmach Debeb Araya, and Dejazmach Sebhat Aregawi.

The relation between the Tigrayans and the Italians was so bad, as stated earlier, that Menelik had placed Meshesha Worqe at Adwa with the additional responsibility of ensuring peaceful coexistence between them.

This arrangement, however, did not last long. When the Italians in Eritrea found out that Meshesha was ineffectual in Tigray, and Mengesha (subdued by constant wars, epidemics and especially by cattle disease which decimated the farm animals and in turn produced widespread famine, which resulted in the dispersion of his army) was no longer a threat to them, they chose to ignore Meshesha, who was placed as a buffer between the two enemies (Italy and Tigray) and to deal directly with Mengesha. Meshesha eventually was obliged to leave Tigray with his five thousand men and settled at Gudo Felasi, in Seraie. He now became a guest of the Italian governor of Eritrea who, much to his chagrin, prevented him from levying taxes in Seraie and Akele Guzai — thus denying him the finances and food supply which he had traditionally been receiving; consequently, his army began to loot the villages, which resulted in the confiscation of their arms by the Italian authorities. In the end, the Italian colonial officials who were afraid of provoking an armed resistance in the region, handed him back all the confiscated arms and he peacefully returned back to Addis Ababa.

Mengesha, on his part, was responsive to the overture made by Italy when he received a letter from King Umberto suggesting that "he could ask the governor of Eritrea, residing at Massawa, for whatever assistance he may desire."[241] He responded positively in a letter to Umberto, dated August 1, 1891, both for economic and political motives.

Northern Ethiopia, comprising Tigray, Begemder, Gojam, Wallo and even Showa, was in the greatest misery during the period 1889 to 1892 because of a lack of grain and the loss of cattle, goats, and sheep due to disease. In such an unforeseen calamity, it is obvious to what straits Ethiopia was reduced: it became impossible to till the land due to lack of working animals.

---

241. Ibid.

In this state of affairs, with the Tigrayan economy in shambles, it was a question of survival which partly persuaded Mengesha to seize upon the Italian offer to import food and ammunition. Mengesha hoped eventually that the blockade imposed by the Italians immediately after they occupied Massawa in 1885 and which had been continuously in effect since 1887 would be lifted.

Mengesha was also disillusioned and his pride was touched by the fact that he was made to share the government of Tigray with his cousin and antagonist Seyum Gabre Kidan and Meshesha Worqe. When he made his submission, he must have expected the same kind of treatment which Yohannes had accorded to Menelik when the latter made his submission in 1878.

The choice of Meshesha Worqe must have cause annoyance, particularly as Meshesha was obliged to reside with his soldiers at Adwa together with Mengesha. The objection to Dejazmach Meshesha by Mengesha and his entourage was deep rooted.

Meshesha was a son of Afe-Negus Worqe, chief justice of Emperor Tewodros, and he himself as a young man was appointed as co-treasurer with Bejrond Kinfe at the fort of Magdalla. His acquaintance with Menelik started from those days when Menelik was kept as Tewodros's captive at Magdalla. When Menelik escaped and returned to Showa in 1865, Meshesha followed him and became a trusted confidant of Menelik. He was sent on several occasions as an envoy of Menelik to Yohannes, notably in September 1887 with Bejrond Atnafe (later Bitwoded) accompanying Abune Matewos, the bishop of Showa, when the latter was summoned by Yohannes while he was planning his campaign against the Italians to Sahati.

Later on, the relationship between Menelik and Yohannes deteriorated to such an extent that they were almost in the brink of war. They positioned their respective armies facing each other on the banks of the Abbay (Nile). At that time Yohannes was corresponding not directly with Menelik but through his uncle Ras Darge, although both Darge and Menelik were responding to his letters. In one of these letters, Yohannes referred to Meshesha Worqe as:

> the person who has played the role of the devil in causing differences between us [Yohannes and Menelik]; who tries to disrupt the empire; who is skilled in all the languages of the world; and who loves to study the languages of devils, is Meshesha Worqe. It is from him...that flows so much evil thought. [242]

Yohannes's view undoubtedly was shared by his heir and son Mengesha and by the close Tigrayan counsellors in the court of Yohannes, such as Alula. It was therefore a blunder, on Menelik's part, to appoint Meshesha and Mengesha simultaneously in Tigray. It was also a mistake to leave Ras Alula (who not only in Tigray but all over Ethiopia had been regarded as a national hero for his defense of Ethiopia's patrimony in the northern province against the Egyptians, Italians and the Mahdists) without any kind of command.

Mengesha and his counsellors appear, therefore, to have contemplated breaking their tie with Menelik, now that his main ally the Italians had abandoned him on account of the dispute that had arisen concerning the protectorate clause of the treaty of Wuchalé.

Mengesha's attempt to be regarded as an autonomous ruler of Tigray rather than as a vassal of Menelik, and the granting of titles and decorations to Gandolfi and his aides, and subsequently conferring the title of Ras on Dejazmach Sebhat Aregawi, certainly indicate Mengesha's aspirations at least for a kingship of Tigray if not for the crown of his father as Emperor of Ethiopia. But it was unrealistic, since the ambition was not backed by force and the Italians made it absolutely clear that they would only treat him as governor appointed by Emperor Menelik.

Ras Mengesha, accompanied by Ras Alula, Ras Hagos and other Tigrayan personalities, met General Giuseppe Gandolfi on December 6, 1891, and concluded the Mereb Convention. According to the Italians, the so-called "Mereb Convention" was simply a ceremony held at Mareb for an exchange of oaths between Ras Mengesha and the prominent personalities of Tigray with General Giuseppe Gandolfi, the Italian governor of Eritrea. There was no formal written agreement. The only document produced was a letter from Ras Mengesha to King Umberto, written at Mereb, on 29 Hidar, 1884 (December 8, 1891) confirming that he and the Italian governor met at Mereb and concluded an oath which declared, "My enemies shall be thy enemies and my friends shall be thy friends."

After the Mereb convention the Italians allowed for a while the import of food purchased in the Eritrean markets and about 35,000 cartridges were sent by Gandolfi (urgently required for security reasons), although Dr. Nerazzani, who negotiated the terms of the Mereb Convention on behalf of Italy, had given an advance warning that Italy would only supply a limited amount of arms and

242. Encampment at Damot (Gojam), 18 Hidar, 1881 (November 26, 1888), Yohannes to Dargue-reproduced in Heruy Wolde Sellassie: unfinished, *History of Ethiopia* pp.81-88, and in my own book, Zewde Gabre-Sellassie, *Yohannes IV of Ethiopia – A Political Biography*, Clarendon Press, Oxford, 1975, Appendix C, pp. 263-269.

ammunition only in the event that Tigray was attacked by the Mahdists, who were their common enemy.

Mengesha's act in concluding the so-called "Mereb convention" was regarded by Menelik as treachery. There is no doubt that Mengesha after his first submission to Menelik at Aguedi, near Mekele, in February 1890, should have obtained permission from the Emperor prior to negotiating and concluding any kind of agreement. But, on the other hand, the so-called "Mereb convention" was in no way comparable to the two secret treaties which were concluded between Menelik and the Italians in 1883 and 1887, during the reign of Yohannes.

Mengesha was also accused later by Nebure Id Wolde Giorgis that, in his correspondence and seal, he styled himself as "son of Yohannes King of Zion Emperor of Ethiopia"; and after the battle of Debre Haila, he had written to Queen Victoria seeking the assistance of the British Government to regain the throne of Yohannes. In actual fact, the letter written to Queen Victoria on 23 Nehasse 1887 (August 28, 1895) only states, "...Now, the Italians have come and occupied my country [dominion]. Do not forget your friendship with Emperor Yohannes."[243] As this letter was written soon after the Italians occupied virtually the whole of Tigray before the national army arrived and fought at Amba Alaghe, it does not necessarily constitute disloyalty to Menelik. Mengesha was desperately, soliciting the assistance of Her Britannic Majesty's Government to liberate his territory from foreign occupation. It was also a common custom, at the time, for important personalities in the realm to state their fathers' names with their titles and there was no restriction on corresponding with foreign powers.

Dejazmach Meshesha, after his return to Addis Ababa, posing as a loyal patriot and Menelik's man who was victimized at the hands of the Tigrayans and the Italians in Eritrea, exacerbated the alienation of Menelik from Mengesha, thus inadvertently fulfilling the principal objective of the Italians. But, before long, Meshesha (whom Massaja referred to as one who spoke English and French, which he learnt from the captives at Magdalla, and described as: "un Faccendiere, o meglio, un imbroglione matricolato,"[244] or a celebrated intriguer and mischievous man) became embroiled in high treason by attempting with Aleqa (later Nebure Id) Admasu to assassinate Menelik and to replace him by his

243. PRO. London – F.O. 78/4784: 23 Nehasse, 1887 (August 28, 1895), Mengesha to Victoria.
244. PRO. London – F.O. 78/4784: 23 Nehasse, 1887 (August 28, 1895), Mengesha to Victoria.

cousin. Fitewrari Gulilate (Tekle Mariam), son of Merid-Azmatch Haile Mikael Sahle Selassie. Meshesha was condemned to death on March 8 1893. The sentence, however, was commuted to life imprisonment and in 1896, on the eve of the expedition to the battle of Adwa, Meshesha was pardoned, and eventually restored to his former position.

Two months after the so-called "Mereb convention" was concluded, Lt. General Oreste Baratieri replaced General Giuseppe Gandolfi as governor of Eritrea, on February 15, 1892, a change which marked a shift of policy on the part of Italy. The entente cordiale between Mengesha and the Italian administration in Eritrea was destined to be of short duration. Baratieri denied Mengesha even the 20,000 sacks of grain which he had purchased earlier from the Eritrean markets for his army's consumption.

The new Pro-Tigrayan policy was doomed to failure for two fundamental reasons:

- First, the colony which Italy had occupied and the territory which she aspired to add to her colony was the home base of Mengesha and Alula regardless of whatever ambitions they might have entertained to regain the crown of Yohannes.
- Second, the Italian government was still uncertain what policy it wished to follow. Antonelli after his unfortunate last mission to Ethiopia was sent to Argentina as minister of the Legation, and from there he continued advocating his view that Italy should continue to pursue its former policy of winning Menelik to her side.

Dr. Leopoldo Traversi, after leaving for Italy with Antonelli the previous February, had returned to Ethiopia in October 1891. At this juncture, Traversi tried hard to calm Menelik by arguing that the so-called Mereb Convention was in no way intended to alienate Mengesha from Menelik; the "enemies" referred to in the Convention were the Dervishes against whom the Italians were engaged in war. Menelik, though not convinced by Traversi's reasoning, nevertheless sent him to Italy in May, 1892, to discuss the matter with the authorities in Rome. As a result, after he convinced Brin, the Foreign Minister, that it was advantageous for Italy to appease Menelik, he returned to Showa in February, 1893 with two million cartridges purchased by the loan of two million lire granted during Ras Makonnen's mission in 1889 and left in the Italian treasury.

Once he obtained the cartridges, Menelik denounced the treaty of Wuchalé on February 27, 1893. In June 1894, Mengesha came to Addis Ababa and made his second submission to the Emperor. Mengesha was pardoned and was received with great pomp and allowed to return to Tigray on June 14, after a short stay.

The next day after the departure of Ras Mengesha, the envoy of the Italian government Colonel Frederico Piano arrived in Addis Ababa to try to persuade the Emperor to accept the Protectorate clause [Article XVII] of the Treaty of Wuchalé and re-establish the cordial relations that had existed between Italy and Showa for nearly two decades. His reception was courteous but cold. While Piano wanted to discuss the Wuchalé treaty, the Emperor simply asked him when he intended to leave and suggested that Dr. Traversi should leave with him. Thus, Piano was obliged to depart, with Dr. Traversi, in July 1894.

Henceforth the issues between the two countries were destined to be settled only by the use of force. Crispi did not take heed of Prince Von Bismarck's sound advice — despite Germany's basic interest in shifting Italy's preoccupation elsewhere, away from the Adriatic, where it led to a conflict with Austria, Bismarck's had said as early as 1887 that he should beware of getting involved in conflict with Ethiopia. [245]

Menelik turned towards France and Russia, leaving aside members of the Triple Alliance which was composed of Italy, Germany and Austria, as well as avoiding Britain, which was a staunch supporter of Italy in warding off French rivalry in Africa.

By purchases, credits and aid, mostly from France and to a small extent from Russia, Menelik had built up his arsenal through his agents and emissaries, both Ethiopians and foreigners, who included such names as Negadras Awegue Hailu, Fitawrari Damtew Ketema, Tessema Mekbib, the Swiss engineer Alfred Ilg, the Armenians Terkis Terziian and Dikran Ebeya; and French merchants such as Bremond, Bardey, Borelli, Baral, Eloi Pino. Chefieux, Labatut, Savoure, Vanderheim, Soleillet, and Arthur Rimbaud, the famous French poet.

The extent of Menelik's total arsenal by 1896, including what he had obtained earlier, principally from Italy, amounted to no less than 190,000 guns, about 2,000,000 cartridges, 46 cannons and a number of machine guns.

The relatively modern rifles, the Fusil Gras, which is known in Ethiopia as "Wujigra" (notwithstanding the fact that 8,000 of these rifles were sold to Menelik's agent Armand Savoure in July 1893 as surplus, when the French army changed from Gras to Labels); and some of the machine-guns and artillery guns

245. German Government Archive – Bonn A.A.A. IbiA Bd, 2 no. 6: Berlin 6 October 1887, Bismarck to Solms (Count Solms was, at this time, the German Ambassador in Rome).

from France, especially the twenty-five cannons which were brought by Cefieux in 1894, enhanced considerably the quality of the weapons at the disposal of Menelik. For example, at the siege of Mekele in January, 1895, when the Ethiopian artillery opened fire at a range of 4,500 meters, no reply could be made, as the Italian guns only carried 3,850 meters at a maximum range, and they were distinctly seen to strike about 800 meters short. [246]

Menelik also built up cordial relations with Khalifa Abdullahi of the Sudan when his relations with Italy deteriorated despite the hostility of recent past that had endured ever since the advent of the Mahdist State.

After the defeat of King Tekle Haimanot of Gojam by the Mahdists at Sar Weha, Menelik himself was ordered by Yohannes to move to Begemder. He remained there from April 18 to May 16, 1888 but they did not fight as the Mahdists retreated. After his return to Showa, Ras Gobana was sent to Wallaga to stop Mahdist-inspired Oromo uprising. Although Menelik was not anxious to become over-involved in conflict with the Mahdists, because this would detract from their ability to engage Yohannes, he could not ignore a direct threat to very rich areas under his fief.

Wachu Dabato, of the Sibu Ganti, and the chief of the Sibu Wambara and Sinasa made treaties with the Mahdists, who had been in the area for fifteen months under Emir Khelil. Mahdist penetration in the south had reached as far as Nonno. At the battle of Sombo Darro, Gobana defeated these dissidents with the help of Dejazmach Moroda, later known as Dejazmach Gabre Egziabher, and his brother Fitawrari Amanté, leading the Leqa Neqamte and the Tuqa clans.[247] Ras Fitawrari Gobana also armed Dejazmach Joté Tullu's troops with muskets and helped in expelling the Mahdists from Beni Shangul, thus liberating the gold mine (the source of Joté-worq or "Joté's gold"), which had hitherto been occupied by the Ansar.

Menelik did not participate with Yohannes in the Battle of Metemma. However, the Mahdist continued their incursion even after Menelik's accession to the throne, on the Metemma side as far as Dembia. When Antonelli came on his last mission to Ethiopia, on February 2, 1891, Menelik suggested that an

---

246. Moltedo, Guido: *L'assedio di Macalle*, as quoted by Berkeley, George. F-H: *The Campaign of Adowa and The Rise of Menelik*, London, 1902, p.199.
247. Cerulli, Enrico: *Folk Literature of the Galas*, Cambridge Mass. 1922, p.82: Trimingharn, John S: *Islam in Ethiopia*, London, 1952, p.24: *Wallaga Ms*, a family chronicle written by the order of Dedjazmatch Gabre Egziabher Moroda, and my personal interview on the subject with Blata Dersa Amente in May 1957.

agreement should be concluded between Italy, Britain and Ethiopia to fight the Mahdists, as they were also threatening the northwestern part of the Italian colony of Eritrea.

The Mahdist had attacked the Italians at Agordat on June 27, 1890, and at Serobelti on June 26, 1892. Again, the Mahdist forces led by Emir Ahmed Ali, governor of Gedarif, had attacked the Italian at Agordat. On December 21, 1893, Major-General Arimondi defeated the Ansars (followers of the Mahdi) and Ahmed Ali, the leader of the expedition, was killed in combat. During this time, Baratieri, the governor, was on a visit to Italy; when he returned and learnt that Mengesha Yohannes had made his peace with Menelik, in May 1894, he attacked and defeated the Mahdists' stronghold at Kassala, on July 17, 1894, and occupied that town in order to avoid a simultaneous attack by both enemies. Baratieri left a garrison of 1,000 men at Kassala under the command of Captain Hilgade.

As early as March 1893, an Emissary of Khalifa Abdullahi was reported to have come to Menelik although the subject of his mission is not revealed. When Menelik heard the news of the Italian occupation of Kassala he held a council to discuss what steps should be taken. It is reported that some of his counsellors pointed out that they should refrain from taking sides, since both were proven enemies. Menelik retorted by saying that: "the Dervishes only raid and return to their country, whereas the Italians remain, steal the land and occupy the country. It is therefore preferable to side with the Mahdists."[248]

To that end he ordered Ras Bitwoded Mengesha Atikem, governor of western Begemder and Ras Meshesha Tewodros, governor of Quara, bordering the Sudan, to explore ways and means of encouraging the Mahdists to continue their attacks on the Italians. Based on their recommendations, Dejazmach Arade was sent as Menelik's emissary to Khalifa Abdullahi with a letter dated Aril, 1895, stating:

> When you were in war against Emperor Yohannes, I was also fighting against him; there has never been a war between us...Now, we are confronted by an enemy worse than ever. The enemy has come to enslave both of us. We are of the same color. Therefore, we must-co-operate to get rid of our common enemy. [249]

---

248. Cerulli, Enrico: *Folk Literature of the Galas*, Cambridge Mass. 1922, p.82: Trimingharn, John S: *Islam in Ethiopia*, London, 1952, p.24: *Wallaga Ms*, a family chronicle written by the order of Dedjazmatch Gabre Egziabher Moroda, and my personal interview on the subject with Blata Dersa Amente in May 1957.
249. Conti Rossini, Carlo: Italia ed Etiopia dal trattato d'Ucciali ala bataglia di Adua, Roma, 1935, pp. 135-136.

Earlier, Yohannes in his letter to Hamdan Abu Anja, the commander of the Eastern Sudan, written from Gojam, on 17 Tahsas, 1881 (December 25, 1888), had proposed:

> I have no wish to cross my frontiers into your country nor should you desire to cross your frontier into my country. Let us both remain, each in his country within his own limits. The inhabitants of my country and your country spring originally from one ancestor. The best and only course to follow which will be of mutual benefit to us is to be united by the bonds of affection against those who come from Europe and against the Turks and others who wish to govern your country and our country and who are a continual trouble to us both.[250]

The Mahdists, however, could not at that time entertain such a proposal. The Khalifa was determined to revive his followers' zeal and to establish his own leadership on a firm footing after a struggle with the Ashraf (the Mahdi's own kinsmen), following the death of the Mahdi in 1885. The Khalifa had written to Queen Victoria, the Sultan of Turkey and the Khedive of Egypt, in April 1887, urging them to accept the only true faith which was his own version of Islam. Thus, even the Sultan of Turkey and the Khedive of Egypt were regarded as nominal Muslims who had obliterated Islam, and were summoned to accept the Khalifa's precepts. It is not surprising, therefore, that Hamdan Abu Anja's reply to Yohannes was:

> As for your request for peace while you remain an infidel this is impossible. There is nothing between us and you, the Italians and the Europeans...Your safety is in Islam and your destruction in your disbelief. [251]

However, after their army was badly shaken at Metemma, despite the death of Yohannes and the growing pressure of the colonial powers on the Mahdist state, Khalifa Abdullahi had become, by this time, susceptible to the friendly overture by Menelik.

As a result, 5,000 Ansars under the command of Emir Ahmed Fadil, governor of Gedarif, arrived 20 kilometers from Kassala, at Gulasit, on February 22, 1896, eight days before the Battle of Adwa: but they were easily repelled as they

---

250. Sudanese Government Archive, Khartoum: Mahdia 1/34, folder 16, Doc. Nos 192-194: Yohannes to Hamdan Abu Anja, dated 17 Tahsas, 1881 (25 December 1888). Yohannes; letter was received on January 11, 1889 according to Holt. P.M., *The Mahdist State in the Sudan, 1881-1898*, (Oxford, 1958) p. 154. The text of Yohannes' letter is found translated into Arabic in Maim Shuqair: *Tarikh El Sudan El Qadim Wa El Hadith Wa Jugrafiyatuhu*, Cairo, undated (circa, 1903), III. Pp.478-479.

251. Jumada I, 1306, A.H. (January, 1889), Hamdan Abu Anja to Yohannes-extracted from Naim Shuqair. *Tarikh El Sudan El Qadim Wa Ei Hadith Wa Jugrafiratuhu*, Cairo, undated (Circo 1903), III, pp. 480-481.

were scarcely equipped with modern arms. Successive attacks made by the Ansars (followers of the Mahdi) subsequently on March 8 and 18, at Sabderat; April 2, at Mocram; and April 3, at Tucruf, suffered the same fate. Nonetheless, the possibility of renewed attacks from the Dervishes caused Baratieri to keep a considerable force based in Kassala.

Based on Egyptian intelligence, on the eve of the Battle of Adwa on February 29, two envoys of the Khalifa Uthman Azraq and Ali El Taishi were present at Menelik's camp in Adwa to discuss concerted action against the Italians.[252] However, after the victory attained at Adwa, Menelik could hardly involve himself in conflict with the Italians just for the sake of the Mahdists. The survival of the Mahdist state itself was, by this time, seriously at stake.

It was alleged, all the same, that Dejazmach Meshesha Worqe, liberated from confinement, was sent after the battle of Adwa with presents to the Khalifa to conclude a treaty. Aleqa Gobaw Desta (later known as Kentiba Gebru) was certainly sent in July 1896 and stayed at the Khalifa's court at Omdurman until the following October. In January 1897, an envoy of the Khalifa was at Menelik's court in Addis Ababa. Sheikh Tolha Ben Jifar, who fought with the Italians at Amba Alaghe, was used as intermediary between the Mahdists and Ethiopia.

But, in Article VI of the Anglo Ethiopian Treaty of May 14, 1897, Menelik declared the Mahdists as the enemy of his country and said he would not allow arms and ammunition to pass through his territory to the Sudan.[253] In compliance with that treaty, a certain European arms dealer, who called himself by a pseudonym "Linoui," was kept in detention for seven months in Addis Ababa and four months in Harar, for attempting to smuggle arms through Ethiopia to the Sudan.

In December 1897, Ras Makonnen and Dejazmach Demissew, the governor of Arjjo, Wallaga, led an expedition against the Mahdists to help liberate the gold-producing territory of Beni Shangul, taken by the use of guns against the traditionally armed ruler of the area Dejazmach Joté Tullu. This expeditionary force was bolstered when Ras Gobana armed Dejazmach Joté Tullu's troops with muskets and helped in expelling the Mahdists from Beni Shangul, thus liberating the gold mine [the source of Joté-worq or "Joté's gold"], which had hitherto been occupied by the Ansar. Thus, on April 30, 1898. Menelik informed

252. Conti Rossini, Carlo: Italia ed Etiopia dal trattato d'Ucciali ala bataglia di Adwa, Roma 1935, pp.135-136.
253. Wylde, August B.: *Modern Abyssinia*, London 1901, p.475 and in Hertslett, Sir Edward. *The Map of Africa by Treaty:* 3rd Edition, London, 1967, Vol II. Pp. 423-424.

John Harrington, the British Minister, in Addis Ababa, that Beni Shangul had now been incorporated into Ethiopia.

In June 1898, Gobaw Desta (Kentiba Gebru) was again sent to the Sudan to negotiate with Khalifa Abdullahi for the return of Ethiopian prisoners in exchange of Mahdists captured by Makonnen. Thus, contact with the Mahdia continued until the eve of the fall of Khartoum and the establishment of Anglo-Egyptian condominium in September 1898.

The Italians vehemently stove to alienate important and influential Ethiopian personalities from the Emperor. In August and September 1894, Prime Minister Crispi and Blac, the Foreign Minister, instructed Baratieri to implement a scheme designed to set up two kingdoms in Ethiopia, the northern part under Ras Mengesha Yohannes and the southern part under Ras Makonnen, both to be placed under Italian protection. Crispi's instruction to Bartieri stated:

> Menelik's inexcusable behavior compels us to prepare from now on a defense plan. As we did with Menelik against Yohannes, we should now encourage pretenders against Menelik. Mengesha in Tigre, Makonnen in have, besides personal ambitions, serious grounds for hatred and revenge against the Emperor. If Menelik disappears, the empire could be divided into two kingdoms, one in the north, and another in the south, under Italy's lofty protection, not to exclude other better combinations for us.[254]

Baratieri tried hard to revive the cordial relations with Mengesha through Mulazzaru, the Italian resident at Adwa. After utterly failing to alienate Mengesha Yohannes, Italy turned through its agents, such as Cesare Nerazzani and Pietro Felter, in Harar to alienate Ras Makonnen. Through Capitano Salvatore Persico and Tenente Gianini they tried to alienate Mohammed Hanfari of Aussa and his son-in-law Abdel Rahman Yusuf, Ras Mikael of Wallo and influential Islamic religious leaders, such as Sheikh Tolha Bin Gefar. Through Count August Salimbeni and Engineer Luigi Capucci they sought to win over Ras Wolle Betoul of Yeju, Wagshum Birru Gabre Medhin of Wag and King Tekle Haimanot of Gojam. On the eve of the battle of Adwa, the Italian authorities even tried to alienate the venerable Ras Darge, uncle of the Emperor, through Nerazzani, by informing him that his son Lij Gugsa Darge, who had been sent earlier to study at Neuchatel, in Switzerland, by Menelik, had come to Ethiopia as an ally of Italy.

---

254. Battaglia, Roberto: *La Prima Guerra d'Africa*, Torino 1958, pp. 572-574; also, cited by Rubenson, Sven: *The Survival of Ethiopian independence*, Addis Ababa, 1991. p.399.

Of all these attempts, the Italian intelligence only succeeded to alienate Mohammed Hanfari and his son-in-law Abdel Rahman Yusuf, Wag Shum Birru, Sheikh Tolha and some Tigrayan chiefs, who were in disagreement with Ras Mengesha such as Ras Sebhat Aregawi and Dejazmach Hagos Teferi of Agame, Dejazmach Ali of Enda Mehoni, and the Etchege Tewoflos, who was head of the clergy during the reign of Yohannes.

Baratieri had suggested to the Italian government the creation of a diversion by invading Harar from Zeila, which was only twenty days from the coast. This would have prevented Ras Makonnen, Governor of Harar, from joining Menelik's army in the north, but the idea was abandoned because the British refused to allow the Italian army to pass through the British territory of Somaliland (where Zeila is located) since to do so would be regarded by the French as allowing the Italians to occupy Harar — an action that goes contrary to the Anglo-French agreement of 1888, in which both countries had agreed not to allow the annex or the establishment of a protectorate over the Ethiopian province of Harar.

Another scheme, to make a diversion by means of an expedition from Assab, was aborted by the annihilation of the Afar fighting force by the Ethiopian army and the logistic difficulties for Italy that such an expedition would entail due to the torrid climate and the vast distance that would have to be covered from the coast to the highland.

On December 19, 1895, the Italian Parliament voted a grant of twenty million lire for war operations in Ethiopia. Between December 25, 1895 and March 10, 1896, a force of 1,536 officers, 38,063 men and 8,584 mules required for artillery, mounted officers and lines of communications, and 100,000 barrels of materiel were disembarked at Massawa. Although some 16,000 of the men and officers did not arrive until after the battle of Adwa, Baratieri had at his command 21,000 men and 56 artillery guns with him at Tigray, and about 10,000 more throughout the Eritrean colony and at his base in Adigrat in February 1896. 255

In the meantime, Dedjach Bahta Hagos (who was one of the staunch allies of the Italians, but who had gradually been disenchanted), instigated by Ras Mengesha, defected at Akele Guzai and waged a war against them from December 14 to 18, 1894. Soon after the Italians quelled Bahta's rebellion.

255. Battaglia, Roberto: *La Prima Guerra d'Africa*, Torino 1958, pp. 572-574; also, cited by Rubenson, Sven: *The Survival of Ethiopian independence*, Addis Ababa, 1991. p.399.

Baratieri crossed the Mereb and marched to Adwa and Axum on December 30, 1894, and then returned to Asmara.

Mengesha resisted the Italian encroachment at the battles of Koatit and Senafe in Akele Guazy, from January 13 to 15, 1895; and subsequently from October 7 to 9, at Debre Haila, in Enderta. In these battles famous heroes such as Dejazmach Tedla Aiba, Dejazmach Araya, Dejazmach Gizaw Haile Mariam, Qegnazmach Teferi Araya, fell on the battlefield. Mengesha, however, was not by himself a match for the Italians even with the small additional force, under the command of Qegnazmach Haile Mariam, who arrived in time for the third encounter at Debre Haila, sent by Menelik to support him. The Italian occupation was extended as far as Amba Alaghe, where their forces fortified the natural fortress.

When the news reached Addis Ababa, Menelik pronounced a war proclamation, assembled over 100,000 men, left his uncle Ras Darge, Dejazmach Haile Mariam Wolde Mikael and Dejazmach Lul Segued to guard the capital, and departed from Addis Ababa for Tigray on October 13, 1895.

While camping at Woreilu on October 29, Menelik dispatched a large segment of the armed forces to join Ras Mengesha Yohannes in the north. This army, under the overall command of Ras Makonnen, was composed of his own Harar contingent as well as those led by: Ras Mikael, Ras Mengesha Atikem, Ras Wolle, Ras Alula, Wagshum Guangul, (who had replaced his father Wag-Shum Birru, when the latter was deposed and imprisoned on suspicion of defection), Fitawrari Gebeyehu, commander of the Emperor's Body Guard or the Emperor's own army, Fitawrari Tekle, commanding a Wallaga contingent, Dejazmach Wolde Abba Seyoum, and Lique Mekwas Adnew.

Similarly, Menelik sent the armed forces of Ras Wolde Giorgis and Ras Tessemma (under the overall command of Azaj Wolde Tsadiq) to Aussa to fight Mohammed Hanfari, who had defected to the Italians. Dejazmach Gabre Egziabher and Dejazmach Joté of Wallaga, Abba Djifar of Jimma and Kawo Tona of Wolaita were sent back to their respective territory to guard the Western regions.

On December 7, 1895, the Ethiopian forces gained a victory after fierce fighting in which both sides displayed valor at Amba Alaghe. The Italian commander Major Pietro Toselli and many men on both the Ethiopian and the Italian sides sacrificed their lives.

On January 20, 1896, the army of Mohammed Hanfari was annihilated by the Ethiopian army. Over 600 Afars perished on the battlefield.

King Tekle Haimanot of Gojam, with his army, joined the Emperor on December 25, 1895; and then, Menelik joined the advance army and Ras Mengesha Yohannes on January 5, 1896, at Tcheleqot. He then proceeded to Mekele, where the Italians had fortified Enda Yesus.

The Siege of Mekele lasted for forty-three days from December 21, 1895, to February 2, 1896. Here, the exceptional talent of Lique-Mekuas Abate and Bed-jrond Baltcha in handling the artillery guns earned the admiration of both their compatriots and their foes. In an attempt to occupy the fort, many gallant Ethiopians died. The Ethiopians, on the advice of Empress Taytu, having occupied the spring from where the water streams into the Italian fortification, the enemy in the isolated garrison started to suffer.

Finally, Pietro Felter (who had been with Ras Makonnen at Harar) was brought from Zeila, where he had been since he was expelled from Harar in September 1895, and was sent to negotiate for their release. As a result of the negotiation, Major Giuseppe Galliano, the commander of the fort, and his men, were allowed to leave on January 23, escorted and assisted by Ethiopians. Thus the Italians who had been under siege, with their guns, rifles and all their belongings, joined the Italian forces at Edaga Hamus, near Adigrat. This act enhanced the prestige of Menelik in the eyes of the world but it was resented by most Ethiopians, who felt the released Italians would swell the ranks of the enemy.

On February 1, 1896, Baratieri left Edaga Hamus and by February 13 he established his headquarters at Sawria, between Enticho and Feres Mai. Menelik also moved away from Mekele and passed through Hauzen and Feres Mai and camped at Yeha, in the vicinity of Adwa. Baratieri sent Major Tommaso Salsa with Captain Annibale Anghera and an interpreter, Gabre Egziabher (who later defected to Ethiopia), to Menelik's camp with a peace proposal requesting renewed acceptance of the Wuchalé Treaty Cessation of territory up to Lake Ashenghe, where the Italian flag had been hoisted.

Major Salsa remained in Menelik's camp from February 6 to 12, and returned to Sawria after he was informed that the proposal was rejected.

In the meantime, the Italians suffered the loss of their prominent Ethiopian allies who had fought with them at Amba Alaghe. Sheikh Tolha disappeared from the war arena after his force was decimated at Alaghe. Ras Sebhat and Dejazmach Hagos Teferi defected on February 12, 1896, with their men and 600 rifles. They fought against the Italians at Mai Meret and moved to the Emperor's camp, with inside knowledge of the Italian lines of communication. Both the

Italian and the Ethiopian camps were becoming impatient and were tired of waiting. Both the Italians and their recruited indigenous soldiers (Askaris) were anxious for action. The Askaris took up a derisive chant: "Eza Adwa Etibluwa Kitments'ekum diya Kitkhediwa," or, "You incessantly talk of Adwa, Adwa — Is it going to come to you, or are you going to it?"

Baratieri was hoping that he could lure the Ethiopians to attack his fortified camp, or that the Ethiopian army would disperse if he waited long enough. The supply situation was becoming acute in both camps. Baratieri was considering a retreat to Adi Qeyih; and on the Ethiopian side a detachment was sent to reconnoiter in the direction of Seraie, but they returned from Mereb as there was neither sufficient water nor food supply to sustain the large army. The temptation to attack the Italians at their fortified camp was abandoned after a council with Ras Mengesha and Ras Alula, who cited their experience at Sahati and Metemma and considered such an act suicidal.

On February 25, Baratieri received a telegram from Prime Minister Crispi, stating:

> This is a military phthisis [progressive wasting disease] not a war; small skirmishes in which we are always facing the enemy with inferior number; a waste of heroism without any corresponding success. I have no advice to give you because I am not on the spot, but it is clear to me that there is no fundamental plan in the campaign, and I should like one to be formulated. We are ready for any sacrifice in order to save the honor of the army and the prestige of the monarchy.[256]

This obviously meant that the authorities in Rome wanted to see some action and initiative, not the defensive posture which Baratieri had espoused.

On February 28, Baratieri called an informal council, comprising his four Major Generals: Giuseppe Ellena, Giuseppe Arimondi, Matteo Albertone and Vittorio Emanuel Dabormida. All were opposed to retreat and favored attack. The spies also brought encouraging news that the army of Menelik was dispersed in search of food.

At 5 P.M. on February 29, Baratieri decided that the army should march to Adwa that evening and make a surprise attack. Accordingly, by 9 P.M., they started the long rugged march from Sawria to Adwa, in three columns. The right flank was led by Dabormida; the central position was led by Arimondi, with Ellena in reserve; and the left flank was led by Albertone.

---

256. Cited in Berkeley, George F-H: *The Battle of Adowa and the Rise of Menelik*, London, 1902. p.256.

The layout of the Ethiopian armed forces was as follows. On the extreme right, facing Enda Abba Guerima, lay the Gojam contingent under King Tekle Haimanot, supported by Ras Worqe. The armies of Ras Makonnen, Ras Mikael, and part of the Emperor's own army (under the command of Fitawarari Gebeyehu) held the central position facing Mount Seloda, while the Emperor himself, with the troops commanded by Ras Wolle, Ras Mengesha Atikem and Wagshum Guangul, were in reserve behind the central column. The extreme left, extending from Adi Aburi to Enda Mariam Shewito, was held by the Tigrayan army under the command of Ras Mengesha, assisted by Ras Alula and Ras Hagos.

The location of Enda Kidane Mehret as shown on the Italians' map did not correspond with reality; this caused confusion so that the left wing of the Italian force commanded by Major-General Albertone was led astray; and without coordinating its movement with the others, it reached the vicinity of Adwa early in the morning. Aw'alom and Gabre Egzy Kassa, the Italian spies, had already informed Ras Mengesha and Ras Alula that the Italian army was advancing. They in turn alerted the Emperor and the other leaders in good time, and the Ethiopians were, therefore, prepared.

As Ras Mengesha Yohannes had been brought the tidings related to the advance of the Italian army on the side of Enda Kidane Mehret, he moved towards that direction, leaving a segment of the Tigrayan army commanded by Ras Alula and Ras Hagos to guard the left flank at Enda Mariam Shewito, and joined with the army of King Tekle Haimanot of Gojam, the segment of the Emperor's own army commanded by Fitawrari Gebeyehu Gora, and the armies of Ras Makonnen, Ras Mikael and Ras Wolle.

These together engaged Albertone's force at dawn and prevented Arimondi's and Dabormida's forces from joining Albertone. The Ethiopians routed the Italian left flank commanded by Albertone by mid morning. They defeated the central force commanded by Arimondi and the reserve force led by Ellena around noon and the right flank led by Dabormida by 4:00 P.M. The Ethiopian forces on the firing line and on reserve moved freely to fight the Italian columns, in turn, until they were all defeated. The Ethiopians inflicted a disastrous defeat on the Italian army at the Battle of Adwa.

Estimates of the number of dead and wounded on both sides and the number of prisoners of war captured by the Ethiopians vary widely. On the Italian side, according to George Berkeley in The Campaign of Adwa and the Rise of Menelik, out of the 17,700 engaged in action, 6,133 were killed and 1,428 wounded, for a total of 7,561 (apart from those permanently missing). The Italians thus lost a huge percentage of their original fighting force.[257] Others have given much higher figures: 7,560 Italians of all rank plus 7,100 indigenous, for a total of 14,660 killed in the battle and in retreat. Of the Italian Generals, Dabormida, Arimondi and Lt. Colonel Galliano lost their lives heroically on the battlefield, while Albertone, after resisting, was taken prisoner. Baratieri and Ellena managed to escape, though the latter was wounded. They retreated to Eritrea with 258 officers and 4,666 Italians of other ranks, and about 4,000 indigenous. All of the Italians' 56 artillery guns and 11,000 rifles were captured by the Ethiopians. The number of prisoners ranged from as high as 4,000 to 2,865, of which 1,865 were Italians and 1,000 indigenous.

The indigenous soldiers who had been recruited by the Italians and were taken as prisoners of war were tried as traitors. Based on the Feteha Negest (The Law of Kings), the traditional Ethiopian code, 406 of them was sentenced to death. The Emperor commuted the death sentence but had their right hands and left feet cut off, a harsh punishment which aroused a great deal of criticism in internal and external public opinion.

On the Ethiopian side, according to some Ethiopian estimates, the number of those killed was as low as 3,867, but others have put the figure as high as 10,000. It is probable that around 7,000 were killed and about 10,000 wounded. Fitawrari Gebeyehu, the hero of Amba Alaghe; Commander of the Emperor's own army, Dejazmach Beshah Aboye; the Emperor's cousin, Fitwrari Damtew Ketema, who just before the war returned from a mission to Russia; Dejazmach Tchatcha; Qegnazmach Abbayneh; his son Qegnazmach Taffese; and Qegnazmach Tegegne Worqu, the Gojam hero of Gallabat and Sar Weha at previous wars against the Dervishes in 1887, were among the prominent men who fell heroically in the battlefield.[258]

On March 4, when Baratieri reached Asmara, he found out that he had been replaced by General Antonio Baldissera, who had just arrived with a fresh force of 15,000 men to be added to the 20,000 already in the colony; and an additional 140 million lire was voted by the Italian Chamber to enable him to carry out the defense of the Colony. This brings the total cost of the war to the Italian treasury to 200 million lire (or 7.75 million sterling). Baldissera immediately sent Major Tommaso Salsa, the resident at Adi Qhuala, to Menelik's camp at Enticho

257. Ibid.
258.Ibid.

on the pretext of seeking permission to bury the dead, but at the same time with the instruction to explore acceptable terms for provisional agreement in the hope of deflecting any desire on the part of Menelik to pursue his victory by crossing over into Eritrea.

Salsa stayed at Menelik's camp from March 12 to 17. The demand for burial was granted without discussion, but as regards the provisional terms, the Emperor requested the cancellation of the Treaty of Wuchalé, the evacuation of Adigrat, and a provisional boundary of Mereb-Belesa-Muna. Salsa returned to Asmara, promising to come back with the Governor's response within a week; he came back on March 25 with a response which accepted the cancellation of the Treaty on condition that the Emperor would not accord the right of protectorate to any other power. Menelik rejected this condition outright as meddling with his autonomous sovereignty.

Before the advent of Major Tommaso Salsa, while Menelik was camping at Feres Mai, and after the negotiation was broken off at Enticho, there was a great deal of talk that the Ethiopian forces would advance to Gurae, in Eritrea. Considerations must have included, first, whether there would be sufficient provision of food and water for the large army and the numerous animals that would be needed; second, news that reinforcements had arrived with Baldissera had reached Menelik but their number were unknown; third, the possibility of repercussion from other powers, with whom the boundaries of the eastern, Western and southern parts of the Empire were still to be demarcated; last, but not least, the exhaustion of the troops and their desire to return to their homes after eight months of the most arduous campaign. Finally, it was decided to abandon the idea of advancing towards Eritrea.

On March 20, Menelik started the return journey from Feres Mai and he arrived at Addis Ababa on May 23. At this juncture, the Russian Red Cross Mission arrived to treat the wounded soldiers and prisoners of war; this eventually led to the establishment of Menelik Hospital in Addis Ababa. In the meantime, on May 18, 1896, the Italians withdrew from Adigrat, which had been encircled by the force of Ras Mengesha.

In Italy, Crispi's government fell on March 15 and his successor, the Marchese Antonio di Rudini and the new Minister of War, General Ercole Ricotti, were not in the mood to avenge Adwa and chose instead to close the chapter, for the time being, by opting for a peace settlement. Accordingly, Dr. Cesare Nerazzani arrived in Addis Ababa on October 6, 1896, as Italy's plenipotentiary, to negotiate and sign the peace treaty on behalf of Italy. Two and half weeks later, on October 27, 1896, the Convention was signed by which:

1. Peace was declared.

2. The Treaty of Wuchalé and the Additional Convention of October 1, 1889 were abolished.

3. Ethiopia was recognized by Italy as an independent sovereign state.

4. Until final arrangements could be made, the boundary of Mareb-Belesa-Muna was to be observed; meanwhile, Italy was not to cede any part of the territory to any other power.

On the same date another convention was signed related to the return of war prisoners, the Italian government agreeing to pay the expenses incurred for their upkeep. Accordingly, Italy paid about ten million lire. By the end of March 1897, or thirteen months after Adwa, all of the surviving 1,759 Italians, including General Matteo Albertone (who had been lodged at the compound of Menelik's palace under the supervision of Azaj Zamanel), returned to Italy.

In conclusion, this author wishes to portray the different sentiments triggered by the events narrated above. On the Italian side, there was a mixed feeling. Those who had been opposed from the start to Italy's colonial adventure considered Adwa a vindication, while those who had been clamoring for Italy's share of colonial possession found it a bitter pill to swallow. Those who had been actively engaged in forging Italo-Showan relations for over a decade understandably felt that they had been utterly betrayed. Leopoldo Traversi, reflecting on these events in retrospect, observed:

> Menelik wanted to gain time and the Empire without incurring serious risks. Fortune favored him; and when he was crowned as King of kings he forgot the benefits and assistance received from us. At the first hurdle he turned against us and revealed the whole of his soul. We, the so-called descendants of Machiavelli, have been derided, made a laughing stock, by this Black King. We are the culprits. [259]

In another passage, comparing Menelik with his predecessor, he commented: "L'imperatore aveva cambiato di nome, ma l'anima etiopica era e sara sempre la stesse, " or, "The Emperor had changed in name, but the Ethiopian soul had been and will always be the same.[260] And in a letter addresses to Colonel Baratieri, dated March 29, 1892, Traversi stated:

> The difference between the deceased and the living Emperor is only one — i.e., one was called John [Yohannes] and this one is called Menelik. [261]

---

259. Traversi, Leopoldo: *Let Maretia,* Milan, 1931, pp. 303-304.
260. Traversi, Leopoldo: *Let Maretia,* Milan, 1931, pp. 419.

In general, despite the cordial relation which was re-established after the Peace Treaty of 1897, the "scar of Adwa," as Gabrielle d'Anunzio called it, lingered in the minds of many Italians and ignited the vindictive sentiment which contributed to the Italo-Ethiopian conflict of the 1930s, and to the realization of Benito Mussolini's dream of building L'Africa Orientale Italiana, or Italian East African Empire.

For Ethiopians, the victory at Adwa instilled a national sense of pride. The unity shown at Adwa was unique; nothing like it had been accomplished in the face of similar perils, such as at Magdalla against the British during the reign of Tewodros; at Guda Gudi and Gurae against the Egyptians; at Dogali and Sahati against the Italians, or at Metemma, against the Dervishes, during the reign of Yohannes.

The victories gained at Amba Alaghe, Mekele and Adwa were achieved by the wise leadership of Menelik and his generals; by the heroism of the warriors in all the wars from Koatit to Adwa; by the sacrifices sustained by the whole army and the camp followers, who managed the transportation; by the peasantry, whose grain and cattle were consumed by the vast army as it passed through and especially at places where it was stations for a considerable time; by the clergy, headed by Archbishop Matewos, who accompanied the army and rendered spiritual inspiration, making it appear almost as a holy war; by the invaluable contribution of the women who played a distinguished role in the whole operation.

First and foremost, Empress Taytu (like her illustrious predecessors, Empress Elleni and Empress Seble Wongel of the 15th and 16th centuries) was the animating spirit and the driving force during all the negotiations; and an active participant in the war arena, leading her own army under the command of Azaj Zamanel. In addition, she supervised her female followers who nursed the wounded, encouraged the fighters, and prepared their food.

It was the sum of all these elements which culminated in the victory of Adwa. As a result, the European powers came to consider Ethiopia a nation to be reckoned with and foreign missions were officially established in Addis Ababa. The demarcation of the frontier on all sides was accomplished in the following years, with the exception of the southeast portion bordering Italian Somaliland.

Ethiopia, to Africans and people of African descent through out the diaspora, became a synonym for independence. Thus we find the "Ethiopian Church" in South Africa early in the twentieth century; the Abyssinian Baptist

261. Traversi, Leopoldo: *Let Maretia*, Milan, 1931, pp. 386.

Church in Harlem, New York; and "Ethiopianism" spread as an ideology to liberate the Black race, expounded by Caseley Heyford in his book, Ethiopia Unbound,[262] at the beginning of the twentieth century; and the Back to Africa movement initiated by Marcus Garvey in the 1920s, which culminated in Ras Teferianism, which flourished in the Caribbean. Independent Ethiopia thus became the living exemplar of an unconquered historic African people and a bastion of prestige and hope to those who were under colonial rule.

262. Hayford, Caseley J.E.: *Ethiopia*

CHAPTER 4. ADWA 1896: WHO WAS CIVILIZED AND WHO WAS SAVAGE?

Negussay Ayele Ph.D.
Professor of African American Studies, University of California, LA

A PROFILE OF COLONIAL EXPANSION IN AFRICA

For Ethiopians in particular and for other continental and diaspora Africans in general, Ethiopia's triumph over European colonialism is a historic occasion when valiant African resistance fighters led by Emperor Menelik, Queen Taytu and many other notables engaged in a series of battles (December 7, 1895 to March 1, 1896), a determined and well supplied European colonial invading force in northern Ethiopia, culminating in the decisive Battle of Adwa. At the end of the day, at Adwa, Ethiopian "victory was complete, the protest effective,"[263] and the news reverberated all over Europe and the United States. However, because of their insulation from global information systems, awareness of the event only trickled down slowly among African peoples and also, to some extent, the Black world in the diaspora. Whenever and wherever the news of Adwa was heard among Black communities, it was received with a sense of pride and joy.

To be sure, Adwa was neither the first nor the last military confrontation between Italy and Ethiopia on Ethiopian soil nor was such martial engagement between African and European forces unique to the Horn of Africa. One could, if

263. Sven Rubenson, "Adwa 1896: The Resounding Protest" in Robert I. Rotberg and Ali A. Mazrui (eds) *Protest and Power In Black Africa:* Oxford, 1970; p.127.

one wished, trace African-European militarized conflicts to the seesaw Punic Wars between Carthage and Rome in the third century B.C., culminating in Hannibal's victory over Roman forces at Cannae (216 B.C.) and his march on Rome (211 B.C).[264] We find nothing of any consequence recorded regarding organized military clashes between Europeans and Africans for the next millennium and a half, until the European slave trade began, off the coasts of West Africa. But, beginning with the Portuguese sacking or rape of Kilwa on the east coast of Africa in AD 1505,[265] military engagements aimed at European territorial presence ensued sporadically all over the continent and reached their crescendo in the heyday of the infamous "scramble for Africa" in the latter part of the nineteenth century. Indeed, one of the oft repeated refrains of nineteenth century colonial predators was, "Whatever happens, we [Europeans] have got the Maxim gun and they [Africans] have not."

By the threshold of the twentieth century, a few tens of thousands of Europeans had subjugated millions of Africans and placed virtually their entire continent — roughly equivalent in area to the United States, India, Western, China and Argentina combined — under colonial control. For the most part, Europeans avoided direct military clashes and used clever tactics to dupe, hoodwink and manipulate Africans into submission for their own "protection." Given that Africa had so recently been Europe's, the Americas' and the Arab world's quarry for the slave trade, Europeans found it easy not just to underestimate Africans but to consider them sub-human, beastly, barbaric, and not worthy of treatment as bona fide human beings endowed with the same moral and civil or human rights and not entitled to invoke laws and principles that govern "civilized" (aka "European") beings. When the Congolese pleaded with a Belgian soldier that they could not go on working in the forests to get rubber because they were literally starving or were being consumed by leopards and other wild beasts, the soldier is said to have told the Africans to go back to the forest because "you are only beasts yourselves."[266] A Herero man bitterly complained to his German hegemon: "dogs, slaves, worse than baboons on the rocks... that is how you treat us..."[267]

---

264. See Emile Bradford, *Hannibal:* New York, 1981.
265. Vide Basil Davidson, *Africa In History:* London, 1984; pp. 188-194. Cf also Robert W. July, *A History o the African People:* New York, 1970; pp. 82-85; A. Adu Boahen (editor) *UNESCO General History of Africa, Vol VII:* Africa Under Colonial Domination 1880-1935: London, 1990; Walter Rodney, *How Europe Underdeveloped Africa:* Washington, D.C., 1974, for more on the subject.
266. Thomas Pakenham, *The Scramble For Africa:* New York, 1991; p. 585.

Expressions like "Africans have no fatherland" had wide currency in Europe and "civilized" Europeans like Prime Minister Crispi said that it was "entirely lawful" to cheat an African. The German pundit Carl Peters said that the African was "a born slave who needs his despot like an opium addict needs his pipe."[268] To European colonialists, Africans were just "niggers," "baboons," "sambos," kaffirs," "savages" etc... These stereotypes governed uncouth European behavior towards Africans in the nineteenth century and were still prevalent in the twentieth.

Were there differences among European colonialists in such behavior? An Ethiopian saying provides the short answer: "It is a futile exercise to attempt to identify the fairest one among a bunch of monkeys." And, monkeys come in the same colors humans use to separate one another by. A longer answer to the question rests with contemporary individual or collective experiences among Africans and Europeans.

To be sure, European colonial penetration did not go militarily unchallenged. Though few and far between, there were instances of African military challenges or resistance to European colonial expansions. For some time the French foreign legionnaires had their hands full with Amazon-like female fighters of Dahomey and the forces of Samori Turay of Western Sudan. The British had their military bouts with Ashanti King Kofi Karikari of West Africa, with Emperor Tewodros of Ethiopia, with the Dervish Mahdi, Mohammed Ahmad and his ansars in the Sudan, with Sheikhh Abdille Hassan in the Somali coast, and with Zulu forces under King Cetshwayo in Southern Africa among others.[269] The Italians perhaps took the worst spanking in Africa (mainly in the Horn) as their much vaunted colonial armies ran into resistance fighters of the likes of Ethiopia's Ras Alula, Emperor Yohannes IV, Emperor Menelik and Taytu — his chess Queen — and Emperor Haile Selassie. Likewise, Sheikhh Abdille Hassan of the Somali coast, Mohammed Ahmed, the Mahdi and his Dervish followers in the Sudan, and Umar al Mukhtar of Libya also proved formidable armed challengers to Italian colonial predators.

---

267. Ibid, p. 602; to put this "savage/civilized" appellation in broader historical context of EuroAmerican/nonEuroAmerican or "White/Black" relations see J. M. Blaut, *The Colonizer's model of the World:* New York, 1993. Cf. also Ali A. Mazrui, *The Africans:* Boston, 1986.
268. Edgerton, above, p. 209.
269. For more on this see Robert B. Edgerton's account of the British-Zulu battles, *Like Lions They Fought:* New York, 1988, particularly pp. 195-213 and Pakenham, above.

In addition, there were also widespread and often protracted general resistance movements and uprisings in parts of Africa during these periods, which were brutally suppressed. It is reported, for instance, that Belgian King Leopold's forces butchered as many as five million Africans in what today is called Congo (formerly Zaire).[270] The Germans also butchered tens of thousands of Tanganyikans (in the Maji-Maji rebellion) and Herero rebels — whom they dubbed "baboons" — in Southwest Africa. The Zulu, Ndebele, Xhosa and other indigenous peoples continued to carry on now hidden, now open, resistance struggles in southern Africa against Boer settler colonialists and/or British and German imperialists during this period. The Battle of Adwa in 1896 was neither the first nor the last military confrontation between European colonial armies and African fighters. However, whereas European colonial forces sooner or later crushed resistance by the Ashanti, the Sudanese, the Zulu, the Herero, the Bakongo, the Ndebele, the Somali and others, their winning streak was broken in Ethiopia. Victory over the Italian invaders at Adwa was decisive and, though its territory was reduced, Ethiopia remained the only independent state in Africa at the time. This unique phenomenon had salutary symbolic meaning to Africans at home and abroad, even as it telegraphed shock and consternation over the self-styled "civilized" European or White world. Time and distance allow for all concerned to reflect upon those events, to bond with their ancestors and acknowledge the legacies and lessons they bequeathed to successive generations.

Furthermore, periodically our knowledge (or lack thereof) about what happened before, during and after the Battle of Adwain the broader context of the colonial scramble in Africa needs once again to be refreshed, corrected or replenished as the case may be from a more distant and more detached vantage point. In the nineteenth century, there were no written indigenous African languages except for Ethiopic and, of course, Arabic for the Arabized parts of Africa. Consequently, a nagging drawback for much of the political historiography of Black Africa is the exclusive reliance on contemporary European, i.e. colonial, writings and renderings regardless of who (Africans or non-Africans) carry on research afterwards. To the extent that there was a written language in this part of Africa and to the extent that some events and correspondences were recorded in the vernacular, we can cross-check colonial historiography and European versions of events against indigenous sources and perspectives.

---

270. Edgerton, above, p. 212.

Specifically, this chapter on the armed confrontation between Rome and Addis Ababa at Adwa in 1896 focuses on a vital and intriguing — but, so far, unexplored — question: who really was "savage" and who was "civilized" in the contemporary peace and war struggles between Africans and Europeans? As we shall see, one factor that made the armed conflict inevitable was the condescending (in today's parlance, racist) attitude Italians exhibited towards Ethiopians.

Struggles in the Horn and the Making of the Adwa Confrontation

In the larger scheme of European colonial adventures in this part of the world, "Adwa was no episode. It was the last dramatic act in a long play, the culmination of a struggle that had begun decades earlier. The Ethiopian protest was slow and patient, but unyielding."[271] Indeed, European colonial encroachments into the Horn were underway very early in the nineteenth century and by the 1840s, an Ethiopian ruler from Tigray, Dejazmach Wube, had had enough of French and British machinations. One of his guests, Amaud d'Abbadie, paraphrased Wube's reaction as follows:

> Take care that you never again tread the soil of my country. The English and you are confined to cursed lands and you covet our healthy climate: one collects our plants, another our stones; I do not know what you are looking for, but I do not want it to be in my country that you find it.[272]

As Sven Rubenson has documented in his classic work, The Survival of Ethiopian Independence,[273] there were many struggles and tugs-of-war between overt and covert colonial agents and indigenous leaders and forces intent on withstanding the devious wiles of Europeans in the Horn of Africa. Europeans represented themselves as ordinary Christians — but "superior" to any other brand of Christianity in Ethiopia or in the Orient. On the other hand, the Ethiopians, who had been Coptic Christians for nearly as long as Christianity had existed and had neither a superiority or an inferiority complex, had assumed — mistakenly, as it turned out — that there were at least certain minimal universal

271. Rubenson, above, p. 129.
272. Sven Rubenson, *The Survival of Ethiopian Independence:* Addis Ababa and London, 1976; p.54
273. Sven Rubenson's book, just cited, remains the best balanced and concise and so far definitive account of Ethiopia's relations with the outside world in the nineteenth century in the English language.

Christian values, principles and standards of behavior to be shared, respected and adhered to by all Christians in relations with one another, be they Europeans or Africans. Consequently, Ethiopians continued to operate from fundamental Christian values, premises and dictates both in peace and in war in their relations with Europeans and continued to appeal to them to behave as Christians. But events associated with the Adwa confrontation between Italy and Ethiopia showed that these latter-day Roman marauders in Africa had a different understanding.

Though the Europeans did not acknowledge it, the Ethiopians in peace and in war bent their words and deeds to the precepts of Christian and civilized conduct. All this notwithstanding, Catholics, Anglicans, Lutherans and other Protestant denominations from America and Europe, including non-colonial Scandinavia, were undertaking large-scale missionary activities in Ethiopia, as in other parts of Africa, to proselytize indigenous Christians to European versions of Christianity. Consequently, some of the bitter conflicts between Ethiopian rulers and Europeans revolved around missionary activities and their often poorly disguised role as the colonial vanguard.[274] Exasperated by recurrent "the flag follows the cross" pattern of European colonial penetration in Africa, one contemporary Ethiopian ruler, Emperor Tewodros, is said to have expressed his indignation in these terms:

> I know the tactics of the European governments when they want to seize a country in the Orient. First they send missionaries, then consuls to support the missionaries, then battalions to sustain the consuls. I am not a rajah from Hindustan to be made a fool of like that; I prefer to engage the battalions at once.[275]

Even though it exhausted every possible means to achieve its colonial objective, it seems that Italy was destined to be "the last of the big powers and the first of the small ones" when it came to European colonial clout as well as the spoils gathered in Africa. This dire condition literally consumed several Italian governments, including Crispi's in the 1890s and Mussolini's in the 1930s. Italy jumped into the colonizing fray in the Horn in the late 1850s using the same venues and ploys as other colonial predators of the era — intriguing consuls and colonially-minded missionaries or, in twentieth century parlance, covert operators. Between the 1830s and the 1890s, agents of British, Italian and French colonialism augmented by Egyptian regional expansionists and individual mercenaries (including Americans, Swiss and others) carried on relentless compet-

274. See Rubenson, Ibid pp. 55-288.
275. Ibid, p. 231.

itive and collaborative political, military, "diplomatic" and religious campaigns to subjugate the Horn of Africa, particularly Ethiopia, which all came to an unexpected climax at the Battle of Adwa. The pace of European colonialist expansion in the Horn was greatly enhanced by the opening of the Suez Canal, in 1869, which also marks the year that a foothold in the African littoral, namely, the Red Sea niche of Assab, was claimed by a Lazarist missionary, Giuseppe Sapeto, on behalf of Italy — which itself had barely emerged as a unified monarchy in 1861.

No part of Africa was regarded as off-limits to European penetration and occupation when the 1884-85 Berlin conference laid ground rules for a more concerted modality of colonial presence in Africa. All the chicanery, duplicity and trickery, the doctoring or eliminating of materials that characterized "treaty making" and the establishment of "protectorates" or "boundary agreements" in Africa were displayed on the Horn. In fact, the Horn of Africa has sustained more intensive and protracted military and political pressures by European colonialists than any other region in the continent.[276] Consequently, the Horn region remains today a political minefield that is chronically destabilized.

Even before 1861, when what was a veritable French "protectorate" region emerged as a unified Italian state — thanks to the revolutionary struggles led by Giuseppe Garibaldi — various missionary and commercial elements (especially from Sardinia) were prowling in the Horn of Africa. Yet, few colonial adventures have experienced so many political fables and military debacles as those of Italy. Prior to their ignominious military debacle in Adwa, for instance, the Italians had bitter experiences with Emperor Yohannes and with his governor in Asmara, Ras Alula. Ever since the Italians were lured into Massawa by the British in 1885, the Ethiopian authorities had tried to get them to evacuate Ethiopian territory altogether or confine themselves to Massawa and not expand into the interior. When the British colonialists were trying to make a case for Italian presence in nearby Sahati, Ras Alula had responded that "the Italians can

276. The Horn region of Africa, particularly Ethiopia, has been subjected to expansionist and colonial military pressures by Ottoman, Portuguese, Egyptian Khedive, British, Italian, and French aggressors. The British and the Italians had launched multiple military engagements with the Ethiopians, the Sudanese and the Somali people in the nineteenth century. Looked at another way, one Ethiopian military stalwart, Ras Alula, personally engaged in thirteen major serious battles against Ottoman/Egyptians, Mahdists, and Italian colonial forces in the Horn between 1875 and 1896. For a brief account of Ras Alula's struggles see Negussay Ayele, "Ras Alula and Ethiopia's Struggles Against Expansionism and Colonialism: 1872-1897" *The Centenary of Dogali* (edited by Taddesse Beyene, et al: Addis Ababa, 1988; pp. 165-195.

come to Sahati only if I can go to Rome as governor."[277] This jousting between Ethiopians and Italians spawned a series of military clashes along the Red Sea coast, culminating in the battle of Dogali where some 500 Italians were killed. The Europeans called it a "massacre" and pressured the Emperor to punish and remove Ras Alula from Asmara. The Italians were adept at the old divide et impera policy of fanning whatever embers of regional, religious, ethnic or internal rivalry existed among ruling groups — or could be developed.

Early on, Italian colonial predators had developed a scheme for their prey called "politica Tgrina" and "politica Sciona," as Antonelli, Crispi, Salimbeni and Baratieri set out to intensify whatever tensions or contradictions they could find in relations between Emperor Yohannes (originating from Tigray) and Negus (King) Menelik of Showa, whose ambition to become Emperor of Ethiopia — immediately, if not sooner — was an open secret. The British, who were more seasoned in the game, had also been busy in the region — aided and abetted by the Egyptians — fomenting and exploiting regional power struggles among Ethiopians, Sudanese and Somalis. The ultimate objective of the Italians was to occupy all of Ethiopia with a pincer movement from their Red Sea beachhead in the north and their Indian Ocean niches on the Somali coast. But, Emperor Yohannes stood in their way; and so they devised strategies for knocking out Ethiopian power structures and challenges one by one, beginning with him. They initiated contacts with Negus Menelik in October 1887 and they proposed that he remain neutral in their conflicts with Emperor Yohannes; for this, Menelik was rewarded with arms and with free access to arms, through Italian-occupied ports on the Red Sea.

Given the fact that, from time immemorial, the way to the imperial throne in Ethiopia was ultimately through force of arms, Yohannes too was able to gain martial preponderance among many aspirants to the Ethiopian Crown. Through his alliance with the British against Emperor Tewodros in 1868, Yohannes overpowered his rivals, including Menelik, and claimed the imperial throne in 1872. With that as a precedent, though it was not necessarily "right," Menelik decided to maximize his chances by flirting with the Italians. In short, it appears that Menelik was ready to agree to go along with this cabal, with a proviso that the Italians "should not occupy any Ethiopian territory" in the process. When this ploy, coupled with increasing regional tensions between Ethiopia and the Egyp-

277. See Zewde Gabre Sellassie, *Yohannes IV of Ethiopia:* Oxford, 1975; p. 223. Cf. also David Levering Lewis, *The Race To Fashoda:* New York, 1987; pp. 104 and ff.

tians and the Dervishes in the Sudan, could not shake Emperor Yohannes, the Italians sought Menelik's active alliance in forcibly removing the Emperor. What Menelik was not supposed to know, of course, was the fact that he would be the next domino to fall under Italian carabinieri boots. Here, Menelik balked; he drew a line ruling out joint attacks with the Italians against the Emperor. Undaunted, the Italians started to spread propaganda intended to reach the camp of Yohannes and indicating that Menelik was going to attack the Emperor. The resulting suspicions made Menelik vulnerable to punitive attack by the Emperor and therefore he was now more beholden to the Italians and their arms deliveries. Such are the circumstances that gave rise to the Wuchalé Treaty of May 2, 1889, which triggered the battle of Adwa was hatched mainly by Antonelli and Crispi.

To put the problem of Wuchalé in perspective, one must recall a couple of momentous events which facilitated the establishment of what was to become the Italian colony of Eritrea and whose expansion to the Mereb and then beyond precipitated the diplomatic and armed struggles between Ethiopia and Italy. First, despite the fact that he had insisted "Massawa is Ethiopian" and that he had "neither the intention nor the power to alienate any territory which properly belongs to Ethiopia,[278] Emperor Yohannes had in effect ceded Massawa to the British/Egyptians and, shortly thereafter the Italians, when he signed the Adwa/Hewett Treaty on June 3, 1884.[279] The second momentous event took place in January, 1888, a year after Ras Alula had trounced the Italian army at Dogali, near Massawa, when Emperor Yohannes mobilized on short notice and personally led perhaps the largest such raza or peoples' militia for any single engagement in Ethiopian history, 120,000 strong — to dislodge the Italians once and for all from Sahati, from Massawa and eventually from all Ethiopian territory. Even as he marched towards the Red Sea coast to deal with the Italian threat in the east, Emperor Yohannes was aware that the Mahdists of the Sudan, egged on by the British and the Italians, were putting a great deal of pressure on the Western front of his empire, burning churches and pillaging villages. But he, perhaps at Ras Alula's behest, had decided to dislodge the Italians first, clear the coastline of any foreign colonial occupation so that he could control the flow of arms to actual or potential rivals, and then deal with the Mahdist threat along the Sudan border.

---

278. See The Centenary of Dogali, above, p.174.

279. For more on this see Zewde, above and Rubenson, *The Survival...* Cf. also Emest Work, *ETHIOPIA: Pawn in European Diplomacy:* New York, 1935.

In an inexplicable turn of events, however, despite the overwhelming force at his command, Yohannes decided not to storm the fortress manned by a few hundred Italians and their local askaris at Sahati. The Italians threw a few flames at nights to scare the Ethiopian fighters encamped around them but did not come out of their fortress. Incredibly, the confrontation at Sahati became a stalemate and in March Emperor Yohannes decided to abort the effort to dislodge the Italians from Ethiopia's coastlines, apparently wishing instead to go back westwards to face the Mahdists. As he left Sahati, he exhorted the Italian commander in the fort and the (Christian) Italians at large. "Has not Christ distributed [the earth] and made peace? Your country is from the sea as far as Rome, mine is from the sea as far as here; this is Ethiopia. There is no reason for us to quarrel.[280]

This inaction had repercussions. That he unilaterally decided to withdraw from Sahati without being attacked or defeated, after whetting the appetites and exacting sacrifices from the largest mobilization ever of the people of Ethiopia, resulted in a diminution of respect for Yohannes's leadership. This eroded his authority and encouraged some of his vassals to maneuver for alternate imperial leadership. Menelik was one who took full advantage of this erosion of support and loyalty to Yohannes.

As we shall see later, this Italian fortress scenario was to be repeated in Mekele but with a completely different outcome.

The 1888 confrontation at Sahati (in which Yohannes blinked) was a turning point in the Italian expansion from Massawa into the interior and the eventual making of its colony of "Eritrea," chipped off from Ethiopia. Over and above his unforced withdrawal of such a vaunted force from a small fortress, without any engagement, Emperor Yohannes made another fateful decision, again unforced, to withdraw Ras Alula — the one military and political leader the Italians and others feared the most — from his post as governor of Hamassein and Mereb Melash, based in Asmara, the town he founded. The Italians then accelerated and consolidated their colonial occupation of the Red Sea Ethiopian coastline, going deeper and deeper into the interior until they entered Asmara unopposed on August 13, 1889. Thus, for all intents and purposes, Emperor Yohannes's withdrawal from Sahati in 1888, coupled with his order for Ras Alula to move out of Asmara, turned out to be a green light for the

280. Rubenson, *The Survival...* p.383.

Italians to expand and consolidate their Red Sea conquests into what, in January 1890, they would declare to be their new colony of Eritrea.[281]

Thus, by the time Menelik signed the Wuchalé Treaty in May, 1889, almost three months after the death of Emperor Yohannes in Metemma, he was faced with a fait accompli of Italian occupation of Ethiopian land up to and including Asmara. To some extent, however, Menelik as King of Showa too was an unwitting accomplice to these Italian incursions into Ethiopian territory along the Red Sea and, in the Wuchalé Treaty, he conceded and confirmed Italian claims to that much Ethiopian territory. The Italians had exploited Menelik's ambition to become Emperor by coupling supply of arms to him with his neutrality in their clashes with Emperor Yohannes in the north, even though he consistently insisted that Italians should not "touch" any Ethiopian land. Thus, like moles (or, as Ras Alula once called them, like rats[282]), the Italians moved from Massawa all the way to Asmara, and their insatiable appetite for more breezy and fertile African land brought them to the Mereb and beyond, deeper and deeper into Ethiopia.

The Wuchalé Treaty and Its Aftermath in Perspective

Most historians and analysts consider the circumstances surrounding Article 17 of the Wuchalé Treaty of May 2, 1989, to have been the proximate cause of the Battle of Adwa. Judged by standards of contemporary foreign relations, the Italy-Ethiopia Wuchalé Treaty of Friendship and Commerce between "il Regno d'Italia e l'Impero d'Etiopico"[283] (the Kingdom of Italy and the Empire of Ethiopia) reads like a typical non-capitulationist international document willingly entered into by two sovereign polities mutually seeking to normalize and enhance positive relations for present and future generations and regimes.

The operative articles of the Treaty were constructed carefully to reflect relative equality and reciprocity between the two signatory states. It is paradoxical that this very document (which was the first and, in the nineteenth century, the only high-level interstate treaty between a sovereign African

281. On this point see Hagai Erlich, *Ethiopia and Eritrea During the Scramble for Africa:* Ann Arbor, 1982; pp. 120-122.
282. Ibid, p.104.
283. The reader may consult Sven Rubenson's monograph, *Wuchalé XVII...:* Addis Ababa, 1964.

country and a sovereign European country) became twisted and subverted by Italian colonial chicanery in which Ethiopia became a "protectorate" (a misnomer which really means colony or possession), a charade that led to armed conflicts between the signatories.

But, before we examine Article 17 of the Wuchalé Treaty, it is important to review the Treaty as a whole. This will provide a more complete context and basis for judging whether the Treaty displays any characteristics of a "protectorate" treaty. The 1889 Wuchalé Treaty, presented below, includes twenty Articles containing provisions that are typical of any contemporary international agreement among sovereign states. (The text of the Ethiopic/Amharic version of the Treaty may be found in the Appendix.)

The Wuchalé Treaty Provisions

1. King Umberto I of Italy and Emperor Menelik II of Ethiopia commit themselves to the [Wuchalé] Treaty of Friendship and Commerce in mutual pursuit of peaceable and friendly relations for themselves and for succeeding generations.

2. There shall be diplomatic and consular exchanges between Ethiopia and Italy which shall operate with the immunities and privileges recognized in Europe.

3. Broad boundary delimitation line from Arafali on the Red Sea coast to the Sudan border with Halay, Segeneiti and Asmara falling within Italian Jurisdiction.

4. Debre Bizen monastery within the Italian zone is to remain Ethiopian territory in perpetuity and to be permanently demilitarized.

5. Ethiopia can import/export merchandise via Massawa by paying 8% port duty.

6. The Emperor can import arms through Massawa free of charge and Italy will provide escort for their safe entry into Ethiopia.

7. There shall be free trade and commercial transit of people between the two countries but no large-scale armed crossing of borders.

8. People of each country can live, move and do business in each other's territory in accordance with the respective local laws and customs.

9. When people from one territory become residents in the jurisdiction of another, they will retain their faith or denomination.

10. Disputes among Italian residents or among Ethiopian residents will be adjudicated by a judge they choose and if the dispute is between Ethiopian and Italian residents the case will be adjudicated jointly by Italian and Ethiopian jurists.

11. In the event Italian or Ethiopian residents pass away within the jurisdiction of one or the other government, their property will be safeguarded until duly claimed.

12. Residents of one jurisdiction who commit capital crimes within another jurisdiction will be tried in their own national courts and in accordance with their own laws.

13. The two Governments agree to extradite nationals wanted for capital crimes.

14. The Ethiopian Emperor shall take all measures to combat slave trading in his country.

15. The Treaty will be in effect throughout Ethiopia.

16. The parties to the Treaty may change or amend the provisions of the Treaty five years after its adoption by giving a one-year advance notice regarding such intent; however, this is applicable to provisions relating to commerce and not to boundaries.

17. For whatever needs the Emperor of Ethiopia may have vis-à-vis European potentates, he can avail himself of the liaison services of the Italian government.

18. In the event that there are two bids for goods or services of equal merit or value offered by an Italian national and by the national of another country, the Italian offer is to be favored by the Emperor.

19. The Treaty shall be written in duplicate in Amharic/(Ethiopic) and in Italian languages and both have equal validity and legal force.

20. For his part Emperor Menelik has hereby signed and affirmed the Treaty in the presence of Italian plenipotentiary Pietro Antonelli, on Myazia 25, 1881 (Ethiopian Calendar) or May 2, 1889 (Gregorian calendar) at Wuchalé, Ethiopia, and it shall be ratified in Rome at the earliest convenience.

While much of the literature so far on the Adwa conflict understandably dwells almost exclusively on Article 17, one can see whence the Italian claim of "protectorate" comes only by profiling the Treaty as a whole.

How did Italy and Ethiopia behave in conditions of active war? Notwithstanding the fact that war is what it always is, the series of battles in the Horn of Africa during December 1895 and March 1896 (generally known as the Battle of Adwa) reveal a unique display of Ethiopian humanity, decency and dignity.

In tandem with the relentless diplomatic offensives, Emperor Menelik did neglect the need for proper military preparedness. He had childhood memories of what it is like to engage a European army, having followed with interest the British Napier Expedition that was launched against Emperor Tewodros in 1868. Like Emperor Yohannes before him, Menelik tended to err on the side of overestimating rather than on underestimating European military organization and firepower. It seems the Italians complemented him, in the opposite direction.

History might judge that, in dealing with Europeans in peace time, Emperor Menelik and most of his courtiers exuded more than a minimum degree of human decency, honor or dignity in dealing with people. Europeans were thought to be "civilized" people of honor who could generally be expected to keep their word, regardless of whether they were dealing with fellow Europeans or with Africans. Likewise, it was assumed that they were imbued with certain universally respected Christian values and principles, that their sense of justice and oppression, of right and wrong, or of independence and bondage, was predictable and universally applicable.

History might judge that in dealing with Europeans in peace time, Emperor Menelik and most of his courtiers might have exuded more than a minimum degree of what in Ethiopia is [chewanet] which may be loosely rendered in English as rudimentary sense of "human decency, honor or dignity" in treating people. Europeans were thought to be 'civilized' people of honor who would generally be expected to keep their words regardless of whether they dealt with fellow Europeans or with Africans. Likewise, it was assumed that they are imbued with certain universally respected Christian values and principles, that their sense of justice and oppression, of right and wrong, or of independence and bondage, was predictable and universally applicable. For example in the Treaty, the courses as well as protection of nationals in each other's jurisdictions and extradition of criminals (10, 11, 12, 13); provisions to amend, change and ratify the Treaty as well as the acceptance of Amharic and Italian to be equally valid languages of the Treaty (16, 19, 20) were distorted to fit the Italian bill. In all these, the most important benefit for the Italians was Emperor Menelik's formal acknowledgement of their territorial possessions on the Red Sea; in addition, of benefit to them was renting the port of Massawa for commercial goods to and from Ethiopia. Their sense of European "civilizing" mission in Africa vis-à-vis the slave trade was also disposed of and they were to gain a most-favored nation treatment when it came to bids (3, 5, 14, 18). For Ethiopia, the beneficial provisions of the Treaty included retaining sovereignty over Debre Bizen monastery, which fell within Italian occupied territory; the Emperor's right to import arms duty free through Italian-occupied Red Sea ports; Italian liaison services for Ethiopia in relations with the rest of Europe (4, 6, 17). Article 15 appears to be redundant and/or inconsequential, unless it was conceived as a continuation of the Article before it.[284]

The Wuchalé Treaty summarized above cannot qualify as a document establishing a "protectorate" (which itself is an oxymoron) agreement between a

284. For more on the background on Menelik's dealings with Italy from 1889 to 1896 see also Harold G. Marcus, *The Life And Times Of Menelik I ...*: Oxford, 1975; pp. 111-173.

sovereign power and a nominal local vassal. What is also ironical about this lethal comedy of errors is the fact that the Emperor did not think the Italian offer of liaison services (in Article 17) necessary to begin with, but he was persuaded by Antonelli that it would be in his (Menelik's) advantage to include it. It was thought that Article 17 would facilitate and enhance Ethiopia's diplomatic activities in Europe, if and whenever the Emperor chose to utilize Italian offer of assistance that is, "serversi," as the Italian rendition has it. But the Italians completely turned Article 17 on its head and purveyed it as Ethiopia's albatross of obligation.

Analysts may not agree which party to the treaty attained more in certain areas but, taken as a whole, it would require a gargantuan feat of imagination to see the Wuchalé Treaty as a "protectorate" agreement. The Wuchalé Treaty is essentially typical of any contemporary friendship and commercial treaties concluded among sovereign states at the time.[285]

Were it not for the fact of a glaring discrepancy in the two versions of the Wuchalé Treaty (Amharic/Ethiopic and Italian), the controversy might not have snowballed into a crisis leading to full-scale international war in the Horn. Without going into details[286] regarding the controversies, we can identify the main issues relating to the Italo-Ethiopian political and diplomatic crisis and Italian deception surrounding the 1889 Wuchalé "Friendship" Treaty. Below is a summary of what may be referred to as "Italy's Chicanery."

Italy's Chicanery

- Fraudulent depiction of the normal Wuchalé Treaty of friendship and commerce between two sovereign states as a "protectorate" treaty to European powers.

285. The most comprehensive compendium on colonial "Treaties" and Protectorate "Agreements" relating to Africa to be consulted is Hertslet, E., *Map of Africa By Treaty:* London, 1967.
286. For a discussion on the making of the Wuchalé controversy see Rubenson, *Wuchalé XVII...* above. An Italian writer joined in the debate with an Italian viewpoint on the Wuchalé Treaty and there have been exchanges on the issue between him and Professor Rubenson. For more on the Italian view see Carlo Giglio, "Article XVII of the Treaty of Wuchalé" *Journal of African History*, Vol. VI, # 3,1965; pp 221-231 and his "Antonelli and Article XVII of the Treaty of Wuchalé" *Journal of African History*. Vol VII, # 3,1968; pp. 445-457. Rubenson has made the pant that he and Giglio have divergent interpretations on the Wuchalé 17 controversy because "I have given much more weight to the documentary evidence preceding the event while Giglio prefers to build much more on the explanations and interpretations presented after the events by those involved." See Rubenson,*The Survival...*, footnote 415 on page 385.

- Acknowledging Menelik as Emperor (King of kings) of Ethiopia in the Treaty but referring to him ambiguously as "His Highness" to European Powers, as if Menelik were one of the many dukes and highnesses under Umberto.
- Recognizing Ethiopian sovereignty under the Additional Convention (intended to persuade Menelik to accede to further territorial expansions inland) signed in Rome five months after Wuchalé but concealing the reaffirmation of Ethiopian sovereignty from the rest of the world.
- Deliberately mis-translating Article 17 of the Treaty from "may avail himself of..." as "has consented to use..." [the services of Italy to represent his international interests], illegitimately converting it into a "protectorate" provision and informing the signatories of the 1885 Berlin Act that henceforth Ethiopia was an Italian "protectorate," so that all communications to and from Ethiopia should be conducted through Italy.
- Concealing subversive communications to European and other powers, and appearing to carry on business as usual between two sovereignties.
- Blaming the "error" on the Ethiopian interpreter, when confronted by Emperor Menelik and Queen Taytu.
- Misrepresenting the boundary line provisions that were to reflect the situation as of the signing of an Additional Convention in Rome in October 1889, and insisting that it included Italian territorial claims up to the time of ratification of the Convention by Emperor Menelik, which was to occur on February 25, 1890.
- Attempting to deny outright that anything was wrong sending different messages to different quarters; trying to make French, Russian and other sources the culprits in any controversies and misunderstandings.
- Having exhausted every ploy they could think of, saying "let us leave everything as is," that is, let's just uphold the way Italy has conceived of the Treaty and conveyed it to the world for five years anyway, in accordance with Article 19, and then review it.
- Declaring that all of Ethiopia was an Italian "protectorate" by virtue of the 1889 Wuchalé Treaty, on the one hand, while on the other hand carrying on territorial conquest hundreds of miles inland.
- There is an Ethiopian saying: "a brazen thief redoubles his insolence to cover up his misdeeds." The Italian diplomats accused Emperor Menelik of breach of treaty and blamed him for the war between Italy and Ethiopia.

This morbidly fascinating Adwa syndrome was perpetrated by one of the "civilized" powers of Europe against a country that it considered to be "savage." The whole episode revolved around Article 17 of the Wuchalé Treaty. According to the wording of the Italian version, in Article 17 Emperor Menelik had compromised his country's sovereignty by "consenting" to use Italy as the middleman in his dealings with Europe. The Ethiopian version, on the other hand, clearly stated that the Ethiopian Emperor could, if he wished, use their good offices (liaison services) in his dealings with Europeans. En passant, one may add that Article 17 says nothing about how relations with the rest of the world were to be conducted by Ethiopia, because Africa was considered to be the exclusive preserve of Europe.

It seems that the Italians did not think the rest of the world would mind, when they learned about the discrepancy. Or, they gambled that if they quickly and quietly consolidated their position and insulated Ethiopia from outside communication (and support), they could weather whatever mild repercussions might ensue. Then, it would be a fait accompli, and irreversible. Besides, is there not something contradictory in the notion of a moral or a just "protectorate" or colonial agreement in Africa, anyway? Consequently, on October 11, 1889, Italy sent formal notifications to European signatories of the Berlin Act that, pursuant to the provisions of "effective occupation" of the Berlin Act, that Ethiopia was henceforth a "protectorate" or colony under Italian sovereignty. This was a suggestion to their fellow colonialists in Europe not to interfere in Ethiopia, in accordance with the Berlin rules of the game; it was also intended to isolate and insulate Menelik from direct contact with the outside world.

Meanwhile, Rome knew that it would have to plod its way through, militarily, sooner or later, to establish actual colonial rule in Ethiopia. That is why Italy was simultaneously pretending to have secured a protectorate over Ethiopia (as far as Europe was concerned) while carrying on territorial expansion into the rest of the country. Most of the European colonial powers promptly accepted the claim or were quiescent about it. Maps of Africa were quickly revised to show Ethiopia in the Italian sphere of influence, an image that continued to persist right up to the end of 1896. But, cleverness can only go so far.

Turkey, Russia and France were the only Berlin signatory countries that did not give outright or unqualified support to Italy's claim. The United States declined to express any stand on the issue, saying that as a non-signatory of the Berlin Act it took note of Italian claims but it did not have to act on them publicly.

Not fully aware of the machinations going on in Europe, Emperor Menelik sent Dejazmach Makonnen 'Abba Qagnew', his next of kin and trusted plenipotentiary, to Rome in the fall of 1890 to collect the ratified copy of the Wuchalé Treaty. Unexpectedly, the Italians cornered and pressured Ras Makonnen to sign, on behalf of Menelik, an Additional Convention to validate current Italian territorial expansion — in violation of the provisions of Article 16 of the

Wuchalé Treaty. In the course of his diplomatic sojourn in Rome, Ras Makonnen learned the strange news of Italy's claim of having taken over his country as a "protectorate." This he learned from his compatriot, Afeworq Gabre Yesus, who read about the affair in the local papers while studying in Italy.[287] When Dejazmach Makonnen tried to broach the matter to relevant Italian authorities, they stonewalled. Upon his return to Ethiopia in February of the following year, the envoy related to the Emperor the disturbing news of Italian duplicity with respect to the Wuchalé Treaty and its relentless territorial expansions. Shocked by the betrayal, Menelik decided to test the diplomatic waters by conveying his case directly to everyone concerned in Europe and elsewhere.

Both at the time he signed the Wuchalé Treaty on May 2, 1889 and shortly thereafter, Menelik had been writing letters to his counterparts in Europe indicating his readiness to forge friendly relations between Ethiopia and the countries concerned. No reply was forthcoming, as had been the case earlier. The Emperor's fears were confirmed when the Italian agent Salimbeni arrived in Ethiopia in July of 1890 with fresh instructions from Rome. Menelik was kindly advised to keep quiet and — to punctuate the point — Salimbeni had the responses to Menelik's earlier letters from Britain's Queen Victoria and the German Kaiser Wilhelm.[288] Needless to say, this sounded a dire note for the Emperor, his Queen Taytu and all Ethiopians. The Kaiser's response was noncommittal but the one from Queen Victoria was more to the point. The Queen cited the Italian interpretation of Article 17 of the Wuchalé Treaty and informed the Emperor that henceforth her government "shall communicate to the Government of our Friend His Majesty the King of Italy copies of Your Majesty's letter and of this Our reply.[289] Lest there be any misunderstanding as to Britain's stand on the question of protectorate, Victoria added that the Emperor need not bother to communicate with her and her government directly, nor to send his envoys to London.

Meanwhile, in an effort to avert the political and diplomatic crisis that was smoldering and to prevent Menelik from internationalizing the Wuchalé faux pas, Italy sent back to Ethiopia Count Pietro Antonelli, the very man who crafted the Wuchalé Treaty in the first place. Antonelli arrived in Addis Ababa in December, 1890. Emperor Menelik and Queen Taytu engaged him in a firm but courteous manner. At this early stage of the crisis, the Italian government could

287. See Afework Gabre Yesus, *Dagmawi Atse Menelik (ET)*: Rome, 1901; p. 70.
288. See Paulos, Ate Menelik, above, p.102 and ff; Rubenson, Wuchalé XVII...I pp14-21.
289. Cited in Rubenson, Ibid, p. 18.

have taken responsibility for the confusion over Wuchalé 17, set the record straight, cut their losses and start afresh. Alas, colonial raison d'état and European ("White"?) pride would not allow it. Instead, Count Antonelli bluffed, prevaricated and even intimidated, compounding the problem once again. The most heated exchanges took place between Queen Taytu and Antonelli, especially when the latter tried to make the Ethiopian translator, Grazmatch Yosef, a scapegoat for his own chicanery and proceeded to scold and insult him in front of his monarch. Queen Taytu took umbrage. Antonelli was out of line, having breached diplomatic protocol and decorum. Antonelli declared that "peace was no more between Italy and Ethiopia." The Queen scorned Antonelli's abusive effort at intimidation and gave him a response in words he could not easily forget:

> Start your war next week if you wish. No one here will be scared of your threat. Go carry out your wish and we will deal with whatever transpires. Do not fool yourself into thinking that there is nobody around here who would commit his feet to the gravel and his chest to the spear in order to save his country. It is not death but honor for anyone to shed his blood for his country. So, let it not be nightfall and too dark for you to travel in order to consummate what you have bragged about and we, of course, shall await you right here.[290]

Antonelli was given a traditional send-off, a mule for his transport, provisions for his journey and escorts for his safe exit from Ethiopia. How blissful it was to deal with "savage" Africans who treated in this manner one who came from far away, called them enemies and brought ill tidings. During the seven years from Wuchalé to Adwa, Emperor Menelik continued to make peace overtures and kept open the lines of diplomatic communication with Italy.

The French, because of their rivalry with Britain and their less than amicable relations with Italy (after all, the French were lording it over Italians until 1861, found it amusing to disrupt the concert of Europe in Africa — a habit they have not abandoned entirely. This was also self serving, as the French had their own colonial designs, namely consolidating a Dakar-to-Djibouti colonial corridor, which included Ethiopia within the scheme. Until its scheme was realized on the ground, it was in France's interest to see to it that Ethiopia, particularly the heartland, was not claimed as a protectorate by any other power. After all, it was the British who first enticed and encouraged the Italians to establish footholds on the Red Sea coasts so that France could not expand into those areas from Djibouti and thus gain maritime strategic preponderance on the Red Sea.

290. Ibid.

The Russians were also interested in the region; they were generally the odd man out in European politics and never managed to join the colonial adventure in Africa, although at times they had some pretensions and at times they spoiled the game for others. Russians and Ethiopians at least shared the Eastern, i.e., Orthodox, variety of Christianity. In the latter part of the nineteenth century, a modest but growing commercial, cultural and diplomatic relationship was growing between Russia and Ethiopia. The Russians sided with Emperor Menelik and cautiously supported his cause, while striving to avoid arousing wrath and protest from their fellow Europeans.[291] Thus, it seems that even if the colonial cabal behind Italy seemed formidable, Ethiopia had at least two powers which (for their own reasons) could play some havoc and provide Ethiopia with moral, diplomatic and other aid. For the Italians, the French and the Russians were nuisances who impeded the process of achieving a consensus behind their "protectorate" claim. For good measure, the Emperor had also developed a sophisticated system of communication abroad using foreign residents and merchants, who relayed mail through networks that circumvented the Italian stranglehold on all his correspondence. For understandable historical reasons, Turkey also had reservations.

Emperor Menelik then embarked on an intensive diplomatic campaign, getting his side of the story across to the rest of the world through informal private correspondence as well as formal letters to European potentates, spelling out who was responsible for the controversy and declaring himself amenable to a peaceable denouement as long as it did not compromise the sovereignty of Ethiopia. In August 1890, Emperor Menelik wrote a very cordial letter to King Umberto, appealing to their common Christian values and calling on the Italian government to repudiate forthwith the false claim of a "protectorate" over his sovereign country. Said Emperor Menelik:

> I did not then [when the Wuchalé Treaty was signed] accept any mandatory engagement, and even today I am not the man to accept it, and you should so much ask me to do so. Now I hope that you will, for the sake of the honor of your friend [Menelik] kindly rectify the error committed in Article 17, and inform other friendly powers to whom you have communicated the Article in question..[292]

Umberto could not, of course, apologize to an African ruler or to reverse the momentum of Italy's manifest colonial destiny. Under the circumstances, Emperor Menelik had no choice but to annul Article 17 altogether and inform the

291. Ibid.
292. Ibid.

Italian government to that effect. The Emperor had written to Queen Victoria and his other counterparts in October 1890, reiterating that Ethiopia was an independent kingdom and debunking rumors in Europe that an Italian "protectorate" had been established over it as an error and "something that degraded ourselves and our kingdom, and we have made the error known to you."[293]

The fact that Ethiopia had its own national script — Ethiopic/Amharic — and its rulers used it in diplomatic and personal communications was an important factor in supporting the Ethiopian side in this controversy. Ethiopians made it a point that the Wuchalé Treaty be written in Amharic/Ethiopic and Italian, both having equal legal validity in interpretation. Fortunately for Ethiopia, quite a few scholars and other professionals had studied the language for some time and were able to read Article 17 for themselves. It was not difficult to figure out within the fuller context of the whole Treaty that it was the Italian version that was flawed.

In April 1891, the Emperor sent an identical letter (also called a circular)[294] to the European powers delineating what he deemed to be Ethiopia's historic boundaries and indicating that he intended to reclaim and consolidate those portions that were not currently under his command. Furthermore, he wished all concerned to know that he would not remain "oblivious in the face of powers coming from across the seas to partition Africa."

After four years of effort to arrive at a negotiated settlement with the Italian government on the Wuchalé Treaty in part (Article 17) or in whole, Emperor Menelik unilaterally scrapped the whole Treaty, in February, effective as of May 1, 1894. Even in his abrogation of the Treaty Menelik's respect for international norms and obligations was remarkable in that despite Italy's rogue behavior, he followed the provisions of Article 16, which stipulated a lapse of five years before such unilateral action could be taken. The Emperor also dispatched diplomatic missions abroad, forgoing the liaison services of Italy. He also established a national mint to replace the Maria Theresa thaler then in use in the country and he applied to have Ethiopia become a member of the Universal Postal Union. Along the way the Emperor and his council, especially Queen Taytu, concluded that most Italians residing in Ethiopia would be either coerced or willing spies for Italy. They were sent back to their country of origin and any further Italian entry into the country was restricted.

293. Paulos, p.145.
294. The facsimile of the Ethiopic text of this circular is reproduced in Paulos, pp106-107.

The Italians gained a slight and ephemeral comfort when their mentors, the British, signed boundary agreements with them involving Sudanese and Ethiopian territory in March and April, 1891, and another one in May 1894. And, as the swords were being drawn for the Italian Armageddon in Adwa the British, the German, Austrian and even the French governments (which also, along with Italy, were major arms producers and dispensers) instituted an arms embargo against Ethiopia. Instead of siding with the aggrieved party, these "civilized" Europeans supported Italy. The prevalent European attitude of the day on the confrontation between a European and an African country was articulated thus, in Paris:[295]

> Ethiopians did not imbibe these human behavioral traits from Europeans but rather from the wellsprings of broad indigenous African values laced with Christian, Muslim or other home-grown precepts and sense of spiritual grounding that yield predictable behavior in interpersonal relationships under certain circumstances. However, in the realm of military engagement, Menelik proved he was nobody's fool, although he was magnanimous to a fault in victory. He commanded his forces with skill, with resolve and with a singleness of purpose. Menelik left virtually nothing to chance in military affairs, although the dice of Lady Luck, mainly in the form of enemy missteps, did on occasion roll in his favor. And, at times, when his court thought that Emperor Menelik's magnanimity or more precisely "Yewahennet/Gerennet," the innocence that emanates from trust), in his dealings with the Italians might jeopardize the country's vital national interests, it seems that divine intervention saved the day.

Pursuant to their longstanding "politica Tigraynya/politica Sciona" divide and conquer policy in December 1891, General Gandolphi, then governor of the newly declared Italian colony of Eritrea, had managed to get Ras Mengesha Yohannes, the titular ruler of Tigray, Hamassein and other areas in Mereb Melash as well as other Tigrayan contenders to take an oath to stand together with Italy in conflicts that threatened their mutual interest and security.[296] It is not certain how much premium the Italians put on this entente cordiale on the banks of the Mereb, where even the hero of Dogali, the bête noire of Italy, Ras Alula wedi Qubi, himself, was in attendance, but the point was to send a message to Menelik, and it was a bitter taste of his own medicine.

Even their de facto colonial border at Mereb was not enough for the Italians. There is an Ethiopian saying to the effect that "the glutton who can't stop eating can't stop throwing up all night." This glutton could not even wait for the ripening of whatever fruits their stratagem might yield politically as they

295. Rubenson, *The Survival*, p. 397.
296. Erlich, Menelik.., p. 170 and ff.

pressed on with their aggressive territorial encroachments into the rest of northern Ethiopia. They were already overextended in the sense that a spate of rebellions in Akele Guzay, Serae and other areas was spilling across the Mereb and muddying the waters in Tigray proper, thus complicating their fragile entente with Mengesha. When the Italian colonial troops had defeated Ras Mengesha and chased him out of Tigray, he pleaded with Emperor Menelik to stop the relentless Italian military advances in northern Ethiopia. With all that, however, the Italian government was being drawn inexorably into an unwinnable situation as several armed clashes erupted on both sides of the Mereb in the mid-1890s. As he continued to monitor these events, Menelik also made sure that far from further antagonizing the Mengesha and the other ruling elites of Tigray, he would continue to make the political environment as conducive as possible for his Ethiopian brethren in the north to ultimately come back to the fold of their motherland.

As pointed out earlier, between 1889 and 1895 the Italians were furiously maintaining that the whole of Ethiopia was their colony, even while expanding their territorial encroachments by conquest. By 1895, they had expanded their area of occupation to the Mereb, beyond what was agreed in the 1889 Wuchalé Treaty; and by December 1895, they were mauling the forces of Ras Mengesha, annexing big swaths of territory across the Mereb river and planting their flag as far south as Ashenge, in Wollo, deep inside the Ethiopian heartland. Meanwhile, without letting up on his diplomatic efforts, Emperor Menelik was also readying himself and his people for the inevitable war with the Italians. On the eve of Adwa, the Emperor could count on the loyalty and commitment of all the important Tigrayan nobles and militants like the famous Ras Alula. The otherwise contentious, ambitious, and rebellious feudal lords in much of his empire were now prepared to close ranks and fight this external enemy. All his efforts at finding a reasonable and respectable peaceful solution to the Wuchalé crisis instigated by Italy having been rebuffed, Emperor Menelik reluctantly resigned himself to defending his country's independence in the only language his interlocutors seemed to understand.

For Italy, the main logistical problem of waging colonial wars in the Horn of Africa was physical distance from the home base and the need to transport troops and supplies over the Mediterranean and the Red Sea and then negotiating the terrain inside the region. Italy produced arms and could acquire practically unlimited supplies from its European allies and sympathizers. Not so for Ethiopia, which neither produced the kind of weapons needed for the kind of war it faced and nor had free access to the sea to import arms, as all the ports were by then controlled by the Italians, the French and the British. And with the renunciation of the Wuchalé Treaty (which was judged by Italy to be tantamount to a declaration of war), the Italian Government enjoined European arms producers not to deal with Ethiopia nor permit the flow of arms to Ethiopia through any ports in the Somali coast of the Gulf of Aden and the Indian Ocean. This scenario was played out again forty years later, when Mussolini invaded. In one of the rarest and strangest of historical ironies, however, since the early 1880s right down to the eve of the Battle of Adwa, the Italians had been supplying Menelik with the arms he used to fight them in Amba Alaghe, Mekele and Adwa in late 1895 and early 1896. The Italians had continued to supply Menelik with arms, from time to time (most of which he paid for), in order to camouflage their "savage" plans to wage war against a people who had done nothing wrong against them. In addition, from time to time, when the Italians sent envoys on phony peace missions, they sent fresh supplies of ammunition or guns to lull any possible suspicions. In the course of battle, the victorious Ethiopian forces also supplemented their ordnance quotas with booty collected from defeated Italian forces. For good measure, Menelik bought and stockpiled whatever he could through the French and Russians, as well as through other private sources, before most of these avenues were blocked.

As to fighting forces, the Italians had a limited supply of Italian soldati or carabinieri; they sought to supplement their ranks by recruiting indigenous elements known as askaris (servants), who could be conscripted to the Italian cause at short notice and required virtually no training; they were used as military guides, spies and fifth column operatives and, of course, as cheap cannon fodder shielding Italians from the brunt of Ethiopian firepower. These native conscripts joined the Italian cause for the promise of a meager daily food ration— a sort of "die-for-a-meal" program. As it turned out, however, Italian policy of using natives to fight natives backfired when, on occasion, the natives mutinied, declaring that "though we eat their [Italian] money, we will not fight our country and our King Menelik."[297] General Oreste Barged, then governor of the Italian colony of Eritrea, and the other commandanti of Italian forces in the Adwa battles were so self-assured that when Baratieri had his final send-off from Crispi and the entire Italian political establishment in August 1895, he boasted

297. Rubenson, *The Survival...*, p. 405.

that he was not only sure of trouncing any Ethiopian resistance but promised to bring a trophy of war — Menelik himself, live, "in a cage," to Rome.

Ironically, perhaps more than in any other European country at this time, Italy had a fairly visible and active anti-colonial anti-monarchy community that chanted the refrain: "Va fuori dell'Africa, non siamo predoni" ("get out of Africa, we are not robbers"), and sought to discourage their country from lurching into endless and fruitless colonial wars. That indeed was also the refrain across the seas in Africa, as Ethiopians were singing:

> Oh, what audacity, Oh, what audacity
>
> To come across in boats to rule the Habesha [Ethiopians]!

Parliamentarian and man of letters Ulisse Barbieri, for instance, had argued that Ethiopia was the victim and not the culprit for Italy's debacles and, if Italy wanted to avenge Dogali, perhaps the best way would be to install five gallows in Rome to hang the five leading Italian military and political leaders, including Crispi himself.[298] When it came to bestowing honors on Italian colonial "heroes," some of the pro-republic and progressive parliamentarians called for honoring Ethiopians, who were the real heroes fighting and dying for their independence.

Whether or not General Baratieri secured enough resources to pursue the war that he initiated and continued, until finally challenged by Menelik himself, is difficult to say. The work of mobilization in Ethiopia was reminiscent of the aborted raza presence under Emperor Yohannes at Sahati in 1888 but it was better supplied and organized. Menelik issued his mobilization proclamation in September 1895, addressed to all his subjects throughout the length and breadth of his empire.[299] The following is an unofficial translation.

> At this time an enemy has crossed our God-given seashore boundaries with the aim of destroying our country and altering our religion. So far, I had been somewhat lax in my response to such incursions because of the plague that has consumed animals and the famine that has exhausted our people. The enemy has taken advantage of our inactivity and has been penetrating like a mole deeper and deeper inside our land.
>
> But now, with God as my shield, I shall not surrender my land to the enemy. O people of my land, I do not think that I have been unjust to you heretofore, and neither have you failed me. Now I ask all of you who are able-bodied to help me with your strength.

298.Cf. Tekle Tsadik, above, p. 281.

299. The reader may consult the Amharic version of the Proclamation in Gabre Sellassie, *Chronicle*, above p. 225.

> If you are physically infirm, give your moral support for the sake of your children, your wife, and your faith. But if you cheat and stay behind when you could have volunteered in this campaign, be forewarned that you have chosen to pick a quarrel with me, in which case I will come back to settle the quarrel. I swear in the name of the Virgin Mary that I shall entertain no intercession on this matter.
>
> As my campaign commences in October (1895), I shall expect to meet organized volunteers from Showa by the middle of October in Wara Ilu.[300]

With that, the Ethiopian Emperor embarked on a thousand-plus kilometer journey northwards from Addis Ababa for his first and last clash with the Italian colonial army (but hardly Italy's first attack on Ethiopia).[301] As both sides were getting ready to do battle, they were also busy forming perceptions and sizing up each other's intentions and capabilities. Each side used spies; the Italians seem to have placed considerable premium on their reports and counsel, most of which, as it turns out, was flawed. On the Ethiopian side, the more modest business of spying behind enemy lines was mainly masterminded by Ras Alula, who had developed intelligence services (especially double agents) in his earlier struggles with the Italians in Mereb Melash. In this, he had the assistance of Ras Makonnen and Queen Taytu. The Italians also used psychological warfare, through their askaris and their envoys who attempted to spread fear and resignation among Ethiopians, saying that European power was like a curse from God, awesome and unbeatable. Another propaganda theme was to disparage Menelik as weak, indecisive and too much under his wife's influence.

The Italians tried to corrupt or otherwise compromise Tigryan and other personages and they spread false rumors that the Emperor's ranks were breaking up, as Ras Mengesha, Ras Mikael of Wallo, Negus Tekle Haimanot of Gojam, Ras Alula and even the Emperor's next of kin, Ras Makonnen, and others were deserting him. It is evident that the Italians deluded themselves into believing such wishful thinking. Besides, some of their supposedly politically savvy envoys also reported to Rome that at Ethiopia was nothing but a "colossus with feet of clay."[302] It appears that Emperor Menelik was one up in this psychological gamesmanship, since he was informed about much of this by his own double agents as well as from his European confidants. After having dealt with them

300. Gabre Selassie, Op.Cit.
301. Not only did Italy fight repeatedly in Ethiopia and the Horn in the Horn of Africa (see note 16, above) but it was to launch another doomed but destructive Fascist invasion of Ethiopia in the 1930s.
302. Rubenson, "Adwa 1896...", p.139.

now for nearly a decade and a half, Emperor Menelik summed up his own perception of Italians and why he dealt with them the way he did so far.

> ...the Italians are impossible to deal with; Power is from God. But from now on no one will try to appease the Italians. I have endured all this until now so that the European powers would know how I have been attacked and not believe me to be the evildoer. This war does not worry me... As for them, the people of Europe who see their troubles will laugh at them.[303]

With that, Emperor Menelik (or, as people fondly called him, Emmeye Menelik, that is, "Menelik, Dear Parent) and his entourage were off to the north.

In the main, we shall leave it to better qualified military analysts and historians to narrate and evaluate the numerical details of the forces involved and the dynamics of defeats and victories in the battles concerned. Figures or estimates of numbers assembled for the series of battles in northern Ethiopia at this time vary considerably,[304] but the bottom line was that Ethiopian resistance fighters were outgunned and Italian enemy forces were outmanned. Herein we shall highlight those dimensions of behavior in wartime that illuminate our focus on who was "civilized" and who was "savage" in the Adwa conflict. Finding instances of brutality and savagery in war is not difficult, but looking for displays of humanity in the midst of war generally is. And so we ask: "Were there instances of humanity, decency and civility in the Adwa series of battles between Italians and Ethiopians that should not be forgotten or buried by the conventional emphasis on casualties, victories, capitulations?"

The armed engagement that has caught the world's imagination was the final day of battle at Adwa on March 1, 1896; that was hardly the only battle that took place between Ethiopia and Italy at the time. There were two battles that preceded Adwa, in Amba Alaghe on December 7, 1895 and in Mekele from December 14, 1895 to January 24, 1896. It is not even clear whether Menelik and his fighters knew beforehand exactly where and when they would first meet the Italian forces. There are even some suggestions that Emperor Menelik was encouraged particularly by Ras Alula and possibly Queen Taytu, as well as by

---

303. Ibid., p.143.
304. Not surprisingly, there are no definitive figures, with even acceptable margins of error, on battle forces or casualties of the Amba Alaghe-Mekele-Adwa series of battles. But, of course, estimates abound. See, for instance, Berkeley, G. F-H., *The Campaign of Adwa and the Rise of Menelik:* New York, 1969, pp. 267-27 and 345-346; Paulos,159-160; Rubenson, "Adwa 1896...", pp. 116-117; Marcus, above, p. 173 for some samples. Emperor Menelik' chronicler, Tsehafi Te'ezaz Gabre Sellassie gives no figures of the battles. Therefore, most everybody just recycle the same estimates cited herein.

Ras Mengesha (who had been pushed by the Italians across the Mereb a few too many times), to aim at the very heartland of Italy's presence in Mereb Melash (otherwise known as the Italian colony of Eritrea). The Italians also prepared themselves for this contingency, which they figured could be either an ultimate objective of the formidable Ethiopian resistance forces or a tactical encirclement of their forces, blocking Italian supply lines that stretched thinly across 300 kilometers.

However, besides the logistical problems and material requirements posed by the choice to go this distance, the Emperor had political compunctions about it. It appears that he was not prepared to violate the border agreement which he, as sovereign, had entered into voluntarily and in good faith. Menelik felt that he had maintained the high moral plane so far vis-à-vis Italy and he was not ready to risk his image, his honor and his "Christian" reputation in Europe and elsewhere by using force to cross into what technically was "Italian territory," thereby behaving just like the Italians. This was a reflection of that Ethiopian notion of human decency and dignity, Yilugnta/Chewannet. Ethiopian rulers both before him (Emperor Yohannes) and after him (Emperor Haile Selassie) shared this view, and were also mindful of their image as Christian and "civilized" rulers. Notable exceptions were Emperor Tewodros and Lij Iyasu, insofar as their relations with Europeans were concerned. While there were several factors that went into the equation of his decisions, the fact remains that after all his earlier protestations against Italian encroachments across the border agreed to in 1889, and despite his decisive military victory in Adwa and at least the theoretical possibility of hot pursuit, Emperor Menelik ended up in 1900 formally accepting Italy's colonial claim up to the Mereb.

The Italian forces did not put up much of a fight in Amba Alaghe; they were easily routed by advance detachments led by Fitawrari Gebeyehu. Those Italians and their askaris who survived fled to Mekele, where there was a well-fortified Italian presence, or to Adigrat, Adwa and across the Mereb. For Ethiopians, the battle at Amba Alaghe was invigorating, and the energized national military juggernaut pressed on towards Mekele, which was far from being a one-sided affair. Reminiscent of their rendezvous with Emperor Yohannes in Sahati in March1888, the Italians had dug in their heels in a well-manned and heavily-armed fortification where they hoped history would repeat itself and Menelik's forces, would in time be forced to withdraw, tired, hungry and frustrated. Sure enough, the Ethiopians lost many lives trying to pound their way into the fort; apparently, they did not have sufficient cannon power for the task. But, as related in a previous chapter, the Italians relied on a water source outside the fort, which they accessed at nights in the cover of darkness. If we take the hagiographies of the saga of Mekele at face value, it seems that Queen Taytu figured out a stratagem to force the Italians out of the garrison. Queen Taytu persuaded her men to guard the water supply on shifts, around the clock, and promised the men that she and the women in the Ethiopian camp would feed them day and night. The Queen went further and pledged that, should these men lose their lives in this mission at Mekele, she would take care of the burial rites and assume personal royal responsibility for the care of their widows and orphans.[305]

It worked. Ethiopian fighters blocked the water sources and although the Italians and their askaris (called bandas, or traitors, in Ethiopia) tried a few times to reclaim them, they could not.

The military engagement at Mekele and its environs started in the middle of December 1895, and Emperor Menelik kept the lines of negotiation open, calling for Italian withdrawal from Mekele and all other Ethiopian territory back to the boundary lines agreed to in Wuchalé — though he was aware of their de facto presence up to the Mereb River. He specifically told the Italians and other interested European observers that he took no pleasure in seeing "Christian blood" on both sides spilt foolishly. The Italians delayed responding to the question of peaceful settlement, buying time to prepare militarily. Supplies and reinforcements were pouring into the port of Massawa at that time, and they also sought to gather more information on Menelik's strength as well as to continue playing one local prince against another. The impasse continued until the first week of January 1896, when the water crisis in the Mekele fortress began to take a heavy toll (especially on the askari, whose rations were cut again and again). Animals stampeded to break out in search of water.

The Italians decided to evacuate their fortress in Mekele. This was sanctioned by Crispi and Baratieri. The order to evacuate, which is said to have been issued under King Umberto's command, was seen in Rome and in the Mekele fort itself as another humiliating defeat. Still, the conditions of the Italian withdrawal had to be worked out with the Ethiopian fighters, who had lost many men, while the Italians had avoided large-scale casualties.

305. Paulos, p.180 and ff; Gabre Sellassie, *Chronicle*, p. 246 and ff; Cf also Chris Prouty comprehensive and lively biography of Queen Taytu, *Empress Taytu and Menelik I* : Trenton, 1986, p. 147 and ff.

The Italian command sent an emissary, Pietro Felter, to Emperor Menelik to negotiate. Felter later related his conversations with Emperor Menelik:[306]

> You [i.e. Italians] have come all the way here to beat us into submission. You claim that you are going to liberate people in Ethiopia from slavery. However, let alone the Ethiopian people, you are not even capable of saving your own wretched rascals self-imprisoned in the garrison. If my own moral fortitude were as wanting as yours, I should have let them all die of thirst. Tell that to Baratieri. But, holy angels in the heavens exhort us to love our enemies. I am a Christian and I am not a king of savage people. Consequently, I will not let these Christians [in the fortress] die... they can evacuate.

With that admonition, Emperor Menelik ordered his fighters to let the Italians and their entourage have access to the water.

Policy debates or manifestations of differences with a monarch are generally not publicly acknowledged, much less recorded, in Ethiopia or elsewhere. Still, it is safe to assume that there may have been some difference of opinion as to how the enemy should be treated in Mekele and the Emperor was later accused of excessive magnanimity (Yewahennet). European commentators seem to have singled out the one-day Battle of Adwa to represent the definitive battle to settle the "protectorate" issue between Italy and Ethiopia because there were more Europeans or "Whites'" killed at the hands of Africans in that conflict than anywhere in the continent to date. In reality, however, the protracted 45-day siege at Mekele claimed more Ethiopian casualties and exhausted their food and ammunition. Upon reflection, it may even be suggested that the turning point of the war as a whole against Italian colonialism and for the survival of Ethiopian independence (Amba Alaghe, Mekele, Adwa) was at Mekele.

Adwa would have been obviated if Italian arrogance and intransigence had been mitigated after their humiliation in Mekele. Menelik called incessantly for peaceful negotiations to prevent the "shedding of Christian blood." For that matter, even Mekele could have been prevented.

Ethiopians defeated the Italians first in Amba Alaghe, and then again in Mekele, and for good measure in Adwa. The reason Adwa is commemorated as a nationwide celebration is because it was after this third mauling that the Italians retreated and suspended armed aggression against Ethiopia — at least for another forty years. In fact, the war could have continued on, in Adigrat and, more significantly, beyond the Mereb until the Italian colonial presence was rooted out entirely. Open hostilities ended in Adwa when, as we have seen, the

306. Paulos, p.187.

Italians were trounced decisively once again and this time they sued for peace and, for a variety of reasons, Menelik did not pursue his victories either to attain certain military objectives or to extract some bigger, tangible and lasting political gains. The fact that the Adwa series of military victories removed Italy's physical colonial presence from most of Ethiopia in the nineteenth century did not translate into a commonly shared stable political freedom. The struggle continued on — and still continues. Not the least of this chain struggles, of course, was the Italian decision to launch another offensive against Ethiopia years later, to avenge their defeat at Adwa.

Whatever the attitudes of his close advisors and adjutants (including Queen Taytu and Ras Alula) might have been, Menelik in fact let the cup of magnanimity overflow even before sure and final victory was attained. That the Emperor allowed the Italian forces to evacuate Mekele without demanding anything immediate and tangible in return is unusual and difficult to understand. In fact, there is no indication that the Italians had demanded any specific conditions for their evacuation, so there appears to have been no external or internal pressure to do what he did. Menelik not only allowed (i) all the Italians and their askaris to evacuate, but also allowed them (ii) to leave with all their arms, ammunition, heavy guns as well as their personal belongings, (iii) to buy or otherwise acquire on the open market all the pack animals they needed for transporting themselves and their weapons across the Mereb, and (iv) although he personally did not converse with him, the Emperor saw to it that commandant Galiano[307] be given a luxuriously saddled fine mule for his own transportation, and he topped all that by (v) instructing Ras Makonnen to insure that the entire fully-armed Italian force be escorted to safety behind colonial lines, with impunity. These, to say the least, were extraordinary gestures of magnanimity. Shortly thereafter, the Emperor also released some of the Italian prisoners of war captured in the earlier Amba Alaghe battle and other skirmishes. Perhaps, to give Menelik the benefit of doubt, he might have thought that by showing such civility, such humanity and such compassion, the Italian authorities (and their European supporters) could not but be impressed, and heed his constant calls for a peaceful solution. However, when he wrote to Umberto, informing him that he had given the Italians a royal escort out of Mekele, the response was, as David Levering Lewis puts it, to dump at Massawa "more than fifty thousand Italian troops in Ethiopia before the end of the year."[308]

307. Ibid., p.188.

Wuchalé and everything associated with it would pale by comparison to what came next. To Menelik's untiring exhortation regarding "the shedding of Christian blood," the Italian colonial establishment came up with new sets of conditions for peace. While still licking their wounds, the Italians demanded that if Ethiopia wanted peace, it should accept the "protectorate" status from Italy.[309]

Italy's unbelievable folly reminds one of Luigi Barzini's comment in his book, The Italians. In their moments of bewilderment, diplomats in Rome used to say: "In Moscow, nothing is known yet everything is clear; in Rome everything is public...yet one understands nothing."[310] Whatever it implies about the Italian psyche, these are not the terms of a peace that a defeated party can demand. The lines were sharply drawn. Menelik's final words to Major Salsa were: "I will never allow an Italian flag to be planted in my country, Ethiopia."

Humanity (Seb'awinnet) and Civility at Adwa and Thereafter

Now, Providence once again smiled on Menelik. Ras Sebhat and Dejazmach Teferi, two very powerful Tigrayan rebels from Agame who had earlier defected to the Italian side because of power struggles with Ras Mengesha, suddenly appeared in the Emperor's camp in mid-February, pledged their loyalty to him and joined the national resistance. With their considerable knowledge of the situation behind enemy lines, they were to prove valuable assets in the ensuing struggle and they wasted no time in disrupting enemy supply and communications lines. On the eve of the Battle of Adwa, Crispi was fulminating in the safety of Rome that, in the Battle of Adwa, Italy would do better in a shorter time than the British Napier Expedition had done against Emperor Tewodros in 1868. And, in a letter to his wife on the eve of the Battle of Adwa, General E. Dabormida, one of the half dozen Italian lead commanders in the Adwa engagement, exuded confidence.

> Our soldiers are very eager to fight while our spies inform us that the Abyssinians are dispirited and all they want to do is go back home... King Menelik has gathered a force of 80,000 and has exhausted much of the resources of the country for

308. Lewis, above, p. 113.
309. These explanations of Italian 'peace' proposals have been drawn from Paulos,191-192 and Tekle Tsadik, 309-310. The Italian version and an English translation of the same are also found in Work, above, pp. 156-161.
310. Luigi Barzini, *The Italians*: New York, 1964; p. 85.

> naught. The ultimate honor of victory is ours but after our minor setbacks in Amba Alaghe and Mekele, one wonders if Menelik will accept our peace terms and go back to where he came from [Addis Ababa] in peace. If he does not, there is no question that, after all that has been sacrificed so far and after putting in place a superior Italian force comprising its finest 20,000 soldiers, who are the best in the world, we will not dishonor Italy by accepting peace proposed by a savage people. The circumstances do not favor the "enemy," although I hope that I will not be deprived of my chances for decorations for valor in fighting in the event that the "enemy" retreats instead of fighting and create logistical problems for us for hot pursuit action.[311]

It should also be noted that there was no let up in Italian efforts at creating political havoc for Menelik. Italian "divide and conquer" tactics included stirring up the Dervishes in the Sudan and inciting an Afar chief, Mohammed, to attack Menelik's forces. They even went to the extent of abducting Gugsa Darge, a young cousin of the Emperor who at the time was studying in Switzerland, and then forced him to challenge Menelik for the imperial throne by smuggling him into the country. The plan, however, resulted in a fiasco for the Italians and it had to be terminated.[312]

On the Ethiopian side the Emperor, Queen Taytu and most of his military leaders asserted that the Italians were simply compounding their problems by their arrogance. By their reckoning, God did not look kindly on Geif, or "wanton inhumanity." There were no expressions of bravado on the part of Ethiopian commanders. Instead, the Ethiopian refrain always noted that, "Power belongs to God." And, the long annual fasting period for Orthodox Christians being February to April, the ecclesiastical establishment of the Church, including the lead Egyptian patriarch, Abune Matewos, was on hand to give a moral boost.

Because the long drawn out impasse in Mekele had drained food supplies for the national resistance fighters, Ethiopia hoped that the next engagement, in Adwa, would be accomplished quickly and out in the open.

An Ethiopian folk saying reminds us: "No matter how sharp the knife, there is always a sharper razor." Thus, they went out of their way to play up, to encourage and to confirm the Italian illusion that Menelik's camp was divided and demoralized and that his key commanders were about to bolt. Let them be sure that the time for Italy to open a surprise attack was now. With Emperor Menelik's approval, Ras Makonnen, King Tekele Haimanot, Ras Mikael and others indicated their readiness to defect and sent letters to the Italian high command purporting to show that a sudden attack by the Italians would create

311. Tekle Tsadik, p. 336.
312. Ibid, p. 341.

confusion that would allow them to desert Menelik and join the Italian side. It seems that the Italians easily swallowed such reports. More wartime disinformation items were churned out: "the Emperor is ill; the Ethiopian forces are scattered all over the countryside looting and pillaging because they are starving; some important chiefs have abandoned the war effort and returned home with their men; there is widespread rebellion in the country..."

Another military ploy used by the Ethiopians was to scatter in various directions, constantly making the Italian high command think that they were getting ready to launch pre-emptive attacks. The most persistent rumor (with a grain of truth but deliberately blown out of proportion) was that a substantial number of fighters were out looking for food supplies, and that these could not regroup if an Italian blitzkrieg were to occur. Apparently, these tactical moves helped Menelik and his resistance fighters get the best of the Italians.

On Friday, February 28, 1896, General Baratieri gathered together his commanding officers to discuss how and when to take the offensive. All Baratieri's lieutenants were upbeat and ready for war and that the moral of the rank and file in the Italian camp was uniformly and unequivocally described as "excellent" At that point Baratieri said, "The Council is full of spirit; the enemy is brave and despises death," and added, "I am expecting further information from spies, who ought soon to arrive from the enemy's camp; when I have it I will come to a decision."[313] Apparently Barateieri had the (dis)information the next day, the gist of which was that, if the Italians were to strike on Sunday (March 1), Menelik and the Ethiopian resistance fighters would be caught in a vulnerable state. A significant number of Ethiopian fighters including the Emperor himself and his lieutenants would be praying in church; Ethiopians tend not to fight or work on Sunday, which is a day of rest and contemplation as well as being an important fasting period. Baratieri gave the fateful order to strike and the Italians, having made their tactical maneuvers all through the night of Saturday, opened fire around five o'clock Sunday morning, just when the faithful generally go to church.

Sure enough, the Emperor and some of his entourage were at St Gebriel Church. As soon as the heavy guns thundered over the hills, the solemn church ceremony came to an end. The patriarch held up his hand cross, prayed, gave his benediction and absolution to the faithful, saying:[314] "My children, this is the day

313. Berkeley, ibid., 259.
314. Paulos, p. 203.

God's Judgment will be revealed. Go forth and fight for the sake of your faith and your monarch. May God forgive all of your sins." With that, those present passed in front of him in a file to take leave of their spiritual leader by the customary kissing of the hand cross.

Unlike the drawn out 45-day siege and standstill at Mekele, the decisive Battle of Adwa was pitched, intensive and very bloody for both sides. As the Ethiopians later said:

> Those from Yeju were more nimble than the spindle
>
> Those from Gondar were more supple than the cheetah
>
> Those from Showa were more graceful than an eagle
>
> Those from Gojam were more stinging than the bee
>
> Those from Tigre were more sinewy than beef jerky.[315]

Though not in such glowing, poetic terms, Italian soldiers in the trenches too had some grudging respect for Ethiopian freedom fighters. Some of them were too old even to stand on their own and fought anyway, leaning on others. The Italians were flabbergasted and unnerved by fearless Ethiopians who, with Italian guns blazing unabated, would dash directly forward with their swords or spears until one of them made it through the gunfire and killed or wounded the colonial enemy. The Italians were categorically defeated.

By the time the battle had subsided, around 4:30 P.M., Ethiopian casualties (dead and wounded) were approximately 20% of those fielded. But overall Italian colonial casualties amounted to at least 70% of those in active battle formation plus some 2,000 Italian soldiers (including one lead general by the name of Albertone) as well as dozens of officers who were taken prisoners to Addis Ababa.[316]

General Baratieri led the hasty and confused retreat to Adigrat, Italian operations headquarters for the war effort against Ethiopia, and then beyond the Mereb. He was immediately recalled to Rome to face a court martial and was replaced by General Baldissera, who was given more funds, more men and more guns for Italian vendetta.

With the Battle of Adwa over, did Menelik have a political agenda with minimum, medium and maximum objectives? A century later, there was still no

---

315. Paulos, p. 209.
316. See Gabre Sellassie, *Chronicle*, p. 265 and ff; Berkeley, p 347 and ff; Tekle Tsadik, p. 495 and ff.

consensus as to what Menelik could or should have done, and why he did (or did not) do it. We are not in possession of substantial indigenous memoirs or other documents that could indicate the specific political blueprint the Emperor followed when he embarked on his campaigns to the north to meet the colonial armed forces. What we have are a few specks from Menelik's correspondences with European powers or letters to his personal spokespersons, buttressed by circumstantial evidence as to prevailing conditions, including speculations and conclusions drawn by colonialists.

There are indications that during the protracted siege of Mekele, Ethiopian fighters were making maneuvers to go across the Mereb behind enemy lines, and the Italians always expected such a move by Menelik. But, at best, these turned out to serve more as decoys to lure the Italians out of their fortifications. The contemporary writer Afework Gabre Yesus says that the Emperor had seriously considered to follow up his victory at Adwa across the Mereb but that such a plan was untenable due to the state of near starvation of the resistance forces that had been in Tigray for three months under extreme deprivation.[317]

Furthermore, advance scouting indicated that the Mereb itself and other rivers behind enemy lines were either completely or partially dried up at the time and hence it would not have been possible to embark on a war to Asmara and possibly all the way to Massawa, where the enemy had maintained well entrenched, well supplied, well fortified forces for nearly a decade.

From a letter Emperor Menelik wrote at the time to the Russian Czar Nicholas, we learn that he had intended to "liberate Asmara" and "all his country" occupied by Italy.[318] As Menelik confirms in this same letter, perhaps a major reason that he did not go across the Mereb was that Rome had let it be known that King Umberto was sending peace proposals and that all hostilities between the two countries should cease until the Emperor heard the new Italian proposals. As far as Baldissera (the new centurion in Asmara) was concerned, the "peace proposal" was just another ploy to gain time, to re-mobilize Italian forces and then engage the Ethiopians there or pursue and attack them from

317. On this nagging issue see Paulos, p. 86 and Tekle Tsadik, pp.469-475; Paulos, pp. 213-215. The report in the Emperor's Chronicle that on the eve of the March 1, 1896 Adwa battle the Emperor's camp had made a decision that "the Italian, decline to initiate the fight the Ethiopian fighters would go into Hamasen" (p. 258); immediately following his victory at Adwa Menelik is also described as having "perched at Inkichew for a while and was sending scouts/spies check out the road through Hamasen (i.e. towards Asmara)."(p. 268.)

318. Gabre Sellassie, *Chronicle*, p. 491.

behind as they were trekking back to Addis Ababa and other parts of the country. Menelik decided to take with him the large number of Italian prisoners and this served several purposes. One was to encourage the Italian government to be serious this time, when it sued for peace. It was also a kind of insurance against an attack by Baldissera, as Menelik had heard was likely. A third purpose was to pressure the Italians to evacuate Adigrat peacefully. And, as in any settlement after a battle, war prisoners, albeit involuntarily, serve as bargaining chips in overall peace settlements.

Ethiopian fighters could have gone on to fight in Adigrat, the last stronghold of the Italians in Tigray after Adwa, but before doing so, they demanded an immediate and unconditional Italian evacuation of the fort. As Menelik and his lieutenants were mulling what to do if Italy started to fight again at Adigrat, the Italian trouble-shooter, Major Salsa, came with a message from King Umberto offering Italy's readiness to sue for peace and therefore for cessation of all hostilities in the area. Meanwhile, Baldissera was actually weighing the possibility of launching another Italian military confrontation, but he gave up the idea and instead evacuated to Adigrat. Baldissera then sent a message to the Emperor, saying that the Italians would withdraw from Adigrat if the Emperor gave his word that Ethiopian forces would not cross the Mereb. It was also stipulated that there would be an exchange of prisoners when Italian withdrawal from Adigrat was in progress.

With Italy formally suing for peace and Baldissera agreeing to pull his troops from Adigrat and hence from all of Ethiopian territory that side of the Mereb, Menelik decided that it was time to head back to his capital. Before he left Tigray, however, the Emperor gave Ras Mengesha instructions to see to it that the Italians evacuate Adigrat promptly and unconditionally and that they release Ethiopian prisoners they held. Emperor Menelik gave Ras Mengesha more men, arms, cash and for good measure some Italian prisoners as insurance lest the Italians have any new thoughts.

It appears that, as far as Menelik was concerned, the northern campaign (which he had taken up reluctantly, in the first place) had by then already lasted for more than six gruelling months, but it had achieved the following modest goals. The victory had enabled him: (i) to make a political statement to Italy and the world at large that Ethiopia, a historic country in Black Africa, was, is and would continue to be, even if reduced in size during the process of colonial aggressions, an independent country equal to any other; (ii) to demonstrate that, at that historical juncture he, Menelik the Second, was its sovereign ruler; (iii) to convince the Italians that their claim to a protectorate over Ethiopia was a non-starter; (iv) to roll back and nullify once and for all Italian territory gained through brazen invasion in all of Tigray and into Wallo; (v) and to show that Ethiopia, although she preferred peace, was prepared to undertake any and all means necessary, including war, if that was what it took to achieve these goals.

The Emperor needed an unequivocal public acknowledgement by Italy of these political realities and hoped that in the process the rest of Europe would henceforth not underestimate his resolve (Endaygemmetu) — that is to say, he should "not be taken for granted." By the time he signed a peace treaty with the Italians, the Emperor's sovereignty over a truncated, landlocked Ethiopia was recognized by Italy and the rest of the world, and maps were revised once again to portray the status quo. Likewise, in Article 2 of the peace Treaty signed in Addis Ababa later in the year (October 26, 1896), it was provided that "the Wuchalé Treaty of May 2, 1889 and the Additional Convention thereto is null and void... for all time.[319]

In the aftermath of Adwa, the European (i.e., White) world's ruling circles were less than amused by the victory of "savage" African fighters over a "civilized" European (White) army and some even suggested that Ethiopians were really not Black Africans. And Emperor Menelik himself was quickly cast as a "Black imperialist" abroad and a domestic "colonialist" at home. They depicted him as one who was more dangerous to his neighbors than the "protecting" Europeans, while at the same time also giving the impression that the scramble in the Horn of Africa was occurring with the full participation or partnership of Menelik. In addition to creating mistrust and tension between Ethiopians and neighboring peoples in the Horn, this venomous propaganda affected the perceptions of some within the country who began to describe Menelik as an internal "imperialist," while others charged him with the "sale" or abandonment of Eritrea to Italian colonialism.

It is not within the purview of the present chapter to go into this important subject but it may be said, with respect to the question of follow-up of the victory of Adwa, that Menelik's options for immediate military pursuit of the Italians across the Mereb were not very viable at the time. However, another option given his stunning victory and the political turmoil in Rome, as well as the holding of nearly 2,000 Italian prisoners of war, would have been to make a

---

319. The Amharic/Ethiopic text of the October 26, 1896 Treaty is found in the *Chronicle*, pp. 539-540.

timely Italian withdrawal from all Ethiopian territory, including all of Eritrea, a condition for signing the "perpetual peace" with Italy.

This, indeed, was intimated mildly in Article 5 of the October 26, 1896 peace treaty, which reads: "until the Ethiopian and Italian governments arrive at a complete agreement" (on all aspects of the treaty such as boundaries, compensation, release of prisoners, etc...) "the Italian government cannot transfer control of any of the territory under its jurisdiction" (i.e. Eritrea) to any other power. Should Italy decide to evacuate the territory altogether it shall return the said territory to Ethiopia."[320] Had Ethiopia been able then to attain a favorable political solution to the problem of continued Italian presence in Mereb Melash (today's Eritrea), then on the heels of its Amba Alaghe-Mekele-Adwa military victory, the political landscape in the region would likely have been quite different. At a minimum, Italy should have been made to pay some political price for its aggression.

Menelik's inability to dislodge the Italians from all Ethiopian territory in 1896 cannot be regarded as the only or the most critical historic cause of the loss of Mereb Melash. The nucleus of the Italian colonial presence in Mereb Melash was formed when Emperor Yohannes was hoodwinked by the British into signing the 1884 Hewett/Adwa Treaty. Despite his intentions, Ras Alula did not or could not follow up his victory at Dogali to chase them out of Massawa once and for all. In 1888, Emperor Yohannes once again had a chance, equal to and perhaps even greater than Menelik's in 1896 (after the Italians were well entrenched in the area), to force the Italians out, militarily or peacefully, but he not only failed to do so but by then removing Ras Alula from Asmara he eventually paved the way for Italian territorial expansion into Mereb Melash.

What Menelik did or did not do in 1896 became the last link in a historical chain of events punctuated by missed opportunities, inability to follow up military victories with political gains, leadership problems, lack of clear political objectives, multiple external pressures, internal elite power rivalries, plagues, famines and natural calamities. One must also take into account the errors and the problems encountered or engendered by successive generations in the past

320. Mereb Melash (Eritrea) continued to be a vexing problem which one hundred years later has degenerated once more — this time in the form of internal armed straggle — into secession by force of arms. This is the bitter political price that the people of Ethiopia as a whole have had to pay despite what happened or of what did not happen at before, during and immediately after Adwa 1896.

one hundred years, in which Adwa is only a part of a cumulative pattern in the making.

Emperor Menelik, the man Italian colonialists vilified as "savage," uncivilized and unworthy of ruling his own people in Africa, continued his humane policy towards the Italian aggressors during and after the battle of Adwa, as he had done in the two previous clashes. In fact, the only act of harsh treatment to blight the Ethiopian record after the battle involved some 400 native askari or banda of bash-bazuk rank who, at the insistence of Ras Mengesha of Tigray, had their right hands and left legs severed as punishment for siding with the enemy. By contrast, Ethiopians and Emperor Menelik in particular treated the Italian aggressors with civility by European standards (probably even better than they could have been treated if they had won the war), over and beyond the call of humanity in war-time behavior. Beyond all Italian expectations, Emperor Menelik and the Ethiopian peoples showed extraordinary humanity, civility and magnanimity to the Italian prisoners despite the litany of Italian chicanery noted in earlier pages.

Ethiopia's Magnanimity towards the Italian Foe

(1) Emperor Menelik never opted for war first but instead always pleaded with the Italians to come to the peace table and to avoid unnecessary "shedding of Christian blood"

(2) He saw to it that Italians within his jurisdiction, even in wartime, were treated humanely

(3) Italian "envoys" (often suspected as spies) who crossed to the Ethiopian side went back safely to Baratieri's camp, while Italians imprisoned Ethiopian envoys routinely

(4) Enemy soldiers — Italian and askari — had proper burials, although the Italians did not provide the same for Ethiopians

(5) As far as possible, personal items and rank insignias of dead or captured Italians were returned to their camps

(6) The prisoners of war taken to Addis Ababa were especially well treated, under the circumstances; the highest-ranking prisoner, General Albertone, was particularly pampered with his own private quarters and servants

(7) The prisoners were given monthly cash allowances, prorated according to rank, when Ethiopians were not paid likewise

(8) The prisoners had visitation rights by anybody from anywhere and at any time

(9) The prisoners had the right and privacy of intercommunication and correspondence

(10) The prisoners had not only access but often priority to any available medical attention, especially for the wounded

(11) High-ranking Ethiopian officials were assigned to care and serve as liaison for the prisoners and the Emperor held hearings on prisoner complaints or rumors of them

(12) Some prisoners were even released outright. Upon hearing about a mother's grief about her son, Menelik is said to have shown deep sorrow and let the son go home, free.

(13) The prisoners were fed, clothed and sheltered better than their Ethiopian captors, who sometimes murmured their displeasure

(14) The religious and other cultural rights of the prisoners were respected

(15) The prisoners were given opportunities and were encouraged (but not forced) to engage in productive activities (i.e. bakery, tailoring, tanning, smelting, masonry, entertainment, etc...)

(16) Once the peace treaty was signed, those prisoners who were ready to go back where they came from were safely escorted by Ethiopian detachments, lest they be randomly attacked by Ethiopians in the countryside; pack animals were also provided for those who could not walk to the coast.[321]

The modern, comprehensive Geneva Convention Relative to the Treatment of Prisoners of War[322] came into effect in 1949, fifty-five years after the Battle of Adwa. Menelik's civility and humanity toward captive Italian soldiers was truly astounding. Even the pro-Italy British chronicler, G.E. Berkeley, grudgingly admitted that "the Italians were probably better treated than would have been prisoners of any native race,"[323] despite Italian reports and claims of

321. This episode of cruel but not unusual punishment meted out to these unfortunate askaris, especially seen against Emperor Menelik's careful and humane treatment of Italian prisoners did not go down well with Afework Gabre Yesus who publicly criticized the Emperor's approval of this kind of punishment on behalf of Ras Mengesha who had been trying to approach the Italians repeatedly. Afework, pp. 102-108.

322. See W. Michael Reisman and Chris T. Antoniou (eds.), *The Laws of War*. New York, 1994; pp. 179219. To put all this in the context of (European) wartime behavior see also John Keegan, *The Face of Battle*: New York, 1976.

cruel treatment of Italian prisoners including starvation, castration, forced labor, etc. In fact, a more honest statement would have been that the Italian prisoners were treated better by their Ethiopian captors than they would have been by their fellow Europeans under similar circumstances. Emperor Menelik reiterated again and again that he wanted to show all concerned that he was not a "savage" king ruling over a "heathen" or barbaric people in Africa but rather a "civilized" and Christian king who ruled a freedom loving, dignified and decent African people with humane values and precepts and a rich cultural history and civilization. And, under his leadership, Ethiopians were willing and ready to enter into voluntary, equitable and mutually beneficial relations with other "civilized" people and their governments, anywhere in the world.

Wax and Gold, and Lessons of Adwa

With a nod to the Reverend Jesse Jackson's poetic maxim that "whoever defines you also confines you," the reader is hereby asked to forget for a moment the conventional (Eurocentric) characterization of who was "civilized" and who was "savage," at least in the nineteenth century. The answer should be straightforward; however, after our profiles of Italian-Ethiopian behavior in war and in peace during the Adwa conflict in the nineteenth century we are entitled to ask the question afresh. Empirical observation of Ethiopian and Italian behavior leads us to a more accurate scientific answer.

The answer in this case is clear. The Ethiopians manifested humane, civilized, decent, dignified and compassionate behavior. The Italians did not. In virtually every respect, their behavior reflected the standard elements of savagery. The outcome of the battles, in terms of who won and who lost, is not part of the equation for determining who was savage and who was civilized. Wars per se can be physically won by savages or by civilized people. From this perspective, successive generations of Ethiopians, other Africans, and Blacks in the diaspora

323. Even Berkeley (above), the British eyewitness chronicler at Adwa who does not hide his pro-Italian sentiments as he parrots the Italian description of Ethiopians as "enemy," nevertheless has grudgingly admitted the humane treatment of Italian prisoners of war by "savage" Ethiopians (p.348). One of the curious manifestations of Italian (European) "civility" that Ethiopians, indeed all Africans, could not understand was how they would cross the oceans and come to different parts of Africa, often unwanted, uninvited and unexpected, then provoke some conflict and call Africans the "enemy."

as well as all other decent people can duly be proud of what happened and how it happened at Adwa in 1896. Ethiopia's legacy of humanity, in addition to the symbolism of victory that it represents against colonial aggression, political subjugation and racist oppression, are precious for successive generations of Africans all over the world, and in a deeper sense for all decent human beings. It is in this vein that the honorable Alfred Nzo, the South African foreign minister, stated that Adwa is important not just for Ethiopia but for all of Africa — and, one may add, for all peoples of African descent everywhere.

The cycles of violence unleashed on the Horn brought untold death, destruction and misery to hundreds of thousands of Ethiopians and Italians for more than half a century, from 1885 to 1941. Crude colonial military invasions of the type we have reviewed in the foregoing pages were supplanted by more sophisticated neo-colonial techniques in the decades since Adwa. In addition, the political repercussions spawned by colonial aggression have also detonated, from time to time, continuing to play havoc in the region to this day.

Adwa has been memorialized as a military victory by a Black African country over a more modern, more developed European colonial army. Less known and certainly less emphasized in colonial and Eurocentric historiography is the amazing saga of humanity, civility and decency of the Ethiopian/African people who were miscast as "savages." Another lesson is how strong, resilient and powerful the Ethiopian people can be when united in the face of a shared threat.

Another lesson of Adwa, repeated in the Fascist invasion of the 1930s, was the fact that colonial predators would not have been able to mount an effective military offensive in Ethiopia, let alone score even occasional successes in battle, without the participation and collaboration of indigenous elements.

And, of course, the exemplary and often crucial role played by Queen Taytu and other ladies in the Adwa-Mekele-Amba Alaghe victory series should be recalled.

Menelik's quarter-century era as Emperor is perhaps one of the most maligned and distorted in Ethiopian history and hopefully a reassessment will be made. The next worst thing to not learning from history is to learn the wrong history. A precondition to a useful review and revaluation of Menelik's rule, his times, his contributions and his failures will be the avoidance of wholesale adulation or wholesale vilification.

An unfortunate consequence of history is that the continuous regional and foreign expansionist and colonial threats has placed a premium on the efficacy of violence, to the point of spawning a culture of political violence which has persisted from generation to generation, to this very day. Ethiopia's political heroes (like those of so many other nations) have been primarily military figures rather than those who build a society. It is easy to overlook the importance of civilian leadership and, even worse not to be concerned with human rights abuses and authoritarian excesses.

Emperor Menelik's many creditable administrative and developmental achievements in the country have hardly been given a passing notice, especially among the foreign-educated elites. Rather than uncritically joining the self-serving anti-Menelik interests, they might reassess his legacy with the academic objectivity they show towards figures like Kennedy, Mao, Nyerere or Nasser, for example. Few Ethiopian emperors or rulers have enjoyed the kind of genuine mass popularity as Emmeye Menelik has. The Emperor's enduring importance to his people has manifested itself in the fact that Adwa Day remains the oldest secular national holiday of Ethiopia and Menelik's monument in the center of Addis Ababa is the longest surviving and only extant monument of its kind, in the capital, originally built and dedicated by his daughter, Empress Zewditu. The Italians buried it, but only under cover of night — for fear of a popular uprising; and modern-day rumors that it might be dismantled brought out the largest peaceful demonstration in Addis Ababa to date. The late doyen of Ethiopian journalism, Paulos Gnogno, has catalogued at least forty items of modernity introduced by Menelik in his book Ate Menelik.[324]

Surely, Menelik deserves much more credit for his initiatives and efforts than he has received so far from his own compatriots. One thing is certain, in his life and rule Menelik was a monarch who was perhaps the most tolerant of criticism, at times even of the opposition,[325] and no one need be afraid of a critical appraisal of him now.

At the same time, it must be recognized that military victory and political success are not always synonymous. We have seen that Menelik could not or did not succeed to extirpate the Italian presence in northern Ethiopia. In fact, it can be argued that politically, the Italians were more successful in the longer run.

---

324. The late Ethiopian journalist Paulos Gnogno has left an engaging and rich profile of Menelik, the man, the king, the warrior, the diplomat, the administrator, in his biography entitled, "Ate Menelik" (Amharic). For a brief interview with Paulos Gnogno shortly before his untimely death, see "I have completed my race" in the Amharic periodical *(Netsbraq)* # 3, Sene 1984 (ED: Addis Ababa, pp. 5-8 and also see for a biographical summary. *Ruuh* Vol.1 # 3 pp. 7-14.

After all, not only did they maintain their colonial presence in Mereb Melash (Eritrea), formalized by a border agreement in 1900, but they also went on to create obstacles for Menelik along the Somali coast, as well.

Another lesson is that the Ethiopian people have invariably suffered in the long run from the short-run rivalries of their rulers and elites, and between and among domestic and external elites. Outsiders have found that the easiest way to pursue an objective in Ethiopia has been either by fomenting new internecine conflicts or by exacerbating and exploiting existing rivalries. Conversely, the ten-month period of the Adwa campaign in northern Ethiopia described in these pages shows that with Hebret or a "cooperative front," if not outright Andennet or "complete unity," Ethiopians were able to beat a modern European military power.

At the threshold of the twentieth century, Ethiopia (described by Emest Work as a "pawn in European Diplomacy[326]) was the only independent African country remaining. Europeans in 1897 rushed to Menelik's palace in Addis Ababa seeking boundary delimitation agreements between Ethiopia and their colonies: Sudan, Kenya and the Somali coasts. Though they called Ethiopia "the last unresolved problem in Africa," behind Menelik's back, he had proved to be "a power to reckon with." Consequently, they stepped on each other's toes streaming into Addis Ababa (mostly uninvited and sometimes unannounced), trying to ingra-

325. Among numerous examples of Menelik's tolerance to criticism and on occasion even opposition one may cite a couple of examples. Some of Menelik's courtiers who were somewhat uneasy about the aging and more or less retired but once powerful warlord, Ras Gobana, apparently concocted some allegation about the Ras conspiring to overthrow the Emperor and demanded that Menelik take immediate action against Gobana. When the Emperor asked for their considered recommendation in light of the grounds they seemed to rely on, the courtiers were split on whether Ras Gobana's punishment should be incarceration or execution. It was up to Menelik to break the tie in favor of one or the other penalty. Menelik however, stunned them by saying, "It has taken me thirty years to make Ras Gobana what he is today. I will not destroy him because of a single infraction on his part because I do not have thirty years to make another Gobana. So, let him be; I have pardoned him" (Paulos, p.408). Again, while he was mortally ill around 1909 and the German doctor in attendance alleged that Menelik had been poisoned and had accused some of his sergeants-at-arms — even Queen Taytu herself. The accused (except the Queen) became fugitives as they feared as they were about to be stoned or hanged by angry mobs. His ill health notwithstanding, Emperor Menelik managed somehow to issue a proclamation enjoining all concerned not to harm, demean or degrade any one of the accused fugitives who were his "children." The Emperor said that if and when they were duly convicted of any crime in the matter he himself would decide how to punish them (Paulos, pp. 561-462).

326. See Rennell Rodd, *Social and Diplomatic Memories*, 1884-1901: London, 1923.

tiate themselves with Emperor Menelik. Menelik is said to have exclaimed, "What do they all want?"[327]

What the European colonialists failed to achieve in Ethiopia in the nineteenth century through direct militarily invasion at Meqdela, Dogali, Sahati, Amba Alaghe, Mekele, Adwa and even Adigrat, they tried to redeem politically. In concert the British, the French and the Italians signed a "secret" Tripartite Treaty a decade after Adwa, in 1906, carving up Ethiopia on paper to match their sled-declared spheres of influence in the event that the country could be destabilized after Menelik was gone.

In the twenty-first century, one may wonder whether those who regretted Ethiopia's qualified escape in the nineteenth century and again in the 1930s from the net of colonialism are finally congratulating themselves that Europe's "last unresolved problem in Africa" has finally been resolved.[328] The country which sacrificed the most in the nineteenth and twentieth centuries fighting for its independence became the only African country in the 1990s to be split up along ethnic fault lines plotted by colonialism in the 1890s. Despite or perhaps more correctly because of the military victories in 1896, the country has been suffering considerable political and economic repercussions ever since.

Perhaps not so paradoxically, it appears that, all other things being equal, had Ethiopia been colonized in whole instead of in parts it would have had a better chance of staying together as a unit, even if it were to deteriorate to stateless status as evidenced in some quarters of the continent. So, despite the travails and sacrifices made to fend off colonialism, the negative effects of the European incursion linger. When a coastal territory chipped off by colonialism

327. Prouty, above, p.192.

328. The raison d'être for the armed struggle that led to the forcible secession of the Eritrean unit from Ethiopia in 1991 is rooted first and foremost in the argument that Eritrea was an entity that was colonized in the same colonial process as virtually the entire African continent, and therefore was entitled to the same rights of self-determination as all colonial entities, despite the decision of the United Nations to federate the territory with Ethiopia. The failure of Ethiopian governments to make the federation a political success degenerated into a protracted armed struggle in the context of the Cold War and resulted in the collapse of the central government in Addis Ababa and the prevalence of secessionist forces in Asmara. Consequently, the Eritrean secessionists succeeded where Africa's Biafrans, Katangans or Shabans as well as northern Somalians and southern Sudanese have not — at least, not yet. In other words, the colonial blueprint that formed the bases of states in Africa still remains sacrosanct in legitimizing the breakaway of Eritrea from Ethiopia and delegitimizing the potential breakaway of southern Sudan from the whole.

becomes the basis for a claim of separate statehood, it hampers the development of the mother country.

In sum, then, the historic events that climaxed in Adwa in 1896 are memorialized for a variety of reasons besides military victory over Italian colonial aggression. Generations of Ethiopians and fellow Africans proudly celebrate Adwa for the display of African civility over European savagery, of Ethiopian humanity, identity, decency, dignity and compassion in the face of Italian enmity, conceit and chicanery.

Emperor Menelik, the man of the hour, rose to the pinnacle of power in his country and to a position of renown abroad. Today, Ethiopians still debate the legacy of Adwa, but the question is not about its significance and its noble place in the country's history. A spurious question has emerged as to which ethnic or regional group is entitled to assume the role of repository of the legacies of Adwa. This attitude represents a descent into that very divisiveness fomented by European invaders, and can only serve their interests. The unmistakable legacy of Adwa is that all Ethiopians qua Ethiopians — and indeed, all Africans — are entitled to bask in its historic glory together.

Chapter 5. Ethiopia: A Bulwark against European Colonialism and its Role in the Pan-African Movement

Getachew Metaferia Ph.D.
Professor of Political Science
Morgan State University

The Significance of Adwa

The battle of Adwa sent two messages, one to the European colonialists and the second to Africans on the continent and in the diaspora. To the European colonialists, it signaled that Africans could effectively challenge their power. To Africans on the continent and in the diaspora, it conveyed a message of hope that subjugation, be it in the form of colonialism, slavery, or other forms of social, political, and economic exploitation, can be overcome through effective organization, consensus-building leadership, and concerted effort.

In the current political environment, Adwa has further significance. Just as Emperor Menelik succeeded in leading Ethiopians to overlook their petty differences and unite to attain a higher goal, so also today Africans can achieve a higher goal through unity and visionary leadership. The goal today should be the attainment of equality, justice, peace, and economic and political empowerment, on the continent and in the diaspora.

This chapter will consider Adwa and its ramifications for the Pan-African movement, examine what Ethiopians and all children of Africa can learn from Adwa, and will focus on the pivotal role that Ethiopia played not only in withstanding European colonialism but also in launching the Pan-African movement. The factors that led to the success of Adwa are inseparable from Emperor Menelik's leadership, governance and military strategies; any analysis must consider them all.

Emperor Menelik and the Battle of Adwa

The success at the battle of Adwa is a testimonial to the quality of leadership that existed at the time. It is important to note that some individuals in Menelik's leadership circle came from widely differing backgrounds. Among his close advisors and ministers were those from humble backgrounds as well as from outside of the Showan establishment.

To name a few, Ras Gobana Datche was an Oromo and one of the highest-ranking generals under Menelik; he was the governor of Wallaga region. When Menelik was absent from the capital, Gobana acted in his stead. Fitawrari Habte Giorgis, another outsider with a humble background, came from the Gurage ethnic group and served as Minister of War. He played an important role during the regency that was established when Menelik was bedridden and unable to govern effectively.

Menelik's palace guard, the corps d'élite, was commanded by Turk Basha Makuria, who was from Tigre and not from the Showan establishment. Furthermore, in this male-dominated society, Empress Taytu Betul was also a formidable force in Ethiopia's politics during Menelik's reign. Empress Taytu's roots can be traced to Semen, Yeju, and Tigre. Educated in Ge'ez, the language of litany, Taytu read and wrote in Amharic and was familiar with the law book Fetha Negest.[329] An astute politician, Taytu was actively involved in state affairs and participated in dictating some important policy papers. Menelik's troops and government functionaries also reflected Ethiopia's socio-cultural profile. There were both Christians and Moslems of various ethnic and geographic backgrounds.

Some provinces were governed by their own hereditary royalty. For example, Jimma-Kafa was ruled by Sultan Abba Jifar; Northern Wallaga, by Dejazmach Moroda Bakare and Southern Wallaga and Beni Shangul by Dejazmach Joté Tullu. Other such rulers of their own regions were Ras

329. Rosenfield, Chris Prouty. *Empress Taytu and Menelik II: Ethiopia, 1883-1910*. Trenton, New Jersey: Red Sea Press, 1986. Also see Harold G. Marcus. *A History of Ethiopia*. Berkeley: University of Berkeley Press, 1994, pp. 80-81.

Mengesha Yohannes of Tigray, Ras Mikael of Wallo, King Kawo Tona of Walaitta, and Negus (King) Tekle Haimanot of Gojam. Their own Abegaz Walsema also ruled the Moslems of Yifat.

Given the level of the socio-economic development of Ethiopia, and a century ago, Menelik's government demonstrated a high degree of inclusiveness and decentralization, which are the hallmarks of representative governance and sound administration. Menelik was a farsighted ruler who let most regions be administered by hereditary leaders (once they accepted his authority) or by individuals nominated by the people. When some of these leaders were excessive in using their authority, Menelik was said to have interceded on behalf of individuals or of the general citizenry.[330] On the other hand, one may observe that the increased centralization and unitary government that was introduced by Emperor Haile Selassie has contributed to some of the problems that have plagued Ethiopia.

The Introduction of Modern Administration and Military Build-up

Major decisions at Menelik's court were based on consultation and deliberation. The nobles, religious leaders, and dignitaries were consulted when decisions on important national policies were made. The role of Empress Taytu is recorded to have been very prominent. Menelik heeded the advice of his councilors; in one instance, in 1879, the council advised Menelik not to resist Emperor Yohannes's advance towards Showa; he refrained from challenging Emperor Yohannes, opting instead to settle the matter peacefully.

Menelik's administration was elaborate and achieved several "firsts" in the recent history of Ethiopia. He was instrumental in introducing modern technologies such as the telephone and telegraph. He also introduced state supported secular education, modern administration, and social and military services. He established the first cabinet posts in Ethiopia's history, put in use a printing press that produced the first regular periodicals, pamphlets, newspapers (Aemiro and Goh) and other documents (as well as religious pieces), and set up a mint that produced coins.[331]

---

330. For a detailed account on Menelik's relation with hereditary leaders, please refer to Paulos Gnogno, *Ate Menelik*. Addis Ababa: Bole Publishers, 1984 Ethiopian calendar.
331. Wagaw, Teshome G. *The Development of Higher Education and Social Change*. East Lansing, Michigan: Michigan State University, 1990. p.3. Refer to Paulos Gnogno, *Atse Menelik*, for the modernization and nation-building efforts under Emperor Menelik, pp. 236-357.

Menelik had a standing palace guard (corps d'élite) whose number ranged from 9,000 to 12,000. In the 1880s the palace guard was comparatively well administered and salaried. The salary of a palace guard, for example, included four amole and seven dawula of grain.[332] Since these palace guards were taken off farm work to serve the Emperor, an additional six dawula of grain was allotted to each dependent of the guard. Furthermore, there was a clothing allowance for their wives and children.[333] Besides this palace guard, Menelik was reported to command an army of some 130,000 men in 1880. In war times the number rose to about 196,000 volunteers from different regions and religions.

During campaigns or wars, the individual soldier provided his own equipment and provision. The provision was normally dry food (chibito), a handful or two a day that lasted for about four days. Women and boys accompanied the solders to cook, carry provisions and weapons and tend to the caravan of mules and horses. George Berkeley,[334] for example, stated that the Abyssinian army numbered 80,000 men accompanied by 30,000 women, servants, and mules.

Menelik was tactful and diplomatic in getting weapons from the different Europeans countries. Although Britain tried to curtail weapons that went to Africans lest they be used against European colonizers, Menelik succeeded in ensuring the flow of weapons from Europe. This flow increased gradually with the rise in the number of European visitors to the court of Menelik, some of whom showered the Emperor with weapons as well as other gifts. Menelik also managed to purchase firearms from European governments and private weapons peddlers. The exact quantity and quality of weapons in Menelik's court, however, is hard to determine. It was reported that Menelik was in a position to arm 50,000 men in 1888 and had a good stock of munitions and accessories.

Menelik's keen interest in modern technology was not restricted to weapons. He was instrumental in introducing Ethiopia to other Western technologies and amenities, such as flourmills, bakeries, and automobiles.[335]

---

332. *Amole* is a slab of salt, which was used as a medium of exchange before the introduction of currency in Ethiopia. *Dawula* is about 20 kilograms of grain.
333. Darkawa, R.H. Kofi. *Shewa, Menelik and the Ethiopian Empire.* London: Butler & Tanner Ltd., 1975.
334. Berkeley, George. *The Campaign of Adwa and the Rise of Menelik.* New York: Negro University Press, 1969.
335. For a detailed account of modern materials that were introduced in Ethiopia during the reign of Menelik, refer to the above-mentioned Paulos Gnogno's book.

Emperor Menelik's reign, on the whole, was also "characterized by greater peace and stability than that of his predecessors."[336]

Italian Strategies and a Prelude to Adwa

Italians managed to gain a foothold on the Red Sea coast of Ethiopia when a local Sultan sold the port of Assab to an Italian concern, Rubattino Navigation Company, in 1869. Italy was the weakest colonial power and a newcomer in the game. At the zenith of the scramble for Africa, the Italian state took over the port from the company (1882) in order to facilitate its military adventure and colonial expansion adjacent to the Red Sea. Such a mercantilist state takeover of a private company assured Italy's bona fide officialized Italy's hold on the region. The Italian aggression then commenced in earnest when it landed troops at the port of Massawa, north of Assab, in 1885.[337] The same year, Menelik diplomatically expressed his opposition to the Italian occupation of the port and notified Count Pietro Antonelli, the Italian emissary to his court, stating that Italy "had no right to the port."[338]

The Italian took advantage of the absence of the Ethiopian governor, Ras Alula Engeda, who was in the Western part of Ethiopia fighting the Dervishes, or the Mahdist (a Sudanese expansionist religious and nationalist movement under the leadership of Mohammed ibn al-Sayid Abdullah), who had ventured to the highland. In the meantime, the Italians were well entrenched in Asmara. Ras Alula was the governor of the northern flank, today's Eritrea, who earlier blocked the Italian move from the seacoast to the highland and defeated them at the battle of Dogali in 1887.[339] From Asmara, the Italians made a gradual move towards the hinterland and occupied Mekele and Adwa in Tigray. In 1895 Ras Mengesha Yohannes, the governor of Tigre who succeeded his father, Emperor Yohannes, challenged the Italian expansion and engaged them in a battle but was defeated. This whole exercise was part of the Italian scheme to eventually control the rest of Ethiopia.

---

336. Pankhurst, Richard. "The Effects of War in Ethiopian History." *Ethiopian Observer*. Vol VII. No. 2, 1963, p. 160.
337. See Ullendorff, Edward. The Ethiopians, London: Oxford University Press, 1965, p.91, and Haggai Erlich, Ethiopia and Eritrea During the Scramble for Africa: A Political Biography of Ras Alula. 1875-1897. East Lansing, 1982.
338. Rosenfield, Chris Prouty, p. 121.
339. See Bahru Zewde. *A History of Modern Ethiopia*. Addis Ababa: Addis Ababa University Press, pp.56-57.

In order to fragment and weaken Ethiopia for the final and decisive onslaught, the Italians stirred up trouble against Menelik in the Afar region. Menelik was thus compelled to divert part of his force there. If they could weaken Menelik enough, he would be easily defeated on the battlefield or would be forced to recognize his vulnerability and accept Italian domination over Ethiopia. The Italians also tried to exploit the differences between Ras Mengesha and Menelik in the colonial tradition of divide and conquer, but they were unsuccessful in that attempt. It is worth remembering here that the British force defeated Menelik's predecessor, Emperor Tewodros, in 1868 because, among other things, the British managed to drive a wedge between Ethiopians. The ruler of Tigre, Dejazmach Kassa Mercha (later crowned Emperor Yohannes of Ethiopia), cooperated with the British against Tewodros. Furthermore, Tewodros also alienated his own people, especially the clergy, and that contributed to his defeat.

Menelik, however, tried to block the Italian expansion diplomatically. When all diplomatic efforts failed, he called up his voluntary army — all the able-bodied people of the land, to join him in his march north to Adwa to evict the Italians from the Ethiopian territory. Those who responded to Menelik's call for national defense against Italian aggression included not only men but also women, young people, priests, elders and even the weak and frail. They all felt that fighting against an invading force was a national obligation and rallied around their ruler. Under the leadership of Empress Taytu, women served as carriers of provisions, and as cooks, nurses, and gun loaders. Empress Taytu herself commanded six thousand troops of her own.

According to George Berkeley,[340] 87,000 men and women marched to Adwa. Of these, there were 25,000 from Amhara, Gondar and Wallo, 15,000 from Tigre, 12,000 from Gojam, and 35,000 from Showa and its southern tributaries and 15,000 from Tigre. Contemporary reports show Oromo horsemen charging the enemy, shouting "Slay! Slay!" The actual number that Emperor Menelik succeeded in raising is variously estimated between 120,000 to 200,000. Menelik also left a large portion of his army behind in garrisons.

When the battle of Adwa broke out, priests at Axum Tsion (Zion), along with those from Showa, encouraged and blessed the fighters while excommunicating those who showed any sign of defection or retreat. Thus, the Ethiopian Orthodox Church played an important and significant role at the Battle of

340. Berkeley, George. The Campaign of Adwa and the Rise of Menelik..

Adwa.[341] Such was the morale, unity of purpose, and the composition of Menelik's force that fought at Adwa.

The Battle of Adwa

The influx of such a large army was a burden on the resources of Tigre, which had already been affected by drought and famine. Menelik ordered a third of the force to provide provisions for itself elsewhere, rather than starve in Adwa. When they moved away from the area, their detour led General Oreste Baratieri to assume that Menelik's force was defecting and he took the opportunity to come out of his fortified bunkers and strike the remaining force. The battle of Adwa thus started on March 1, 1896.

That Italian initiative proved to be based upon a wrong calculation and exposed a flaw in the Italian intelligence gathering. Menelik also succeeded in keeping the number of his troops a secret. Prior to the Battle of Adwa, Italian intelligence assumed that Menelik would not bring more than 30,000 men as far as Tigre. Even then, the Italians thought that most of his Rases (generals) would be allied with Italy and would betray Menelik. Finally, the Italians were also provided with misinformation or disinformation by their indigenous "informants," such as the claims that Menelik was struck by lightning; had lost his power of speech; and had been assassinated during a palace coup. Furthermore, the Italians assumed that Ras Makonnen, one of Menelik's most able commanders, was friendly to the Italians and would defect to them. Ras Makonnen was the father of the future Emperor of Ethiopia — Haile Selassie. He also had visited Italy in 1889 in regard to the Treaty of Wuchalé. To the Italians' surprise, much of the critical information they had turned out to be incorrect. Moreover, the Italian support in Lasta was turned around and the ruler joined Menelik; so also did the Kings of Gojam and Wallo and the Moslems of Afar.

Adwa thus played host to the largest African and European armies ever to have engaged in battle. The Italian army was the largest colonial force ever to encounter an African army. The Ethiopians, besides the advantage they had in intelligence and familiarity with the terrain, had numerical superiority, deep commitment and high morale. The Ethiopian tactic of encircling the enemy also lent them an advantage over the Italian army; conversely, the Italian forces had the advantage in military training and the use of modern weapons, such as

341. Please refer to Richard K. P. Pankhurst, a special issue on the Battle of Adwa in *Ethiopia Observer*. Vol. I, no. 11, October 1957.

mountain artilleries. The Italian army numbered 17,700, out of which 10,600 were White and the rest (7,100) were askaris or natives from Italian colonies, mainly Eritrea.[342] At the end of that decisive battle, almost 8,000 Italians and 4,000 askaris (Eritrean recruits) were killed. The rest were reported as missing or captured. The outcome of the battle shocked both the Italian public and officials, and ignited large-scale public demonstrations against the Italian government. In some cities, including Rome, the army was called in to protect government officials and buildings. Universities and theaters were indefinitely closed in Rome because of the continued public demonstrations. Adwa was thus a blow to the Italians not only militarily but also with regard to morale. The shock wave destabilized the Italian government.

Two days after Adwa, Prime Minister Francesco Crispi's cabinet resigned. The Ethiopian success at Adwa also shocked the rest of Europe and forced some countries to a grudging respect for Ethiopia and see her as a power to be reckoned with. In London, *The Times* newspaper referred to Ethiopia as a "barbarous foe" and deeply regretted the defeat of a European army by a "native" force. After the decisive Battle of Adwa, however, it declared that the Ethiopians were a "civilized power both in the way they made war and in the way they conducted their diplomacy."[343] The French newspaper La Liberté declared that "All European countries will be obliged to make a place for this new brother who steps forth ready to play in the Dark Continent the role of Japan in the Far East."[344]

The Ethiopian success at Adwa was gained at a human cost of 7,000 dead and 10,000 wounded. The victory arrested the colonization of Ethiopia by Italy; but the Italians were not totally ejected from Ethiopia's northern territory — Baher Negash, or today's Eritrea. The realities of that time hindered Menelik from evicting the Italians from the northern territory that historically had been attached to Ethiopia. Menelik was faced with several constraints and opted to return to Showa. Some of the reasons for turning back rather than eradicating the Italians once and for all, could be summarized as follows:

342. The Italian army was said to be the largest when compared to other colonial powers that faced an African army.
343. Pankhurst, in special issue on the Battle of Adwa, "Diplomatic Relations with Europe, 1861-1896," *Ethiopia Observer*. Vol. I, no. 11, p.359.
344. Pankhurst, ibid., p. 366.

1. Menelik's forces were running short of provisions. The amount they could transport was, after all, limited. The Tigre region, where Adwa is located, was unable to sustain so many troops with local produce.

2. Ethiopia's fighting force heavily depended on the weather conditions. Expeditions and wars were traditionally conducted during the dry seasons. The month of March, which is close to the early rainy season in Ethiopia, is not an ideal period to conduct war or undertake any major military campaign. During war periods, while the leaders usually camped in tents, the troops were left in the open air, subjected to variations in the temperature. The mobility of solders and pack animals was also heavily hampered during the rainy seasons.

3. Health was another point to be considered. The breakout of any epidemic disease, such as cholera, could have been catastrophic, not only to the troops but to the regional population as well.

4. In terms of military strategy, it would have been a losing proposition to proceed on to Baher Negash (Eritrea) to dislodge the Italians from there. Menelik's force would have been stretched thin; already weakened, they would have been unable to withstand another military engagement without a recovery period and new supplies. It was reported that Menelik wanted to march on Asmara and Massawa and dislodge the Italians but he was advised by his loyal Eritrean intelligence sources (especially Ato Gabre Eigzieabher and Basha Aw'alom)[345] that the Italian force was entrenched and ready to defend Asmara, Massawa, and Keren.

The Italians were reported to have alerted about 43,000 well-equipped men in Eritrea in case Menelik proceeded to that region. On March 3, 1896, the Italian Foreign Minister assured the Parliament in Rome that Italy had reinforced its positions in Asmara and Massawa in order to avoid the repeat of Adwa. It would have been disastrous for Menelik to reengage, bringing tired troops against a well-entrenched, well-supplied and well-equipped army after a long march and an earlier battle.

Finally, there was also a suspicion that the local rulers might support the Italians to undermine Menelik. Although Ras Mengesha Yohannes defied the divisive scheme of the Italians and did come to assist Menelik, he challenged Menelik after Adwa (in 1898). Local rivalries could only be set aside for so long. Given the logistics, tactical constraints, and realpolitik, it would have been unwise for Menelik to move on Asmara and Massawa. A march to the north

345. See Paulos Gnogno, p. 214.

would have exposed Menelik's southern flank and would have made him susceptible to any attack, thus jeopardizing even the gains achieved at Adwa.

Had Adwa gone the other way — had Italy succeeded in defeating the Ethiopian force — the whole of Africa (excluding Liberia) would have been under European control and domination. The defeat and full colonization of Ethiopia would have also dealt a final blow to the psychology of Africans on the continent and those in the diaspora. Africans and those of African descent have rallied around Ethiopia since the 18th century — both in its generic and in its specific reference.

Ethiopia, in its generic term, is a reference to all Blacks and to Africa. In its specific term, it is a reference to the Kingdom of Ethiopia, the sole independent African country during that period. Ethiopia thus symbolizes resistance and a bulwark against European domination and subjugation of Africa and the Africans. Some argue that just as Japan later had a psychological importance for Asians when it defeated Russia, a "White" nation in 1905, so also Ethiopia held special importance to all Africans after Adwa. Adwa defused the myth of African inferiority and European superiority. Even a pro-Italian British historian, George Berkeley, admitted that the Battle of Adwa marks "the first revolt of the Dark Continent against domineering Europe."[346] It is, therefore, important to learn about Ethiopia's relation to the Black Nationalist movement, Pan-Africanism, which withstood Euro-centric onslaught of various dimensions such as colonialism, slavery, apartheid, and socio-cultural subjugation.

The Ethiopian Connection to the Pan-African Movement

Ethiopia's prestige in Africa, as a consequence of her triumphant success in repelling invasion and in having remained unconquered throughout the centuries, is practically unfathomable. To Africans in general she stands as a granite monument, a living exponent and testimony of the innate puissance of the Black race, the shrine enclosing the last sacred spark of African political freedom, the impregnable rock of Black resistance against White invasion, a living symbol, an incarnation of African independence.[347]

Ethiopia's relation with the diaspora Blacks, as well as Africans on the continent, is tied to the Pan-African movement. The word Ethiopia is used in

346. Berkeley, George, p. viii.
347. Daniel Thwaite, The Seething African Pot A Study of Black Nationalism 1882-1935. London: Constable and Co. (1936), p. 207.

Biblical literature as a reference to all Blacks. Later it was associated with and is used in reference to the African nation-state of Ethiopia. The nomenclature "Ethiopia," initially in the broadly defined Biblical interpretation and later in a country-specific concept, did play an important role in shaping the Pan-African movement and in the struggle against colonialism, slavery and subjugation. It is important, therefore, to offer an explanation of the Pan-African movement.

Pan-Africanism is a belief in the common historical, racial and experiential background that all Blacks share. This global racial identity transcends territorial political boundaries[348] and holds that the destiny of all Blacks is intertwined. The Pan-African concept as well as the movement was born and nurtured in the Western world in the 18th century. At that time, the goal of Pan-Africanism was to regain the racial identity and pride of Black people that was lost because of slavery, colonialism, and social oppression.[349] The liberation of Africa, the emancipation of all Blacks of the diaspora, and the unity of Black people were, therefore, at the core of the movement. That was why, in the twentieth century, proponents of Pan-Africanism such as Marcus Aurelius Garvey argued that Pan-Africanism knew "no clime, boundary or nationality." Marcus Garvey's Back to Africa Universal Negro Improvement Association was seen as a revolutionary idea by Whites although it instilled confidence in diaspora Blacks.

In order to articulate and bring to fruition the concept of Pan-Africanism, several congresses were held in Europe. The driving forces behind the various Pan-African conferences such as the ones that were convened in London (1900, 1921, and 1923), Paris (1919), New York (1927), and Manchester (1945) were diaspora Africans: African Americans and Afro-Caribbeans. Henry Sylvester Williams, a barrister from Trinidad, called for the 1900 Pan-African conference (he coined the word "Pan-Africa") and William Burghardt DuBois, from the US, convened the 1919 Pan-African conference. Both individuals played important roles in organizing as well as influencing the conferences and setting the vision for the movement.[350] These and many other intellectual proponents of the Pan-

348. Edmondson, Lockseley. "Pan Africanism and the International System: Challenges and Opportunities," in W. Ofuatey-Kodjoe (ed.), *Pan-Africanism.* Lanham: University Press of America, pp. 285-316.

349. Drake, St. Clair, "Pan-Africanism, Negritude, and the African Personality" in William John Hanna (ed.), *Independent Black Africa: The Politics of Freedom*, Chicago: Rand McNally & Co., 1964, pp. 530-541.

350. Shepperson, George, "Notes on Negro American Influences on the Emergence of African Nationalism," *Journal of African History*, I, 1960, pp. 299-312.

African movement believed that their Africanness and the destinies they all shared as Blacks were the foremost aspects of their lives.

When the Pan-African movement started, African countries, with the exception of Ethiopia and Liberia, were under colonial rule. Hence, Africans from the continent did not play significant roles as leaders in the conceptualization of the Pan-African movement nor in the subsequent Pan-African conferences. It was during the dawn of independence and in the subsequent periods that Africans played important roles in the Pan-African movement. After the independence of a few African countries, the venues for Pan-African conferences also moved to Africa.

The Philosophy of Ethiopia and Ethiopianism in the Pan-African Movement

The genesis of the Pan-African movement can be traced back to the different political and religious movements called Ethiopianism or the Ethiopian movements.[351] Ethiopianism, or Ethiopia as a concept, was a generic reference to the Black race or to the continent of Africa. Later, the name Ethiopia came to refer to the specific geographical area of what was originally called Abyssinia or the kingdom of Ethiopia.[352] The concept of Ethiopianism or Ethiopia as a generic reference to the Black race emanated from the Old Testament, which prophesied that "Ethiopia shall soon stretch forth her hands unto God" (Psalm 68, verse 31). This messianic prophecy, Ethiopianists believed, is a covenant between the Black race and God that He will deliver the Black race from slavery and oppression and bring together all the children of the African diaspora. In the 1920s, a West African nationalist newspaper stated that, "when we speak of our prospects we speak of the prospect of the entire Ethiopian race. By the Ethiopian race we mean the sons and daughters of Africa scattered throughout the world."[353] Ethiopianism hence became a kind of religion for some Blacks through which they saw a ray of hope in the wilderness of history.

This messianic and quasi-religious movement gave hope to its followers; a hope in the rise of Africa and the coming together of her scattered children. Followers of Ethiopianisim believed that during the ascendance of Africa and the

351. See Drake, St. Clair. The Redemption of Africa and Black Religion. Chicago, 1970.
352. Chirenje, J. Mutero. *Ethiopianism and Afro-Americans in South Africa, 1883-1916*. Baton Rouge: Louisiana State University Press, 1987, pp. 1-2.
353. Asante, S.K.B. *Pan-African Protest: West Africa and the Italo-Ethiopian Crisis 1931-1941*. Longman Group Ltd., 1977, p.14. Originally appeared in editorial of *Gold Coast Leader*, 1 November 1924.

coming together of African people, God would punish those who had caused her misery. "The enemy" is a reference to the colonizers of Africa and the ensuing enslavement and diaspora of its people. God, it was thought, would doom Western civilization, for its action directed against Africa.[354]

This messianic movement of Ethiopianism, or the notion of Ethiopia as a generic reference to all Black people, was indeed a psychological boost engendering new confidence in its followers. They believed that they were special people and superior to the other races. Ethiopianism glorified Africa and Africans of the past. Its vision was that God would redeem Africa; its people would free themselves from bondage and recapture their lost glory and civilization. Ethiopianism thus was both a spiritual hope and an important ingredient in Black messianic insurrection.

The Ethiopian millennium was further advocated by the 18th-century Swedish philosopher Emmanuel Swedenborg. His followers, both in Europe and in the US, believed that Blacks were the race that God and nature had endowed with the greatest aptitude for Christianity. Whites, according to Swedenborg, were too cerebral and self-seeking, while Africans were affectionate and had an altruistic temperament, the right soil for the full flowering of Christian faiths and virtues. Swedenborgians believed that the prophecy of Ethiopia stretching forth her hands unto God meant that the redemption of Africa would realize the Kingdom of God on earth.[355] This philosophy had also considerable impact on White American abolitionists and some Christian missionaries to Africa.

Indeed, Ethiopianism inspired the birth of the Pan-African movement. The early American Pan-Africanists such as W.E.B. DuBois, Marcus Garvey, George Padmore, and West Africans such as Casely Hayford were influenced by Ethiopianism and its universal fraternity. As Wilson Jeremiah Moses wrote in his book, *The Golden Age of Black Nationalism*, "Ethiopianism had become not only a trans-Atlantic political movement, but a literary movement well-known among all Black people from the Congo basin to the mountains of Jamaica to the sidewalks of New York."[356] Robert Alexander Young, in his *Ethiopian Manifesto*, published in February 1829, made one of the earliest calls for nationalism by African

354. See in Moses, Wilson Jeremiah, *The Golden Age of Black Nationalism 1850-1925*. Hamden, Connecticut: Archon Brooks, 1978, pp.158-159 as quoted from David Walker, *Walker's Appeal in Four Articles* (1829) and Henry Highland Garnet, *An Address to the Slaves of the* United States of America. Troy, New York: 1848.

355. Frederikson, George M. *Black Liberation*. New York: Oxford University Press, 1995, pp. 62-63.

356. Wilson Jeremiah Moses, Ibid., p.24.

or Ethiopian peoples. In the same year, David Walker's Appeal to the "colored citizens of the world, but in particular, and very expressly, to those of the United States of America" was one of the early publication that stimulated nationalist and Pan-African ideology.[357]

Political conservatives such as Booker T. Washington, though ideologically different from his contemporary DuBois, a proponent of Ethiopianism and Pan-Africanism, was aware of this African connection and attempted to exploit it for African progress.[358] Washington, in the spirit of Pan-Africanism, advocated for African industrial education, self-improvement, and the establishment of Tuskegee-type schools in Africa.[359] Washington was the principal of Tuskegee Normal and Industrial Institute in the US. He believed in self-help and education for Blacks that would qualify them for good jobs. Accordingly, he established a technical school in the then German colony of Togo, which was modeled after Tuskegee. Nine Tuskegee students and faculty were dispatched to Togo to show Africans how to raise better sheep or to develop superior cotton cultivation methods.[360] Ethiopianisim and its brainchild, Pan-Africanism, thus brought together African-American intellectuals and community leaders who belong to different political bents in the post-Reconstruction era.

The second reference to "Ethiopia" is as an identifier for the current geographic region of Ethiopia. Ethiopia was more of a sovereign country than the other two independent Black countries of that time, Liberia and Haiti, which were politically independent but were economic appendages of the US. At the time of the movement, Haiti was heavily indebted to US companies and Liberia was more or less dominated by the Firestone Rubber Company.[361] Ethiopia was the only independent Black country that successfully resisted Euro-based cultural and political domination. Hence, it became a symbol of independence and hope for Blacks in the continent and those in the diaspora. Then, it further boosted the morale of all Blacks by defeating the Italians in 1896. Ethiopia, as one

357. For Robert Alexander Young's *Ethiopian Manifesto* and Walker's *Appeal* see in Sterling Stuckey, *The Ideological Origins of Black Nationalism*, Boston: Beacon Press, 1972.
358. Fredrickson, George M. *Black Liberation*, p. 145.
359. Washington, *Booker* T., "Industrial Education in Africa," *Independent*, LX (March 15, 1906), 616-19, as quoted by W. Manning Marable, "Booker T. Washington and African Nationalism," *Phylon*, Vol. XXXV, NO. 4, 1974, pp. 398-406.
360. Quoted from W. Manning Marable, *Phylon*, vol. xxxv, No. 4, 1974, p. 399. Also see John W. Robinson. "Cotton Growing in Africa," in BTW, ed. *Tuskegee, Its People, Their Ideals and Achievements*, New York, 1905, pp. 185-99.
361. Please see Dubois, W.E.B., "Inter-racial Implications of the Ethiopian Crisis. A Negro View," *Foreign Affairs*, Vol. l. 4, No. 1, October 1935, pp. 85-6.

West African newspaper put it, "remained the only oasis in a desert of rank subjugation from the avaricious hands of foreign domination."[362] Most Blacks at that time believed in the "Ethiopian millennium," based on the Old Testament and Bible references. The victory at Adwa enhanced the symbolism, with Ethiopia representing and strengthening the messianic belief in such a Millennium and in the eventual demise of European colonialism.

Thus, Ethiopia proper became a symbol of independence and resistance against colonialism. It was increasingly associated with Black nationalism and resistance movements. Ethiopia and Ethiopianism became a rallying point and remained the unifying core for Africans of the diaspora and later for Africans in the continent in their struggle for independence. That symbol of resistance also influenced African Americans in their political struggle to free themselves from slavery. Later, it inspired Henry McNeal Turner of South Carolina to denounce White injustice and to call for racial separation. Bishop Turner advocated the repatriation of African Americans to Africa. He visited Africa in 1893, 1895, and 1898 and was instrumental in establishing the underground intellectual movement in Africa during World War II.[363] For example, he helped found Black churches in the US and separatist Ethiopian movements in South Africa, and effectively articulated the political importance of church-based Ethiopianism.[364]

The influence of the Ethiopian movement was not restricted to the realm of politics. When Black churches broke away from White churches, they named their churches African, Abyssinian or Ethiopian. That was to assert their independence, cultural purity, and affinity with Africa, and their belief in the Old Testament as well as the New. The quest for independence of Black churches from the White churches in the US dates back to the 1790s, when African Americans seceded from St. George's church, a Methodist Episcopal church in Philadelphia, and established African Methodist Episcopal (AME) church. Later, in 1800, the Abyssinian Baptist Church, the largest African American church, was established in New York. In 1809, African Americans in Philadelphia seceded from White Baptist churches and formed the Abyssinian Baptist Church.[365]

In West Africa, Ethiopianism was the driving force in nationalist movements such as Sierra Leone's Native Pastorate, in 1861. Similarly, Ethiopian

---

362. Asante, S. K. B., *op.cit*, p. 15 as was written in the *Gold Coast Independent Accra*, 18 January 1936.
363. Moses, Wilson Jeremiah, *op.cit.*, p. 24.
364. M. Fredrickson, George, *Black Liberation*, p. 77.

churches were established and declared religiously independent in the Transvaal province of South Africa in the early 1890s, by Mangena Maaka Mokone.[366] After seceding from the Wesleyan church because of discrimination against Blacks, Reverend Mokone established a church named the Ethiopian Church of South Africa on November 5, 1893. Other priests such as Reverends Gilead Xaba and James Dwane seceded from the Wesleyan church and joined Rev. Mokone. Rev. Kanyane also succeeded from the Anglicans and joined the Ethiopian Church. Similar Ethiopian churches were established in other southern African countries such as Zimbabwe.[367] These independent Ethiopian churches operated according to "African ideals, methods and objectives, by and for Africans."[368]

Furthermore, radical-minded African Americans, including American socialists, used "Ethiopia" to symbolize resistance against the establishment. In the 1930s, the Ethiopian Peace Movement in Chicago was one such political organization. In Africa, the Ethiopian Movement of South Africa challenged the status quo. These churches and organizations provided the platform for articulating Black concerns and mobilizing Black resources to benefit and uplift the ossified Black underclass.

Ethiopia and Ethiopianism, therefore, represented a movement that rejected the political, cultural, and religious domination of Blacks. In the US the movement was directed against the Establishment and slavery; in Africa, Ethiopianism was an expression against racial domination by White settlers as well as against colonial rule. Ethiopia and Ethiopianism was a heresy in the mind of the oppressors, colonialists, settlers, and enslavers, who associated it with Black militancy. Ethiopianism challenged the status quo and demanded equality and respect for Blacks. It challenged the fundamental economic and political modus operandi of the time, and threatened the exploiters who lived off the unjust economic and political system. As a movement, Ethiopianism emboldened Blacks to rise up and challenge social injustice, racial discrimination, and colonial domination.

---

365. Isaacs, Harold R., *The New World of Negro Americans*, New York: The John Day Co., 1963. p. 149. Carter G. Woodson, *The History of the Negro Church*. Washington, D.C., 1921, pp.86-90. See also in George Shepperson, "Ethiopia and African Nationalism," *Phylon*, Vol. XIV, (1953) pp. 9-18.
366. Ayandele, E.A., Holy Johnson: Pioneer of African Nationalism 1836-1917. London, 1970, pp. 34-47.
367. Chirenje, J. Mutero, p. 44.
368. Asante, S.K.B., *op.cit.* p.10 and Clarence G. Contee, "The Emergence of DuBois as an African Nationalist," in *The Journal of Negro History*. 50, 1969.

Ethiopia and Ethiopianism was also romanticized and glorified by Black poets. Many poems and literary works have been written on Ethiopia and Ethiopianism. One such piece, by Frances Ellen Watkins, depicted the innocence of Ethiopia and her closeness to God:

> Yes, Ethiopia yet shall stretch
> Her bleeding hands abroad;
> Her cry of agony shall reach
> Up to the throne of God.[369]

Ethiopianism was not restricted to social, political, religious, and literary realms. It also influenced Black entrepreneurs. The Ethiopian Progressive Association, for example, was established in the US to provide the economic leverage that Blacks needed to influence government policies and legislation affecting Blacks both in the US and abroad. To increase its economic influence, the association purchased stocks and became involved in other economic enterprises.[370] Thus, followers of Ethiopianism cut across classes: they ranged from factory workers to intellectuals, the clergy, and businessmen.

Ethiopia's Preoccupation with Development, Political Independence and National Survival

While the Black world was attracted to Ethiopia figuratively, Ethiopia and its leaders had more concrete business to attend to. As a result of its unique geographic position, bordering a significant sea-lane, the Red Sea, and its proximity to the most important land bridge, the Isthmus of Suez, its frequent communications and preoccupations for centuries had been with visitors and merchants from Greece, Syria, and Arabia. Europeans were especially interested in tracing the mystical Christian Kingdom, believed to be Ethiopia, and the legendary saintly monarch Prester John. They hoped that the discovery of this kingdom would bring a strong ally to their religious crusade against the Ottoman Empire which occupied the Holy Land, Jerusalem.

In general, Ethiopian history abounds with literature, religion, paintings, and cultural influences from these ancient countries. Their influences did not dominate but were subordinate to Ethiopian experiences. Ethiopian kings, for

---

369. See in Brawley, Benjamin, *Early American Negro Writers*. Chapel Hill, North Carolina, 1935. Also see in Wilson Jeremiah Moses, *op.cit*, p.158.
370. Ibid., 219.

example, allowed European missionaries and religious leaders to teach in Ethiopia only as long as their religion did not supplant the Ethiopian Orthodox Church, as there was no separation between Church and State. In one instance, when Emperor Susneyos was converted to Roman Catholicism in 1632, he was forced to abdicate his throne and Jesuit missionaries were expelled from the country.

Be that as it may, communications with European countries and the frequency of visitors increased, especially after the opening of the Suez Canal in 1869. The century was also identified with European imperialism and state-sponsored mercantilism. This European onslaught threatened Ethiopia's independence and preoccupied its leaders. Furthermore, the infamous Berlin Conference of 1885 laid the groundwork for the partitioning of Africa among European powers. Ethiopia remained independent because of its leaders' shrewdness, the state administrative and military structure, and the geographical inaccessibility of the country.

While Europe was stepping up its efforts to colonize Africa and the rest of the world, European countries were essential sources for the technology and goods that Ethiopia badly needed, both for its national defense and for development efforts. Ethiopia, therefore, maintained ties with Europe out of necessity. Emperor Tewodros (1855-1868), who was a visionary ruler for his time, wanted to accelerate the process of nation building. The emperor's unrelenting efforts to develop his country led him to a conflict with the British. He detained British and other European technicians whom he suspected of being Egyptian agents; they failed to manufacture for him the military weapons that he needed and appeared to be working to undermine Ethiopia's territorial integrity. The British dispatched (1867-68) Sir Robert Napier (later Lord Napier of Maqdala, 1890) from India in order to free the British citizens. Tewodros' army was no match for that of the British and he was betrayed by his own people, especially the clergy. He took his own life at the Battle of Maqdala, rather than surrender to the British army. The battle of Maqdala resulted in the burning of churches and the looting of the country's priceless treasures and manuscripts. It also robbed Ethiopia of a forward-looking leader and created a political power vacuum until Emperor Yohannes IV emerged in 1871.

After Tewodros, it was Emperor Menelik (1889-1913) who began, in earnest, the modernization of Ethiopia. He, too, employed foreigners to assist him in that endeavor. Emperor Menelik, for instance, "welcomed Europeans of all descriptions, arms merchants, missionaries, both Protestant and Catholics, travelers and explorers..."[371] to assist him in his modernization efforts. Menelik sponsored the introduction of modern technologies to Ethiopia.

With Christianity as the state religion, the rulers' good relationship with Christian Europe gave them more security, surrounded as they were by non-Christian states. When the Somali Ahmad ibn Ibrahim (known in Ethiopia as Gragn Mohammed — the left handed) ran over the highland and devastated churches and shrines in the 1530s, during the reign of Libne Dengel (1508-40), Christian Portugal dispatched a 400-man army. The Turkish Pasha in turn assisted Ahmad ibn Ibrahim. Emperor Lebne Dengel's son, Gelawdewos, finally defeated Gragn's army in 1541. The Turks also continued to occupy Ethiopia's coastal regions around the Red Sea and Harar in the east. Similarly, in 1875, the Egyptian army launched a three-pronged attack on Ethiopia and after their initial defeat made a second unsuccessful attempt a year later. The Mahdists in the Sudan were also a continuous threat, and Emperor Yohannes IV (1871-1889) was killed in Metemma (north-west Ethiopia) while fighting the Dervishes — followers of the Mahdi, as mentioned earlier.

Thus, historically, Ethiopia has been at war almost continually, and its political independence has continuously been threatened. The Berlin Conference of 1884-5 further threatened Ethiopia's independence; in the 1880s the Italians began their encroachment on the Red Sea coast of Ethiopia.

The noted Ethiopianist Richard Pankhurst compiled this history of twelve battles within twenty-six years with foreign countries, between the defeat of Tewodros (1868) and Menelik's victory over the Italians in 1896. After Adwa Ethiopia had a period of relative peace and development for forty years, until the Second World War. After Menelik consolidated the Ethiopian territory, there were no further military expeditions.

The following are the twelve battles that occurred in Ethiopia, 1868-1896.[372]

---

371. See in Darkwah, R.H. Kofi, *Showa, Menelik and the Ethiopian Empire.* London: Butler & Tanner Ltd., 1975, p.64.
372. Pankhurst, Richard, "The Ethiopian Army of Former Times." *Ethiopian Observer.* Vol. VII. No. 2, 1963, p. 151. Pankhurst quoted A.B. Wylde, *Modern Abyssinia,* 1901, p. 44 (publisher not quoted) as his source.

Battle Sites	Adversary	Month/Year
Maqdala	British	April 1868
Gundet	Egypt	November 1875
Gura	Egypt	March 1876
Kufit	Dervish	September
Dogali	Italians	January 1887
Gondar	Dervish	April 1887
Wagera	Dervish	August 1888
Gallabat	Dervish	March 1889
Coatit	Italians	January 1895
Senafe	Italians	January 1895
Amba Alaghe	Italians	Dec. 1895 -Jan. 1896
Adwa	Italians	March 1896

Because of Ethiopia's strategic geographic location, it was often under attack. Hence, Ethiopia's leaders looked to "friendly" European countries that would provide them with modern weapons and the know-how to produce them. They skillfully played one European power against the other, especially beginning in the nineteenth century, while welcoming European technology from all sides. Ethiopia used France against both British and Italian expansionism, and it used Britain against Italian expansionism. In the latter part of the nineteenth century similar strategic needs compelled Emperor Haile Selassie to befriend the US. He hoped that this new global power could enhance his position, develop the country, and help fend off Ethiopia's historical enemies. The US allied with Ethiopia because it fitted its global and regional strategy of the Cold War era; in other words, anything to keep the Russians out.

The rapid modernization of a non-European and monarchic Japan also attracted the interest of Emperor Haile Selassie, and Ethiopian intellectuals as well.[373] Imperial Japan, especially after the introduction of the Imperial Constitution (also called the Meiji Constitution), 1889-1947, was determined to make Japan a rich and modernizing country. This attracted the interest of Ethiopian monarchs, beginning with Emperor Menelik. These preoccupations, political and cultural survival and nation building, meant that the Pan-African movement was not initially given priority by Ethiopian leaders.

The Implications of Adwa to the Diaspora Africans

Yet, as indicated above, Ethiopia played a significant role in the Pan-African movement. The movement forged Africans and people of African descent into a unified force against oppression, colonialism and racial domination. Although intellectuals spearheaded the movement, it gradually became a mass movement for a noble cause. The civil rights movement in the US and the anti-colonial struggle in Africa and the Caribbean are extensions of the Pan-African and Ethiopian movements. Black movements of the 1890s were associated with Ethiopia because of Ethiopia's civilization, long political independence and rich historical and cultural legacy.

The success of Ethiopia against Italy has major implications for both Africans in the diaspora and Africans in Africa. First, it disproved the misconception of the inferiority of the Africans. Some of the classical writers, from Herodotus to the followers of social Darwinism, had stigmatized Blacks as inferior.[374] That belief, among others, presupposes that the African is a "savage" who cannot hold his ground in the face of European brains and power. Ignorance of Blacks and their achievements has contributed to the myth of African inferiority and the falsification of their history and achievements.[375] Adwa disproved the inevitability of the superiority of European armies. Adwa also was evidence that, given the right leadership, unity of purpose, and a galvanization of resources, Africans can protect and promote their national interest. This espe-

---

373. Kebede Michael's book in Amharic, *Japan Indet Seletenech* (How Japan Modernized), published in the 1960s, was used as a reading in Ethiopian schools. This indicates the extent of the fascination of Ethiopians with Japan's modernizing without sacrificing its tradition. See also Bahru Zewde, "The Concept of Japanisation in the Intellectual History of Modern Ethiopia", in *Proceedings of the Fifth Seminar of the Department of History*, Addis Ababa, 1990.
374. Refer to Joseph Harris, *Africa and their History*. New York: Meridian, 1998, pp. 1-19.
375. Cheik Anta Diop, *African Origin of Civilization*, edited and translated by Mercer Cook, Chicago: Lawrence Hill, 1974.

cially is a crucial issue today when the ineptitude of African leaders is most often blamed for the economic, social, and political predicaments that the continent faces; in fact, these conditions have more complex causes.

In the Western Hemisphere, especially in the US, African Americans were relegated to second class citizenship and racism worked against the interests of people of African descent. Adwa, at that time, played a positive role in uplifting the morale of the colonized and the racially oppressed Africans in the continent and in the diaspora. It challenged the status quo. In the US, the struggle gradually culminated in the civil rights movement that, at least on paper, guaranteed racial equality. In Africa and in the Caribbean, it emboldened the freedom fighters to increase their efforts in opposing colonialism and its vestiges.

Ethiopia was associated with freedom, independence and liberation. At a time when the rest of Africa was under colonial rule, Ethiopia also lent support to African freedom fighters. In the United States and the Caribbean states, the Rastafarian movement of the 1930s is a testimony to the respect given Ethiopia by Black people worldwide. Rastafarianism symbolized and is associated with the persona of Emperor Haile Selassie (Ras Tafari). When fascist Italy attacked Ethiopia (1936-1941), African Americans rallied around and lobbied the US government to establish a positive foreign policy towards Ethiopia.[376] They stood behind Ethiopia although they "had only a limited financial ability and political influence with which to translate their concern into concrete assistance."[377] The war resulted in the growth of pan-African movement and helped build Black pride.[378] To the dismay of Black Americans, Western governments directly or indirectly supported the aggressor, fascist Italy, and Ethiopia became a sacrificial lamb. Emperor Haile Selassie appealed to members of the League of Nations, then declared that history would remember their inaction. Europe soon faced utter destruction at the hands of the forces of Fascist Italy and Nazi Germany.

Afro-Caribbeans and Africans on the continent also voiced their support for Ethiopia and volunteered to join the war on Ethiopia's side, even though they were under European colonialism themselves. After all, the struggle to defend Ethiopia was part of their own struggle to overthrow colonialism. The rape of Ethiopia served as a galvanizing force similar to the success of the Battle of

---

376. Joseph E. Harris, *American Reactions to war in Ethiopia1936-1941.* Baton Rouge: Louisiana State University, 1994.
377. Red Ross, "Black Americans and Italo-Ethiopian Relief 1935-1936." *Ethiopia Observer.* Vol. XV, no. 2, 1972, p. 122.
378. Ross, p. 129.

Adwa, which had psychological, social, and political implications for all Africans, and especially for African Americans of the time.

Yet, despite a proud history of unified action within Ethiopia and in the greater Black community worldwide, today, internal and external forces have worked against Ethiopia and have marginalized it despite its vast potentials.

Ethiopia and Blacks of the diaspora

While Blacks, mainly in the diaspora, used Ethiopia as a symbol of resistance and identity, Ethiopia itself was struggling to maintain its political independence and survival, as it had done for centuries. Beginning with Emperor Menelik II, in the nineteenth century, leaders extended special invitations to skilled Blacks in the diaspora to return home. And many did come back to work and live in Ethiopia. Their contributions to Ethiopia's development, especially in the areas of health, education, training, and development programs, are significant. Ethiopia also benefited from the expertise and goodwill of people from Armenia, Greece, Egypt, and the Middle East in establishing "a rule qualitatively different from governments... in sub-Sahara Africa."[379]

The first African American who arrived at Emperor Menelik's court was a highly educated young Haitian named Benito Sylvain. Sylvain came to Ethiopia around 1897, seeking the assistance of Emperor Menelik to create an international Black organization to help ameliorate the condition of the Black race, according to Robert P. Skinner. Skinner was a US Consul-General in Marseilles, France, who recommended to President McKinley in 1900 that the US establish economic ties with Ethiopia.[380] In 1903, President Theodore Roosevelt commissioned Robert Skinner to negotiate a commercial treaty with Emperor Menelik.[381] US-Ethiopian economic ties thus commenced in 1903. Benito Sylvain later became Aide-de-camp to Emperor Menelik and represented Menelik at the London Pan-African Conference in 1900. Emperor Menelik's efforts and his contributions to the welfare of Blacks worldwide were acknowledged at that meeting and Menelik was made an honorary member of the Pan-African Association.[382] An Afro-West Indian from Guadeloupe, Dr. Joseph Vitalien, also served as Menelik's physician in early 1900, along with his Italian physicians, Drs.

379. Marcus, Harold G. *A History of Ethiopia.* Berkeley: University of California Press, 1994, p.78.
380. For the US diplomatic mission to Ethiopia, refer to Harold G. Marcus, "A Note on the First United States Diplomatic Mission to Ethiopia in 1903," *Ethiopian Observer*, Vol. II, No. 2, 1963, pp. 165-168.
381. Skinner, Robert p. *Abyssinia of To-Day.* New York: Negro University Press, 1906, p. ix.

Alfieri and Traversi. Dr. Vitalien was instrumental in establishing the Menelik Hospital in Addis Ababa.[383]

Blacks increasingly looked towards Emperor Menelik and Ethiopia after Adwa. In 1903, William H. Ellis, a Black Wall Street stockbroker from Texas and an admirer of Menelik, travelled to Ethiopia with his wife to pay homage, at the invitation of Ras Makonnen. Ras Makonnen had met Ellis in London, while representing Ethiopia at the coronation of King Edward VII.[384] Ellis' visit to Ethiopia was international news, reported by New York World; Cleveland Times; New York Times, New York Daily News, Pittsburgh Post and the Washington Post.[385]

Menelik's invitation of Blacks and his admiration of Presidents Abraham Lincoln and Theodore Roosevelt, and the steel magnate and philanthropist Andrew Carnegie impressed Ellis. When Menelik heard that Andrew Carnegie was assisting African Americans to "gain a higher sphere of civilization, knowledge, virtue and morality and educating them on higher plans," he wrote Carnegie a letter and wished him that "God give him power and strength to fulfill all his good wishes."[386] Carnegie reportedly had the letter framed; then he wrote back a patronizing letter on January 11, 1904 and signed it, "His majesty's obedient servant." It was also reported that Menelik wept when he heard about Abraham Lincoln's effort to free the slaves.

Ellis convinced Menelik to agree to a Treaty of Amity and Commerce between Ethiopia and the US.[387] Robert Skinner signed the treaty with Menelik on December 27, 1903. Ellis received permission to establish a textile factory in Ethiopia but the project was abandoned after Menelik's death.[388] Fifty years later, on May 22, 1953, Ethio-American relations were further enhanced under Emperor Haile Selassie when a 25-year Treaty of Amity and Economic Relations was signed. The US thus became actively involved in Ethiopia's economic, educational, and military development in the post WWII period.

---

382. See in Esedebe, p. Olisanwuche, *Pan-Africanism: the Idea and Movement, 1776-1963.* Washington, D.C.: Howard University press, 1982, pp. 48-53.
383. See in Pankhurst, Richard, "Menelik and the Utilization of Foreign Skills in Ethiopia," *Journal of Ethiopian Studies.* Vol. V, No.1, January 1967, pp. 65-67.
384. "The American Promoter in Abyssinia" in *World's Work*, vol. 7, March 1904, p. 4602.
385. Paulos Gnogno, pp. 381-383. The date for *The Washington Post* was not furnished.
386. Pankhurst, *Ethiopia Observer.* Vol. XV, no. 2, 1972, p. 93.
387. Rosenthal, Eric. *Stars and Stripes in Africa.* London, 1938, p.244.
388. Paulos Gnogno, p. 384.

Cold War Era

Once again, Emperor Haile Selassie extended invitations to skilled Blacks in 1922 and 1927, to "come back to the homeland." He invited especially engineers, teachers, physicians, and other professionals and promised them free land and high wages.[389] Such calls attracted many African Americans and Afro-Caribbeans. Black Jews such as Rabbi Arnold Josiah Ford, originally from Barbados, arrived in Ethiopia in 1930.[390] Rabbi Ford traced his genealogy to Sierra Leone and Nigeria on his father's side; to Ethiopian Jews, people of the Bete Israel, on his mother's side.[391] Rabbi Ford was the musical director of the Universal Negro Improvement Association (UNIA) founded by Marcus Garvey. He married Mignon Loraine Innis in Ethiopia in 1933. (The lady had gone to Ethiopia in 1932 in response to an appeal for volunteers.) Mignon Loraine Innis was born in 1905 on a sugar plantation in Barbados, immigrated to the US in 1921, and lived in New York, where she was influenced by the philosophy of the UNIA. Then, together with Albertha Thomas, she established the first coeducational school in Ethiopia (Bete Ourael School in 1941). The school was renamed Princess Zenebe-Worq School, in 1943, after the five-year Italian occupation was terminated. Mignon Loraine Innis (affectionately referred to as Mrs. Ford by her former students), died at the age of 90 in Washington, D.C., on January 14, 1995, and was buried in Ethiopia according to her wishes.

Ethiopian Invasion by Fascist Italy and the Solidarity of Blacks in the diaspora

Pan-African solidarity was challenged during the Second World War when fascist Italy attacked Ethiopia in October 1935. The Italian leader Benito Mussolini, in violation of the League of Nation's covenant to which both Ethiopia and Italy were signatory, attacked a member country. The Italian force employed poison gas on defenseless Ethiopians to subdue them and colonize the country. Mussolini used many excuses to attack Ethiopia; he claimed that Italy intended to bring Christianity to Ethiopia — Christianity had been introduced to Ethiopia in the 4th century. He also claimed he would penalize Ethiopia for

389. Refer to Amy Jacques Garvey, *Garvey and Garveyism.* Kingston: A.J. Garvey, 1963, p. 99.
390. Scott, William R. *A Study of Afro-Americans and Ethiopian Relations: 1896-1941.* A Ph.D. dissertation, Princeton University, 1971.
391. An interview with Rabbi Ford's son, Yosef Ford, who was an active member of the Ethiopian Community Center in Washington, D.C. He died in Washington, D.C. in 2001 and his body was taken to Addis Ababa and laid to rest next to his mother's.

practicing slavery — slavery had been outlawed in the country and was on the decline. Actually, Mussolini's declaration of war against Ethiopia was in revenge for the shame Italy had faced at Adwa; Mussolini intended to bolster Italian nationalism and fanned the populist imagery of ancient Rome. This was similar to Giuseppe Mazzini's Risorgimento movement of the 1840s, which was intended to awaken Italian nationalism.

While the war against Ethiopia was also a measure undertaken to address the sagging Italian economy of the Depression era, it was at the same time a manifestation of Mussolini's racial chauvinism, to which the Western countries acquiesced. In this regard Padmore, in an article entitled "Ethiopia and World Politics," quoted the Rome correspondent of the London Times that "Mussolini is not only defending the rights of Italy, but he is upholding the prestige of the White race in Africa." Another British journalist, of the liberal paper News Chronicle, stated "Great Britain cannot afford to jeopardize her friendship with Italy simply in order to defend Ethiopia on the basis of abstract justice."[392] Along with Britain and France, the US government denied support to Ethiopia in order to appease Mussolini.[393]

Mussolini's invasion of Ethiopia, however, outraged Blacks throughout the world. The noted African American historian, John Hope Franklin, noted that "Ethiopia was a Black nation, and its destruction would symbolize the final victory of Whites over Blacks."[394] Opposition to fascist Italy's aggression as well as support for Ethiopia came from both Blacks and liberal Whites. However, the main thrust came from Blacks — Africans, African Americans, and Afro West Indians.[395] Organizations were established throughout the world to help rally support for Ethiopia[396] and to appeal to the League of Nations, the British Foreign Office and the US Department of State on behalf of Ethiopia. The official

392. Padmore, George. "Ethiopia and World Politics," *Crisis*, Vol.42, No.8, 1935, p. 157. Also see Magubane, pp. 142-143.
393. For the role of the US during the Ethio-Italian war, refer to John H. Spencer, *Ethiopia at Bay: A Personal Account of the Haile Selassie Years*. Algonac, Michigan: Reference Publishers, Inc., 1984, p. 36.
394. Franklin, John Hope and Alfred A. Moss, Jr., *From Slavery to Freedom*, New York: McGraw Hill, Inc. 1994, pp. 433-434.
395. Some of the African, African Americans, and Afro West Indians who spearheaded the opposition against Italian aggression against Ethiopia were Jomo Kenyata (Kenya), Dr. Peter Millard (British Guiana), Mrs., Amy Ashwood Garvey (ex-wife of Marcus Garvey), Samuel Manning (Trinidad), Muhammad Said (Somalia), John Payne (African American), G.E. Moore and S.R. Wood (Ghana), Miss Sylvia Pankhurst (Britain), George Padmore (Trinidad), and I.A.T. Wallace-Johnson (Sierra Leone). See in p. Olisanwuche Esedede, *op.cit.* pp. 115-124.

organ of the National Association for the Advancement of Collared [*sic*] People (NAACP), Crisis, and the National Urban League's Opportunity, wrote in their editorials condemning the rape of Ethiopia by fascist Italy. The national Black press extensively covered the Ethio-Italian war, promoted Pan-Africanism in America and helped thousands, if not millions of African Americans rally to the support of the Ethiopians.[397]

Many Blacks saw the attack and final occupation of Ethiopia by fascist forces as an insult to their race in general. Jomo Kenyatta, who was to become president of neighboring Kenya, commented from exile in London that "Ethiopia was the sole remaining pride of Africans and Negroes in all parts of the world"[398] and must be defended. In the US, the Italian invasion of Ethiopia highly politicized the African Americans and gave them a sense of involvement in world events.[399] African American volunteer pilots, John Charles Robinson (nicknamed the Brown Condor of Ethiopia) and Hubert Fauntleroy Julian (originally from Trinidad and called the Black Eagle of Harlem), went to Ethiopia to fly the only two airworthy planes Ethiopia possessed during the war. After the war, Robinson was involved in the reconstruction efforts in Ethiopia and trained Ethiopian pilots until his death in 1954. He was buried in Addis Ababa.

During the Ethio-Italian war, the US government's persistent restraints and harassment prevented African Americans from participating in the war on Ethiopia's side.[400] Tension also grew between African Americans and Italian Americans when Blacks launched a boycott of Italian vendors and smashed shop windows owned by Italians.[401] Public rallies were held in American cities in

396. Some of these organizations were the International Council of Friends of Ethiopia and the Provisional Committee for the Defense of Ethiopia (New York), the International African Friends of Abyssinia, and the Ethiopian Defense Committee (West Africa); Comite International Pour la defense du peuple Ethiopien et de la Paix (France); Nederlandsche Vereeniging Voor de Vrijmaking Abessynie (Dutch Society for the Liberation of Ethiopia) in Holland; Friends of Abyssinia (Venezuela); Friends of Abyssinia League, Circles for the Liberation of Ethiopia and the Abyssinia Association in Britain. Ibid. pp. 116-119. C.L.R. James also founded friends of Abyssinia in London and members included Jomo Kenyata, I.T.A. Wallace-Johnson, George Padmore, and Kwame Nkrumah.
397. Scott, William R. "Black Nationalism and the Italo-Ethiopian Conflict, 1935-1936," *The Journal of Black History*, Vol. LXIII, No. 2, 1978, p. 120.
398. See Jomo Kenyatta's article, "Hands off Abyssinia," *Labor Monthly*. London, XVII, 9 September 1935, p. 536.
399. Franklin, John Hope and Alfred A. Moss, Jr., *op.cit.* p. 433.
400. Harris, Joseph E. African-American Reactions to War in Ethiopia 1936-1941, p.54.
401. *The New York Times*, July 13 and 14, 1935.

support of Ethiopia. About 20,000 people, for example, marched in Harlem on August 4, 1935 and displayed Ethiopian flags.

After the EWF was established, its official organ, The Voice of Ethiopia, played a pivotal role in mobilizing African Americans in support of Ethiopia. The paper carried slogans such as "It is Better to Die Free than Live in Slavery"; "Black Men Everywhere! Remember Liberty Is Not Obtained By Begging For It! Unite And Get It"; "Ethiopia Must Remain Free"; "Save Ethiopia, Right Will Prevail — Persevere!" "Black Men! Let Us Get Together and Save Ethiopia"; "Demand That Haile Selassie I Be Sent Back to Ethiopia As Emperor At Once"; "Over 400,000,000 Members Of The Black Race United Can Obtain Justice For Ethiopia," and "No Black Man Shall Shed His Blood For Europe Until Ethiopia Is Free." Warren Harrigan wrote, "If Black men in America and in the West Indies and in other parts of Africa are men in reality and in truth, they cannot fail to come to the assistance of their brethren in Ethiopia."[402] The paper further urged African Americans to learn the Ethiopic alphabets and announced, "Black Men! Let Us Keep Our Ancient Culture In Our Hands. Learn This!" Articles were also featured in the paper. Matthew E. Gardner, for example, had an article entitled "Do Inter-racial Movements Serve Any Useful Purpose?" One advertisement announced that the "Recently established Juvenile Unit of the Ethiopian World Federation, Inc., Local No 1, will render its First Performance on Sunday, May 7, 1939 at the Ethiopian World Federation Auditorium, 2667 Eighth Avenue (cor. 142nd St.) New York City."

Thus the Ethio-Italian war turned out to be a "racial war" wherein Black nationalists supported Ethiopia and Whites who believed in imperialism and racial supremacy lent their support to Italy. The champions of Italy did not even mind the gassing of millions of innocent Ethiopians. The Crisis, in one of its editorials, called on African Americans to organize common action on behalf of Ethiopian people. It also associated the struggle of the Ethiopians with the universal struggle of the Black race for national freedom, economic, political and racial emancipation.[403] Dissatisfied with news reports in Ethiopia by White reporters, African Americans dispatched a Black war correspondent, J. A. Rogers.[404] In the Caribbean, thousands petitioned their governments to be allowed to fight for Ethiopia, but such requests were denied by Britain, the colonial ruler of most of the Caribbean countries. After the war many African

402. *The Voice of* Ethiopia, May 27, 1939.
403. *Crisis*, Vol. 42, No. 8, July 1935, p.214. Also see in Magubane, *op.cit.* p. 171.
404. Magubane, Bernard, *op.cit*, p. 171.

Americans and Afro-Caribbeans left for Ethiopia to assist in the reconstruction and development efforts of the country.[405] Melaku Bayean was instrumental in building bridges between African Americans and Ethiopians in the spirit of Pan-Africanism. He inspired African American technicians to help build modern Ethiopia in the spirit of Emperor Haile Selassie's nationalism.[406]

Meanwhile, millions of Ethiopians took to the jungles and mountains and resisted the Italian army. Hundreds of educated Ethiopians were targeted and wiped out, especially after the assassination attempt on the Italian viceroy, Gen. Rodolfo Graziani, on February 19, 1937. At the same time, Italians were busy sewing seeds of hatred and division among Ethiopians, according to the long-standing colonial adage of divide and rule. The country was divided ethnically and religiously, and animosity and suspicion were incited. In spite of all, Ethiopians resisted the Balkanization of the country and the Italians were finally ejected from Ethiopia in May 1941, after five years of occupation. Once again, as Daniel Thwaite stated, Ethiopia stood as "a granite monument, a living exponent and testimony of the innate puissance of the Black race... the impregnable rock of Black resistance against White invasion, a living incarnation of Africa's independence."[407] As Bernard Magubane also stated, if this attack on Ethiopia had succeeded, it "would have been the last nail in the coffin of Black humanity. It was an attack on the principle of national rights for the African peoples everywhere."[408]

Post World War II Ethiopia and Its Role in the Pan-African Movement

As mentioned earlier, Africans of the diaspora who resided in the West, especially in the US and the Caribbean, dominated the first three Pan-African congresses. They played a pivotal role in articulating racial equality and promoting the universal oneness of all Blacks, the mutuality of interests in the liberation of all Blacks, and the regaining of Black identity.[409] The visions of these

405. For Britain and the US banning of travel visas to African Americans applying to serve in Ethiopia during the Italian invasion of Ethiopia see Richard Pankhurst, "Ethiopia and the African Personality," *Ethiopia Observer*, III, 1959 and see Jerrold Robbins, "The Americans in Ethiopia," *The American Mercury*, XXIX, May, 1993 as quoted by William A. Shack, *op.cit.*.
406. See comments in *The Voice of Ethiopia*, June 3, 1939, p.2. It was reported that Emperor Haile Selassie stated that Ethiopia needed some Western technical advancement, but not Western civilization.
407. Thwaite, Daniel. *op.cit.*, p. 207. Also see in Magubane, *op.cit*, p. 165.
408. Magubane, Bernard, op.cit p. 168.

Pan-African congresses were not only gradually crystallized but also put to the test during the Italian-Ethiopian war. The solidarity and experience gained during the Second World War, especially for the Black fighters, intensified Black awareness and the demands for social equality and political independence in their respective countries.

The post World War II era witnessed the independence of African countries and the Caribbean, especially in the 1950s and 1960s. Ghana became the first African country to gain its independence, in 1957. In the US, where resistance against social justice for Blacks ran deep, civil rights movements were intensified quantitatively and qualitatively. Escalated mass mobilization and social pressure led the US government to correct some of the social, economic, and political injustices directed against its minority citizens, especially African Americans. In 1964, with the passage of the Civil Rights Act by the US Congress, drastic corrective measures were taken to redress social inequalities and injustices meted out to African Americans.

Demands for political independence and equal rights for all Blacks can be traced at least in part to Ethiopianism and the Pan-African movement. Churches, especially those named after Abyssinia, Ethiopia or Africa, have played important roles in the US, the Caribbean, and West, Central, and Southern Africa in raising Black consciousness and demanding social equality and political independence.

Beginning with the fourth Pan-African congress in Manchester (1945), Africans started playing major roles and there was an increased demand for the liberation of Africa. Jomo Kenyatta and Kwame Nkrumah, who soon returned home and led resistance movements and later became leaders of their countries, Kenya and Ghana respectively, were active participants in the Manchester Pan-African conference. The venue of Pan-African conferences also shifted from European to African cities. Immediately after the independence of Ghana, Nkrumah convened a meeting of independent African states in Accra from April 15 to 22, 1958. The Sixth and the Seventh Pan-African Congress also convened in Dar es-Salaam, Tanzania (1974) and in Uganda (1994), respectively.

Ethiopia once again started playing an important role in African politics and in the realization of the Pan-African dream. Along with seven other independent states — Egypt, Ghana, Liberia, Libya, Morocco, Sudan, and Tunisia,

409. Mezu, S. Okechukwu. *The Philosophy of Pan-Africanism.* Washington, D.C.: Georgetown University Press, 1965.

Ethiopia formally convened a Pan-African conference in Accra in 1958. At the sixteenth United Nations General Assembly in 1962, Ethiopia introduced the idea of an organization of African states. The following year Ethiopia's Emperor Haile Selassie made history by hosting 32 heads of African states that gave birth to the Organization of African Unity (OAU).[410]

That summit of leaders of African countries experienced some snags because of philosophical as well as political differences. There were those (like Kwame Nkrumah of Ghana) who advocated the immediate political unity of all independent African countries, and others who argued that economic integration should precede political integration. Nkrumah was influenced during his university years in the US by Pan-Africanists such as Garvey, who advocated the total unity of Africa. The divisions between independent African countries were sharp. The political division between the Casablanca, Brazzaville, and Monrovia groups threatened the unity of Africa and the Pan-African dream. The political division also threatened the core of the Ethiopian movement which was the unity of Africa and Africans.

Eventually, Ethiopia succeeded in convening the first continental organization in Africa, averting the divisional crisis. The Emperor's efforts and the respect he commanded among the leaders were instrumental in the birth of the OAU in May 1963. The OAU was seen, after a long process, as the culmination of the Pan-African movement as envisioned and desired by the early proponents: Henry Sylvester Williams' "Pan Africa," Marcus Garvey's "Africa for the Africans," and the goal of William Burghardt Du Bois' advocacy of Africa's total independence.

The Prospect of Ethiopianism and Current Conditions of Ethiopia

After the 1920s, Ethiopian churches declined and members left for other churches — some joined the Zionists and Pentecostal churches that are opposed to political activity, and concentrated on faith healing and religious ecstasy. They also preached loyalty to the state and shunned any political involvement.[411]

---

410. Legum, Colin. *Pan-Africanism: A Short Political Guide.* New York: Frederick A. Praeger, 1962. Also see Richard Cox, *Pan Africanism in Practice.* London and New York: Oxford University Press, 1964.
411. Fredrickson, George, pp. 88-92.

After the October 1917 revolution in Russia, the advent of socialism not only negated religion but also supplanted Ethiopianism by advocating the unity of the proletarians of the world through Communist internationalism.

Marxism gave its followers utopian promises and messages of salvation for the working and marginalized group in the class struggle between the proletariat and the bourgeoisie. While opposed to religion, "the opiate of the masses," it came up with a religious coloration in its own right.

In Africa a home-grown version of socialism tried to articulate the political philosophies of certain African leaders but failed to gain roots beyond their political confines. The African Socialism of Julius K. Nyerere, the Humanism of Kenneth D. Kaunda, and the Negritude of Leopold Sedar Senghor picked up the struggle and articulation when Ethiopianism faded away. Such philosophies of cultural self-determination and identity definition lasted as long as the individual leader was in power.

Although most of modern-day Africa has not yet produced political giants who are vibrant and widely respected, the demise of apartheid and the emergence of Nelson Mandela are remarkable developments. Nelson Mandela's philosophy of forgiveness, political accommodation, and the unity of all South Africans in order to build a nation are inspirational for all other African countries. While some African leaders, shunning the philosophy of Pan-Africanism, engineer religious and ethnic conflicts and advance ethnocentric politics, they are urged to draw a lesson from Mandela's accommodation policy and the early leaders of the Pan-African movement. Again, African leaders should be urged to promote the culture of peace, tolerance, political accommodation, while avidly protecting the interests of their peoples.

The current problems facing the African continent (the core of the Pan-African movement) are indeed perplexing and serious. Africa has gained its political independence. Yet, there is a serious hurdle to overcome. The satisfactory fulfillment of basic human needs: shelter, food, health, and a decent life for its citizens; the guaranteeing of democratic and basic human rights; the development, effective utilization, and retention of its human resources,[412] the

412. The retention of developed African human resources in the continent is a problem. Unless Africa retains its brainpower by providing economic and political security for its citizens, the Pan-African dream will hardly be realized. For the theoretical argument and empirical study regarding this issue, please see Getachew Metaferia and Maigenet Shifferraw. *The Ethiopian Revolution of 1974 and the Exodus of Ethiopia's Trained Human Resources*. Lewiston, New York: The Edwin Mellen Press, 1991.

meaningful cooperation and symbiotic economic relations among all African countries, as envisioned in the OAU's Lagos Plan of Action,[413] and the assurance of sustainable economic development will be some of the issues to be grappled with in the 21st century. The post-independence optimism of African countries of the 1960s has not lasted long. Africa, beginning in the 1970s, experienced an economic downward spiral and was quickly marginalized in the global political economy.

While this marginalization has its genesis in both endogenous and exogenous forces which are outside of its control,[414] the question of the 21st century will be how these impediments to development can be overcome, self confidence regained, and sustainable development, equality and human rights for all citizens guaranteed.

Meanwhile, the association of Ethiopia with Black independence, the generic concept of Ethiopianism in reference to the Black race, and the Pan-African concept that transcends political boundaries seem to have eroded. First, the political and economic crises in Ethiopia as manifested in the civil wars and the subsequent draught and hunger (1973–74, 1984–85, 1987–88) that claimed the lives of thousands have gravely affected Ethiopia's image internationally. A country that development experts hoped would be a bread basket for the region ended up a basket case because of political conditions and environmental degradation. The successive famines (politicized by the Ethiopian government) and neglect by some aid donors (especially the US under President Reagan) jeopardized the lives of millions.[415] Ethiopia or Ethiopianism, as a Pan-African concept relating to the Black race, has lost its relevance.

Second, African Americans have shifted their international appeal for Black brotherhood/sisterhood to national struggles, domestic politics, and parochial interests. Political and economic empowerment has become the driving force for most African Americans in the post Pan-African movement. Furthermore, because of the conservative shift in the US political institutions beginning the 1980s, African Americans are preoccupied in protecting some of

---

413. OAU, *The Lagos Plan of Action For the Economic Development of Africa 1980 -2000*, Geneva: ILO, 1981. This is Africa's economic blue print set for the continent's integrated economic plan by the OAU until the year 2000.
414. Getachew Metaferia. "The Politics of Hunger and Poverty in Africa." Occasional Papers series, Vol. 1., Nos. 1-4. Washington, D.C.: The Institute for Afro-American Scholarship, 1990.
415. Varnis, Steven L. *Reluctant Aid or Aiding the Reluctant?* New Brunswick, New Jersey: Transition Publishers, 1990.

the civil rights legislation and constitutional guarantees that have been gained since the 1960s. Hence, Pan-Africanism has lost its appeal for many African Americans. The zeal, however, is still alive within the Rastafarians, where it has taken a semi-religious bent. In the US, Pan-Africanism has gained new followers in a few African American academic circles in a form of Afrocentrism or Afrocentric education.[416] Some public schools in the District of Columbia also started offering Afrocentric education in 1994 (Webb Elementary School and Joel Elias Spingarn Senior High School) in an effort to "shift the focus from Europe to Africa as the cradle of culture and learning."[417] This is a belief, in the tradition of Pan-Africanism, in the pivotal role Africa has played in all human endeavors despite the attempt by some scholars to diminish its contributions or to question Afrocentric education in general.[418] Such an outlook is a manifestation of intolerance for multiculturalism in a mosaic society and a refusal to acknowledge the various contributions of Africa to humanity in general.

During the 30th year celebration (June, 1993) of the March on Washington by the late Reverend Martin Luther King, Jr., organizers of the march hoisted a trio of the US, Ethiopian, and African American flags in one. This indicates that the Pan-African movement and the role Ethiopia played in the movement are still remembered by some.

Meanwhile Ethiopia, the focus of the Pan-African movement, is undergoing some changes itself:

First, the government in Ethiopia that assumed power in 1991, after the overthrow of the military regime of Mengistu Haile Mariam, seems to downplay Ethiopia's past history. It speaks as if Ethiopia's history does not span more than a century. This is a classic example of leaders who try to rewrite history to fit in their own agenda and interest.

Second, the government is ethnocentric in its domestic policies, has gerrymandered administrative boundaries based on ethnicity (similar to what the Italians did during their occupation of Ethiopia), and pitted one ethnic group against the other. This represents an intent to destroy the Ethiopian identity, built over centuries, as it would not serve the interests of the current leaders of Ethiopia and Eritrea.

---

416. According to Asante, Afrocentric theory is "a reconnection in our minds, of Egypt to Africa." See in Molefi K. Asante, *op.cit.*, p. ix.
417. *The Washington Post*, February 21, 1995, B6.
418. For a criticism of Afrocentric education see Arthur M. Schelesinger, Jr., *The Disuniting of America*. New York: W.W. Norton & Company.

Third, it has encouraged, for example, without a public debate and a clear mandate from the Oromo ethnic group, the substitution of the Ethiopic alphabet by the Roman. This indicates that the government has failed to recognize Ethiopia's achievement in developing its own script over the centuries. This is another contribution of Africa to the world. First language literacy is important and must be encouraged, as it is a democratic right. But the substitution of Roman for Ethiopic alphabet should have been submitted to the public for discussion and debate, as this will have a wider ramification for the Oromo people.

Finally, during the 1992 regional election, candidates who ran for regional offices as Ethiopians were discouraged unless they ran as ethnics and carried an identification card bearing their ethnic backgrounds. This, unfortunately, is a reversal and a negation of the Pan-African movement that started more than a century ago. From all indications, the current government in Ethiopia, under the Ethiopian People's Revolutionary Democratic Front (EPRDF), dominated by a minority ethnic group, seems to have an aversion to the long history of Ethiopia and is devoid of transparency and democratic governance. It is riddled with corruption and crony capitalism. The Tigray People's Liberation Front (TPLF), the core of EPRDF, controls the economy and all institutions of the country. The government lacks grassroots support because of its grave shortcomings. It has pitted one ethnic group against another in the fashion of the Italian divide and rule policy that it tried to implement in Ethiopia. This, we hope, is an aberration and will be short lived. A significant number of Ethiopians appear to be opposed to the ethnicization and fragmentation of the country along ethnic lines. The situation is far removed from the coalition and consensus building period of Menelik — the hero of Adwa. Hence, Ethiopia is presently at a political crossroads and its long history is put to a test. The introduction of ethnic or "tribal" politics is a dangerous trend for Africa. The future for Africa, in the post Pan-African era, depends on how wisely it pulls together and utilizes its resources in order to satisfy the basic needs of its citizens. If the rulers are not visionary and statesmen, they are bound to put Africa on a dangerous course.

Chapter 6. British Reactions to the Battle of Adwa: As Illustrated by The Times of London for 1896

Richard Pankhurst, Ph.D.
Founding Director, Institute of Ethiopian Studies
Addis Ababa University, Ethiopia

The British attitude to Italian imperialist aims before and after the Battle of Adwa may be illustrated from the pages of The Times newspaper, which then, as so often, reflected official British thinking — and of course helped to form it. The object of the present chapter is to examine how the events of the time were presented and interpreted in that august newspaper. All quotations in this chapter are from pre- and post-Adwa editions of The Times of London.

European Thinking Prior to the Battle

By the last days of February 1895, it was apparent to The Times and its readers that the Italians were advancing militarily into northern Ethiopia and that Italy's colonial ambitions might be opposed by the French, who, according to some accounts, were siding with Ethiopia. Towards the end of the month the newspaper had published a revealing report from its Rome correspondent. This asserted that the Italian Government was aware of "a secret treaty" between France and Ethiopia, in which the French agreed to support the Ethiopian ruler, Emperor Menelik, in order to disaccommodate Italy.

This assertion provoked considerable irritation on the part of the French. The *Paris Temps* immediately denied what it called this "extraordinary" report, while a dispatch from The Times Paris correspondent indicated that colonially-minded sections of French public opinion, though opposed to Italy as a rival colonial power, were unwilling to side with the invaded country because it was situated on the African Continent. The Paris correspondent declared:

> No one here — with the sole possible exception of one or two dimwitted persons or a few habitually malevolent minds — wishes for the success of the Abyssinians at the price of the discomfiture of a civilized nation, from which it is quite possible to differ in aims and opinions without cherishing any ill-will when that nation is face to face with a brave but barbarous foe.

Despite these words, the Paris correspondent admitted that there was a tendency in French circles to be "rather kindly disposed" toward "the presence of serious difficulties for Italy in Africa." He was, however, confident that the "somewhat bitter complaints" about French sympathy for Menelik, as expressed by Italian politicians, would "induce no revival" of French hostility against Italy.

Reactions to the Battle

It was in such an historical context that news broke of the Battle of Adwa, and of the unexpected Italian debacle. Report of these events did not appear in the British press until five days later. When the news finally appeared, on March 6, it came as a great surprise, which was the more remarkable in that it coincided with a report that the Government of Francesco Crispi had collapsed and that Italy was embroiled in a major, and seemingly intractable, political crisis. The news story thus had a double bill: an unexpected military disaster for a European power in far-off Africa, and political turmoil in a much nearer and hence better known European capital: Rome.

News of the Ethiopian victory changed British thinking on that country almost overnight. The Times, which, as we have seen, had only a few days earlier referred to the Ethiopians as a "barbarous foe," chided the Italian commander General Oreste Baratieri, on March 8, for imagining that he was confronted with "undisciplined and ill-armed savages." The paper declared that the Ethiopians were "a civilized power both in the way they made war and in the way they conducted their diplomacy."

The Times was, however, at first mainly preoccupied with the political crisis in Italy. Discussing the Italian situation, it observed, on March 6:

> Though the Crispi Government cannot be held directly responsible for the Italian defeat..., it was certain that General Baratieri's blunder would bring about its overthrow... Signor Crispi's action appears to have the approval of moderate men...

> but the extreme Left, enraged by the curtailment of its opportunities for vituperation, has not been able to control its temper either within the Chamber or outside.
>
> The sitting seems to have closed in hopeless confusion, while Radical Deputies placed themselves at the head of excited mobs, marching through the streets with loud cries for the impeachment of the fallen Ministers. It is, happily, difficult for human nature to remain long at fever heat. The very violence of these demonstrations tends to shorten their duration, so that after a certain amount of shouting, gesticulating and anathematizing, we may expect the Piazza Colonna to regain its wonted calm and the people to regain the rational consideration of events.

Reporting that the Marquis di Rudini, a contemporary Italian leader, had set up what was to prove a merely interim administration, the newspaper alluded to other Italian problems and declared:

> While the excitement in Rome arises naturally out of the profound chagrin with which a sensitive people receives the news of a great calamity, there are threats of disturbance in other parts of Italy which are of a more disquieting character. In Sicily there is chronic disaffection, which, it will be remembered, was not long ago suppressed or driven under by Signor Crispi. His fall in circumstances so deplorable will undoubtedly prove a great encouragement to all the disorderly factions... It must therefore be hoped by all friends of Italy that, whether under the Marquis di Rudini or another, a Government may be promptly formed capable of steadily maintaining the authority of the law.

Despite the supposed hopes of such "friends of Italy," riots were reported from Rome, Naples, Milan and the other principal cities, and a telegram even reached London reporting Crispi's assassination.

On the following day, March 7, it was, however, learnt that the assassination report was unfounded. A Times editorial commenting on this happily declared: "the good name of the Italian people has not been dishonored in its hour of trial by the crime of a maddened mob." The same article went on to observe that what it termed "the Italians of to-day" were "the descendants and the heirs of the people whose Senate thanked an erring and defeated General after the crushing disaster of Cannae because he had not despaired of the Republic." The newspaper added that it would "not permit" itself "to discuss the possibility that the [Savoyan] dynasty may be threatened," as "a revolution in Italy would be unspeakably calamitous to the country itself and would menace the tranquility of the whole of Europe." Such arguments, it is interesting to recall, were to be voiced again in Britain almost half a century later when it was argued that action by the League of Nations might bring Mussolini's invasion of Ethiopia in 1935 to a halt and thereby threaten the Italian monarchy, which had close friends in London and several other European capitals.

The Times, thinking in 1896 in similar terms, advised the Italian people not to display "ingratitude" to King Umberto, whose father, it recalled, had "played so noble a part in winning and consolidating Italian unity and freedom" — a reference to the Risorgimento, or earlier struggle for Italian unification. Turning more specifically to Italo-Ethiopian relations, the paper most revealingly advised a policy of caution and compromise as best calculated to serve Italian interests in Africa. Elaborating on the paper's point of view, the article argued:

> What is to be deprecated in the interests of Italy is the hasty and inconsiderate adoption of a policy of extremes. Some of her counselors support the present outcry of the populace for an immediate and unconditional retirement from Abyssinia. Others exhort her at all costs to wipe out what is represented as a stain upon her honor by renewing her military and financial efforts on a greater scale than ever. Both courses, in our opinion, are equally unwise. A complete and precipitate withdrawal would be surely and speedily repented, and the responsibility for it would be urged against the King's Government at no distant date by those whose interest it is to create trouble. On the other hand, it is absurd to say that the honor of Italy can only be secured by undertaking the conquest of Abyssinia — a task which would not be hopefully attempted in the existing state of public opinion. Her [Italy's] true policy would appear to be that of withdrawing from the mountain region where General Baratieri met his ruin, as well as from Kassala, where she is threatened by the Dervishes, and holding Massawa with the dominating positions in the neighborhood, as a pied-à-terre from which to watch events. Thus the present might be made safe while the future would not be compromised.

However "natural" the Italian impulse "to pour in men and munitions" to avenge the Adwa defeat, the political horizon was "not so clear," The Times added a few days later, that Italy could "afford to entangle herself in adventures which there is no hope of carrying to a successful issue except by means of exhausting expenditure and persevering effort." Meanwhile the Parliamentary crisis dragged on in Italy, and fuller news of the debacle of Adwa began pouring in. On March 9, The Times had much to say on both subjects. Discussing the battle, detailed news of which had at last reached England, the newspaper went to considerable length to point out Baratieri's tactical errors. Continuing its pro-Italian stance, it repeatedly referred to the Ethiopian army as "the enemy," and "the Showans" — though all the principal Ethiopian provinces had in fact been included in Menelik's armies at Adwa.

The Times' account of the engagement, and of the Italian debacle, illustrates the essentially pro-Italian stance of the newspaper and indeed that of the British establishment in general. The report reads as follows:

> The latest accounts place the Italian loss in the battle.... at a figure so high that we cannot but hope there is a serious mistake somewhere. It is estimated at no less than 7,000 White and 2,000 native troops, though what proportion of the missing

are killed and how many are prisoners it is at present impossible to say. As the total number of troops engaged in the attack is given as 15,000 and cannot have been very easily in excess of that number, the disaster has clearly been one of quite exceptional magnitude. One-half the forces, and, if the figures are correct, much more than one-half, seem to have disappeared. Italians will find a melancholy consolation in the fact that their troops fought with desperate gallantry. One division seems to have been practically destroyed where it stood, after inflicting enormous loss upon the enemy. It was probably owing to the severity of their punishment that the Showans abstained in a manner otherwise unaccountable from a pursuit which might have rendered the catastrophe even more appalling. They have evidently now followed up their victory, for Adigrat is invested, and the position of its garrison renders the whole situation infinitely more difficult to deal with. Adigrat is not upon the direct line of retreat, and General Baratieri seems to have been too hard pressed either to turn aside and avoid leaving the road to Asmara open to the Abyssinians, or even to give the garrison timely notice of its impending isolation. With 600 sick in hospital its movements were seriously hampered, and the enemy seems to have been within a few kilometers before the commander was aware of his danger. From the tone of his message it may be doubted whether he is even now acquainted with the full extent of his disaster, for he speaks cheerfully of having a month's provisions. So far as can be judged at the present there is little chance of relief reaching Adigrat within a month in face of what is plainly a forward movement on the part of the Abyssinians.

While the Italian troops displayed splendid valor, their generals seem to have set at defiance all the elementary rules of warfare, and especially of mountain warfare. The Showan army was posted upon an elevated plateau to the number, it is said, of 80,000 men. General Baratieri must have had abundant opportunities of learning of their equipment and the use they could make of it, consequently he can hardly have imagined that he was dealing with undisciplined and ill-armed savages. Yet he behaved as if nothing were in front of him but a rabble which would melt away on contact with disciplined troops. He attacked that plateau with three divisions, marching through three valleys or ravines, and therefore completely isolated and incapable of mutual support. He neglected the elementary rule never to engage your forces in a defile without occupying the hills that command it. The rocky heights that effectively separated his columns were taken possession of by the Showans with the utmost facility, because they practically entered on the level. They could therefore flank each of General Baratieri's divisions, which struggling in the narrow passes, had no room for the evolutions required to offer even such defense as was possible against such odds. To attack such an enemy at all on the front was a serious blunder, but to attack in that particular manner shows an almost incredible disregard of the rudimentary principles of military science. The motives which impelled General Baratieri to push forward regardless of the danger to which he exposed the reinforcements he knew to be on the way, and to make his ill-judged attack without awaiting their arrival, almost baffle conjecture. It would, however, be well to await further details before attributing his impatience purely to personal motives. Italy is not the only Power which on political or religious pretexts interests herself in Abyssinia, and it is just conceivable that there were political motives for pressing the unfortunate General to score some success if possible, even at the serious risk of failure.

Turning from military events in Africa to the political situation in Italy, the paper announced that Signor Saracco, one of the Italian political figures of the day, had failed in his efforts to form a cabinet, and continued:

> On the immediate question of the policy to be pursued in Abyssinia, the Cabinet will have to come to a decision which, whatever its nature, will arouse opposition from one side or another. Each of the three possible policies has its advocates. With a large section of the nation the whole Abyssinian enterprise is unpopular, and nothing short of complete abandonment would satisfy some critics. On the other hand, the feelings of a high-spirited people are profoundly stirred by the crushing reverse at Adwa, which too many will seem to call for the most determined efforts to regain the position that has been lost. Between these two is the middle course which we have ventured to urge upon the Italian Government, that of rigorous concentration within an area capable of being defended without excessive effort.

Elaborating on this proposal, which reflected the official British attitude at this critical juncture of affairs, the editorial concluded: "Italy need not abandon any of her claims or renounce any project that careful consideration may show to be feasible. But in the meantime a defensive and waiting policy seems to be clearly indicated alike by military and political motives." The Times, once again expressing the official British attitude, also expressed deep regret that a European army had been decisively defeated by a "native" force.

The paper now emphasized the difference between the Ethiopians and other inhabitants of Africa, then also confronted with imperialist pressure. They should, the paper urged, not be confused with "savage tribes incapable of making a stand against a regular European attack." Discussing the outcome of the military campaign in East Africa, the newspaper added: "It was true that, in some respects, the military disaster seems to be less crushing than was supposed. The Abyssinian generals do not appear to have followed up their victory with the vigor enjoined by all the masters of the art of war. Hence the actual destruction of the Italian forces is less complete than it might easily have been and has been assumed to be." Moreover, considerable numbers of stragglers were turning up at Italian headquarters. The newspaper commented:

> Unfortunately this is about the only gleam of consolation that can be found in the story of a most disastrous enterprise. Though the men remain, the army has sustained a deadly blow. Such a reverse, accompanied by heavy loss of artillery, cannot but prove demoralizing to any force and especially to one largely composed of native levies. The more we learn about the matter, the more serious does it become from this point of view.

All this merely served to strengthen the newspaper's thesis that it would be "unwise" for Italy to attempt a policy of immediate revenge. The article added:

"Were the Showan army to make an energetic forward movement, it would be difficult to assign limits to the embarrassments of the Italian Government." Actually, as we know, Menelik rightly or wrongly — this point was later to be much debated — stopped his advance at the Ethio-Italian frontier existing at the time. This was the border which Ras Makonnen had signed in Rome on October 1, 1889, in the Additional Convention to the Treaty of Wuchalé, of May 2 of the same year. This subsequent Convention line was based on trickery in that the Italians had advanced their frontier beyond the position they occupied when the Treaty of Wuchalé was originally signed.

The attitude of The Times was thus one of friendship for the aggressor, qualified only by a criticism of Italian tactical mistakes. The newspaper thus declared that the Italians had "to do more than merely reconsider the plan of operation followed, under considerable pressure from home, by General Baratieri." They had also, the paper declared, "to revise their whole policy towards Abyssinia," and if "on mature consideration" they thought it "necessary to attempt the conquest of the country, they must make up their minds to efforts very much greater and more exhausting than they have hitherto contemplated." Elaborating on this train of thought, from an essentially European perspective, the editorial concluded:

> It is felt at this moment, in every European capital, that the position in Italy is critical, and her action is watched, if with varying sympathies, at all events with unvarying closeness of attention. A mere African expedition against nomad tribes would not affect her general position or call forth all this anxiety. It is seen that she is involved in an enterprise of a totally different kind, which, if persevered in, cannot but profoundly affect all her European relations. Her allies of the Triple Alliance are exhibiting the most unmistakable symptoms of concern.

Turning to the specifically British attitude to Italian colonial ambitions in Africa, the newspaper was brutally frank:

> The sympathies of this country cannot be thought doubtful for an instant. Englishmen have a sincere and enduring friendship for Italy, while English policy regards her as an essential and most valuable factor in the political equilibrium of Europe. Her aims in Abyssinia we in this country regard without the faintest tinge of jealousy, while her general well-being, political and financial is earnestly desired.

The fact that The Times had admitted that Ethiopia was a "civilized power," both in her methods of warfare and in her diplomacy, renders cynical the sympathy the paper accorded to Italy in its unprovoked aggression as well as the assertion that the latter country "need not abandon her claims" but should bide her time to strike again at Ethiopia at some favorable opportunity. Italy's claim to govern Ethiopia was entirely without foundation, being based, it will be recalled, on a discreditable trick — the inclusion in the Italian version of the Treaty of Wuchalé of words which did not appear in the Ethiopian version.

British sympathy for Italian aggression had, in fact, three motives: (1) hope that Italian expansion would prevent the French from obtaining influence in part of Africa; (2) desire to win Italian support in the Mediterranean; and (3) fear lest the defeat of a European power by an African nation would create unrest in British colonies. When order was at last established in Italy, The Times of March 11 devoted a leader to the situation. This article expressed its thankfulness that the Italian Government appeared to have adopted the "moderate" course of action the paper had itself been recommending, and declared:

> After the first outburst of national grief and disappointment men [in Italy] are settling down to calm and earnest consideration of the condition of affairs... Popular demonstrations against the dispatch of reinforcements to Massawa have given place to a general conviction that, whatever decision may be ultimately arrived at as to Italian policy, it is indispensable that General Blandisher [the new Italian commander in Eritrea] should receive all the support he may deem necessary... Those responsible, whether immediately or proximately, for the disaster at Adwa, will undoubtedly be called to account in good time. But for the moment the more pressing duty is to effect the relief of the garrisons at Adigrat and Kassala, and to offer the Negus [i.e. Menelik] a front sufficiently formidable to make Italy once more mistress of her actions in Erythrea.

The article then continued:

> The fact must be faced, although it is nowhere more sincerely deplored than in England, that events in Abyssinia constitute a grave embarrassment for Italy, no matter in what way they may be dealt with... Italy is most unfortunately involved in a difficulty which cannot be immediately shaken off by anything she can do; and to that extent she is hampered in any other enterprise she may desire to pursue.

The paper repeatedly deplored Italy's seriously weakened position resulting from Adwa, but recognized that there was little that could be done about it, at least in the short term.

A Close Watch on the Russians

The essentially sympathetic interest shown by The Times in Italy's expansionistic activities in Ethiopia led the newspaper to keep a close watch on events in the country throughout the months after Adwa. The St. Petersburg Correspondent, for example, reported in April that some 12,000 rubles had been collected in Russia for an "Abyssinian fund," but that the Italian authorities were obstructing a Russian Red Cross mission to Ethiopia which had been dispatched at a cost of 130,000 rubles. "The consequence," the paper explained, was that "the [Russian] nursing sisters, with part of their baggage, have been ordered back to Russia, and the rest of the party are obliged to make a much longer and very difficult journey though desert country with no prospect of arriving at Menelik's camp before the rainy season... These painful details have been officially announced at a special meeting of the Red Cross Society."

Russia, we may note, was in fact the only European power to champion Ethiopia at the time of Adwa. The Tsars, who saw the Ethiopians as fellow Orthodox Christians, had no colonial ambitions in Africa and were, moreover, anxious to discomfort the Italians, who were then the allies of the Germans and Austrians, who constituted a rival European power group. Later in the month of April, The Times reported the dispatch of a Russian scientific mission to Ethiopia led by M. Dimitroff, which was closely followed by General Svedoff, together with "several military officers" and a priest.

The newspaper, which watched such developments with disapproval, thereupon published a strong editorial attacking and ridiculing the Russian activity. The article commented sneeringly that the Russian Red Cross chaplain had brought with him "20,000 small crosses of the Orthodox pattern," complained that the officers were seeking "to stir the troubled waters for sinister reasons," and warned the statesmen of the French Republic that "the Imperialism of the Tsar might be more dangerous to their Red Sea colony [Obock, later Djibouti] than that of their Italian neighbors." The paper declared:

> The sudden development of Russian interest in the Abyssinians is a subject for the curiosity of Europe... Russia, it is true, is not more noted in the annals of philanthropy for any unusual eagerness to succor than for zeal in ministering to their spiritual necessities. As a rule her works of mercy, both corporal and spiritual, are rigidly restricted to members of the Slav race. But as she has manifested lately an unexpected concern for the religious welfare of the subjects of King Menelik, it is quite natural that she should likewise display an exceptional solicitude for his wounded soldiers.... Russian military officers have proved most effective missionaries before now, and perhaps the Abyssinians may hearken to them for the present.... Several of the Balkan States have enjoyed in an unexpected fashion, the beneficence of the Tsar. Servia wanted money. Montenegro wanted rifles, and the ruler of Bulgaria had cravings to be recognized by the Powers....
>
> The Russian adventure in the domains of King Menelik seems rather worthy of Count Ignatieff (the leader of Russia's "military party" advocating the manifest destiny of Holy Russia and general Slav expansion)... It is not, perhaps, very likely to succeed, but if it does succeed nobody will have more cause to regret its success than France. The Republic will find the Tsar a much more unpleasant neighbor to Obock than the Italians.

THE ITALIAN GREEN BOOK

The Times' interest in Ethiopia, and in the Battle of Adwa, came to the fore again in May when the paper gave publicity to the publication in Rome of an Italian Government Green Book on the campaign. Though the volume had been devised by the Italians, according to the paper, to blame their debacle on lack of support from Britain, the document was important, the paper showed, in that it also contained interesting diplomatic revelations. It revealed in particular that the British Government had agreed, on the eve of the battle, to allow the Italian army to land at the British Somaliland port of Zeila and pass through British Somali territory for the express purpose of diverting Ethiopian forces from the northern front in order to defend Harar.

The Times strongly criticized the publication of the Green Book on the grounds that it was calculated to stir up anti-British feeling in Italy and was arranged to bring into "undue prominence" the points of difference between the two powers, so that "the substantial agreement on essentials was in no small danger of being ignored." On the specific project of an Italian campaign against Harar, the paper commented:

> The point of most interest to ourselves in the document is the account they give of the negotiations opened up by Italy in respect of Zeila. The Italians, at one period of the campaign, believed that by landing troops at that port and marching them in the direction of Harar, they could distract the attention of the Abyssinians and divert their forces from the theater of operations further north. General Ferrero, the Italian Ambassador in this country, was instructed to ask our permission for the landing of the troops. The British were quite willing and even anxious to give the Italians any aid they rightly could give them, but the objection to the proposal was obvious. It was that the column operating from Zeila might be driven back upon Somaliland. Were we to endanger a British possession from a desire to assist a friendly people?

Moreover, The Times noted, there was a further diplomatic obstacle — the opposition of France. Explaining this, the paper continued:

> France regarded the project with intense jealousy, and we were naturally reluctant to give her any just grounds of offence, either of a general kind or arising from our agreement with her in regard to Harar itself. These topics were discussed with the freedom usual in diplomatic conversations of a confidential nature between Lord Salisbury and General Ferrero, in London, and between Sir Clare Ford and Baron Blanc, in Rome... The project was well received, and in January of the present year [i.e. 1896] Lord Salisbury assented to the passage of the Italian troops through Zeila while making reservations to spare any just susceptibilities on the part of France. At various points in the negotiation of this extremely difficult and complex affair, our Government were not able at once to accept the view of the Italians, and on one occasion especially Baron Blanc, in conversation with the British Ambassa-

> dor, in Rome, signified his annoyance in very plain terms. Exaggerated language was employed, and in possible contingencies action was spoken of which, doubtless, it was never intended to carry out. These conversations have been published in the Green Book, and it is difficult to suppose that they can have been published with any object but one. That object certainly was not to inform the Italian people as to what the relations between Great Britain and Italy really were at the close of the Crispi Administration.

Those relations," the paper concluded, "were always friendly, as they are friendly now. They depend on interests too deep and solid to be affected by petty questions in remote parts of Africa. Our friendship rests upon our common interests and our common objects in the Mediterranean, and while those remain it can never be shaken."

The above passage is revealing. It sums up the basic late nineteenth century British attitude to Italy. It was this attitude which dominated the position of the British Government, and of The Times, in relation to the Battle of Adwa and its aftermath.

Chapter 7. Racist Discourse about Ethiopia and Ethiopians before and after the Battle of Adwa

Harold G. Marcus Ph.D.
Distinguished Professor of History
Michigan State University

The Ethiopians' victory at Adwa was a strategic success that permitted Menelik (r. 1889-1913) to reconstruct and enlarge the old Solomonian state. For the Black diaspora, the shining Ethiopian triumph signified present dignity and future possibilities. For Europe, the Italian disaster was a surprise which caused Westerners to reconsider their notions about Ethiopia. European discourse about Africa was characteristically racist, ethnocentric, and ignorant.[419] Concerning Ethiopia, there were, however, elements of an alternate discourse[420] that stemmed from the long-standing mythology in Europe about Prester John; from the existence in the Ethiopian highlands of an ancient Christianity; and from travelers' reports of a prosperous and salubrious land.[421]

---

419. The essay's theme has also been discussed in the author's article "The Black Men Who Turned White: European Attitudes Towards Ethiopians, 1850-1900," *Archiv Orientale* 39 (1971): 155-166.
420. Not to be confused with a counter discourse, described by Richard Terdiman as one created by the oppressed to oppose the dominant or hegemonic discourse. See Richard Terdiman, *Discourse/Counter Discourse: The Theory and Practice of Symbolic Resistance in Nineteenth-Century France* (London, 1985), p. 65.
421. J.H. Arrowsmith-Brown, trans. and ed., and Richard Pankhurst, annot., Prutky's *Travels in Ethiopia and Other Countries* (London, 1991), chapters 15-32; C.F. Beckingham and G.W.B. Huntingford, eds., *The Prester John of the Indies*, Vols. I, II (London, 1961); Harold G. Marcus, *A History of Ethiopia* (Berkeley and London, 1994), p. 14. For a controversial analysis, see John Sorenson, *Imagining Ethiopia* (New Brunswick, 1993), pp. 21-27.

In the mid-nineteenth century, for example, Cornwallis Harris commented on "the green and lovely highlands of Abyssinia" (actually, Showa), with its "rich and thriving cultivation." He admired each "fertile knoll...with its peaceful hamlet" and "each rural vale...traversed by its crystal brook." He esteemed the teaming herds and flocks, the mountain breezes "redolent of eglantine and jasmine," and the fields emitting "the aromatic fragrance of mint and thyme [and] spangled with clover, daisies, and buttercups." Birds, of course, "warbled among the leafy groves, and throughout the rich landscape reigned an air of peace and plenty," which Harris attributed to the leadership of King Sahle Selassie (r. 1813-1847).

The Negus, the Englishman wrote, also sought to return Christian rule to areas south of Showa that had been separated from the Solomonian Empire in the 16th and 17th centuries. Yet, Harris editorialized that the King's expansionism was motivated by "revenge...and the insatiable love of plunder inherent in the breast of every savage." His regal brutishness was matched by his subjects, who evinced a "spirit of merciless destruction" towards their enemies, since to die while on campaign against "the accursed Gentile" ensured "a high reward in heaven." Harris found it barbaric that priestly absolution before battle led to "ruthless slaughter [and] savage atrocity... [in] the name of the Most High."[422] He had probably not heard of the Prussian battle cry, "Gott mit Uns!" and other such slogans, nor of the practice of chaplains accompanying European and American armies to offer soldiers religious solace and justification before battle.

The European alternate discourse appears in the writings of Charles E.X. Rochet d'Héricourt. He understood Ethiopian Christianity as a sophisticated, flourishing religion that had cooperated with the state to organize a complex society and to sustain Ethiopian nationalism. He regarded its ideology and its support as necessary contributing factors in the inevitable modernization of Ethiopia. As d'Hericourt put it: "In religion lies the surest point of contact which we have with the Abyssinians; it will once again join Abyssinia to the general civilization of the world."[423] Not so certain was the German Hermann Steudner, who believed that achievement stemmed from proper education, discipline, cleanliness, industriousness, frugality, and the like. Since Ethiopian Christians did not behave like good Lutherans, he questioned the teachings and the the-

422. W. Cornwallis Harris, *The Highlands of Ethiopia*, 2nd ed. (London, 1844), Vol. I, pp. 352, 354, 400; Vol. I I, p. 182; Vol. 111, pp. 369-370.

423. Rochet d'Hericourt, "Les Moeurs religieuses dans le royaume de Choa," *Bulletin de la Société de Géographie* 3e s., 4 (1845): 3290.

ology of the Orthodox Church.[424] Gerhard Rohlfs, another German, had such a thoroughgoing disregard for Ethiopian Christianity that he described the church and its clergy as "inhospitable, greedy, rude, and filthy."[425]

The Austrian Werner Munzinger, an agent of Egyptian imperialism in Ethiopia, also disliked Ethiopian Christians, doubtless because they resisted their country's dismemberment. He rationalized Ethiopian Orthodoxy as a form of African fetishism, more formalistic than ideological, and thus could argue that Islam was more adaptable to modernity.[426] As another German explained, "dogma alone does not make a people civilized," and then cited the ingestion of raw meat as evidence of Ethiopian barbarism.[427] One wonders if eating steak tartar (generally made from horse meat) made the French less Christian and civilized. God alone knew the deleterious effects wrought on the culture of North Sea Germans through devouring a local specialty made of raw chopped beef and herring! Finally, in 1874, an Austrian wrote that the Ethiopians liked the Maria Theresa dollar (thaler) because "The image of the Empress in a low cut dress and with full bosom has an appeal that corresponds to the Arabian taste."[428] He completely ignored the Ethiopians' long familiarity with the coin and its intrinsic value in silver. And, of course, he never asked why the Austro-Hungarian treasury struck such sexy specie. Maybe it corresponded with Mittel-European tastes.

European discourse generally was deeply racist, even in apparently positive commentary. In 1868, an anonymous writer in Globus characterized the Ethiopian soldier as "brave, fearless...and efficient," but "in his own way," obviously not up to European standards. He cautioned nonetheless — the paradox at work again — that the Ethiopian army should not be underestimated as an adversary, even if it would be unable to confront "an infantry with European training, in an open field, as the riflemen cannot cope with artillery; besides, this army will never get accustomed to European tactics [italics mine]."[429] This ludi-

424. Hermann Steudner, "Raise von Adoa nach Gondar, Dec. 26, 1861 -Januar 1862," *Zeitschrift fur algemeine Erdkunde* 15 (1863): 121-124, 128.
425. Gerhard Rohlfs, "Nach Axum Ober Hausen and Adua," *Zeitschrift der Geselschaft fur Erdkunds zu Berfin* 3 (1867): 487.
426. Abyssinian and die Europier," *Globus* 13 (1868): 49, 51.
427. Ibid.,255
428. Richard Andree, "Zur geographischen Verbreitung des Maria-Theresia-Thalers," Mitteflungen der K. and K. Geographischen Geselschaft in Wien 17 (1874: 270.
429. Aus dam Kriegerleben der Abyssinier," *Globus* 13 (1868): 10.

crous assessment ignored the severely transected, mountainous terrain of highland Ethiopia, to which local tactics and strategy were admirably adapted.

It seems likely the Italians were misled by the pervasive European racism of the day and the generally negative discourse that characterized most Western writings about Ethiopia. They were also deceived by European assessments of Menelik II (King of Showa, 1865-1889; Emperor, 1889-1913), who was viewed as only a nominal Christian, whose habits were "in general sullied by paganism."[430] His methods of governing were "inadmissible in civilized lands." He and his uneducated people were narrow minded bigots with a xenophobic dislike of Europeans, although — that paradox again — Menelik was "too clever to show his true feelings." His brutish nature was revealed to one sensitive soul when he refused to buy over-priced goods and took what he wanted at an equitable price.[431] Sebastiano Martini speculated that the King's materialism might lead him to agree to transform Showa into some form of dependency.[432] Italians generally believed that Ethiopians were incapable of acting out of patriotism or nationalism or developing and following policy, and the notion that Menelik might be using Italy as a pawn in his various political struggles was simply unthinkable.[433]

After he became emperor in 1889, Menelik used an Italian request to define Ethiopia's frontiers (the ultimate aim of which was transparent) for his own nationalistic reasons. In his circular letter to the powers in 1891, he defined Ethiopia's frontiers as Khartoum in the north, the upper Nile basin in the west, Lake Victoria in the south, and the coast from Suakin to Cape Guardafui.[434] The various chanceries totally disregarded his statement and divided eastern Africa according to their own designs. After the battle of Adwa, when European countries were forced to reckon with the obvious power of Ethiopia, Menelik ignored their territorial arrangements and negotiated on the basis of uti possidetis. When Western diplomats mentioned a prior agreement, he argued, "Myself, I

430. Charles Bourrit, "Concernant le Voyage d'exploration de M. J. Borelli dans le Choa et la région de l'Omo," *Le Globe* 28 (1889): 158.
431. Jules Borelli, "Souvenirs d'un voyage dans les pays des Gallas du sud et Sidama," *Bulletin de Société Khediviale de Géographie* 3 (1889): 150-151. Sebastiano Martini, "Terzo Viaggio de. Cap. S. Martini allo Scioa" *Cosmos* 6, 11 (1880-1881): 70.
432. Sebastiano Martini, "Terzo Viaggio de. Cap. S. Martini allo Scioa" *Cosmos* 6, 11 (1880-1881): 70.
433. Harold G. Marcus, *The Life and Times of Menelik I*, 2nd ed. (Lawrenceville, NJ, 1994), pp. 128, 190
434. Menilek to Rodd, Addis Ababa, 14 May 1897, FO 403/255.

have never heard of it until you told me. Neither of the two Governments [has] sent it to me."[435]

The Italians chose, however, to disregard the subtleties of Ethiopian diplomacy and consistently offended Ethiopian sensibilities with their barely disguised imperial ambitions. Leopoldo Traversi warned his countrymen not to interfere ignorantly in Ethiopia's internal affairs lest Italy be dragged into a war, "which will cost us millions and millions and many soldiers. Abyssinia will not be defeated with twenty or thirty thousand men."[436] A long-time German resident of Adwa cautioned that in face of external threats, Ethiopia was able to mobilize men and resources to meet the challenges.[437] In agreement, Henry Morton Stanley advised against intervention in the interior, suggesting instead that Italy strengthen Eritrea economically and attract Ethiopia's trade to its markets and ports. Ultimately, the inland empire would become dependent on the Italian economy and fall under Rome's hegemony.[438] Meanwhile, Menelik built a larger Ethiopian state and used the new revenues to strengthen its defenses. Even the Italians sold or gave him weapons, which astonished many of his compatriots. A post-Adwa ditty well sums up their feelings:

> What kinds of fools are they, in Europe? Why do they make their instruments of death and give them to us? With guns which they have brought, with cartridges they have brought, Menelik has roasted and exploded the foreign barley![439]

When Italian aims became obvious by 1894, a nation-wide revulsion against White men arose. Menelik exploited such primordialism in his mobilization proclamation of 1894, which was also calculated to strengthen the religious solidarity of Ethiopian Orthodoxy in the face of Roman Catholicism:

> Enemies have now come upon us to ruin the country and to change our religion.... Our enemies have begun the affair by advancing and digging into the country like moles. With the help of God I will not deliver up my country to them. Today, you who are strong, give me of your strength, and you who are weak, help me by prayer.[440]

---

435. Leopoldo Traversi, "Estratti di Lettere dallo Scioa," *Bollettino dela SocietA Geografica Italiana* XXIV, 7 (July 1887): 497-498.
436. Kamill Russ, "Aufzeichnungen in Bezug auf den Aegyptisch-Abessinischen Kreig," Petermann's Geographische Mitteilungen 23 (1877): 157.
437. Felice Schiber, "Giudizi di Stanley sull'Eritrea," *Revista Geografica Italiana* 4 (1894): 584-585.
438. Enrico Cerulli, "La Poesia Popolare Amarica," *L'Africa ltaliana* XXXV, VIII (August 1917): 175.
439. O. Baratieri, *Mémoires d'Afrique* (1892-1896) (Paris, 1899), p. 75.
440. Ibid.

In response to his call, "every tukul and village in every far-off glen in Ethiopia was sending out its warrior."[441] The emperor mobilized nearly 100,000 soldiers, composed of 80,000 riflemen, 8,600 cavalry, 42 artillery and machine gun batteries, and about 20,000 lancers, spearmen, and swordsmen, who were ready to take over the rifles of those who might fall in action. On the Italian side were 20,000 men, about half European troops, the rest Eritrean men armed with obsolescent rifles, machine guns, and artillery. Notwithstanding his obvious numerical superiority, Menelik wisely chose not to attack Italian fortified positions and risk repeating Yohannes's tactical mistake at Sahati in 1888. Instead, he camped near Adwa and hoped that the Italians would bring the war to him, allowing him to envelop and overrun the smaller force. By late February 1896, as food and forage grew scarce, it seemed a failing strategy: Menelik shortly would have been compelled to retire southward and concede an important part of Tigray to the imperialists, who would have won an important psychological victory. The same scenario could have repeated every year until, finally, the emperor would not have been able to resurrect his army for yet another campaign and Ethiopia would have fallen to the Italians by default. And that was the strategy General Baratieri had in mind; he was quite willing, therefore, to wait out the confrontation. He was, however, under pressure from premier Francesco Crispi, who believed that one Italian soldier was the measure of ten Ethiopians — all evidence to the contrary notwithstanding — and from his overconfident brigadiers, who believed that they could easily defeat the Ethiopian generals — all evidence to the contrary notwithstanding. And so, against his better judgment, Baratieri ordered a forced march on the night of February 29: "the night was black and there was profound silence."

Menelik learned about the Italian troop movement between 4:00 and 5:00 A.M., when he and his generals were at Sunday mass. As one Ethiopian explained: the enemy "had marched all night, hoping to surprise us, when our soldiers were worshipping God." He watched Menelik order his army to stand to arms, the soldiers dash to their units, and the priests administer communion. He heard the amassed Ethiopian troops yell out, "for the Motherland! For the faith!" At 6:00 A.M., the Ethiopians attacked before the Italians had fortified their new positions in the heights above their encampment. By mid-day, the emperor's

441. The last two paragraphs were based on "la Bataille d'Adowa d'après un récit Abyssin," *Revue Française de l'Etranger et des Exploration*, XXI, 215 (Nov. 1896): 656-658; Sven Rubenson, "Adwa 1896: The Resounding Protest," in *Power and Protest in Black Africa*, edited by Robert Rotberg and Ali Mazrui (New York, 1970); Berkeley, *Adowa.*

army had enveloped and overwhelmed the smaller Italian force. Our Ethiopian source commented simply that, "The machine guns of the Negus, the Remingtons, the Fusil Gras did their work of death." The Ethiopian success at Adwa revealed conclusively that, inconceivable as it was to Europe, an African power could overcome the challenge of modern European imperialism; and five days later the Italians recognized the fact by suing for peace.[442]

Now, Europeans had to rationalize Menelik's victory, and they turned inevitably to the alternate discourse without abandoning notions of racism, since such an admission would conflict with the teleology of modern European imperialism. Instead, they characterized Ethiopians as White, and they found several convenient observations upon which to build a new Ethiopian typology. Writing in 1884-85, Denis de Rivoire had written that Ethiopians "were men of quick intelligence with pure traits, although bronze [italics mine], with an elegant appearance, with a graceful carriage, [and with] civilized customs." From this evidence, he concluded that Ethiopians were members of "the great Caucasian family."[443] In 1890, a German traveler suggested that Caucasian admixture was responsible for the generally light Ethiopian skin color.[444] Another German commented that the Ethiopian had great reservoirs of energy and considerable quickness of mind, "which I have never witnessed among Arabs, Egyptians, Nubians, and Negroes."[445] The meaning could not have been clearer.

Following these precedents, post-Adwa discourse characterized Menelik and Ethiopia in positive terminology. A French author found that the emperor had excellent personal habits: he rose early, worked hard, was disciplined, all characteristics which Europeans considered their own.[446] No longer a semi-barbarian, he was found to be a dignified and energetic man "of intelligence and...character."[447] Many characterized him in superlatives: his activity was

---

442. Denis de Rivoire, "L'Abyssinie pittoresque et commerciale," *Annales de l'Extreme Orient et de l'Afrique* 7 (1885-1885): 65.
443. Karl Dove, "Kulturzonen von Nord-Abessinien," *Petermanns Geographische Mitteilungen, Erganzungsband XXI* (1889-1890): 16.
444. Georg Schweinfurth, "Einige Mitteilungen Ober seinen diesjAhrigen Besuch in der colonia Eritrea (NordAbessinien, 2 Juli 1892)," *Verhandlungen der Geselschaft fur Erdkunde zu Berlin* 19 (1892): 343.
445. "Abyssinie: A la cour de Menelik," *Revue Frangaise* 21, 210 (1896): 345
446. James Rennell Rodd, *Social and Diplomatic Memories, 1884-1901*, 2nd series (London, 1923), pp. 162163.
447. Count Gleichen, *With the Mission to Menelik* (London, 1896), p. 152; Michel Morphy, *Le Commandant Marchand*, Vol. III (Paris, 1900), p. 1628.

"superhuman"; he was "extraordinarily" well acquainted with world affairs, engineering, and science; he was a "prophet...a mystic...a modern man...a military genius."[448] A US diplomat described him in terms generally reserved for great Americans: "Menelik," he wrote, "has created the United State of Abyssinia — a work for which he was endowed by Nature with the constructive intelligence of a Bismarck, and the faculty of handling men... [with the] sheer amiability of a McKinley."[449] In this discourse, basically racist observers viewed phenomena within the terms of their own experience and proved unable to grant ordinariness to Black people. If usually inferior people accomplished anything, they necessarily had to be superhuman, extraordinary, and astonishing; and they had to embody the elements of a genius, a prophet, and a McKinley.

The Ethiopian military and nobility were similarly transformed. The latter became valorous in war, magnanimous in victory, and enjoyed "all of the qualities which distinguished ancient chivalry."[450] Such men led the now magnificent Ethiopian soldier, who was hardy, strong, durable, disciplined, indefatigable, happy, and courageous. He could march hundreds of kilometers without any noticeable exertion, was an excellent marksman, and apparently could subsist on minimum rations without any appreciable drop in efficiency.[451] [In 1901, Augustus Wylde summed up the post-Adwa discourse about the Ethiopian army: "Now that they are armed with modern rifles and modern artillery [and using] tactics admirably suited to the country they inhabit, they will prove a foe that will tax the resources of any first-class power..."[452]

Many Westerners searched out characteristics in common with Ethiopia. They found them, of course. Prince Henri d'Orleans suggested that pride and love of country, those twin Gallic virtues, accounted for Ethiopian success.[453] Hughes Le Roux was impressed by the depth of Ethiopian nationality, which made it impossible for most Ethiopians to conceive of living elsewhere.[454] Two

448. Robert p. Skinner, *Abyssinia of Today* (London, 1906), p. 14.
449. Sylvain Vignéras, "La Mission Lagarde en Abyssinie, Impressions de Voyage," *Le Tour du Monde*, n.s. 3, 2 (1897): 244.
450. Albert Hans, "L'Armée de Ménelik, *Revue des Deux Mondes* 135 (June 15, 1896): 871; A.E. Pease, *Travel and Sport in Africa* (London, 1902), Vol. III (London, 1902), p. 3; A. Donaldson Smith, "Expédition through Somaliland to Lake Rudolf," *The Geographical Journal*, VIII, 2 (August 1896): 127.
451. Wylde, Modern Abyssinia, p. 421.
452. Henri d'Orléans, "Le Transvaal et l'Abyssinie," *Buletin de la Soci6t6 de Geographie de Marseile* 24 (1900_: 43-44.
453. Hughes le Roux, "L'Abyssinie," Bulletin de la Société de Géographie Commerciale de Bourdeaux28, 3 (3 Fev. 1902): 151.

British officers, who had fought alongside Ethiopians in the Ogaden, reported that Ethiopian soldiers had "a very profound sense of nationality."[455] After Adwa, most Europeans willingly agreed that Ethiopia constituted "A civilized nation of an immense intelligence, the only one that is civilized without wearing trousers and shoes."[456] Yet, Ethiopia was not accepted without reservations. Herbert Vivian railed that the Ethiopians went too far when they presumed to arrogate to themselves a superiority over civilized countries."[457] Most Westerners, even the more positive, regarded Ethiopia as a country half-way between savagery and civilization. As the Austrian Baron Kulmer explained, Greek and Armenian businessmen were invariably successful in Ethiopia because they were closer to the Ethiopians in mentality than were Western Europeans.[458] An American Presbyterian missionary posited that his church should quickly convert and educate Ethiopians, who then would be dispatched "from the lofty plateau and go into all the distant parts of Africa....[they] would not have to bridge the distance that separates the White man from the Black."[459] So, even in its hour of greatest triumph, Ethiopia was not afforded full equality.

The discourse of anti-Ethiopian racism would reach its apogee in 1935-36, when Mussolini's attack revealed his "profound hatred and contempt for the Abyssinians," whom he could not bring himself to treat "on an equal footing."[460] But I shall have to return during its centenary in 2035 to analyze the discourse surrounding that war.[461]

454. James Willes Jennings and Christopher Addison, *With the Abyssinians in Somaliland* (London, 1905), p. 189.
455. Friedrich J. Bieber, "Reise durch Athiopien and den Sudan," *Mitteilungen der K.K. Geographischen Geselschaft in Wien* 53 (1910): 338.
456. Herbert Vivian, *Abyssinia* (London, 1901), p. 248
457. Kleine Nachrichten," *Globus* 94 (1908): 292.
458. Statement by Dr. Lambie, 21 Feb. 1924, from Minutes of the First Annual Meeting of the Abyssinian Association of the United Presbyterian Church of North Africa, *Archives of the United Presbyterian Church*, New York City. This racist view was also present in the 1980s. See also Georgi Galperin, *Ethiopia: Population, Resources, Economy* (Moscow, 1981), p.29.
459. See Georgi Galperin, *Ethiopia: Population, Resources, Economy* (Moscow, 1981), p.29.
460. Drummond to FO, Rome, 3 Jan. 1935, PRO, FO 371/19000; Ivone Kirkpatrick, *Mussolini: A Study in Power* (New York, 1968), p. 310.
461. A well-known Africanist scholar, Harold Marcus suddenly passed away on January 15, 2003, after this book to which he contributed this study was well underway.

CHAPTER 8. CONTEMPORARY ETHIOPIA IN THE CONTEXT OF THE BATTLE OF ADWA, 1896

Mesfin Araya Ph.D. Professor of Political Science
York College, City University of New York

It was 1 March 1896, a Sunday, about 4 o'clock in the morning. The night was black and the silence profound. The camp, between Adwa and the mountains, slept. The Emperor and Empress were up, having left their tents without ceremony, to go to religious services. Everyone was deep in prayer and contemplation when a courier ran in and threw himself on the ground before the emperor. There was a rumbling, a muffled thunder of troops on the move... More messengers arrived and finally the Emperor realized that danger was imminent. Trumpeters sounded assembly and in very short order the troops were ready....The green-yellow-red flags were dipped before the crucifix. As dawn illuminated the scene, the army got underway with its customary shouting.... At exactly 6:10 A.M. General Albertone...heard a fusillade...The battle of Adwa had begun.... The fighting was intense in every sector, but the war was essentially over by 12:30 P.M.... As The Spectator commented...: "The Italians have suffered a great disaster... greater than has ever occurred in modern times to White men in Africa"....Adwa was the bloodiest of all colonial battles.[462]

Colonel Piano's perception of Ethiopia as "Colossus with feet of clay"[463] was dramatically proven wrong. What is the historical and contemporary signif-

462. Chris Prouty, *Empress Taytu and Menelik II* (Trenton, NJ, The Red Sea Press, 1986), pp.155 & 157.
463. Sven Rubenson, "Adwa 1896: the Resounding Protest" in Robert I. Rotberg and Ali A. Mazrui (eds.) *Protest and Power in Black Africa* (New York, Oxford University Press, 1970), p.139.

icance of that fateful event in the history of Ethiopian people? Adwa's significance goes well beyond Ethiopian borders. There were many African Adwas in the history of colonial incursions. The short-lived victory of the Zulus, the great resistance of the indomitable Matabele, and the Shona revolt are a few examples. What makes the Ethiopian Adwa unique is that, as a success story, it is able to invoke and sustain a sense of Pan-Africanism among the Black race. Beyond its Pan-Africanist content, it was a major factor in bringing political crisis to the homeland of the enemy: Francesco Crispi, the architect of the war, fell; and the Commander of the Italian troops at Adwa, General Baratieri, was brought to trial. Finally, the victory at Adwa gave Europeans a clear signal never to provoke Ethiopia again. The author will not dwell on the international significance of the battle of Adwa, as it has been retold many times. What is attempted here is something quite different.

In Western tradition, death is perceived as terminal. In the African tradition, on the other hand, to die, to use Ali Mazrui's phraseology, is "like changing your address:"[464] the dead continue to participate in the lives of the living — hence, the African tradition of ancestor worship. Underlying that philosophy is the inseparable link between the past and the present: the past as the present and the present as the past. History, especially oral history, occupies a significant place in African tradition. The Adwa victory, therefore, ought to be an occasion to recall our ancestors for consultation, to engage them in discussion, in our time of national crisis; or, if you will, to have an open therapy session with our ancestors, confronting them as they confront us. This would require on our part a profound reflection, honest and intense participation. The author's discussion will move from the present to the past, and vice versa, through comparison, imagined dialogue, and anecdote.

Two arguments are advanced here. First, Adwa represents a bold critique on the current ethnic politics in Ethiopia — be it from the point of view of a history of a people in general or from that of a ruling class in particular. Second, Adwa has its own contradictions which still plague Ethiopia; contradictions whose resolution is also contained in Adwa itself.

---

464. Ali Mazrui, *The Africans, a Triple Heritage*, (Boston, Little Brown & Co., 1986), p.45.

ADWA AS A HISTORY OF A PEOPLE

In his breakfast meeting with American scholars on October 20, 1995, Ethiopian Prime Minister Meles Zenawi is reported to have said that, "Ethiopia's peoples have to sort out their identities before mobilizing their energies to build a new nationalism."[465]

That statement by the first post-Mengistu Prime Minister is in stark contradiction to the real, lived, experience of Ethiopian people. Ethiopia's victory at Adwa would never have been possible if the people had indeed a crisis of identity. It is not difficult to imagine how the history of Ethiopia would have turned out if the people were locked in their respective ethnic particularism in the face of foreign aggression. On the contrary, they mobilized their energies and collectively descended on the enemy like "an infernal whirl."[466] Adwa was a country-wide upheaval, and "every tukul and village" responded to the call. The long and arduous march signifies a remarkable experience in the collective memory of a people.[467] Adwa was truly a people's war where women's participation was no less significant than the men's: they carried military supplies on their backs; harassed the enemy; and those who had access to the Italian camp supplied information. Quoting an anonymous source, Chris Prouty vividly describes the role of women in the battle.

> The Empress collected the ten or twelve thousand women in the camp and issued water jugs to all of them. This army of another kind filled their jugs at the river and were ready to carry water to those who fought, wherever they stood. Hundreds of women remained in camp prepared to care for the wounded.[468]

According to Sven Rubenson, there was even a "resistance in the Eritrean rank and file against entering the battle. The Italians are reported to have surrounded their Basha buzuks [Eritrean recruits]' before the battle to prevent desertion," as the latter was reported to have said: "though we eat their money, we will not fight our country and our King," an interesting historical commentary on the EPLF argument that Ethiopian nationalism is a myth created by the country's dominant ruling group.

---

465. Harold G. Marcus, "A Breakfast Meeting with Meles", *Ethiopian Review* (December, 1995):33.
466. David Levering Lewis, The Race to Fashoda: European Colonialism and African. Resistance in the Scramble for Africa (New York, Neidenfeld & Nicolson, 1987), p.103.
467. Menelik's army is said to have marched 1,000 kilometers, according to Sven Rubenson, *The Survival of Ethiopian Independence* (London, Heinemann, 1976), p.406.
468. Prouty, Taytu and Menelik, p.156.

Indeed, one can imagine countless peasant men and women, Adwa veterans from various ethnic backgrounds, defiantly replying to the Prime Minister, "You may have a crisis of identity; as for us, we fought for freedom as a united people; we could not do otherwise!" Was Meles unable to appreciate the shared determination, the collective struggle of a people for self-determination, that was symbolized according to local tradition by "one individual, a poor man with a crippled hand who on his own initiative...went to Baratieri" to spread false information on the condition of the Ethiopian army?[469]

Neither could the Ethiopian resistance movement during the Fascist occupation of 1936 to 1941 have sustained itself without the spirit of Adwa. The history of Adwa served the patriots as self-reference — a reservoir from which to draw national pride and courage.

Viewed as a history of a people, therefore, Adwa signifies a single inescapable truth, one which the current ethnic politics tries to undermine: Ethiopia may be a mosaic of nationalities, but its people also have a collective, shared history that binds them together. Adwa represents a supra-ethnic and supra-regional consciousness in search of collective freedom.

The current divisive politics of ethnicity is indeed largely the making of Ethiopia's contemporary political elites whose self-reference seems alien to the spirit of Adwa. If we closely observe the regionalist and ethno-nationalist politics of the last twenty years, a single truth emerges: none of them began as a grass-roots movement; all of them were movements from above to create separate identities; and those who succeeded were largely aided by the repressive machinery of Mengistu Haile Mariam.[470] Indeed, time will tell whether such artificial creations will have permanence, or the collective history of Ethiopian people will once again forcefully reassert itself.

Adwa as a History of a Ruling Class

The history of the battle of Adwa can also be analyzed at the level of the Ethiopian ruling class. Here, again, may be a lesson for Ethiopia's contemporary political elites. Adwa signified the role of leadership. The battle could never have been won if there had been internal divisions within the ruling class — the kind of internal division that made a critical difference in the history of colonial incur-

469. Sven Rubenson, "Adwa 1896", p.126.
470. Ibid., p.121.

sions in the rest of Africa and that, throughout history, in every part of the world, has weakened nations and served the interests of foreign rivals.

Indeed, the victory of Adwa was partly due to the internal unity of the ruling class, whose members closed ranks in the face of foreign aggression. A good example is that of Ras Alula and Menelik. If Alula had been a Tigrayan nationalist first, he could have easily struck a deal with the Italians. Yet, despite his hostility to Menelik's newly acquired power, he was able to see the larger picture and closed ranks with the latter. As Alula recounted to Augustus Wylde: "I...turned to King Menelik as the only man who could restore order, and since that time I have thrown all my influence on his side, in order to unite [Ethiopia] once more."[471] A remarkable consciousness and vision, especially from the point of view of a ruling class.

Menelik was an exceptional leader.[472] As Augustus Wylde says, "Emperor Yohannes was like a child compared to him."[473] His diplomatic skills, "...spinning out in his mind," as David Lewis says, "a politics for all comers and for all seasons," and his remarkable ability of building consensus within his multi-ethnic ruling group, of co-opting the dissatisfied members through marriage and reward, are indeed indicative of effective leadership. The Italian attempts at provoking divisions within the Ethiopian ruling class were effectively pre-empted.[474] As Rubenson writes, Menelik's call to arms had been obeyed throughout the realm. All his vassals, except those who had received security tasks elsewhere, had either preceded him or joined him in his march to the North.[475]

It must also be recalled that the defection of former Italian allies, Ras Sibhat and Dejazmach Hagos Teferi, and their subsequent agitation inside their districts in Tigray are indicative of class solidarity. Baratieri had to admit that "he really did not know at all who would be with him, neutral, or against him."[476] Indeed, the internal cohesion of the Ethiopian ruling class at Adwa was striking, especially in the context of the current political crisis in Ethiopia.

471. For details, see Mesfin Araya, "The Eritrean Question: An Alternative Explanation", *The Journal of Modern African Studies* (March 1990):79-100, and Robert D. Kaplan, *Surrender or Starve: The Wars Behind the Famine* (Boulder, The Westview Press, 1988).

472. Haggai Erlich, *Ethiopia and Eritrea During the Scramble for Africa: A Political Biography of* Ras *Alula, 1875-1897* (East Lansing, African Studies Center and the Shiloah Center for Middle Eastern and African Studies, Tel-Aviv University, 1982),p.188.

473. As quoted in Lewis, *The Race to Fashoda*, p.12.

474. Ibid., p.128.

475. Rubenson, "Adwa", p. 117.

476. Rubenson, Survival of Ethiopian Independence, p.405.

Today's Ethiopian political elites show every characteristic of a weak class, fatally undermined, as Frantz Fanon would say, "by its...incapacity to think in terms of all the problems of the nation as seen from the point of view of the whole of that nation."[477] Internally, they are divided by regionalism and ethnicity. The ruling elites set out to form a firing squad to defend what they call the "New Ethiopia" and ended up in a circle. Today their guns are aimed at each other: the conflict between EPRDF and OLF, and EPRDF and the Liberation Fronts in the Ogaden area are good examples. The opposition forces are no less internally divided, as the mode of struggle of many of them is defined by the political discourse of the EPRDF. Several of them are organized on either ethnic or regional basis. At a more general level, Dr. Beyene Petros' simultaneous official position as the president of the Alternative Forces and as the chairman of the Southern Peoples' Coalition — two loyalties in one person — is no less an indication of internal fragmentation. Only recently has a pan-Ethiopianist party Kinijit [CUD] been created — out of splinter groups. Not surprisingly, for those who know Ethiopia and Ethiopians well, this has paid dividends: the party has for the first time swept the city of Addis Ababa and all major urban areas from the ruling EPRDF in the May 2005 national elections.

The fragmented vision of Ethiopian political elites may give foreign powers an opportunity to fish in troubled waters. Esayas and Meles have opened their doors wide to US and Israeli interests in the Horn of Africa. Ignored as they are by the latter two, the Oromo nationalists seem to have attracted German interest (the Germans are currently the strongest patrons of Oromo Studies in the Western world); the Moslem group may attract petro-dollar interests; and the Amhara nationalists may get sympathy from the Russians.[478] Indeed, Ethiopia may well end up becoming a playground for foreign interests: a direct assault on the spirit of Adwa.

In the celebration of Adwa's victory, one can imagine a brief confrontation between Ras Alula, the venerable Ethiopian nationalist, "the husband of Kassala and lover of the sea,"[479] and Meles, the champion of ethnic politics.[480]

---

477. Frantz Fanon, *The Wretched of the Earth* (New York, Grove Press, 1968), p.154.
478. Interestingly Russian Embassy's political Counselor in Addis Ababa is said to have visited the AAPO's head office and held talks with the First Deputy President. See Ethiopian Register (March 1996): 5.
479. As quoted in Erlich, p.196.
480. The words in Meles' answers are collected from the various interviews he has given.

Meles Zenawi started his struggle as a Tigrayan, not as an Ethiopian. The TPLF led by Meles Zenawi currently rules the country and but it started as a separatist movement intended to spawn a sovereign Tigray, not to liberate Ethiopia from Mengistu's dictatorship. If there were nationalities issues to be resolved, they need to be resolved in the context of a united Ethiopian state. The Adwa veterans, peasant men and women from all over, knew enough to look at the big picture; can today's elites not do as well?

Ras Alula would add a message to the opposition forces in exile. The battle of Adwa was fought on the ground, inside Ethiopia, together with the humble people, and not from a pedestal, or a comfortable seat in the balcony; and following Frederick Douglass, he would conclude:

> Those who profess to favor freedom and yet [refuse to struggle at home] are men who want crops without ploughing the ground, they want rain without thunder and lightening. They want the ocean without the awful roar of its many waters.[481]

Post-Adwa

Although Adwa's victory marks a high point in the collective struggle of the Ethiopian people, it also had its own contradictions from which present-day Ethiopia has yet to extricate itself meaningfully. The era that Adwa's victory initiated needs to be confronted for what it is, with a sober and critical mind.

At the battle of Adwa, Ethiopian people fought collectively, with great determination, to defend their freedom from external domination; but they also lost part of their collective identity when Eritrea remained colonized. The Eritreans, particularly the highlanders, had hoped that the victory of Adwa would also deliver their salvation.

Forced by a combination of circumstances — the specter of pre-Adwa famine, the fear of an unending winnable colonial war of attrition, and his own concern of power consolidation in the South and Southwest — Menelik did not heed the advice of Ras Alula, who advocated the extension of the war to the Ethiopian frontier province of Ethiopia (then known as Mereb Melash), which had been forcibly colonized and named Eritrea by the Italian expansionists.[482]

---

481. From Philip S. Fomer (ed.) *The Voice of Black America vol.1*, (New York, Capricorn Books, 1975) p.222.
482. Erlich, pp.188-195.

The difference between the two was a difference between a realist and a dreamer.

The point here, however, is that what was a sound strategy for Menelik was a disaster, a tragedy, for highland Eritreans, especially when we recall that the prelude to the battle of Adwa had begun in Eritrea with the anti-colonial revolt of Bahta Hagos, in 1894. In their own words, this is what highland Eritreans said, in their hour of desperation, as Emperor Menelik signed the treaty of Wuchalé with the Italians legitimizing their occupation: "We, the people of Hamasein, [are] doomed forever."[483] They helplessly longed for the mythical Tewodros (the unifier of Ethiopia in the mid 1800s after the total fragmentation of the country during the Era of the Princes) who could deliver their salvation. So, they sang:

> We have been told that Tewodros would come.
> Where is He?
> Without witnessing his arrival
> Darkness fell upon us
> Where is the staff of Moses, that destroyed the Pharaoh?
> Only God knows.[484]

Fifty years after Adwa, the people of Eritrea fought as Unionist Ethiopians to regain what they had lost. As a result of their struggle, the United Nations federated Eritrea with Ethiopia. But four decades later, they were led astray by the EPLF leadership which falsely claimed to represent them — though it had its own private agenda.

The contradictions of post-Adwa can also be analyzed at another level. Berkeley writes:

> The warriors who fought at Adwa won a fresh lease of independence for their race — whether this is a gain to the world and whether they or their descendants will take advantage of the chance thus obtained is a problem of the future.[485]

That chance has been seized and monopolized by the ruling class. For the people, the last hundred years have been a history of betrayal of the promise that Adwa held. Although the Ethiopian people struggled against Italian aggression in the name of collective self-determination, they have been denied that same right by their own homegrown rulers.

---

483. Johannes Kolmodin, *Traditions de Tsazzega et Hazzega, Textes Tigrigna* (Rome, 1912), p.263. The translation is the author's.
484. Ibid., p.263.
485. Berkeley, *The Campaign of Adowa*, pp.259-260.

Ethiopia may not have been colonized, but it has never escaped the European influence that wreaked havoc in the African continent: the modern state and money economy — signifying Ethiopia's steady integration into a market driven globalized world. Under Menelik's reign, the ruling class consolidated its power and increasingly began to "shed its martial character of pre-Adwa days and developed business instincts. A series of profitable partnerships were struck between its members and the expatriate merchants and concessionaires,"[486] and the process of privatization of land began in earnest. For the ordinary Ethiopian people who directly and indirectly participated at the battle of Adwa, the modern state and its economic relations brought the intensification of both class and cultural oppression — more glaringly in the South, the newly incorporated region. The collective misery of the Ethiopian people was indeed articulated by Gebra-Heywet Baykadagn, "the intellectual pace-setter of his age,"[487] when he called for reform.

Haile Selassie's reign only accelerated, at both political and economic levels, the era initiated by Adwa's victory. But at a time when the people needed to have a sweeping but meaningful social change, Mengistu Haile Mariam emerged. After terror, wars, and famine, the people longed for peace, reconciliation, and democracy — only to have history produce Issayas Afeworki and Meles Zenawe Zenawi (the former lording it over the Eritrean people and denying them their basic human rights; and the latter recklessly experimenting with the tinder box of ethnicity that might, if not smothered quickly, could destroy the Ethiopian nation state once and for all). As things stand now, we see the same pattern of collective misery of a people, largely spawned and sustained by a tiny, greedy, ruling minority represented by the overseers of the EPRDF

---

486. Bahru Zewde, *A History of Modern Ethiopia, 1855-1974*, (Athens, Ohio University Press, 1991), p.98. For creeping modernization under Menelik's reign, see pp.85-108. Bahru seems to contradict himself when he writes that "The relatively more progressive elements of the feudal ruling class also sought to reconstitute feudalism on a new and more solid foundation"(p.92). On the contrary, Menelik's state of post-Adwa signified the gradual decline of the traditional "feudal state" and the emergence, albeit staggeringly, of a variant of capitalist state. The ruling class may have been traditional in its origin, but its members were fast adapting to the changing circumstances, i.e., the steady process of Ethiopia's integration into international capitalism — the logic of international capitalist process exerting a determining pressure upon Ethiopia's development and form.

487. Bahru Zewde, "The Intellectual and the State in Twentieth Century Ethiopia," *New Trends in Ethiopian Studies. Papers of the 12th International* Conference of Ethiopian Studies, vol.I, Michigan State University, 5-10 September 1994 (Red Sea Press, Lawrenceville, N.J., 1994):483.

empire — a huge party-controlled business enterprise in full charge of all aspects of the Ethiopian economy.

The rulers in Asmara and Addis Ababa, like their predecessors, have failed to provide an "intellectual and moral leadership," a failure which has come to surprise even their staunch supporters. Their regimes are engaged in the "Politics of the belly," as EPLF and TPLF own and control not only business enterprises but also land, rendering their respective political organizations a status of powerful national landlords and CEOs of giant industrial corporations. Clive Thomas writes:

> In post-colonial situation, control of the state power was the basis through which the petty bourgeoisie sought to confirm its social position as a ruling class — In the process of consolidating itself as a ruling class, members of the petty bourgeoisie took on political roles and managerial positions in the State enterprise.[488]

Those descriptions aptly fit both the EPLF and the TPLF since their victories in 1991. They are engaged in authoritarian politics stifling free speech (both have imprisoned hundreds of journalists) and denying individual freedom (both have arrested, jailed, tortured and killed dissidents).

In the Ethio/Eritrean political culture, especially in the highland regions, the socio-economic and political institutions lacked internal liberal tendencies. At the village level, the risti/rist property system was a despotic economic institution, where the individual was subsumed under the collective interest of the community, as deeply anchored institution of kinship system, the property relations hindered the process of individuation. At the national level, patrimonialism and violence remained the foundation of politics, as the Christian highland saying goes; "The King (or to use modern parlance, the politician) wades in blood to his throne."

Policy initiatives were invariably exercised by the state, constantly stifling the free development of commerce and industry. Class power and state power overlapped, depriving the state even a semblance of autonomy, necessary for peaceful and democratic reforms; and in such conditions, violence remains the necessary catalyst of change. Despite its modern trappings, the state under Haile Selassie, and Mengistu Haile Mariam, were strongly embedded in those traditions.

Although EPLF and TPLF claim to have ushered a new era, the state that they "reconstructed" is modeled in the image of their predecessors. The EPLF

488. Thomas Clive.*The rise of the authoritarian state in peripheral societies.* New York:Monthly Review press,1984,pp.60-62.

and TPLF had to use violence to capture state power, and they remain primarily concerned with maintaining and consolidating it. Kenneth Jowitt writes:

> Populists attempt to achieve national homogeneity through political mobilization rather than social mobilization. Political mobilization consist of elite efforts to activate people, to direct their actions and affect — at particular targets — without, however, directly challenging the social identity, or institutional commitments of those activated. Reliance on political mobilization as the basic means of social change results in the superimposition of new elites on largely unreconstructed social institutions, and new political loyalties on existing ones. Social mobilization [on the other hand] consists of elite effort to undermine existing institutional frameworks and social identities — and create alternative ones.[489]

Both EPLF and TPLF were — in their histories as liberation fronts — engaged in mere political rather than social mobilization. There is evidence that both Fronts were engaged in political mobilization in areas of land, gender, and political reforms. The parallel armed state that the Fronts organized in the northern mountains was the driving force rather than an open and democratic popular movement. Despite their successful capture of state power, however, they remain plagued by multiple socio-economic and political problems: the issue of persistent poverty, the crisis of inter-elite integration, the question of democracy and problems of inter-state relations.

Indeed, the era initiated by Adwa has yet to be transcended, and the resolution is contained in Adwa itself. The people voted with their feet as they marched to fight at Adwa — a noble act of supra-ethnic and supra-regional consciousness. Their desire to fight foreign domination at Adwa inherently contains a desire to fight any oppression; indeed, it embodies a criticism of their own condition of existence. That collective desire for freedom can, therefore, be activated against their own internal oppressors. To that effect, Ethiopian as well as Eritrean intellectuals — committed to the public cause — can act as catalysts in advancing an alternative social discourse anchored in the collective history of the people-an alternative social discourse aimed at building a new and democratic Ethiopia where the various cultural groups can enrich their collective history in freedom and equality. That task must remain central in the 21st century.

Ethiopian nationalists have lamented the fact that Meles Zenawi's provisional government willingly landlocked Ethiopia when it let the port city of Assab be made part of independent Eritrea despite an overwhelming struggle by

---

489. K. Jowitt."Scientific Socialist Regimes in Africa: political differentiation, avoidance, and unawareness" in C. G. Rosberg and T.M. Gallaghy[eds.] *Socialism in Sub-Sahara Africa*, Berkeley: Institute of International Studies,1979,p.152.

the Afar people to oppose separation from the mother country. Others who support Eritrea disagree. The author would like to end his remarks with a brief comment on the nature of the debate that the Assab question has provoked. A critic of nationalism/ethno-nationalism once argued:

> Men and women did not choose collective identification as they choose shoes, knowing that one could only put on one pair at a time. They had, and still have, several attachments and loyalties simultaneously including nationality, and are simultaneously concerned with various aspect of life, any of which may at any time be foremost in their minds, as occasion suggests.[490]

What does that mean? It means that the politics of nationalism/ethnonationalism — which is currently unsettling the Horn of Africa — must not be seen as something that is fixed for all time, immutable, unchanging, defying the human experience in history. It must rather be seen in terms of experiences of relationships. Those who want to fix group identity do so only by trying to subvert, intimidate, and silence other identities. That is seen in the behavior of the regimes in Addis Ababa and Asmara. Cultural politics is always related to the question of power, and that is why identity politics always carries within itself a crisis of representation.

It is true that group identities are always contested. However, the current trend is towards accommodation and union and not to engender disintegration. For example, if we look at European history, with the religious and political wars leading to the formation of nation-states, currently they are moving toward a larger union. In addition, in the case of African Americans who despite their separate identity rooted in the history of slavery, lynching, and racism, they have not espoused separatism.

Back in Africa, look at the social disintegration of Somalia, whose people possess a common religious and linguistic identity — a rare phenomenon in the entire continent of Africa. Look at the checkered history of Eritrea itself, which was once an Italian colony, an autonomous region of Ethiopia and currently a new nation state. Those who perceive the politics of nationalism/ethno-nationalism as a fixed, permanent phenomenon need to think twice. Viewing the politics of nationalism/ethno-nationalism in terms of experiences of relationships has profound and radical implications. When it comes to the politics of nationalism/ethno-nationalism, nothing is historically given; separatism is not inevitable, nor is the act of separation is a fixed, permanent phenomenon. As a broad and open way of thinking, this perspective enables us to create conditions for

---

490. Eric Hobsbawm. *Nations and Nationalism since 1780, program, myth reality*. Cambridge: Cambridge press, 1992, p.123.

dialogue among the past, present and future. It helps us to focus on what matters on the ground: a conscious attempt at building relationships, brick by brick, if that is necessary. And that being said, it would be useful to present some brief comments on the nature of the debate the Assab question has provoked.

There are at least three schools of thought regarding the question of Assab, i.e., the ultra-legalists, a reference to the government of Meles Zenawe Zenawi whose major argument is that according to colonial treaties, Assab belongs to Eritrea; the Rectifiers, who claim that Assab has never legally been part of Eritrea; and the Unionists, who see the independence of Eritrea as altogether illegal, and call for the return to unity.

How do we explain the position of Meles' government? Its central argument has its historical roots in the original sin of TPLF which, motivated by military and political expediency, had initially accepted the EPLF argument that theirs is a "colonial question" -which means that the case of Eritrea is different and unique in that it was colonized by the Italians and was transferred to Ethiopia by the UN without the consent of the majority of the Eritrean population. Yes, this was driven by military and political expediency, precisely because the Tigrayian elite — given their cultural and historical ties — accepted the "colonial question" of Eritrea. It was the same TPLF which, during the Transitional Government, used the Eritrean residents in Ethiopia as political functionaries in government bureaucracy and Kebeles, as a voting constituency during the regional elections. It was also the government of Meles which unconditionally handed the people of Eritrea to a single political party, the EPLF, leaving in the cold the ELF organization which had started the liberation war in the first place. Meles had no concern whether or not the referendum in Eritrea was to be conducted in an open and democratic environment, and yet, under totally changed circumstances, it was again the same government that deported Eritrean residents in Ethiopia when a war broke out between the two countries in 1998. The checkered behavior of Meles's government points to one direction: its stance on the Assab question (leaving it to Eritrea, instead of claiming it for Ethiopia) is driven merely by the search to stabilize and consolidate his own power. His government could not have acted differently.

Regarding the so-called Rectifiers and the Unionists, their arguments may be used to rally political support against the government of Meles; and indeed, that is precisely their intention. Their motivation is not entirely dissimilar to that of Meles and his clique. Vividly in the foreground of the arguments is the question of power as they evade the larger question of democratization in the entire region. The true nature of the arguments of the two schools of thought becomes even clearer if we review the past behavior of their leading elements.

They fail to understand and appreciate the legitimate and historical grievances of the people of Eritrea. This is especially true of the unionists, who simply argue that Eritrea has always been part of Ethiopia or, as the Rectifiers seem to imply, that Ethiopia as a matter of national interest needs a sea outlet. It is interesting to note that both elements did not show much sympathy or give support to the Eritrean people, especially during the seventeen years of brutal war which was unleashed by the government of Mengistu Haile Mariam, nor did they protest when Eritrean residents in Ethiopia were deported in gross violation of their human rights.

Focused as they are on the question of power, what these three schools of thought clearly evade is the very problem that caused the question of Eritrea, or the Assab issue, to be raised: the absence of democratization. With democratization in the region, even the separate existence of Eritrea (let alone Assab) is likely to be rendered superfluous.

We need a sense of historical perspective that sees nationalism/ethnonationalism in terms of experiences of relationships, and how those experiences affect relationships. That perspective could only alert us to the need of building a positive experience of Ethio-Eritrean interaction; and the rich historical/cultural repertoire that the two societies share could only make the task less difficult. To that effect, our guarantee is to struggle for and attain the democratization of the two societies.

Indeed, the historical wounds that mark the Ethio-Eritrean relationship, rooted as they are in Menelik's decision not to drive the Italian colonialists into the sea after his brilliant victory at Adwa, and the legacies of the fratricidal war the Eritreans and the Ethiopians waged from 1961 to 1991, and the meaningless and destructive border war of 1998-2000, should not be construed as the end of the story. Nevertheless, the continuation of the rapidly increasing positive developments after all this depends on how the two people go about treating them. For this, the democratization of Ethiopia and Eritrea is the best guarantee. Fortunately, that nascent force is slowly emerging in both countries, though applied somewhat asymmetrically. It must be sustained, enhanced, and consolidated. What is and ought to be on the agenda is not a single issue-oriented struggle, but the fostering and nurturing of the larger question of democratization. The story of the two peoples is not yet over. That is why Ethiopians and Eritreans, nay, all Africans, need to be wise, understanding, and tolerant so that they would be able to chart ways of reconstructing their relationships in a community spirit. Needless to say, to succeed, they will have to invoke the moral fiber that spawned the remarkable triumph at Adwa.

CHAPTER 9. ETHIOPIAN HISTORY AND CRITICAL THEORY: THE CASE OF ADWA

Maimire Mennasemay
Ph.D. Humanities and Philosophy Dawson College/Fellow: Center for Developing Area Studies, McGill University

RETHINKING ADWA

The uniqueness of Adwa lies not in the defeat of a European power by an African country, but in the fact that Adwa is, to use Alain Badiou's term, "a Truth-Event": a singular event that exceeds the circumstances out of which it emerges such that what appears impossible becomes real, giving rise to radically new political problems.[491] In this sense, from the cracks of the fragmented order of regional princes and rulers that characterized Ethiopia in the pre-Adwa period emerged a new self-perception of the inhabitants of the diverse regions of the country as a nation, making Ethiopians visible as a people, and opening up, unlike any other conflict Ethiopia has known, a radically new and troubled future within whose horizon Ethiopians are still living.

Adwa is the first event in Ethiopia's history that interpolated Ethiopians as national subjects whose identity transcended ethnicity, gender, religion and

491. Alain Badiou, *L'être et l'événement*, *Paris*, Seuil, 1988, pp. 25-29, 202-204, 221-225. I am using this term in a slightly different sense to convey the uniqueness of Adwa in Ethiopian history, in terms of the conditions that made it possible; the event itself, which could be seen as totally unexpected given the lop-sided advantage the Italians enjoyed in terms of armament; and, more importantly, the radically new historical horizon it opened up, generating fundamentally new problems, to wit, the issues of internal freedom, of modernization, and of national unity.

social class, such that in the post-Adwa period it was no longer possible to continue the traditional mode of economic and political relations as if nothing had happened. For the secret of Adwa, the part which is still alive and is the engine that has been driving the history of the post-Adwa period, is that the unity of Ethiopians against external oppression was rooted in internal oppression, and out of this unity, and the victory against a foreign aggression, was born a new political subject — Ethiopians — unwilling to accept in the name of tradition the pre-Adwa system of oppression. Its demand to be recognized as a political subject triggered Menelik's timid reforms,[492] Haile Selassie's "passive revolution,"[493] the Derg's "socialism," and the EPRDF's "ethnic federation";[494] but none of these succeeded to radically change the rules of political inclusion in so far as all of them have fallen short of creating the political order that expresses the sovereignty of every Ethiopian as clearly as the victory of Adwa expressed the sovereignty of Ethiopia as a nation.

Adwa is thus an important watershed in the history of Ethiopia. The conditions that made it possible gave rise to intellectual and political challenges that are more difficult to meet than defeating the Italian army. In order to grasp the significance of these challenges and the impact of failures to meet them, it is necessary to make an analytical distinction between the external and internal aspects of Adwa. The external aspect deals with the relations between Ethiopia and Italy and the emergence of Ethiopia as an African power in the age of European colonial expansion.[495] The internal aspect refers to the social practices and constitutive meanings that made the victory of Adwa possible and prepared the ground for the rise of new political conditions and questions.

The author will argue in this chapter that this internal aspect of Adwa provides an opening for a critical reflection on the Ethiopian predicament, and that

---

492. Harold G. Marcus, *The Life and Times of Menelik I: Ethiopia 1844-1913*, Oxford: Clarendon Press, 1975.

493. A. Gramsci, *Selections from Prison Notebooks*, New York, International Publishers, 1973, pp. 106-120. According to Gramsci, a "passive revolution" is one which preempts the radical transformation which a given historical situation is ready for by a reform brought about by the traditional elite that enables them to maintain their political and cultural control.

494. EPRDF stands for the Ethiopian Peoples Revolutionary Democratic Front. It is a collection of ethnic parties, organized and led by the TPLF, the Tigrayan People's Liberation Front. It is widely recognized that the EPRDF is a fig leaf that the TPLF uses to hide the fact that it has a monopoly of political and economic power by using the ethnic parties within the EPRDF as surrogates for its rule in the ethnic states that make up the federation.

the failure to seize this event for a critical re-appropriation of Ethiopian history has deprived Ethiopia of the opportunity to complement the "military" victory of Adwa with an "intellectual and political" Adwa. The outcome of this failure has been a destructive understanding of the citizens of the country as "objects" of development and revolutions and the subsequent decline of Ethiopia into one of the poorest and oppressed countries of the current century.

The Absence of an "Intellectual Adwa"

The failure to deal with the economic, social and political decay that has taken root in Ethiopian society could be examined from various perspectives. But there is one aspect which, if not fundamental, is at least one of the main reasons that accounts for this failure: the kind of knowledge Ethiopians have brought to bear on their country's unending economic, social and political crises, and, consequently, the kind of knowledge that were and are driving the country's political options and practices aimed at overcoming these crises. Ethiopians did not complement the "military Adwa" with an "intellectual Adwa"; consequently, modern Ethiopian history is indelibly marked by their failure to apprehend their country's realities in ways that identify the real aspirations of Ethiopians and the real possibilities embedded in their life circumstances. This intellectual failure, and the inevitable erroneous political analysis and practices it has spawned, is integral to the crises in which Ethiopia is now immersed, and has prevented them from articulating productively the people's aspirations with their own social practices. Ethiopians might be in a better position to understand and perhaps overcome these intellectual and political failures were they to conduct an immanent critique of Adwa as an internal process, as well as of the social and political contradictions that have emerged from it and have spilled over into the present, with a view to uncover the subterranean emancipatory themes embedded in the conditions that made it possible.

However, an effort to uncover these emancipatory themes is bound to fail unless it is mediated by an approach that allows them to take a critical distance

495. Harold G. Marcus, op. cit. Sven Rubenson, *The Survival of Ethiopian Independence*, Addis Ababa: Addis Ababa University Press, 1978. G. F. H. Berkeley, *The Campaign of Adowa and the Rise of Menelik*, New York: Negro Universities Press, 1969. Ernest Work, *Ethiopia, A Pawn in European Diplomacy*, New Concord, Published by the author, 1935. Tekle Tsadik Mekuria, *Atse Menelik ena Ye -Ethiopia Andennet*, Addis Ababa, Kuraz Asatami Dirijit, 1983 (Ethiopian Calender) Gabre-Selassie Welde Aregai, *Tarike Zemen Ze-Dagmawi Menelik*, Addis Ababa, Berhan ena Selam, 1959 EC.

from Adwa and its aftermaths. And Ethiopians do not as yet have such a critical approach or theory internal to applied social practices. This does not mean that they have to borrow wholesale theories that others have produced as responses to their own social and political questions precipitated by their particular histories. Rather, it means that Ethiopians have to mine, like all societies who have successfully determined the direction and content of their lives have done, their own history and social practices in order to develop the theories needed to comprehend and overcome the internal adversities that the country presently confronts. One way of achieving this "historical awakening," or retrieving the emancipatory aspirations and ideas that still inhabit the country's history as tasks that are "not yet" accomplished, is through a critical reflection on the tasks of emancipation that the previous generations have initiated but not completed and whose failures still inhabit the country's present as open wounds. To bring out the necessity for such a critical reflection, the author considers the various questions that Adwa raises if theorized as an internal event, the different modes of production of knowledge — both internal and borrowed —that have prevented them from producing an emancipatory understanding of the country's citizens and their conditions, and, finally, reflect on Adwa as an unfinished internal battle that Ethiopians have to complete in order to produce knowledge that can effectively transform Ethiopians and their country in a way that makes possible the redemption of the hopes of the past and the achievement of democracy in the present.

The Primacy of the Internal Aspect of Adwa

The victory of Adwa created conditions that incubated new questions about national unity, equality and freedom. Though at the time, these ideals were understood primarily as independence from foreign domination, the recognition of these ideals as a justification for resisting external oppression nevertheless sowed the political seeds that in the long run transformed these ideals into goals to be pursued internally. It is this historical "richness" of Adwa, produced by the conjunction of external and internal political and social processes, which made Adwa the first "modern" and "national" historical event.

The internal circumstances, which led to the success of Adwa, contained within themselves the emergence of new political and social forces. Showa, the Amhara-Oromo synthesis that emerged as a powerful political force in the 19th century, was the pivot of the resurrection of the Ethiopian State. This state building was at the same time inscribed in the process of the anti-colonial struggle undertaken by Menelik against the territorial ambitions of Great Britain, France and Italy. Menelik's success in thwarting the designs of these colonial powers and his success in rebuilding the Ethiopian state — a goal that both Emperor Tewodros and Emperor Yohannes IV pursued diligently, but without success, and for which both sacrificed their lives — created new and contradictory political, social and economic constellations.[496]

Menelik responded to the new conditions by introducing some reforms, which led Marcus to note that, "In relation to his own social background, Menelik was a progressive man. He thought in liberal terms..."[497] His reign saw the introduction of a taxation system and of Ethiopia's first national currency; the initiation of new laws, such as the law of property inheritance, which took into account the changing nature of the economy; the establishment of the cabinet system of government; the opening of modern schools and hospitals; the building of the Addis-Djibouti railway line, still the only one in Ethiopia; the installation of telegraph and telephone systems; and other measures designed to respond to the needs created by the new political, social and economic developments.

However, the political, social and economic contradictions created by the resurrection of the Ethiopian state — the issues of freedom, equality and unity and of the increasing economic polarization between the peasants and the land owners — were in no way met, let alone resolved, by Menelik's very timid reforms. With the gradual insertion of Ethiopia into the world capitalist market in the post-Adwa period, these contradictions matured into serious political, social and economic crises; and, until now, no Ethiopian regime has been able to resolve them.

As a victory against an external power, much has been claimed regarding Adwa's relevance to Africans and people of African descent. Berkeley described it as "the first revolt of the Dark Continent against domineering Europe."[498] "The racial dimension," writes B. Zewde, "was what lent Adwa particular significance. It was a victory of Blacks over Whites." [499] This may be true, rhetorically

496. H. Marcus, *A History of Ethiopia*, Berkeley: University of California Press, 1994, p. 104
497. H. Marcus, *The Life and Times of Menelik I* p. 199. For the discussion in this paragraph see also pp. 174-213 and Paulos Gnogno, *Atse Menelik* Addis Ababa, 1992 (GC).
498. G. F-H. Berkeley, p. viii.
499. B. Zewde, *A History of Modern Ethiopia 1885-1974* Addis Ababa, Addis Ababa University, 1991, pp. 81.

and symbolically. Historically, however, the victory of Adwa did not become the spark that ignited the fire of anti-colonialism in Africa. The war against Nazism, the Russian and Chinese revolutions, Ghandi's non-violent movement in India and nationalist uprisings elsewhere had more ideological and political impact on anti-colonial struggles in Africa than the victory of Adwa.

As to why Adwa's impact on the African anti-colonial struggle never went beyond rhetorical references may be considered from various perspectives. Among these, however, stands out the fact that Adwa was reduced to its external aspect, that is, to an inter-state military conflict. The primacy given to this aspect of Adwa put the emphasis on the policies and actions of the ruling elites, thus expunging from it the emancipatory ideas that informed the motivations and aspirations of the men and women who, in making the victory possible, hoped for a better life.

But in Ethiopia, the new constellation of interests and social contradictions that emerged from Adwa eventually introduced into the stream of Ethiopian politics, via the question of external oppression, the issues of internal oppression. These issues are still present, embodied in relentless poverty, in ethnic politics and conflicts, and in the exclusion of the majority of Ethiopians as active political subjects from the decisions that affect their present and future conditions of life. Indeed, even an understanding of who the Ethiopian people are can no longer arise from just calling the country's citizens as Ethiopians, for the ethnicization of politics ushered in by the EPRDF[500] regime has shaken the certainty of the Ethiopian people's identity. It is the very category of "Ethiopian" that is currently contested. Who are we? Just a collection of ethnic groups, unwillingly squatting besides each other, preparing and waiting for the right time to implement what the 1994 Ethiopian constitution calls the right to secession?[501] Or, does Adwa — as the event that brought together the conditions that eventually gave birth to the idea of modernity in Ethiopia — prefigure a way of becoming Ethiopian such that the Ethiopian people's present doubts and conflicts are transitional expressions of the difficult unfolding of this modernity? Answering these questions requires that Ethiopians go beyond an empiricist account of the origin, conduct and outcome of the war, and uncover the immanent aspirations and motivations, the common and inter-subjective

500. The Ethiopian Peoples Revolutionary Democratic Front.
501. Article 39, 1, of the 1994 Constitution reads, "Every nation, nationality and people in Ethiopia has an unconditional right to self-determination, including the right to secession.

meanings,[502] that have made Adwa an event that overflows into the present and have a dominant presence in the people's collective memory.

Adwa, Collective Memory and Emancipation

It is almost an axiom of historical interpretation that "The past is intelligible to them only in the light of the present; and Ethiopians can fully understand the present only in light of the past."[503] However, the Ethiopian people's past and present cannot be rendered intelligible by conflating the past with the present. The past has its questions and concerns that differ from those of the present. The temporal distance between the past and the present is not an empty, homogeneous and mechanical time; it is the result of the effective history that has taken place in between. The in-between is articulated by various conflicts and contradictions, some old and dying, and others new and developing. To understand the present in which Ethiopians live then requires that Ethiopians elicit what is worth inquiring about it through a question-answer dialogue between the past and the present, mediated by the issues that Ethiopian history has precipitated as the focal points of the current circumstances, such as the rise of ethnic politics and the people's incapacity to create a democratic order, or even to feed themselves.

Adwa serves as an indispensable key for opening the door to such an inquiry. However, Ethiopians have to deal with Adwa as it inhabits the Ethiopian people's collective memory rather than as it is described in their official history, which narrates Adwa as a series of facts and reduce historical consciousness to a story of the events of the past.[504] Consequently, the current

502. C. Taylor, *Philosophy and the Human Sciences*, Cambridge, Cambridge University Press, 1988, pp. 15-57. "Common meanings are the basis of community. Inter-subjective meaning give a people a common language to talk about social reality and a common understanding of certain norms, but only with common meanings does this common reference world contain significant common actions, celebrations, and feelings. These are objects in the world that everybody shares. This is what makes community," p. 39. Though constitutive meanings are not immediately accessible to agents, they nevertheless are the grounds for the possibility of the existence of social practices in definite ways. And they are thoroughly historical. G. Funke, "Phenomenology and History" in M. Natanson, *Phenomenology and the Social Sciences*, vol. 2, Evanston: Northwestern University Press, 1973, pp. 3-102.

503. E. H. Carr, *What Is History*, New York: Random House, 1967, p. 69; H-G. Gadamer, *Truth and Method*, New York, Seabury Press, 1975, pp. 258-274, 333-341; Paul Ricoeur, *Temps et Récit*, Paris: Seuil, 1983, pp. 117-129. For an anti-empiricist and interpretative understanding of inquiry in the social sciences, Charles Taylor, op. cit., J. Habermas, *Knowledge and Human Interests*, Boston: Beacon Press, 1971.

knowledge of Adwa, and indeed the knowledge of Ethiopia's past as told in the country's official history, has not facilitated the production of a critical historical consciousness capable of preparing them to understand the world in which Ethiopians live. Nor has it made them capable of fulfilling the urgent task of rethinking the country's social practices as vehicles for translating the people's own aspirations for freedom and prosperity into the categories of modern ideas, values, institutions such that these categories express the Ethiopian people's own historical destiny in the modern world.

Despite this, Adwa has however resisted being reduced to a fact that merely inhabits the past precisely because, unlike the official history that has reduced it to a fact, collective memory has invested it with a singularity that has made it the historical happening par excellence that every Ethiopian, educated or not, knows as an event that surpasses all other events, and as a promise, however inchoately it is felt, of a different Ethiopia that is still unrealized. It is precisely this singular place it occupies in the Ethiopian collective memory as a "Truth Event" that has made Adwa the source of a spontaneous historical consciousness and the only historical event over whose appropriation the ruling elites have been fighting over since 1896. The Imperial Regime, the Derg and present day monarchists see in Adwa the legitimization for the existence of a homogeneous nation, the ethnic nationalists see it as the affirmation of Ethiopia as a "colonial power," and the TPLF considered it, at first, as a Tigrayan victory in which Menelik would have played a minor role, but then re-appropriated Adwa as the symbol of Ethiopia's resistance to foreign aggression during the 1998-2000 Badme conflict between Ethiopia and Eritrea. [505]

To appreciate the role of Adwa in the country's collective memory, it is necessary to clarify the meaning of collective memory. Collective memory is the

---

504. Consider the most widely used history textbooks: Tekle Tsadik Mekuria, *Atse Menelik ena Ye -Ethiopia Andenet*, Addis Ababa, Kuraz Asatami Dirijit, 1983 (EC) Gabre-Selassie Welde Aregai, *Tarike Zemen Ze-Dagmawi Menelik*, Addis Ababa, Berhan ena Selam, 1959 (EC) Paulos Gnogno, *Atse Menelik* Addis Ababa, 1992 (E. C).

505. The Meles regime had a nucleus of intellectuals, well represented at the Adwa Centenary Conference, 26 February–1 March, 1996, Addis Ababa, who consider Adwa as a Tigre-Italian conflict. A representative view is that of Iyasu Gayim who writes that the Italian Army "was crushed by the Tigrayans, who were assisted by Emperor Menelik." Quoted in Sven Rubenson, "The Falsification of History: When, Who and Why," *Ethiopian Register*, 3, 3 March 1996, p. 35. See also the daily discussion of this issue in *Addis Zemen* in the weeks preceding Yekatit 23, 1988 E. C., and the identification of the war against Eritrea with the war against Italy in *Addis Zemen*, after the capture of Adwa by Ethiopian forces.

past living in and informing their common and inter-subjective meanings. It is embedded in customs, myths, beliefs, institutions, and social practices; it is expressed in stories of struggles, of victories and defeats; it narrates the people's hopes and aspirations and the unfulfilled promises of the past. Collective memory "is one of the great stakes of developed and developing societies, of dominated and dominating classes, all of them struggling for power or for life...[It] is an essential element of...individual or collective identity...collective memory is not only a conquest, it is also an instrument and an objective of power."[506] Being the intersubjective dimension of the impersonal process of history, collective memory is inevitably complex, multiple and contradictory.

As one may see from the debate on the "colonial" nature of the Ethiopian state, to be discussed below, Ethiopian collective memory is complex and multiple because it is shaped by the concerns, interests and needs of the different classes and communities living under conditions of social, political and economic iniquities and struggles; it is variously interpreted by political actors to legitimate or condemn past and present events, projects and conditions. It is contradictory because, far from being homogeneous, it bears within itself ideas, values and practices that both affirm and challenge the dominant power relations. It is what one may call a "systematically distorted" narration of events, experiences, beliefs and aspirations.[507] But if subjected to a critical reflexive reading, it delivers the repressed and hidden aspirations for freedom, equality and social justice.

The Struggle for Collective Memory

Seen in this light, the Ethiopian collective memory has always been and still is an object of struggle for defining the past, the present, and the future. Each ruling elite appropriates the past from its perspective, and narrates it as the

---

506. J. Le Goff, *History and Memory*, New York: Columbia University Press, 1992, p. 97–98. Le Goff, an eminent member of the Annals school of historiography, emphasizes the importance of the dialectics between collective memory and history. In this essay, my discussion of the role of collective memory in human emancipation is indebted to his.

507. J. Habermas, "Toward a Theory of Communicative Competence" in H. P. Dreitzel, ed., *Recent Sociology No. 2: Patterns of Communicative Behavior*, New York, Macmillan, 1970, pp. 115-148. According to Habermas, the "asymmetrical distribution of chances for the legitimate satisfaction of needs" arising from the asymmetrical arrangements of economic and political power generates repression leading to distorted communication.

collective memory of the people with a view of legitimating the political regime it imposes on the people.

The ruling elites' effort to control the collective memory of Ethiopians is reflected in the way Ethiopian history is flattened into a one-dimensional narrative centered on the state. Those in power evacuate the historical depth of the previous generation's deeds and replace them with a "drum-and-trumpet" history — a narrative that reduces the history of Ethiopia to a succession of struggles between princes and kings, occludes the daily struggles of the people against poverty and oppression, silences their hopes of a better life, and marginalizes their acts of resistance as brigandage or shiftanet.

Adwa is probably the event in Ethiopian history that has been drained the most of its unique historical depth and transformed into one of the numerous "drum-and-trumpet" events that are strung out in the hegemonic narrative of Ethiopian history to form a linear, monovocal and unitary national story that is claimed to have started with Menelik I, son of Queen Saba and King Solomon of Israel. In this scheme, Adwa is reduced to a military victory against foreign aggression and is fixed in the hegemonic narrative uniquely and only as an externally oriented event, as an affair between two states Ethiopia and Italy. What is forgotten in this narrative is what Adwa raised between the lines — the issue of what kind of a nation Ethiopia would be in the context of the inequalities of power that characterized this first ever pan-Ethiopian identity-formation process that brought together peoples from every corner of the country and successfully transcended their regional and ethnic identities to construct Ethiopians as a people fighting for their freedom.

Still, the ruling elites' hegemonic history does not exhaust the themes that animate the Ethiopian collective memory. The resistance to domination and the aspirations for freedom, equality and justice run through it as its "unofficial," or repressed content, as lore, popular poems and songs and stories. From the perspective of emancipation, this "unofficial" content stands in a relationship of metonymy to "the true history of the past," and points to the "buried potentialities of the present."[508] insofar as this "unofficial" content connects with the present circumstances and intimates the existence of these aspirations as potentialities "not yet" realized. This "not yet" invites them to "shape an unfinished world" in light of the yearnings of the previous generations for a better life. And

508. For this quote and the quotes in the following sentence, P. Ricoeur, *Hermeneutics and the Human Sciences*, Cambridge: Cambridge University Press, 1981, p. 295.

when Ethiopians fail to actualize this "not yet," the "unofficial" content of the Ethiopian people's collective memory continues to lead a subterranean existence. Prevented from actualizing itself, this "not yet" returns cyclically to the foreground of Ethiopia's national life, exploding into a political crisis that is more intense and more destructive with each new re-enactment, as one could see in the increasing intensification of political conflicts from the first coup d'état in 1960, to the rise of the Derg in 1974, and the subsequent descent into ethnic politics in 1991. Unless the struggle for emancipation, which lies repressed in the country's collective memory, is not brought to light and actualized as a consciously pursued political objective, the future of Ethiopia will continue to be no more than modernized variations of past oppression and poverty. Adwa stands at the juncture of this problematic insofar as it is appropriated by the ruling elites as a "drum-and — trumpet" event whereas its "unofficial" content of unfulfilled promises hovers in the Ethiopian people's collective memory as a "yet-not" presence.

Freeing Adwa from its "drum-and-trumpet" straight jacket, and indeed the Ethiopian past and present, Ethiopians need an indigenously rooted critical theory, that is, "a reflective theory" which gives Ethiopians "a kind of knowledge inherently productive of enlightenment and emancipation."[509] It is the absence of this kind of critical knowledge, capable of guiding the country's social practices, and not the lack of struggles for freedom and justice, that has made it impossible to bring about an "intellectual Adwa" or an authentic understanding of the present society and a "political Adwa" or a victory against internal oppression. This failure has landed them in the cul de sac of poverty, inequality, dictatorship and ethnic politics, more than a century after Adwa. To grasp the source of this failure and the importance of creating knowledge capable of liberating the seeds of emancipation sown at Adwa, Ethiopians need an indigenous critical theory.

THE NEED FOR CRITICAL THEORY

Though Ethiopians have escaped, through the victory of Adwa, the destructive experience of prolonged colonialism suffered by many African coun-

509. R. Geuss, *The Idea of A Critical Theory*, Cambridge: Cambridge University Press, 1981, p. 2. See also, J. Habermas, *Knowledge and Human Interests*, Boston: Beacon Press, 1971, pp. 191-317.

tries, they share with them the tragic experience of being objectified, observed, described, and analyzed by others working from within historical horizons with which Ethiopians have not been, and are not as yet, in a dialogical relationship. What is currently available to them is a monological dialogue — a dialogue conducted from within the framework of one of the communicating parties, that is, the West, without any actual "inter-subjective consensus" on the terms of the dialogue.[510] As a result, though Western academics have studied the Ethiopian people's cultures and history extensively, Ethiopians still are, as St. Augustine, the African bishop, would have put it, a question to themselves.

The possible answers to which Ethiopians are and what they are capable of becoming cannot but be enucleated from the Ethiopian people's history. But these possible answers are not mere data to be directly apprehended. Rather, they are buried in the Ethiopian people's collective memory and social practices; they are fully enmeshed with all the contradictions, the hegemonic interests and ideas, and the "unofficial content" or the repressed dimensions that characterize the country's collective memory. To have access to them requires the Ethiopian people's own reflective labor. Without such reflective labor, the people's understanding of themselves and of their society will lack authenticity and fail to translate itself into an active force capable of overcoming the oppression and poverty that has been the lot of the Ethiopian people for centuries.

The Lack of Internal Understanding

To be sure, Ethiopia is flooded with externally produced knowledge-claims that purport to respond to the social and political questions precipitated by Ethiopian history. The issue is not whether the knowledge others have produced on them is true or false. This is a question of a different order. Rather, the question is: Has borrowed knowledge — modernization, Marxist, neo-liberal, and ethnic theories — led to emancipatory social practices in Ethiopia? The answer is no. Despite the billions of dollars of foreign aid received since 1945, the thousands of foreign advisors and technical assistants lodged in almost every area of the economy and in every branch of government, and the generous borrowings of both theoretical and applied knowledge, Ethiopia is still one of the most backward countries, to use the correct term rather than a euphemism, on the planet.[511]

510. J. Habermas, *Moral Consciousness and Communicative Action*, Cambridge, MIT Press, pp. 43-115.

One may wonder why knowledge that has brought so much social and economic transformation in the West seems to be so ineffective in Ethiopia. The difference lies in that this knowledge emerged from within the life-world of Western societies as responses to their doubts, questions and problems, as activities of self-examination and self-interpretation, as ways of seeing more clearly into the opacities generated by their social practices. But this knowledge, introduced into Ethiopia as borrowed knowledge, brings with it historical and cultural presuppositions that are alien to Ethiopian history and culture. It cannot transform the society unless it is critically mediated by the people's values, institutions, and the common and inter-subjective meanings that are constitutive of who Ethiopians are. Inevitably, borrowed knowledge, un-subjected to critical mediation, has made the society progressively more opaque and rendered the country's political, social and economic problems more and more intractable.

This does not mean that reason and science, as they developed in the West, are irrelevant to us. The relativism that considers these as inherently ethnocentric must be rejected. The question for them is: Did Ethiopia experience the kind of self-examination and self-interpretation that authentic knowledge requires and imposes? She could have, but she did not, because Ethiopians have limited themselves to mere borrowing of the end-results of European reason and science. This borrowed knowledge exists for them as a disparate collection of ready-made tools rather than as ways of active understanding of themselves and their conditions. This unmediated borrowing and the attendant lack of self-examination have blinded them to the potentials that lie within the Ethiopian people's history, traditions and society, has crippled them as historical agents, making them incapable of determining the country's future in ways that are consistent with the people's aspirations.

One important consequence of uncritically borrowed knowledge is the imposition of Eurocentric theory of historical change. This condemns Ethiopia to define its future in terms of the Western experience of social transformation, leading them to policies that mimic the West's experience of development in order to solve the country's non-Western problems. But the West itself has not developed by mimicking others; rather, it has done so through an internal understanding of its conditions and of the adversities it has to overcome. True, the West borrowed the "0," the numerals, and algebra from the Arabs, but it did not try to mimic Arabic or Islamic civilization; it took the art of making paper, gun-

511. UNDP, Human Development Indicators, 2004.

powder, and the compass from the Chinese, but it did not mimic Chinese civilization. Not surprisingly, then, borrowed knowledge, which in Ethiopia exists primarily as unmediated and uncritical knowledge, has the opposite effect in the country: It has not expanded and transformed their self-understanding; it has not enabled them to build a society of freedom, prosperity and social justice. It has on the contrary inflicted incalculable harm on Ethiopians. A number of issues need to be clarified to understand the difference between the productive and emancipatory outcome of Western knowledge in the West and its authoritarian and impoverishing impact in Ethiopia.

Europeans have gained an internal understanding of themselves through the double process of self-study and the study of others. Given the obviousness of the first, let me deal with the second. The knowledge created by Europeans from studying non-Europeans has expanded their fund of knowledge and deepened their understanding of their own histories, societies, and of themselves by using the "other" as a detour or a foil for rediscovering themselves in a new light. The history of Western social sciences shows that "other-understanding is always in a sense comparative," that there is no "view from nowhere" which gives one an "objective" understanding of the other on the model of the natural sciences.[512] That is, the knowledge that others produce about them is part and parcel of their activities of self-understanding. Malinowski, the anthropologist, encapsulated this idea when he wrote, "What is the deepest essence in my investigations? To discover what are his [the native's] main passions, the motives for his conduct, his aims...His essential, deepest way of thinking. At this point Ethiopians are confronted with specific problems: for example, what is essential to the Ethiopian people?"[513] The self-understanding Westerners draw from such comparison articulates itself as theory internal to their history and society, that is, internal to their common and inter-subjective meanings. Consequently the knowledge that drives their social practices is not experienced as alien to their life-world; rather, it enriches and drives it towards new horizons. Such is not the case with us.

Our fund of self-knowledge is nowhere comparable to that of the West. In addition, due to the historical ascendance of the West, what the West has produced about them confronts them externally as knowledge on us. As knowledge

512. C. Taylor, *Philosophical Arguments* Cambridge, Harvard University Press, 1995, pp. 146-164 (emphasis added) on some of the questions that arise when studying other societies and cultures. This of course raises the issue of monological dialogue. See J. Habermas, "Toward a Theory of Communicative Competence."

that narrates them from the Archimedean point of the constitutive meanings of another society, it is external to and disconnected from the constitutive meanings of their social practices. It thus loses for them its reflexive and critical character. Nor is the comparative dimension available to them as a source of self-understanding insofar as their knowledge of European society, history and culture is not the result of what Ethiopians themselves have discovered about the West but rather of what Westerners themselves have produced as knowledge of themselves. Ethiopians know about the West what the West tells them about itself. Though Ethiopians borrow a lot from the West, Ethiopians could say that Ethiopians do not know the West well enough to develop a comparative knowledge of themselves. This combination of lack of self-knowledge with a knowledge of the West that merely repeats what the West says about itself has reduced them to being undiscriminating and insatiable consumers of Western knowledge as "prêt à porter" rather than being creators of emancipatory knowledge. As a result, the "revolutions" and "reforms" that have been imposed on them since 1960 are hardly related to the inter-subjective and common meanings that inform their life world. It is not surprising then that the theories that animated their revolutions and reforms and their outcomes make them often feel and indeed make them act as if Ethiopians were aliens to their own cultures, history and society.

The internal obstacles to critical reflection embedded in Ethiopian cultures reinforce this dependence on external knowledge. With the exception of the flicker of rationalism in the sixteenth century,[514] Ethiopian intellectual traditions are dominated by naïve realism and elite-centered discourse. Neither the first nor the second is able to provide the critical conceptual tools needed for

---

513. B. Malinowski, *Diary in the Strict Sense of the Term* New York, Harcourt, Brace and World, 1967, p. 119. Consider also, for example, the role played by the Enlightenment's idea of the "noble savage," Margaret Mead's anthropological study of "sexuality," Picasso's "African masks," Levi Strauss's "savage mind," etc. in the self-understanding of Europeans. The study of other societies and cultures, from Montaigne through Locke, Rousseau, Weber, down to Claude Levi Strauss; the travel literature of the past four centuries; the place of "natives" in Western literature; and comparative social science studies, have served and continue to serve as a foil for the West's self-reflection and self-understanding. See also, Edward said, *Orientalism*, London, Routledge, 1978. In the case of Ethiopia some studies which play the same role are, Michel Leiris, *La Possession et ses aspects théâtraux chez les Ethiopiens de Gondar*, Paris, Plon, 1958. Donald L. Levine. *Wax and Gold*, Chicago, Chicago University Press, 1972.

514. Zera Yakob (1599-1692), initiated a critical rationalist method, *Hateta*. However, Ethiopians have yet to build on this beginning. C. Sumner, *Classical Ethiopian Philosophy*, Los Angeles, Adey, 1994.

grasping and overcoming the contradictions that have emerged from the circumstances that made Adwa possible.

Consider the current ethnicization of Ethiopian politics. It is in part rooted in the naïve realism dominant in some of Ethiopia's indigenous intellectual traditions of social interpretation. According to this naïve realism, there are ethnic groups, each with its own ethnos, culturally homogeneous, and providing a fixed background of essential norms and beliefs which would determine one's identity as an Oromo or an Amhara or a Tigre, and so forth.[515] When this naïve realist conception of ethnic groups meets Western empiricist anthropological and historical studies of Ethiopia, it generates a "modern" discourse which upgrades the naïve realist conception of the ethnie to scientific respectability, thus naturalizing ethnicity. It is this process of reification of ethnicity that informs the 1994 Constitution and the creation of the current ethnic federation made up of ethnicstans, that is, each ethnie its own state.

A double play is taking place here. The social sciences, which developed as discourses of self-reflection of Western societies, naturalize their local naïve realist ethnic description of social groups as Oromo, Amhara, Tigrai, Somali, and so forth, and make them available as a comparative foil for understanding in a new light the Western process of citizen identity-formation, while this same knowledge, accepted by them "as is," reinforces the boundaries between ethnic groups and inhibits the full emergence of the modern Ethiopian identity that was gestated in the conditions that led to the convergence of Ethiopians as a people in Adwa. That is, the empiricist reading of their society reinforces their naïve realist self-understanding and sharpens the boundaries of ethnic identity.

Second, a similar dead end is reached with the scheme of interpretation offered by the other aspect of their indigenous intellectual tradition: the elite centered appropriation of their past and present which tends to reduce history

515. Abba Bahrey, "History of the Galla" *Some Records of Ethiopia, 1593-1646*, That this kind of naïve realism was the dominant discourse in the formative period of Ethiopian modernity, that is, in the immediate post-Adwa period, is discernable in Bahru Zewde`s discussion of the political writings of intellectuals of this period. Bahru Zewde, *Pioneers of Change in Ethiopia: The Reformist Intellectuals of the Early Twentieth Century*. Oxford, James Curry, 2002. C. Beckingham and G. W. B. Huntingford. eds., London, Hakluyt Society, 1954, pp. 111-139. The ontologization of ethnicity by the EPRP, Meison, the Meles regime and ethnic nationalists fully shares the naïve realism that informs Abba Bahrey's "History...." But it is more justifiable in his case, since he was describing a relatively new situation. But to adopt the same view after 400 years of history is to consider the present population of Ethiopia as fossils of groups that existed centuries ago. See discussion below.

to the biographies of rulers and hagiographies of religious people.[516] This intellectual tradition, which espouses a "drum-and-trumpet" approach to events, is related to the naïve realist aspect of their intellectual tradition. It conflates power with the holders of power, and the nature of power with the biography of the powerful. In this tradition, the narration of the deeds of and the struggles between the powerful replace reflections on the social forces, circumstances and processes that drive political power and political relations. As a result, the deeds, aspirations and motivations of the men and women who through their labor, commerce and sacrifice have constituted Ethiopia as a historic community are absent from their intellectual traditions as harbingers of emancipatory practices, hopes, values and ideals.

When this elite-centered tradition of social interpretation meets borrowed knowledge such as modernization, development, Marxist, and other social science theories, it reinforces the Ethiopian ruling elites' self-understanding as the bearer of imported salvation to Ethiopians — socialism according to Mengestu, and ethnicism according to Meles. Compounded with the massive support the Ethiopian state — be it monarchic, military, or ethnicist — gets from the international state-based system, and fortified by its role as the gate-keeper of economic, political and cultural relations with the outside world, this conjunction of the traditional and of the social-scientific bolsters the ruling elites' traditional understanding of Ethiopians as mere predicates of their rulers. Thus reified, Ethiopians appear as a discrete collection of ethnies, without a collective consciousness of being a people. Currently, then, ethnicity, an ever-changing aspect of their life and history is reified as a natural fact. [517] However, this reification creates its own question: But how is it that Ethiopians have in fact acted in Adwa, as a people? As the question is made possible by the denial that Ethiopians are a people, the denial itself provides the answer: that the "unity" of Ethiopians is a façade that hides a colonially imposed state. Thus is born the "colonial thesis."

---

516. D. Levine, Wax and Gold, pp. 271-2; Tadesse Tamrat, *Church and State in Ethiopia: 1270-1527*, Oxford, Clarendon Press, 1972. See also P. Garretson, cited in H. Erlich, *Ethiopia and Eritrea During the Scramble: A Political Biography of* Ras *Alula, 1875-1897*, Michigan. The dominance of this approach was already commented upon in the post-Adwa period by Gabre Heywat, one of the prominent intellectuals of the era. According to Bahru Zewde, Gabre Heywat identifies in his writings "two types of historians in the past: the official chroniclers and the clerical historians," and condemns their dominant mode of historical explanation which is to resort to benign or malignant supernatural powers. Bahru Zewde, op. cit. p. 142.

The Poverty of the "Colonial Thesis"

It is not then surprising that more than a century after Adwa, Ethiopians end up with a borrowed political theory, that of colonialism, that ontologizes ethnic identity and falsely represents Ethiopia as a collection of discrete, ethnic communities, brought together by "Amhara colonialism." This is the "colonial thesis" or "the nationalities question" that is central to the discourse of "radical" Ethiopian intellectuals since the 1960s, [518] who, in their effort to go beyond their traditional naïve realism and elite centered discourse, borrowed wholesale the theory of colonialism that Europe generated as knowledge of its own self-understanding and self-criticism.

Born out of a lack of an internal understanding of their history, this borrowed theory has wrought havoc on contemporary Ethiopia, leading to the creation of ethnic liberation fronts, the secession of Eritrea, the creation of ethnicstans within Ethiopia, and the institutionalization of ethnic politics in the 1994 Constitution.[519] However, the gaps between the presuppositions of the colonial thesis and the conditions that made Adwa possible are so great that the colonial thesis had to be recast using ad hoc theoretical epicycles.

---

517. Consider for example the ontologization of ethnic identity by P. T. W. Baxter, "The Creation and Constitution of Oromo Identity', in K. Fukui and J. Markakis, eds., *Ethnicity and Conflict in the Horn of Africa*, London: James Curry, 1994, pp. 167-186; H. S. Lewis, "Ethnicity in Ethiopia: The View from Below..." in C. Young, ed., *The Rising Tide of Cultural Pluralism*, Madison: The University of Wisconsin Press, 1993, pp. 158-178. This ontologization of ethnicity is espoused by the MELES REGIME and ethnic nationalists. See A. Jalata, *Oromia and Ethiopia: State Formation and Ethnonational Conflict, 1868-1992*, Boulder, Lynne Reinner, 1991. Holcomb B. and S. Ibsa, *The Invention of Ethiopia*, Trenton, Red Sea Press, 1991. This ontologization of ethnicity is now enshrined in the 1994 Constitution penned by the TPLF, itself an ethnic liberation movement.
518. Addis Hiwet, *Ethiopia: from autocracy to revolution*, London, ROAPE Occasional Publication No. 1, 1975, p. 3; B. Habte Selassie, *Conflict and Intervention in the Horn of Africa*, New York, Monthly Review Press, 1980. A. Jalata, *Oromia and Ethiopia: State Formation and Ethnonational Conflict, 1868-1992*, op. cit. Holcomb B. and S. Ibsa, *The Invention of Ethiopia*, op. cit. The Ethiopian Students Movements of the '6os, MEISON, EPRP, ethnic movements such as the OLF, the EPLF, and the current Meles regime, have resorted to the concept of "colonialism" as the lens through which to read Ethiopian history. The concept of "colonialism" is used in a vague and impressionistic way and is metaphorically based on the European experience. In all cases it boils down to describing the integration of the surrounding areas by the center, a historical process of state building that characterizes all states. Such acts of state building are by their very nature violent and involve relations of domination and exploitation. See C. Tilly, ed., *The Formation of National States in Western Europe*, Princeton, Princeton University Press, 1975.

The Ptolemaic method of the colonial thesis

The Marxist concept of colonialism is derived from the logic of capitalist reproduction.[520] But traditional Ethiopia did not have a capitalist mode of production. Because of this hiatus between the borrowed theory and the Ethiopian historical forms of production, analysts of "Ethiopia as a colonial power" zealously apply the Ptolemaic method of "saving the phenomenon," to borrow the expression of the pre-Copernican astronomers, by adding "epicycles" to the Marxist theory of colonialism until the reality fits the dogmatically imposed theory. In a statement that conflates the historical processes expressed in different modes of productions and social formations, Addis Hiwet writes that, "The same historical forces that created the 'Gold Coast,' the 'Ivory Coast,' the Sudan and Kenya were the very ones that created modern Ethiopia"; and he adds, "the conceptual tool that best describes the whole social-economic structure" of Ethiopia is "military-feudal-colonialism."[521]

This military-feudal-colonialism "conceptual tool" is an epicycle added to Marxist theory. It "saves the phenomenon," but it does not render a historical event of Adwa intelligible. The historical novelty of a "national Ethiopian" army at Adwa (the first pan-Ethiopian army in history) is unaccounted for; the term "feudal" conveniently conflates the differing European and Ethiopian modes of land ownership and occludes the specificity of the Ethiopian social formation; and "colonialism" is tagged on in a way that invites the reader to transfer the

---

519. The interpretation of Ethiopian history as colonial history appears to be now the official line. Dr. Negaso Gidada, the President of Ethiopia, on March 2, 1996, at Mesquel Square said: "Emperor Menelik invaded the people in southern, eastern and Western Ethiopia and imposed upon them a brutal national oppression... The expansionist invasion that Menelik had carried out had caused the massacre of numerous people, inflicted on the rest humiliation and national oppression." This is a point repeatedly made by Mr. Dawit Yohannes, the Speaker of the House in various official and non-official pronouncements. An interesting aspect surrounding the celebrations of Adwa is the use of Emperor Yohannes IV and Emperor Menelik II by the opposing sides as symbols for what each stands for, though it must be said that those who praise Menelik do not in any way denigrate Yohannes whereas those who favor Yohannes seem to paint Menelik as a "colonialist." See also Dawit Yohannes, the former legal adviser of Meles Zenawi and current Speaker of the House, who claimed, "Ethiopians say there is no country called Ethiopia..." *Financial Times*, May 5, 1995.

520. Sholomo Avvineri, ed., *Karl Marx on Colonialism and Modernization*, New York, Anchor Books, 1969.

521. Addis Hiwet, *Ethiopia: from autocracy to revolution* pp. 3-4. For other examples of such "epicycles" see Holcomb B. and S. Ibsa, *The Invention of Ethiopia*, pp. 11-26. On the use of epicycles to "save the phenomenon," see P. Duhem, *Le Système du monde- Histoire des doctrines cosmologiques de Plato à Copernic*, Paris, Vrin, 1917.

European historical process of capitalist expansion to Ethiopia's qualitatively different territorial self-definition. The "militaryfeudal-colonialism" epicycle thus reduces a complex historical process to some of its visible aspects — the existence of military campaigns and of a traditional economic system that is non-capitalist — in order to generate a "Marxist" theory that is tailor-made to explain the formation of the Ethiopian state as a "colonial" enterprise. Even this distortion of Marxist theory is inadequate to hide the shortcoming of the "colonial" thesis. To compensate for this inadequacy, the adepts of the colonial thesis add another "epicycle" by smuggling in a Weberian conception of the state into their Marxist analysis.

According to Weber, "the state is a political entity" that "claims the monopoly of the legitimate use of physical force within a given territory."[522] Emperor Menelik's use of force in the process of the Ethiopian state-building is thus read as an "illegitimate use of physical force" outside a given territory, to wit, "Abyssinia," suggesting that what Emperor Menelik was engaged in was colonization and not the unification of peoples that in some sense were within the same historical horizon. Such a reading, however, is based on the questionable assumption that Weber's concepts — state, political entity, and legitimacy — can immediately cash into Ethiopian politics, without any critical discursive mediation that grasps the specificity of Ethiopian history. Weber had in mind European history when he wrote, "the state is a political entity" whose extent is limited to the "territory" that is subject to the state's "legitimate use of physical force." But the Weberian way of conceptualizing the relationships between state and political entity does not grasp adequately the specificity of Ethiopian politics as seen in Ethiopia's own history.

Only partially did the existence of Ethiopia's identity as "a political entity" depends on the "physical force" of the state. For centuries, factors other than physical force have also been crucial in the constitution of Ethiopia as a shared historical and political space. Cultural, economic, social, religious and mythological factors as well as commerce, political alliances, and demographic movements have played important roles in the creation of Ethiopia as a shared historical space. Historically, the reach of the "physical force" of the Ethiopian state has always been in constant flux, due to internal conflicts and external aggressions, mainly Egyptian, Turkish, and Italian. Throughout the period of

522. H. H. Gerth and C. Wright Mills, eds. *Max Weber*, New York: Oxford University Press, 1970, p. 77. Emphasis in original.

expansion and contraction of the Ethiopian state, the capacity or the incapacity of the state to project its "physical force" was not articulated in the collective memory of Ethiopians as the essential factor that defined Ethiopia as a "political entity." During most of the history of Ethiopia, the boundaries between the Ethiopian "territory" and the Ethiopia "state" did not always coincide. The constitution of Ethiopians as a people and the formation of Ethiopia as a "political entity" cannot thus be reduced to the fluctuations of the reach of the "physical force" of the state. A recent illustration of this asymmetry between Ethiopians and the Ethiopian state is the secession of Eritrea. From the historical perspective, the secession produces two states for one people.

What has to be recognized is that the Marxist concept of colonialism and the Weberian concept of state are not mere discursive tools applied universally to any history, as the laws of physics are to any part of the physical universe. Social practices and their outcome, human history, is not inert matter. The Marxist and Weberian concepts emerged in a historical context deeply entwined with the rise of capitalism and, as Weber shows, of utilitarian or means-end rationality, and are integral to the West's effort to make its historical actions and processes less opaque to itself. The historical context that produced these concepts neither overlaps nor is similar to the historical context out of which emerged Adwa and the conditions that made it possible.

The reading of Ethiopian history in terms of these concepts is not an innocuous error. In politics, words matter. The application of these borrowed concepts and the theories that articulate them has not only clouded their self-understanding and made their society and history opaque to Ethiopians; it has also brought untold suffering in generating policies and solutions which have driven Ethiopia deeper into poverty and oppression. The history of "modernization" in Ethiopia shows the impotence and the danger of theories when they have no roots in the history of the social practices they try to explain.

The radical inadequacy of the concept of "colonialism" and its underlying theory to make sense of Ethiopian historical and existential realities could be seen from a different angle by considering the qualitative differences between the European and the Ethiopian historical experiences that the "colonial thesis" conflates. If Ethiopians take the case of the relationships between the Amharas and the Oromos, relationships described as "colonial" by the adepts of the colonial thesis,[523] and compare them to those that existed between Britain and her African colonies, Ethiopians note telling differences.

A Counter-Evidence to the Colonial Thesis

Colonialism is a total phenomenon of domination.[524] As such, its distinguishing feature is the use of social, political, economic and spatial exclusions of the colonized as the basis for the organization of political power, social and economic institutions, and space, symbolized by the quintessentially colonial practice — racial segregation. Is this the experience of the Oromos and the Amharas?

To start with, both the Oromo and the Amhara share, for the most part, the same geographical and historical space; this of course is not true, for example, of Britain and her African colonies. As a result, the personal, social, political, economic interrelationships between the Oromo and the Amhara are so widespread that no clear cultural and demographic boundaries can be established between the two. Indeed, millions of Ethiopians in Showa, Wallo, Gojam, Harar, Wallaga, etc., trace their ancestors to both groups, something one can hardly say about the British and the Ashanti, or the British and any of the African peoples they colonized. The Oromo and the Amhara were so intertwined politically, culturally and economically that the Oromo language was at one time during the Zemene Mesafint (1769–1855) a court language in Gondar; no African language remotely came close to enjoy such a status in London. Indeed, during the Zemene Mesafint, the Oromo elite were the kingmakers in Gondar; Africans were nowhere close to the seats of British power, let alone kingmakers in London. The intermarriages between the Amhara and the Oromo ruling elites were and are still extensive; nothing similar has ever happened between the British and, say, the Buganda or the Swazi royal families, or between the British and African ruling elites. Thousands of Amhara, from nobles to peasants, educated and unlettered, served loyally, both in peace and wartime, Oromo ministers and generals.[525] This would be like having thousands of Englishmen, nobles and

523. A. Jalata, *Oromia and Ethiopia: State Formation and Ethnonational Conflict*, op. cit. Holcomb B. and S. Ibsa, *The Invention of Ethiopia*, op. cit. P. T. W. Baxter, "The Creation and Constitution of Oromo Identity', op. cit; H. S. Lewis, "Ethnicity in Ethiopia, op. cit. ; H. S. Lewis, *A Gala Monarchy: Jimma Abba Jifar, Ethiopia 1830-1932*, Madison, University of Wisconsin Press, 1965.

524. Georges Balandier, *Anthropologie Politique*, Paris, PUF, 1978.

525. Among the most illustrious of the Oromo generals are Ras GOBANA and Fitawrari HabteGiorgis. For the names of some of the prominent leaders, see *Tobia*, 4, 6 Megabit 1988 (EC) and *Tobia*, 4, 8, Sene 1988 (EC). On the Zemene Mesafint, see Mordechai Abir, *Ethiopia: The Era of the Princes*, op. cit.

commoners, loyally serving African ministers and generals in England itself, something that never happened, and cannot happen under a colonial system.

This demographic and cultural interpenetration is recognized in their collective memory. As Markakis notes, "the Tigre are apt to refer to the Amhara ... as half-Galla."[526] Ethiopians consider this claim a truism. The Oromos and Amharas share numerous cultural markers in their daily lives, ranging over such things as food, clothing, customs and mores, beliefs, myths, religions, vocabularies, social institutions, and styles of communication. It is the extensive and profound symbiosis between the Amharas and the Oromos that made possible Menelik's reconstruction of Ethiopia as well as the anti-colonial victory of Adwa. One of the conditions that made Adwa possible and gave birth to modern Ethiopia is the Amhara-Oromo synthesis.[527] It is very difficult to claim that Great Britain is an English-Ashanti or an English-Kikuyu synthesis either ethnically, or politically, or culturally.

What this brief comparison suggests is that the very idea of comparing the history of Europe's colonization of Africans with the Ethiopian historical process of state-building over an already historically shared space is the result of borrowed theory which in its externality to Ethiopian history imposes a crude empiricism which reduces all oppression to colonialism. The "colonial" thesis takes the complex and contradictory social practices and meanings out of the

526. J. Markakis, *Ethiopia: Anatomy of a Traditional Polity*, Oxford, Clarendon Press, 1974, p. 48.

527. That historical processes have led to a profound interpenetration — cultural, social, economic, political and demographic — among the major Ethiopian ethnic populations, and especially between the Oromos and the Amharas, is noted by historians. See Mordechai Abir, *Ethiopia: The Era of the Princes*, London: Longmans, 1968. H. Marcus, *A History of Ethiopia*, Berkeley, University of California Press, 1994, pp. 30-84; R. L. Hess, *Ethiopia: The Modernization of Autocracy*, Ithaca: Cornell University Press, 1970, p. 13. C. Clapham, *Transformation and Continuity in Revolutionary Ethiopia*, Cambridge, Cambridge university press, 1988, pp 216-217. The Amhara-Oromo synthesis is an important element of their collective memory, something, for example, the Italians were unable to see both in 1896 and 1935. R. Greenfield, *Ethiopia: A New Political History*, London: Pall Mall, 1965, p. 230, "The Italians appear not to have understood that leading families were as often Galla as Amhara, or were a mixture of both, and constitute a class, not an ethnic group. " Within Ethiopia this Amhara-Oromo synthesis is recognized by the Tigrayan reference to Amharas as "half-Galla." See J. Markakis, Anatomy of a Traditional Polity, op. cit pp. 46-7. This seems to be true for the ruling classes also. P. Marital de Salviac, Un peuple antique au pays de Menelik; Les Gala, Paris, 1902. De Salviac noted in 1902 that it was difficult to find an Ethiopian lord or prince who did not have one or more "Galla" ancestors p 241. The Oromo played a prominent role in the rise of Showa. Without Oromo leaders of the caliber of Ras GOBANA and Fitawrari Habte Giorgis, Menelik would probably not have succeeded in rebuilding the Ethiopian Empire so swiftly.

historical processes that formed the Ethiopian polity and reduces it to an extension of European colonial history. In so doing, it transmogrifies their past into the gravedigger of the present and submits the future to arbitrary and destructive actions, precisely because the unmediated and uncritical borrowing of such theories invariably leads to treating Ethiopia as a tabula rasa.

Ethiopia as a "Tabula Rasa"

With Adwa reduced to a military victory against a foreign invader and later misread as a moment in the unfolding of the so-called "Abyssinian colonialism," Adwa's internal dimension as an event that incubated (in the actions of the common people who united to defeat the threat of external oppression) the possibilities of resistance to internal oppression is stifled. With this silencing of Adwa as a bearer of a better future, the past is treated as if it has nothing to say on the kind of future Ethiopians would like to construct. The people are thus invariably treated as a tabula rasa for social and political experiments such as the "socialist experiment" of Mengestu and the "ethnic experiment" of Meles.

Both experiments necessitated the use of destructive violence against the people because both were radical negations of what Ethiopians have accomplished historically: Mengestu imposed collectivism on a society that has historically developed a way of life rooted in the acceptance of individual merit;[528] Meles imposed ethnic identity as a criterion of political association on a society that has already started moving at Adwa from closed ethnicity to fluid ethnicity and has initiated the restructuring of Ethiopia as political space for all ethnicities.

Not only Ethiopians but Ethiopian territory is treated as a tabula rasa, as an empty, ahistorical, geometrical space that can be divided into so many abstract units. The Derg did it with its arbitrarily drawn regions, and the Meles regime is doing it with its artificially drawn ethnicstans or ethnic "Killils." This kind of map-making which treats Ethiopia as if it were a territory without history, and denies the deeply rooted, historically formed regional identities, assumes that the historical sedimentation of social practices which transformed Ethiopian territory into a thick historical space can be simply willed away. But it cannot. Both the Derg and the Meles regime had to resort to repression and violence to erase the historicity of Ethiopian territory and to reduce it to a blank

528. See Messay Kebede. *Survival and Modernization, Ethiopia's Enigmatic Present: A Philosophic Discourse.* Lawrenceville, NJ: The Red Sea Press, 1999, chapters 4 and 5 for an excellent discussion of the role of individual merit in Ethiopian culture.

slate on which "socialist" or "ethnic" spatial structures may be imposed arbitrarily.

Treating a historical entity as a tabula rasa is a strategy of oppression practiced by colonial powers, as one could see from the arbitrary colonial boundaries imposed on Africans and the Bantustan policy of the White minority Apartheid regime in South Africa. Paradoxically, the current minority ruling elite, the TPLF, has adopted the strategy of the Boers who, to impose their ethnic minority rule, also treated South Africa as a tabula rasa and imposed ethnicization as a basis for the territorialization and distribution of political power, ethnically fragmenting and disorganizing the population, and thus protecting the Boers' monopoly of power. Indeed, the 1994 Constitution engineered by the TPLF has unsettling similarities with the 1959 promulgation of the Bantu Self-government Act which proclaimed that "The Bantu people of South Africa ... form separate national units on the basis of language and culture," and declared that ethnic groups are "national units," giving each ethnic group the option to eventually become "independent."[529] However, all the essential institutions of power were in the hands of the Boers, clearly indicating that the "self-determination" the Boers were offering to the various ethnic groups was nothing but a disguise for a policy of divide-and-exploit.

Similarly, the TPLF-penned 1994 Constitution fragments Ethiopians into "nations, nationalities, and peoples" (art. 8) and gives each ethnic group "the right to secession" (art. 39). The parallel between the Apartheid regime and the regime imposed by the TPLF is noted also by S. Huntington who, though a friend of the EPRDF regime, writes on the ethnicization of politics in Ethiopia: "[T]he TGE redrew regional boundaries in Ethiopia so as to create ethnic-based regions where none previously existed. As a result, the EPRDF...made ethnicity the controlling consideration in national politics...This attempt to classify people by ethnic background is reminiscent of practices which used to exist in...South Africa. It seems totally contrary to a political process one of whose purpose is to promote a common Ethiopian national identity. It also seems inappropriate in a country in which a substantial portion of the population is of mixed ethnic

---

529. P. Harries, "Exclusion, Classification and Internal Colonialism: The Emergence of Ethnicity Among the Tsonga-speakers of South Africa," in Leroy Vail, *The Creation of Tribalism in Southern Africa*, London, James Currey. p. 104. Dunbar T. Moodie, *The Rise of Afrikanerdom: Power, Apartheid, and the Afrikaner Civil Religion*, Berkeley, University of California Press, 1975; Robert M. Price, *The Apartheid State in Crisis: Political Transformation in South Africa 1975-1990*, New York, Oxford University Press, 1991.

background...The combination of ethnic territorial units and ethnic parties, however, cumulates cleavages and can have disastrous effect on national unity and political stability." [530]

The TPLF's complete and unqualified adoption of "colonial theory" is at the root of the policy of wiping away their ancestors' effort to construct a history common to all — Adwa being the highlight of this construction — and of the collective consciousness and identity whose emergence in Adwa came, as Ethiopians shall see below, as a surprise to Europeans in general, and to Italians in particular. Out of this "table rase" treatment of Ethiopia came forth the recognition of Eritrea as an Ethiopian "colony," the creation of ethnic liberation fronts as "anti-colonial" movements, and the reorganization of Ethiopia as an ethnic federalism wherein each ethnistan enjoys the right of secession.

But the history of societies that have tried to make "table rase" of the past, Pol Pot's Cambodia being the extreme case which brings out clearly the pathological essence of such a practice, indicates that such a path leads into a dead end where politics invariably morphs into violence. Even thinkers as dissimilar in their philosophies as Edmund Burke and Karl Marx agree on this point. Burke condemned the practice of the man who thinks that he can "consider his country as nothing but carte blanche, upon which he may scribble whatever he pleases."[531] From a radically different angle, Marx noted, "Men make their own history, but they do not make it just as they please; they do not make it under circumstances chosen by themselves, but under circumstances directly encountered, given and transmitted from the past."[532] Both argued, from different perspectives, to be sure, that one reaps political tragedies when one acts as if there is no historical context to one's political actions. The "socialist revolution" of the Derg and the "ethnic revolution" of the TPLF confirm these somber observations.

It must be emphasized that both "revolutions" are the political outcome of the "colonial thesis" or the "nationalities question." The quandary with this thesis is that it cannot grasp the historical trajectory that made the unity of Adwa possible; it cannot reveal the contradictions that emerged from Adwa; it

530. Samuel Huntington, "Political Development in Ethiopia: A Peasant-based Dominant-Party democracy?" *Report to USAID/ETHIOPIA on Consultations with the Constitutional Commission 28 March — 1 April 1993*, dated 17 May 1993. pp. 15-16. TGE stands for the Transitional Government of Ethiopia set up and controlled by the TPLF after it took over Ethiopia by force of arms in 1991.

531. Quoted in R. Harrison, *Democracy*, London, Routledge, 1993, p. 67.

532. K. Marx, *The Eighteenth Brumaire of Louis Bonaparte*, New York, International Publishers, 1969, p. 15.

cannot explain why and how these contradictions developed over the last century into a political and economic system that inflicted systematic harms on all Ethiopians; it cannot account for the repeated failures of reforms and revolutions undertaken to resolve these contradictions. This failure should not be surprising, for a distorted reading of one's history is a recipe for political and social disorientation, confusion and alienation, surreptitiously transforming one's actions into acts of subversion of one's declared goals.[533] The only conclusion one can draw from this history of failures is that the "colonial thesis" or the "nationalities question" has no handle on the problems and contradictions of Ethiopian society because the thesis is patently false.

To show the falsity of the "colonial thesis" is not however to deny the oppression to which Ethiopians have been subjected for centuries. Ethiopian rulers have inflicted on the people sufferings which are probably no less painful than the ones European colonialism has inflicted elsewhere. That these sufferings were and are still inflicted by Ethiopian rulers does not make them more palatable. However, the way these sufferings and their causes are conceptualized conditions the nature of the political actions that are required to overcome the sources of these sufferings. This is precisely why Ethiopians need a critical theory that has the conceptual resources that could make their history and society intelligible without making them alien to their own history and society.

Those who conceptualize the historical process of Ethiopian state building, Adwa being one of its highpoints, in terms of "colonialism" conflate two historically distinct phenomena — state-building (internal oppression) and colonialism (external oppression).[534] Whereas colonial power is an alien presence that can be removed by attaining independence — and modern African history indicates that independence does not equate with freedom, equality and social justice — the overcoming of internal oppression cannot be accomplished without the transformation of the state into a democratic one. The current ethnicization of Ethiopian history and the politicization of ethnic self-determination as the right of secession do not in anyway deal with the issue of internal oppression and democratization.[535] Ethnic secession simply changes the identity of the oppressor. What is lacking in such an approach is a critical understanding of Ethiopians as a historical subject.

---

533. J. Owensby, *Dilthey and the Narrative of History*, Ithaca: Cornell University Press, 1994, p. 137. The EPRDF regime's policy is curiously reminiscent of Ubu Roi's fantasy, "S'il n'y avait pas de Pologne il n'y aurait pas de Polonais!" A. Jarry, *Ubu*, Paris: Gallimard, 1931, p. 130. The equivalent being, "If there is no Ethiopia, there won't be any Ethiopians."

IV. "Regions," or Reading Ethiopia from Within

To make sense of their past and present, Ethiopians need to discard the colonial thesis and consider the Ethiopian polity as it manifested itself at Adwa. Ethiopian unity at Adwa, expressed in the creation of the first national trans-ethnic army in Ethiopia's history, was the outcome of a "longue durée"[536] historical trajectory whose internal dynamic of national integration was articulated in terms of "regions,"[537] such as Gojam, Wallo, Showa, Wallaga, Sidama, Tigre, Harar, etc. The regions were mostly trans-ethnic, historically formed political domains. Its inhabitants and the inhabitants of other region saw every region as an organic part of a larger historical entity — Ethiopia. The ruling elites of the regions saw themselves primarily as members of the ruling class of Ethiopia. They used their regions as a platform for participating effectively in the national power structure rather than as a platform for ethnic closure. A singular outcome of this political orientation is the trans-ethnicity of the Ethiopian ruling class. Consequently, these regions are present in the collective memory of Ethiopians

---

534. Secessionist claims are based on the confusion between internal and external oppression. For a discussion of this see, C. W. McClellan, *State Transformation and National Integration: Gedeo and the Ethiopian Empire*, East Lansing: Michigan State University Press, 1988, p. 3, "What these secessionists refuse to admit is that their own subjugation was part of a much larger anticolonial struggle. Given the circumstances of the late 19th century, these peoples undoubtedly would have been subjugated, if not by an emergent Ethiopia, then by one of the surrounding European powers, most likely Britain or Italy. Eritrea in fact did go to the latter." Dr. Werku Aberra drew my attention to a similar stand taken by the Marxist economist, S. Amin, *Unequal Development*, New York, Monthly Review Press, 1976, pp. 332-333. He comments positively on Menelik's conquest of "the southern half of present-day Ethiopia...before the arrival of the Europeans" by contrasting it to "the wretched dependent societies established by colonialism in Africa." p. 332. However, one cannot dismiss the fact that Menelik's state building involved the violent imposition of state structures on peoples and areas which though within the Ethiopian historical space were nevertheless autonomous in many respects.

535. On the absence of a necessary relationship between democracy and independence, see C. Taylor, "Why do Nations Have to Become States?" S. G. French, ed., *Confederation: Philosophers Look at Canadian Confederation*, Montreal, The Canadian Philosophical Association, 1979, pp. 19-35. Indeed, the case of Quebec in Canada is instructive for demarcating the issue of independence from that of democracy. Quebec citizens have, in two referenda, in 1980 and 1995, rejected those who see their membership in Canada in terms of colonial relations, and they have defeated the independence option because they believe, and rightly so, that enjoying democracy is not necessarily a function of having an independent state. African post-colonial states provide ample proof of this. The secession of Pakistan from India, of Panama from Colombia, of Eritrea from Ethiopia has not resulted in democracy.

as diverse expressions of the Ethiopian historic community. Adwa is one of the manifestations of this "region" based Ethiopian unity and identity.

The outcome of this nation-region dialectics is an Ethiopian self-definition that portrays Ethiopia as a regionally rather than ethnically organized historical entity. Generally, a person was identified primarily by his or her region of origin and only secondarily by his or her ethnic background. One saw oneself and was seen by others as a Wallaga or a Walloyé, or a Showan, and so forth, to which some attached an ethnic or clan affiliation and others did not. With few exceptions, an ethnic label dissociated from its regional grounding had, and still has, limited meaning. This was because each "region" had its distinctive historical configuration and its unique "personality" of which ethnicity was only one of many strands, making regional identification rather than ethnicity the dominant mode of expressing one's identity. Even during the Zemene Mesafint, ethnicity was not a politically significant factor.[538]

This point cannot be overemphasized. Historically and sociologically, "the Amhara label has little meaning in the context of traditional provincialism, since the Amharinya-speaking population has been divided into clearly defined provincial units which serve as the foci of provincial attachments and provide the framework for collective action in defense of area interests."[539] The same may be said of the Oromo.[540] Though there are ethnic groups in Ethiopia, ethnic closure

---

536. F. Braudel, *Ecrits sur l'histoire*, Paris, Flammarion, 1969, pp. 41-83.

537. I use "region" in the sense of "terroir." The concept of "terroir" includes the idea that the geography of political practices is historically formed, that a given territory like Wallaga or Wallo is not a neutral geometric space but a historically thick ground formed by political practices. I use the term "terroir" to designate what some call "region." But the term "region" does not grasp the historical nature of what Ethiopians call "Hager Bet" as clearly as the term "terroir." The Amharic term "Hager Bet" refers neither to "Gosa" nor to "Zer" but rather to a non-ethnic conception of a commonly shared human space. Such an approach shows the destructive nature of treating a territory as a geometric neutral space that can be cut up for political expediency as the Italians and the Derg before and the Meles regime now have done. J-F. Bayart, *L'Etat en Afrique*, Paris, Fayard, 1989, p. 322, for the concept of "terroir."

538. D. Crummey, "Society and ethnicity in the Politics of Ethiopia During the Zamana Masafint" *International Journal of African Studies* vol8, 2, 1975, pp. 271ff.

539. J. Markakis, *Ethiopia: Anatomy of a Traditional Polity*, pp 46-7.

540. C. Clapham, *Transformation and Continuity in Revolutionary Ethiopia*, pp. 216-7, "Underlying the absence of any united Oromo action at the time of the crisis of the regime in 1977-78 was the difficulty of identifying any politically coherent Oromo identity, and the same problem has likewise reduced the effectiveness of the OLF since that time. " And then goes on to show how in fact the Oromos, like the Amharas, articulate their identities in terms of provinces rather than in terms of ethnic-genealogical identification.

has not been a goal pursued by any of them. Indeed, ethnic politics is not historically the major content of the political actions and processes that formed the Ethiopian polity. Regions, with overlapping and interacting ethnic cultures, were the frameworks of interest definitions and collective actions, and the leaders of these regions were primarily interested in influencing or appropriating the power at the center rather than pursuing ethnic separation. A telling example of this is Ahmad ibn Ibrahim, known as Ahmad Gragn, who in the first half of the sixteenth century tried to conquer the whole of Ethiopia rather than consolidate his power in Adal and secede from the Ethiopia of the time.[541]

The nation-region dialectic was the basis of the national unity that emerged at Adwa as Ethiopia's "modern" form of national identity. But this cannot be fully grasped in terms of "multi-ethnicity." The latter presupposes a billiard-ball view of ethnic groups which conceptualizes them as self-enclosed entities, existing side by side without interactions other than the ones occasioned by the struggles for domination.[542] The notion of "multi-ethnicity" is mechanical and reductive and does not grasp the historical particularity of the Ethiopian polity, that is, its trans-ethnicity — the interaction of people of diverse origins; the mix and overlaps of cultures and beliefs; the inter-penetration of social practices and of social spaces. But trans-ethnicity does not mean cultural homogeneity and political harmony. It is, as Ethiopian history shows, a

541. Joseph Cuoq, *L'Islam en Ethiope*. Paris, Nouvelles Editions Latine, 1981, pp170-176.

542. For a critique of the conception of culture as "separate, bounded and internally uniform," see M. Carruthers, *Why Humans Have Cultures: Explaining Anthropology and Social History*, Oxford, Oxford University Press, 1992. There is an amazing blindness to the inter-ethnic character of Ethiopian cultures among those who espouse a billiard-ball conception of *ethnies* in Ethiopia. This is due to the fact that some who study Ethiopia still work with the 19th century idea that cultures are internally homogeneous and have fixed boundaries. This leads one into adopting a billiard-ball conception of ethnic groups and prevents one from seeing that the trajectory of Ethiopian history offers something quite different. This old conception of culture is what underlies a comment such as: "Where Oromo culture was fragile, Amhara culture was durable. Where the Oromo were inclined to associate with one another as equals, the Amhara were disposed to rule." D. N. Levine, *Greater Ethiopia*, Chicago, The University of Chicago Press, 1974, p. 164; or "The Gallas had little to contribute to the Semitized civilization of Ethiopia; they possessed no significant material or intellectual culture..." E. Ullendorf, *The Ethiopians*, London, Oxford University Press, 1973, p. 73. Some ethnic nationalists in Ethiopia generally espouse the billiard-ball conception of *ethnies* of 19th century anthropology, which by the way, was the legitimating knowledge of colonial practices such as "indirect rule" or the artificial creation of tribal chiefs in areas where there were none. Many African countries are paying a heavy political price from the institutionalization of such a billiard-ball conception of ethnic groups. The most tragic examples are Burundi and Rwanda.

process of interactions that has both regional and national levels and that is permeated at each level by the conflicts and contradictions generated by the various forms of domination and exploitation practiced by the local and national ruling elites. But these conflicts and contradictions were also instrumental in weaving a national identity by creating deeply intertwined interests, putting in motion the transformation of closed and territorial ethnic identities into fluid and non-territorial ethnicities, making the Ethiopian space a commonly shared trans-ethnic space. In such a historical context, emancipation need not, and cannot, presuppose ethnic or territorial secession; rather, it underlines the idea that emancipation of the local cannot but be a function of the emancipation of Ethiopians as a whole. This of course requires a conceptualization of the people that recognizes them as historical agents.

V. Conceptualizing the Ethiopian People

Adwa is an event that reveals Ethiopia in its generic multiplicity. To grasp the historical identity that unifies this multiplicity Ethiopians need to abandon the current conceptualization of Ethiopians as raw matter on which the rulers imprint their will to serve their own interests. The conditions that made possible Adwa impose the imperative of conceptualizing Ethiopians in a way that grasps the historical agency embodied in that event. But, the post-Adwa historical experience, the rise and fall of Haile Selassie and the Derg, and the irruption of ethnic politics in 1991, show that the historical agency that manifested itself at Adwa cannot be taken for granted. It needs to be critically retrieved if contemporary emancipatory practice is to have roots in the soil of Ethiopian history and successfully overcome the resistance of those whose interests are not served by the redemption of the hopes for freedom and social justice of their ancestors.

A conceptualization of Ethiopians from the perspective of emancipation presupposes making a distinction between the understanding of Ethiopians as historical agents and Ethiopians objectified as the "masses" or "ethnies" by the ideological constructions of the ruling elites. But a conceptualization that reflects the interests of emancipation cannot be achieved in a mechanical way by simply changing one's perspective from that of the ruling elite to that of the people, because the self-understanding of the Ethiopian "people" is also partly infected by the hegemonic elite-centered discourse and is therefore an understanding which is systematically distorted, as the ethnicization and fragmentation of the Ethiopian democratic opposition to tyranny demonstrates since the 1960s.

Throughout history, the ruling elites have used Ethiopians for the accumulation of power and wealth. Ethiopians have resisted this oppression, mostly in localized revolts and as shiftas.[543] In the elite-centered discourse, the resistance to the rulers' oppression and exploitation — the silent and the vocal, the armed and the unarmed, the secular and the religious — is marginalized, distorted, repressed, or demonized. The reigning ideology has, since Adwa, defined the people in terms of the interests of the ruling elites, creating internal chasms and barriers, divisiveness and mutual suspicions among Ethiopians, and has sapped the development of a unified nation-wide resistance against internal oppression comparable to the one achieved at Adwa against external oppression.

Two contradictory aspects of the Ethiopian ruling elites' ideological conceptions of Ethiopians are worth considering. The first is that which, contrary to the experience of Adwa and all the historical evidence, treats Ethiopians as a homogeneous population. This simplification was the basis of the Emperor Haile Selassie's and the Derg's destructive policies of centralization that denied the diversity expressed in the regional embodiment of Ethiopian political life. Under Haile Selassie, this led to the abolition of the Ethiopian-Eritrean federation and to the repression of demands for autonomy in Gojam, Tigray, the Ogaden, and Bale, all historically defined regions. Forced centralization was pursued by the Derg with even more destructive zeal. And yet, the sort of "feudal federalism" of historically defined regions that was at the basis of the national unity that made Adwa possible shows that centralization and homogenization are not prerequisites for national identity and unity. The sense of Ethiopian identity at Adwa emerged through the recognition of the region — based nature of the Ethiopian polity.

The second aspect is that which denies the historical existence of a commonly shared Ethiopian political, economic and cultural space and treats Ethiopia as a mere aggregate of discrete ethnic groups. This simplification is the basis of the ethnic essentialism that has led to the EPRDF's ethnicization of space, history, and politics. Here also, the experience of Adwa shows that ethnic essentialism is alien to the self-understanding of Ethiopians, for the successful mobilization of various ethnicities into a single national resistance movement

543. G. Tareke, *Ethiopia: Power and Protest — Peasant Revolts in the Twentieth Century*. Cambridge: Cambridge University Press, 1991.

against the Italian invasion indicates that being Ethiopian was the content that gave meaning to the participants' actions irrespective of their particular origins.

The difficulty now is that Ethiopians cannot abandon the hegemony of the elite-centered ideology and adopt a people-centered approach without unmasking and dismantling the systematically distorted political culture that has, in part, permeated the people's own self-understanding. The failure to found democracy in Ethiopia, despite the monumental sacrifices made by Ethiopians since 1960 suggests that Ethiopians do not as yet have a critical theory capable of generating an understanding that demystifies the elites' hegemonic ideology and conceptualizes the people, both in their plurality and in their unity, as a single historical subject, as agents who created Ethiopian history, and as agents who can accomplish their own emancipation and create their own future.

Historically then, the "internal" battle of Adwa revolving around the issues of freedom, equality and social justice is far from settled. It is time then to set aside Adwa as a victory over an external enemy and rethink it as an unfinished battle against the internal enemies that keep the people of Ethiopia in bondage.

Adwa: The Unfinished Battle

A critical appropriation of Adwa offers a starting ground for a historically rooted critique of their political ideals, projects and practices; provided that Adwa is rendered intelligible as an event whose principal significance resides in its internal rather than its external dimension.

That this internal dimension is the real issue with which Ethiopians have to contend in the post-Adwa period did not escape the perspicuous Wylde in 1896. He wrote, "Before the country settles down to modern civilization...a civil revolution must take place, and which may not be far distant. There are all the elements now ready in the country to make this uprising and it will be no doubt the great turning point in its history, and whether Abyssinia is to remain a despotic monarchy or to enjoy freedom of a better and more enlightened rule."[544]

Indeed, Adwa created the circumstances that led to the birth of a modern political critique. In the 1920s and '30s, what Wylde called "the elements" triggered the first indigenous and critical political reflection. The issues of feudalism, development and governance were discussed by intellectuals such as

544. A. B. Wylde, *Modern Abyssinia*, London: Methuen, 1901, p. 3. Emphasis added.

Gabre Hiywet Baikedagn, Asbe Hailu, Afework Gabreyesus, Blata Deressa, and others.[545] These writers were, in the words of Bahru Zewde, "among the most articulate group of intellectuals that Ethiopia ever had."[546] To appreciate the qualitative change that emerged in the post-Adwa political horizon, one must note the shift from personal loyalty (loyalty to the ruler) to loyalty to one's country that emerged in some of these writings, particularly in that of Baqqala habta-Mikael.[547] Their critique of the traditional organization of power and their new outlook on politics were trenchant for their time. Even more significant is their effort to articulate their critique in a national language, Amharic, rather than in a European language, as was the practice in the European colonies, thereby making their ideas accessible to the indigenous reading public.

It is not therefore surprising that, for the first time in the history of Ethiopia, Adwa opened an internal discursive space for a critique of power that dealt with Ethiopia as a whole. The Ethiopian intellectuals in the immediate post-Adwa period availed themselves of this political-theoretical opening that Adwa offered and developed their critique of the prevailing order in a way which was rooted in the constitutive meanings of Ethiopian social practices and institutions.[548] In the 1920s and '30s an "intellectual Adwa" was in the offing. A new consciousness of the possibility for extending the historical agency awakened in the war against the Italian invasion to the internal battle against oppression was in gestation. But this beginning of the Ethiopian Enlightenment was cut short by the 1935-1941 Fascist invasion.

The promising beginning of critical reflection instigated by the "elements" that emerged from Adwa did not have time to flower. In 1937, after the attack of Abraha Deboch and Moges Assgedom against the Italian Viceroy, Marshal Graziani, the Blackshirts were unleashed on the educated class. As Greenfield noted in 1965, twenty-eight years after the massacre of the Ethiopian intelligentsia, "Ethiopia has not yet recovered from this cruel blow. Two to three hundred educated young Ethiopians...perished with the thousands of ordinary folk who were murdered. Today amongst the educated there is to some extent a missing generation. Had they lived...?"[549]

---

545. For an exhaustive discussion for the writings of the intellectuals of the immediate post-Adwa period, see Bahru Zewde, *Pioneers...* op. cit.
546. Ibid. p. 209.
547. Ibid., 197.
548. Ibid, pp. 162-207.
549. R. Greenfield, *Ethiopia: A New Political History*, London, Pall Mall Press, 1965, p. 240

The post-fascist restoration of the Crown was not accompanied by the rebirth of the intellectual ferment of the 1920s and '30s. Rather, the intellectual vacuum created by the "missing generation" facilitated the Emperor's policy of co-opting intellectuals and refashioning their ideas to strengthen his grip on power. To this purpose, he articulated modern ideas with traditional modes of social interpretation, foreign capital and imported weapons. The Emperor's successful centralization of power was a defeat of the potential for radical change — both practical and theoretical — insofar as the social and political contradictions, which were calling for radical reforms, were sidestepped by Haile Selassie's "passive revolution."[550]

But the underlying instability of the system continued to grow, spurred now by the increasing integration of Ethiopia into the world capitalist market, making the need for an indigenous, critical and reflexive understanding of Ethiopian society to guide emancipatory actions even more urgent.

After the failed coup d'état of 1960, there was a feverish quest for a theoretical understanding capable of transforming Ethiopian reality. But contrary to the intellectual ferment of the 1920s and '30s, there was, this time, a massive and uncritical dependence on external theories, mainly Leninism and Maoism, and especially, as discussed earlier, on the imported theories of "colonialism" and the "nationalities question." Ethiopian social practices, past and present, were subjected to concepts that were internal to the histories of Russia and China; and, contrary to the practice of the immediate post-Adwa intellectuals who reflected and wrote on Ethiopian issues in Amharic, the language analyzes the intellectuals in the '60s and after was more often than not English, a language disconnected from the constitutive meanings of Ethiopian social practices. The disconnection of these borrowed theories from the inter-subjective and common meanings of Ethiopians may be gauged from the fact that even literate Ethiopians needed a special dictionary to understand the theoretical analyses that were supposed to guide the social practices of the people![551] In this "radical" discourse Ethiopian peasants were depicted as a suffering mass but never as the active agent of historical transformation. This role was reserved to the English-language theorizing elite.

To take up Greenfield's question, "Had they [the intellectuals of the 1920s and '30s] lived...," would the generations of the 1970s and '80s have had at their

550. Gramsci, op. cit, pp. 106-120
551. Teramaj Mezgebe Kalat; Yesensa-HAssab Kalat Mefcha, Central Matemia Bet, Addis Ababa, 1978 (EC).

disposal an indigenous tradition of a systematic critical discourse that could have saved Ethiopia from the tyrannies of Leninism, Maoism, and ethnicism? Would the latter generations of intellectuals have been better equipped to criticize, fertilize and sublate the borrowed theories in ways that could have transformed them so that they could have measured up to the specificity and complexity of Ethiopian history and society? These are difficult questions to answer. But the questions underscore the urgent need for reviving the process of critical, internal reflection that was initiated by the intellectuals of the 1920s and '30s; not so much in terms of the content of their ideas, for Ethiopians now live in circumstances that bear within themselves new questions and challenges, but rather in terms of their methods that put primacy in raising questions internal to the social practices and history of the Ethiopians in a language that cashes into their inter-subjective and common meanings. This is the unfinished "intellectual Adwa" that needs to be resurrected and brought to fruition if Ethiopians are to be spared another round of destruction in their struggle against the new forms of oppression and exploitation introduced by ethnic politics and globalization. An internally generated emancipatory theory needs historical depth if it is to capture the hearts and minds of Ethiopians. A critique of Adwa as a historical process of national resistance to external oppression out of, which emerged the questioning of internal oppression, offers this historical depth.

VII. A Preliminary Critique of "Adwa the Unfinished Battle"

From the perspectives of the thousands who participated in the campaign of Adwa, the resistance to the Italian invasion embodies the aspiration for freedom, equality and unity as well as the rejection of colonialism. It stands at the beginning of modern Ethiopia as the first national blow against oppression, albeit in its external form. The manifest content of the Ethio-Italian conflict, the military victory that the ruling elites ensconce, is a completed event. Its latent content, that the ruling elites occlude but which is the force that has been driving the political struggles of the entire post-Adwa period, is the unfulfilled promise of freedom, equality, and social justice. This unfulfilled promise has worked itself into the present as an unfinished task of their history.

Adwa and the Quest for Freedom and Equality

Adwa is probably the first battle in their history in which Ethiopians from every corner of the land participated to resist foreign aggression. "[T]he great upheaval was proceeding from the Tigrayan Mountains of the North to the Gallas and Somalis in the South; every tucul and village in every far off glen of Ethiopia was sending out its warriors in answer to the war-drum," wrote Berkeley.[552]

The fighting force that Menelik marshaled was indeed made up of peasants from the eastern, western, southern, central and northern regions of Ethiopia.[553] Some may say that the peasants did not have much choice, and that they had to obey the orders of their lords on pain of being punished. Though there might be a measure of truth in this claim, to consider this as the only reason for why soldiers and peasants from the four corners of Ethiopia went to fight at Adwa betrays one of the assumptions that informs the elite-centered narration of Ethiopian history — that Ethiopians are a tabula rasa, a predicate of their rulers, a people whose motivating purposes in life are of external origin, to wit, their rulers.

Hess notes that, "No study of this period can pretend to be serious unless it takes into account the aspirations of the Ethiopian monarchs..."[554] But for such a study to be worthwhile, such a narrow perspective is insufficient for it leads to an elite-centered discourse whose distorting outcomes Ethiopians have already pointed out. Rather, a wider perspective that includes the aspirations of the common men and women who participated in the campaign allows them to discover, in the gaps that separate the motivations of the rulers from the aspirations of the people, the hopes of the common people for whom fighting in Adwa was also an act of faith in a better future.

True, the motivations and goals of the "monarchs" are more easily accessible to the scholar insofar as the rulers have a monopoly of institutional memory recorded in documents and monuments. Such records are rare with regards to peasants. Their hopes for a better future, their yearning for freedom from poverty and arbitrary rule are inscribed in their stories, values, beliefs, social practices, and deeds. Not recognizing the collective memory in which these are embedded as the repository of the peasants' hopes for a better world is reducing them to the

552. Berkeley, p. 126.
553. Wylde, pp. 199ff.
554. R. L. Hess, "Italian Imperialism in its Ethiopian Context," *The International Journal of African Historical Studies*, VI, 1973, p. 102.

status of passive victims of their conditions. It is precisely because the reforms and revolutions that have been imposed on Ethiopians are based on the reduction of peasants to a mere suffering mass, in need of liberators, and on the refusal to recognize them as the agents of their own social transformation, that Ethiopian peasants are still victims of repeated famines, absolute poverty and lack of freedom.

If one then wants "to be serious," to borrow Hess's words, one has to take into account the collective memory of the people and enucleate from them the aspirations, however inchoate they might be, which motivated the common men and women to fight in Adwa, fully understanding the grave risks to limb and life they were taking in confronting an enemy which they all knew had superior weapons. Treating them as a mass, as a people without an inner life, mechanically obeying their masters, is to succumb to the ruling elites' objectifying conception of the Ethiopian people; it is to consider them as humans without hopes and dreams of a better life. But this cannot be, for they could have indeed chosen not to fight or fight on the opposite side.

In 1896, Ethiopia did not have a European-style tightly organized and highly disciplined army, with officers exercising strict control over the conduct of their soldiers. Ethiopians came by foot, carrying their weapons and supplies, from every corner of the land, to risk their lives in Adwa. Such valorous actions do not spring spontaneously from the soil, nor can they be explained in terms of mere obedience. The current ethnicist reading of Ethiopian history as a process of "colonization" cannot explain the crucial role-played at Adwa by soldiers from the western, eastern and southern regions, without whose remarkable exploits the victory of Adwa would not have been possible.[555]

This massive mobilization of Ethiopians cannot be reduced either to a mere military campaign, a forced zemecha. If Ethiopians do so, Adwa appears as a silent monument in their history, a glorious one to be sure, but with no connection to the concrete history of the people — the aspirations and struggles for freedom and equality. The massive mobilization of Ethiopians at Adwa expresses more than the simple desire to resist foreign aggression. It signifies the yearning for and the pre-appearance of a future of freedom and equality. In sacrificing themselves to defeat an external oppressor, in rejecting Italian oppression, those who fought in Adwa sowed the seeds of the rejection of oppression tout

555.Tekle Tsadik Mekuria, chaps. 25 and 28.

court. This is the latent content of Adwa, the driving force of the diverse forms of political resistance and revolts from 1896 to the present.

Adwa and the Quest for National Unity

One can also see in the actions of the people who flocked from all corners of Ethiopia to Adwa, the practical emergence of a new and an indigenously rooted modern principle: that regional, linguistic, religious and ethnic difference need neither be denied nor be transformed into identity prisons. This sense of belonging to the Ethiopian historic community did not operate in opposition to the local self-definitions that Ethiopians of diverse region had. On the contrary, the circumstances that made Adwa possible reflected the recognition that particular self-definitions could be fully articulated and expressed as dimensions of Ethiopian identity.

Ethiopian history has always been characterized by competition, hostility, division and wars between the various nobles and kings. "Rivalry and disunity," writes Rubenson, "were, indeed, prevalent facts in the shaping of Ethiopian politics..."[556] This is a political tradition which in many cases saw Ethiopian ruling elites use foreign forces as pawns to further their own interests: Emperor Tewodros had to confront alone a foreign army with whom Dejazmach Kassa, the future Emperor Yohannes, collaborated to ensure the fall of Tewodros; Emperor Yohannes did not receive the support of Emperor Menelik in his fight against the Dervishes for Menelik was more interested in clearing a path to the throne by making his rival fall; and both Tewodros and Yohannes paid with their lives their lonely stand against their foreign enemies.

The novelty of Adwa lies in the fact that for the first time in Ethiopia's history, all the important political forces agreed to sacrifice their particular interests and stood together in order to ensure the independence of Ethiopia. When the Italian aim of dismantling Ethiopia — in the words of the Italian foreign minister Blanc, "An Ethiopia subdivided into various states, none preponderant and all equally dependent upon us..."[557] — became clear, those Ethiopian leaders who in the traditional fashion considered using the Italians as pawns to promote their particular interests abandoned their relations with Italy. The Italian governor of Akele Guzay, Bahta Hagos, deserted the Italians. Ras Sebhat and Dejazmach Hagos Teferi abandoned their alliance with Italy and

556. S. Rubenson, p. 404.
557. Quoted in H. Marcus, *The Life and Times of Menelik I*, p. 170.

defected to Menelik. Ras Mengesha stopped flirting with Italy and joined the Ethiopian fold. Eritrean auxiliaries refused to go to battle against "our country and King.'" [558] The Italian scheme to engineer a split between Muslims and Christians also came to naught.

The Italians, and subsequently, the European powers, were forced to recognize that something whose existence they denied — a modern Ethiopian national identity[559] — was manifesting itself at Adwa. But entrapped as they were in their European prejudice and unwilling to recognize a different historical form of "modern national identity," they categorized Ethiopian nationalism in a negative manner. Thus General Baratieri explained it away as a unity motivated by "hatred against the Whites."[560] Baratieri, of course, got it wrong. While the Italians denied the existence of an Ethiopian nation by dichotomizing it into "Galla and Abyssinia," "Christians and Muslims," the inter-ethnic Ethiopian troops effectively put an end to Italy's ambitions, affirming in their deeds that Ethiopians saw themselves as a nation.[561]

True, some may object that there were other motivations behind the maneuverings of the political leaders who joined Menelik. There might well be: human motivations are never simple. Whatever might have been the intentions of those who joined the Ethiopian fold after flirting with the enemy, such intentions do not necessarily exclude the motivation that arises from these leaders' self-definition as Ethiopians. Moreover, one should not discount the persuasive force of their peasant-soldiers' self-understanding as Ethiopians and their

558. S. Rubenson, p. 405.

559. Some may object to my use of the terms "modern," "nation" and "nationalism" to describe Ethiopian events that took place in 1896. Such an objection is based on a "diffusionist" conception of modernization. But the failures of modernization theories and of the practices premised on them have given credence to the idea that there are different kinds of and routes to modernity and its constituent elements may differ from society to society insofar as the inception and development of modernity express in important ways the historical trajectory of each society. The literature on this issue is enormous. For an interesting reflection, see J. F. Bayart, op. cit. ; J. Manor, ed., *Rethinking Third World Politics*, London: Longman, 1991.

560. S. Rubenson, p. 405.

561. It is interesting to note that currently all those who deny that contemporary Ethiopia is a nation expressing an inter-ethnic identity prefer to use the name "Abyssinia," a term, first used by the Portuguese (1535-1541) and whose knowledge at the time was limited to north-west Ethiopia. This appellation was then used by European colonial powers to signify and legitimate their designs to split southern Ethiopia from northern and central Ethiopia. See the Treaties between England and Germany (1890), and Italy and England (1891). "To be called 'an Abyssinian' is still resented by the Ethiopian," observed Berkeley in 1902, p. 4, fn. 1.

resentment in seeing their leaders side with an enemy bent on destroying the independence of Ethiopia.

Thus, at Adwa, a new principle was recognized and inscribed in the Ethiopian political landscape — that national identity and interests sublate political, regional, religious, and ethnic identities and interests (without, however, denying the legitimacy of such identities and interests).

Emperor Menelik, described by Berkeley as "a typical Jacob [who] will work seven years or twice that time to accomplish an object," and by Sanderson as "a subtle and far-sighted diplomat with, at times, an almost Bismarckian capacity for keeping several irons in the fire," and by Ras Alula, a scion of the Tigrayan nobility and no friend of Menelik, "as the only man who would restore order, and...unite [Ethiopia] once more,"[562] played an important role in the forging of this unity, an achievement that Baratieri described as a "miracle,"[563] and whose surprise at this manifestation of Ethiopian nationalism is indicative of Italy's, and Europe's, misreading of Ethiopian history.

But Emperor Menelik did not conjure up this unity out of the blue. Nor was the national unity that manifested itself at Adwa an accident. Rather, it was successfully achieved because there was already a dense, evolving historic community aware of its common and shared destiny. It was the outcome of a "longue durée" historical process whose internal dynamic of national integration was, as indicated earlier, articulated in terms of regions. Though rooted in asymmetrical power relations between the various regions, Adwa articulated a national rather than an ethnic conception of self-determination, and marked the indigenous emergence of a modern conception of a nation as an "imaginary community," to borrow Benedict Anderson's expression.[564]

This "imaginary community" has, however, its own historical content. It eschews the destructive notion of a homogeneous nation — the assumption that was the basis of the policies of centralization adopted by Emperor Haile Selassie and the Derg. In denying the autonomy of the region or regions on which Ethiopian unity is founded historically, centralization sowed the seeds of disunity. On the other hand, the historically formed Ethiopian nation cannot be recog-

562. G. F. Berkeley, p. 15; G. N. Sanderson, "The Foreign Policy of Negus Menelik," Journal of African Studies, 1964, 4, p. 93; Ras Alula quoted in Haggai Erlich, Ethiopia and Eritrea During the Scramble for Africa: A Political Biography of Ras Alula, 1875-1897, East Lansing: Michigan State University, 1982, p. 189.

563. Berkeley, p. 104.

564. B. Anderson, *Imagined Communities*, London, Verso, 1983.

nized in terms of the notion of ethnic-genealogical identity either. The "regional" bases of this "imaginary community" had distinct historical personalities, understood and accepted as a variation on the Ethiopian theme. Consequently, the current (EPRDF's) effort to erase these regions, and their historically formed Ethiopian content, and replace them with ethnicstans cannot but lead to destructive conflicts for the same reasons — the denial of the historical personalities of these regions — that led to the failure of centralization. The secession of Eritrea, the Badme war between Ethiopia and Eritrea, the ethnic conflicts in southern Ethiopia, and the ethnic massacres in the Gambella region[565], the ethnicization of political competition to an extent that the incumbent Prime Minister, Meles Zenawi, has tried to win the 2005 elections by raising the specter of an Ethiopian "Interahamwe,"[566] could be seen as harbingers of similar destructive trends in the future.

Adwa, Anamnestic Solidarity, and Democracy

When their knowledge of the past is a mere collection of events with no discernable meaningful connection amongst them, the best Ethiopians could attain is a spontaneous historical consciousness. But this offers no consistent vision of the present and future, precisely because the present and the future appear to be blank slates on which anything could be written. In this sense, "The ability to define the meaning of the past grants power to define the meaning of the present and future."[567] It is then not surprising that one of the most persistent ideological position of the EPRDF regime was to define the meaning of the Ethiopian past as a collection of ethnic conflicts and, correlatively, to redefine Ethiopia as a colonial entity that came into existence in the nineteenth century. In the words of Dawit Yohannes, the former legal adviser of Meles Zenawi and current Speaker of the House, "Ethiopians say there is no country called Ethiopia..."[568] To extricate themselves from this trap of spontaneous historical consciousness, Ethiopians have to develop a critical historical consciousness, capable of helping them grasp the Ariadne thread of resistance to oppression that runs through centuries of Ethiopian history, from the collapse of the Axumite empire, through the fall of Zagwe dynasty, the turmoils of the

565. Targeting the Anuak: Human Rights Violations and Crimes against Humanity in Ethiopia's Gambella Region, Human Rights Watch March 2005 Vol. 17, No. 3(A).
566. Associated Press, May 5, 2005.
567. Steven Best, *The Politics of Historical Vision.* New York, The Guilford Press, 1995, p. xii.
568. *Financial Times*, May 5, 1995. See also footnotes 28, 30, 32.

Zemene Mesafint, the internal conflicts that characterized the regimes of Tewedros, Yohannes, Menelik, Haile Selassie, the Derg, down to the Meles regime.

Ethiopian history is characterized by numerous local conflicts and by individual rebellions (shiftas), or region-based revolts of peasant men and women against the exploitation and oppression of their lords. It is certainly the case that peasant revolts in Ethiopia have been local. "None of the revolts," writes Tareke in one rare and impressive study of peasant revolts in Ethiopia, "was capable of upsetting the whole system of social organization, nor was that its goal."[569] This is true of all the past peasant struggles in Ethiopia. Still, the interpretation that limits the meanings of these rebellions to acts that "seek to protect a vanishing world"[570] suffers from the empiricist refusal to practice a hermeneutics of hope capable of extricating from the revolts of the down-trodden and from "the accumulated rage born of the frustrated hopes of the past" [571] the aspirations for a life free from oppression. That Ethiopian peasants have often expressed their hopes in idioms of a golden past age may be true; that their vocabulary for articulating their hopes for a better world is incompatible with the modern vocabularies of emancipation may also be true. But to infer from this that what the peasants want is the recreation or maintenance of a "vanishing world" is a fallacy that flows from the empiricist assumption that what the peasants say are brute data whose meanings are transparent. It is this assumption that prevents them from enucleating from the peasants' resistance the aspiration for a life without unnecessary suffering that is expressed in the "non-synchronism"[572] inscribed in their conception of a past golden age as a source of solutions to contemporary problems. The deeds of the peasants, whatever the immediate meanings attributed to them might be for rebelling against their lords or for fighting at

---

569. G. Tareke, *Ethiopia: Power and Protest — Peasant Revolts in the Twentieth Century*. Cambridge: Cambridge University Press, 1991, p. 199.
570. Ibid. p. 3.
571. E. Bloch, "Dialectics and Hope," *New German Critique*, 1976, 9, pp. 3-10.
572. E. Bloch, "Nonsynchronism and the Obligation to its Dialectics," *New German Critique*, 1977, 11, pp. 22-28.

Adwa, were internally biased towards hope in the future;[573] they were expressive of aspirations for a better life.

The dissociation of resistance to external oppression — Mekdella (1868), Gundet (1875), Gura (1876), Dogali (1887), Mettema (1889), Adwa (1896) — from resistance to internal oppression, and the empiricist reading of various "local" revolts as discrete and unrelated acts, reduces their history into cyclical local conflicts and make it a concatenation of allegory events and fortuitous incidents. Such a reading of their history which does not go beyond narrating the facts as objectively given discrete data prevents them from recovering from their history the emancipatory themes that run through it and excludes the powerful potential of memory as a force for emancipation.

In order to avoid rendering their history into a purposeless succession of events, external and internal acts of resistance must be unpacked to uncover the common threads of emancipatory intention that connect them. Ethiopians need to bring together the struggles against the various forms of oppression that characterize the Ethiopian historical landscape so as to show that the Ethiopian tradition of rebellions and shiftas and the successful campaign of Adwa do indeed express shared latent aspirations for freedom from oppression and poverty. Adwa offers an excellent entry point into such an inquiry, because, where as one may argue that resistance to external aggression such as Mekdella (1868), Gundet (1875), Gura (1876), Dogali (1887), Mettema (1889), did not go further than recreate the existing political order, an argument which this author believes fails to see the inner link of these events to the idea of oppression tout court, Adwa cannot be so easily contained as a mere victory against external aggression that ensured the stabilization of the old order. As Ethiopians have seen earlier, it uniqueness lies in that it could be seen as a "Truth Event,"[574] insofar as it opened up, for the first time in Ethiopian history, a new political horizon and a novel struggle for a different and better future, a struggle with which Ethiopians are still entangled. A serious obstacle to recovering the emancipatory force of this struggle, and to achieving the freedom and prosperity Ethi-

573. Ibid. That peasants use the idioms of a golden past age imposes upon the student the obligation to enucleate the emancipatory intention born by these idioms. The reference to a golden age expresses the quest for a "better future" or a "better life" that is not fulfilled in the past and is "not yet" realized. The idioms of a golden past age express the continuation of the inherited memory for a world without unnecessary suffering.

574. Alain Badiou, op. cit. See footnote 1.

opians have yearned for since Adwa, is its isolation from the myriad acts of resistance to oppression and exploitation which punctuate Ethiopian history.

It is only by discovering and recovering the threads of emancipation that wind themselves through the labyrinth of the various acts of resistance to internal and external oppression that Ethiopians can bring intelligibility and universality to the innumerable conflicts that characterize the history of Ethiopia. Otherwise, the past events of Ethiopia appear devoid of purpose and direction, or, as Hegel put it writing about us, "In...Africa, history is in fact out of the question. Life there consists of a succession of contingent happenings and surprises. No aim or state exists whose development could be followed; and there is no subjectivity, but merely a series of subjects who destroy one another."[575] Hegel's description of Africa may be an expression of the ignorance of the history of the continent that characterized his epoch. But the point he is making could also be understood to mean not that events have not taken place in Africa, but, rather, more importantly, that these events have not been appropriated by Africa's people in a way which shows freedom as the purpose that animates the deeds of their ancestors.

The issue is thus not lack of deeds but their refusal to recuperate them in their actions to further the struggle for emancipation, and thus render them intelligible. What Ethiopians lack is "anamnestic solidarity" [576] — a solidarity with their ancestors through an active remembering of their struggles and a commitment to bring about to fruition their unfulfilled hopes for a more humane world. From this perspective, what for them is still the living core of Adwa is not the victory over Italy, but rather that this victory was rooted in an exclusive order which had no place for the great majority of those who fought and sacrificed their lives and made possible the victory. In failing to see this still active meaning of Adwa, Ethiopians fail to see the interconnections between it and the seemingly disparate struggles against local oppressors, and between these and their current predicaments, and treat Ethiopian history as a mere "succession of contingent happenings and surprises." In the process, Ethiopian unity loses the liberating sense it inherited as its telos from, to use Donald Levine's expression, the "in-gathering" of Ethiopians at Adwa. If what Hegel said about them in 1830

575. Hegel, *Lectures on the Philosophy of World History*, Cambridge, Cambridge University Press, 1975, p. 176.

576. Christian Lenhardt, "Anamnestic Solidarity: The Proletariat and its Manes," *Telos* 25, 1975, pp. 133-54. The reader will note that I am using Lenhardt's concept in a more expanded sense.

still seems to ring true in light of their compulsive treatment of Ethiopia as a tabula rasa, the responsibility is ours and not their ancestors'. Ethiopians lack the historical consciousness and the anamnestic solidarity without which their democratic project will be like a house of cards that will collapse at the slightest political tremor.

Ethiopian Democracy and Critical Theory

The absence of critical reflection internal to Ethiopian society and history has currently left them with knowledge that is just enough to make them see the extent of their failures without however giving them the intellectual tools that permit them to understand and overcome them. This tragic situation of being impotent witnesses to their own descent into tyranny, ethnic politics and poverty presents a stark contrast to the vitality and imagination that ensured the success of Adwa.

Questioning, observing, describing and analyzing one's own society and history in a way which is rooted in and interpolates one's own social practices, inter-subjective meanings and collective memory generates a liberating potential that being observed, described and analyzed by others does not. When Ethiopians are being studied, they are the objects of the intellectual curiosity of others who are producing knowledge to extend the knowledge fund of their society and to deepen their self-understanding. When Ethiopians study themselves, and make themselves the audience of such studies, they become reflexive subjects struggling to uncover the questions and ideas that will help them overcome the internal and external adversities that keep them in bondage.[577] In the process, they develop an internal intellectual tradition that provides criteria of relevance and truth, standards of discourse and judgment, that allow them to identify, conceptualize and discuss critically their historical experiences and contemporary issues from within their life-world. Such an internal critical intellectual tradition makes questions about ends central to their reflection and generates a culture

577. Messay Kebede. Survival and Modernization, Ethiopia's Enigmatic Present: A Philosophic Discourse. Lawrenceville, NJ: The Red Sea Press, 1999. 460pp. This is probably the first book by an Ethiopian that offers a systematic and critical reflection on the kinds of self understandings that are available to Ethiopians from within their history.

that internalizes democracy as a fundamental value without which Ethiopia will continue to be mired in a sea of oppression and poverty.

"Immaturity" as an Obstacle to Democracy

There is something immeasurably important in engaging in such a critical reflection. By systematically reading their history and social practices internally and critically, and by trying to understand the sources and implications of their understandings and self-understandings, Ethiopians will definitely overcome one of the most difficult obstacles in their quest for democracy and prosperity — the obstacle that Kant identified as "immaturity."

"Immaturity," wrote Kant, "is the inability to use one's own understanding without the guidance of another. This immaturity is self-incurred if its cause is not lack of understanding, but lack of resolution and courage to use it without the guidance of the other. The motto of enlightenment is therefore: Sapere aude! Have courage to use your own understanding."[578]

Adwa demonstrates that their ancestors were more "enlightened" and mature than them insofar as they had the "resolution and courage" to use their own understanding. It is this kind of "resolution and courage" that led them to triumph against both external and internal adversity — a powerful enemy and internal division. their post-Adwa history, on the other hand, clearly shows that in uncritically espousing Eurocentrism — the reading of their history, politics and society in terms of theories borrowed uncritically from the West — Ethiopians have retreated into "immaturity." Unlike their ancestors, Ethiopian intellectuals of today lack the "resolution and courage" to use their own understanding; they uncritically borrow answers that others have developed for their own specific historical questions. As a result, the potentialities for freedom, equality and social justice that inhabit their collective memory are left unrealized.

Facing the Dark Side of History

A recovery of Adwa as an "internal" event is an invitation to appropriate critically their history — that which led to Adwa and that which emerged from it — and to enucleate the emancipatory themes with which it is pregnant. But a recovery of the unfulfilled hopes of the past from their present vantage point will

578. I. Kant, "What is Enlightenment?" in H. Reiss, ed., *Kant's Political Writings*, Cambridge: Cambridge University Press, 1980, p. 54.

inevitably fail if it is not conducted as a critical, reflective long march through the effective history that lies between the present and the past. Such a long march through their history will force them to confront the painful questions Ethiopians have so diligently repressed: Why and how have Ethiopians made possible the tragic unfolding of their modern history into a landscape of poverty and oppression? Such a question is productive only and only if Ethiopians are willing to embrace all of their history frankly and critically.

To embrace Ethiopian history frankly and critically means to see it as both "a document of barbarism"[579] and a document of civilization, and thus understand why many of their compatriots consider Ethiopia as a prison from which they have to escape. It is to recognize how their past is rendered unbearable by their neglect to critically reflect on it, to extirpate its repugnant elements, and to overcome the relations of domination and exploitation that are the dark side of their history and the hidden face of Adwa. Critical theorizing demands that Ethiopians embrace their history as both a history of oppression and of struggles for freedom. Otherwise, Ethiopians will be caught in an endless cycle of failures, political violence and injustice.

Conclusion: From Adwa to Democracy in the Third World

Ethiopian history is representative of Third World history; but, in general, history is in an important sense "an unending dialogue between the past and the present."[580] Adwa is not just an event that transpired somewhere in the distant past; it looms in the collective memory of Third World peoples because their present circumstances are in dialogue with the internal consequences of Adwa. That is to say, as long as the peoples of the Southern Hemisphere do not consciously and critically appropriate the subterranean dialogue between their past and present history, they will continue to be blind to the underlying social and political causes that make and unmake their lives and their countries. Indeed, if that is the case, the peoples of the Third World will remain helpless, uncomprehending victims.

---

579. W. Benjamin noted that "There is no document of civilization which is not at the same time a document of barbarism." This is true of their history as it is true of all other histories. W. Benjamin, *Illuminations*, New York: Schocken Books, 1976, p. 256.
580. E. H. Carr, *What Is History?* New York: Vintage Books, 1961, p. 35.

Many lands were under foreign occupation in 1896, but at Adwa, the peoples of the South triumphed over colonialism. Nevertheless, today many nations remain weak because of internal divisions. Ethnic politics and religious fundamentalism can do incalculable harm when they destroy that unity of purpose that is required to found a solid national state. An equally alarming force, the imposition of globalization and its ideology of the primacy of the market, cheapens the day-to-day life of the common man. Neither the forces of the global market nor ethnic politics, religious fundamentalism nor political terrorism is driven by the quest for democracy. Rather, they serve to perpetuate a state of neocolonialism by keeping many "developing" nations weak and needy. If social justice is to come to the peoples of the Third World, including Ethiopians, they must learn from past successes and failures.

Appendix: Amharic Version of the Wuchalé Treaty

የኢጣልያ፡ንጉሡ፡ዑምበርቶ፡በስሙ፡መንግሥቱ፡
የኢትዮጵያ፡ንጉሠ፡ነገሥት፡ዳግማዊ፡ምኒል
ክ፡ለኢትዮጵያ፡መንግሥትና፡ለኢጣልያ፡መ
ንግሥት፡የሚጠቅም፡ለልጅ፡ልጅ፡የሚኖር፡
ሰላምና፡ዕርቅ፡ለማጽረጋ፡የፍቅርና፡የንግድ፡
ውል፡ተዋዋሉ። የኢጣልያ፡ንጉሥ፡ከንቴ፡አን
ቶኔሊን፡በኢጣልያ፡መንግሥት፡ዘውድ፡ኒ
ሻን፡ከማንዷቄሬ፡ተብሎ፡የተሾመ፡በእልፍ
ዘርና፡በሞሪስ፡ንሻን፡ከባሊዬሬ፡ተብሎ፡የ
ተሾመ፡ተመርጦ፡እንደራሴ፡ሆኖ፡ወደ፡ንጉሠ፡
ነገሥት፡ምኒልክ፡መጡ፡ሥልጣኑ፡ተቀብሎ፡
የተላከ፡የተቀበለውንም፡መጡ፡ሥልጣን፡
በንጉሠ፡ነገሥት፡ምኒልክ፡ፊት፡በርጓፒ፡
የተቀበለ፡ከለሆነ፡ንጉሠ፡ነገሥት፡ምኒል
ክ፡የኢትዮጵያን፡አልጋ፡የወረሱ፡እርሶዎ፡ሹ
ልሞኑ፡ደጃዝን፡ከዚህ፡ቀጥሎ፡የተጻፈውን፡የ
ውል፡ከኢትዮጵያ፡ንጉሠ፡ነገሥት፡ምኒልክ፡
ጋራ፡ተዋዋልን።

መጀመርያ፡ክፍል።
በኢጣልያና፡በኢትዮጵያ፡ንጉሠ፡ነገሥት፡
መካከል፡በወራሾቻቸውም፡በሕዝባቸ
ውም፡እነዚህንም፡በተጠጉ፡ሕዝብ፡መካ
ከል፡ሰላምና፡ፍቅር፡ሳይጓጐል፡ለዘወትር፡
ለልጅ፡ልጅ፡ይኖራል።

፪ተኛ፡ክፍል።

እነዚህ፡፪ቱ፡እሁን፡የተዋዋሉት፡ነገሥታት፡
በየአገራቸው፡በምዕልኒዎቻቸው፡ይነጋገሩ

ሎ፡ ፩ዱ፡ ከ፩ዱ፡ አገር፡ ቈንስልም፡ የቆንስል፡ ወኪ
ልም፡ መሾም፡ ይቻላቸዋል፡፡ እነዚህም፡ ሹሞቹ፡
እንዲ፡ ኤዎሮፓ፡ ነገሥታት፡ ሥሬት፡ መሾፈርና፡
መከበር፡ እዲጉድልባቸውም፡፡

፫ተኛ፡ ክፍል፡፡

በነዚህ፡ በ፪ቱ፡ ነገሥታት፡ ወሰን፡ ጠብና፡ ክር
ክር፡ እንዲይነሣ፡ በውቅ፡ የተሠፈሩ፡ ከ፪ ወገ
ኖቹ፡ ፪ ፪ ሽማግሎች፡ ልክው፡ በማይጠፋ፡ ም
ልክት፡ የሓዘቱን፡ ድምበር፡ ይወስናሉ፡፡ ከ፪ወ
ምበፊ፡ ወዲህ፡ የሚጨምሩት፡ አገሮች፡ እነዚህ፡
ናቸው፡፡

የዲጋው፡ አፋፍ፡ ከኢትዮጵያም፡ ከኢጣሊያ፡ ማኸ
ል፡ ወሰን፡ ይሆናል፡፡

ከራፋሌ፡ ዣምሮ፡ ኳለዪ፡ ሰገነዪቴ፡ አስመራ፡
፫ቱ፡ የኢጣሊያ፡ መንግሥት፡ መንደር፡ ይሆናሉ፡፡

ዳግመኛ፡ በቦግስ፡ በኩል፡

አዲ፡ ነፋስ፡ አዲ፡ ዋንስ፡ በኢጣሊያ፡ ድምበር፡ ው
ስጥ፡ ይሆናሉ፡፡

ከአዲ፡ ዋንስ፡ መንደር፡ ዣምሮ፡ ከምሥራቅ፡
ወዲ፡ ምዕራብ፡ በቀና፡ ይከፈላል፡፡

፬ ክፍል፡

የዲብረ፡ ቢዘን፡ ገዳም፡ ከነጕልቱ፡ ከነርስቱ፡ የኢ
ትዮጵያ፡ መንግሥት፡ ርስት፡ እንደሆነ፡ ይቀራል፡፡
የጦር፡ እምብ፡ መሆን፡ ግን፡ አይቻለውም፡፡

፭ተኛ፡ ክፍል፡፡

ከምጽዋ፡ የሚወጣ፡ የንግድ፡ ዕቃ፡ የሚገባም፡
የንግድ፡ ዕቃ፡ ከ፻ ፰ በገቢ፡ ዕቃው፡ እየተገመገመ፡

ሽንቢ፡ ፩ጊዜ፡ ይከፍላሉ።

፮ተኛ፡ ክፍል።

የጦር፡ መሣርያ፡ ንግድ፡ በምጥዋና፡ በኢትዮጵያ፡ መካከል፡ የሚመላለሰው፡ ለንጉሠ፡ ነገሥት፡ ብቻ፡ ይፈቀድላቸዋል። ሲያስመጡም፡ በለማፋቶም፡ የቢዲቢዎን፡ ለኢጣሊያ፡ ሹማምት፡ እየላኩ፡ ያስመጣሉ። ነፍጡንም፡ የያዘውን፡ ሰፈር፡ ከምጥዋ፡ ጀምሮ፡ እስከ፡ ኢትዮጵያ፡ ድምበር፡ ድረስ፡ የኢጣልያ፡ መንግሥት፡ ወታደሮች፡ ዘበኛ፡ ሁነው፡ ይሸኛሉ።

፯ተኛ፡ ክፍል።

የነዚሁ፡ የ፪ቱ፡ ውል፡ ያደረጉ፡ ነገሥታት፡ ዜጎች፡ የንግድ፡ ዕቃቸውን፡ ይዘው፡ ያ፩ዱ፡ ከ፩ዱ፡ አገር፡ መሄድ፡ መምጣት፡ ይቻላቸዋል። በየመንግሥቱና፡ በየወረዳው፡ ባለው፡ ሹም፡ ጥቃነት፡ የሱ፡ ጥበቃቸው፡ ይመላለሳሉ። ነገርግን፡ ከ፪ቱም፡ ወገኖች፡ የጦር፡ መሣርያ፡ የያዘ፡ ብዙ፡ ሁኖ፡ ከ፩ዱ፡ ድምበር፡ ወደ፡ ፩ዱ፡ ድምበር፡ መተላለፍ፡ ተከልክሎ፡ አለ። እንዲሁም፡ ማለት፡ ፩ዱ፡ ያ፩ ከብት፡ እንዳይዝርፍ፡ በሁሉም፡ ነገር፡ እንዳይነካካ፡ ተከልክሎ፡ አለ።

፰ ክፍል፡

የኢጣሊያ፡ ሰዎች፡ በኢትዮጵያ፡ የኢትዮጵያ፡ ሰዎች፡ በኢጣሊያ፡ የኢጣሊያ፡ መንግሥት፡ በሚገዛውም፡ አገር፡ ቢሆን፡ እንዲገቡ፡ ልማድ፡ መግዛት፡ መሸጥ፡ መከራየት፡ ይቻላቸዋል።

፱ ክፍል፡

የነዚህ፡የ፪ቱ ነገሥታት፡ዜጎች፡፩ዱ፡ከ፩አገር፡ቢ
ሄድ፡በየሄዱ ማኖሪያቸው፡ይኖራሉ።

፲ኛ፡ክፍል።

የኢጣሊያ፡ሰውና፡የኢጣሊያ፡ሰው፡የተካሰሱ፡እ
ንዲሆን፡እነዚያ፡በመረጡት፡ዳኛ፡ያለዚያም፡
ተያይዘው፡ምጥዋ፡ወርደው፡ይዳኛሉ።
የኢጣሊያና፡የኢትዮጵያ፡ሰው፡የተጣላ፡እንደ
ሆነ፡ግን፡የኢትዮጵያ፡መንግሥት፡ወኪልና፡የኢ
ጣሊያ፡የምጥዋ፡ሹም፡እንድነት፡ሁነው፡ይዳኛሉ።

፲፩ኛ፡ክፍል፡

የኢጣሊያ፡ሰው፡በኢትዮጵያ፡የሞተ፡እንደሆነ፡
የኢትዮጵያ፡ሰው፡በኢጣሊያ፡አገር፡የኢጣሊያም፡
መንግሥት፡በሚገዛው፡አገር፡የሞተ፡እንደሆነ፡ከ
ሟቹ፡መንግሥት፡ወገን፡ገንዘቡን፡የሚቀበል፡ሰ
ው፡እስኪመጣ፡ድረስ፡የ፪ቱ፡ነገሥታት፡ሹማምን
ት፡ገንዘቡን፡ጠብቀው፡ያስቀምጣሉ።

፲፪ኛ፡ክፍል።

በማናቸውም፡ኋጢአት፡ተከሶ፡የተያዘውን፡የኢ
ጣሊያ፡ሰው፡በኢጣሊያ፡ሹማምንት፡ይዳኛል፡ስለ
ሆነ፡ግን፡ታላቅ፡ኋጢአት፡ሰርቆ፡የተገኘን፡የኢ
ኢጣሊያን፡ሰው፡ፈጥነው፡ይዘው፡ለምጥዋ፡ሹማ
ምንት፡መስጠት፡ነው። ደግሞ፡በኢጣሊያ፡መንግ
ሥት፡ግዛት፡የኢትዮጵያ፡ሰው፡ታላቅ፡ኋጢአ
ት፡ሠርቆ፡የተገኘ፡እንደሆነ፡በኢትዮጵያ፡ዳ
ኛ፡ይዳኛል።

፲፫ተኛ፡ክፍል፡

የኢትዮጵያ፡ንጉሠ፡ነገሥትና፡የኢጣሊያ፡ን

ጉሥ፡ ብርቱ፡ ኃጢአት፡ የሰራ፡ ሰው፡ ከንጉሡ፡ ግዛ
ት፡ ወጥቶ፡ ፩ ግዛት፡ ሸሽቶ፡ የሄደ፡ እንደሆነ፡ ፪ቱም፡
እያሰሩ፡ ይልካሉ።

፲፬ተኛ፡ ክፍል፡

የባርያ፡ ንግድ፡ በክርስቲያን፡ ሃይማኖት፡ የተ
ከለከለ፡ ስለሆነ። የኢትዮጵያ፡ ንጉሠ፡ ነገሥት፡
በሚችሉቸው፡ ነገር፡ ሁሉ፡ በግዛቸው፡ ባርያ፡ እ
ንዳይነግድ፡ ይከለክላሉ።

፲፭ተኛ፡ ክፍል።

ይህ፡ አሁን፡ የተደረገው፡ ውል፡ ለኢትዮጵያ፡ ሁሉ፡
መንግሥት፡ ውል፡ ነው

፲፮ተኛ፡ ክፍል፡

ይህ፡ ውል፡ በተደረገ፡ ካ፭ ዓመት፡ በኋላ፡ ከ፪ቱ፡
መንግሥት፡ አንዳቸው፡ ውል፡ ለመጨመር፡
ወይም፡ ለመለወጥ፡ የፈለጋቸው፡ እንደሆነ፡
ከ፩ ዓመት፡ በፊት፡ አስቀድሞ፡ መናገር፡ ይገባ
ቸዋል። ነገር፡ ግን፡ የንግድን፡ ውል፡ ብቻ፡ ማ
ስጠንቀቅ፡ ይቻላቸዋል፡ እንጂ፡ ዘሬ፡
ሬም፡ የተለየውን፡ የድምበር፡ ወሰን፡ ማፍረስ፡ እይ
ቻላቸውም።

፲፯ተኛ፡ ክፍል፡

የኢትዮጵያ፡ ንጉሠ፡ ነገሥት፡ ከኤዎሮጳ፡ ነገ
ሥታት፡ ለሚፈልጉት፡ ጉዳይ፡ ሁሉ፡ በኢጣሊ
ያ፡ መንግሥት፡ እጋዥነት፡ መላላክ፡ ይቻላቸዋ
ል።

፲፰ተኛ፡ ክፍል፡

የኢትዮጵያ፡ ንጉሠ፡ ነገሥት፡ ከሌላ፡ መንግ

ለስ ት ፡ ሰዋ ች ፡ ጋሬ ፡ ባ ግ ባ በ ባ ጓ ግ ዔ ፡ ነ ገ ር ፡ ለ መ
ወ ዋ ል ፡ ዋ ፈ ል ጉ ፡ እ ን ዲ ሆ ን ፡ ከ ፉ ፡ እ ማ ር ወ
ሲ ይ በ ቁ ፡ ይ ይ ች ም ፡ ዉ ል ፡ ፯ ዋ ሆ ኑ ፡ እ ን ዲ ሆ ኑ ፡ ለ
እ ጣ ሊ ይ ፡ ሰ ወ ፡ ይ ሰ ዉ ታ ል ።

፲ ሃ ኛ ፡ ክ ፍ ል ።

ይ ሀ ፡ እ ሁ ን ፡ ባ ተ ይ ረ ገ ወ ፡ ዉ ል ፡ በ እ ግ ዜ ር ኛ ፡ ና ፡
በ እ ጣ ሊ ይ ፡ ቋ ን ቋ ፡ ት ክ ክ ል ፡ ሆ ና ፡ ተ ገ ል ብ ጠ ፡ ሲ ፡
ይ በ ቃ ፡ ሀ ተ መ ን ፡ ም ስ ክ ር ፡ ይ ሆ ና ል ።

፲ ክ ፍ ል ።። ይ ሀ ፡ እ ሁ ን ፡ ይ ተ ጸ ፈ ዉ ፡ ዉ ል ፡ በ ር ባ ን
ክ ፡ ባ ግ ፡ ሬ ጥ ና ፡ ይ መ ነ ቀ ታ ል ።።

ነ ገ ር ፡ ባ ግ ፡ ህ ሁ ፡ ዉ ል ፡ ከ ን ት ፡ ጢ ተ ሮ ፡ እ ን ዱ ፈ ል ፡
በ እ ጣ ሊ ይ ፡ ጓ ጉ ፡ ለ ስ ም ፡ ከ ን ጉ ፡ ሰ ፡ ፲ ግ ለ ት ፡ ም ፩ ፡
ል ክ ፡ ባ ሬ ፡ ቀ ዋ ወ ለ ወ ፡ እ ት ፡ መ ወ ፡ ጫ ር ሰ ዋ ል ።።
በ ም ዛ ይ ፡ በ ፬ ረ ቀ ግ ፡ በ ዝ ህ ዉ ፯ ዋ ወ ት ፡ ም ሕ ሬ ፡
ት ።። በ ዉ ጫ ለ ፡ ሰ ፊ ር ፡ ተ ጸ ፈ ።።

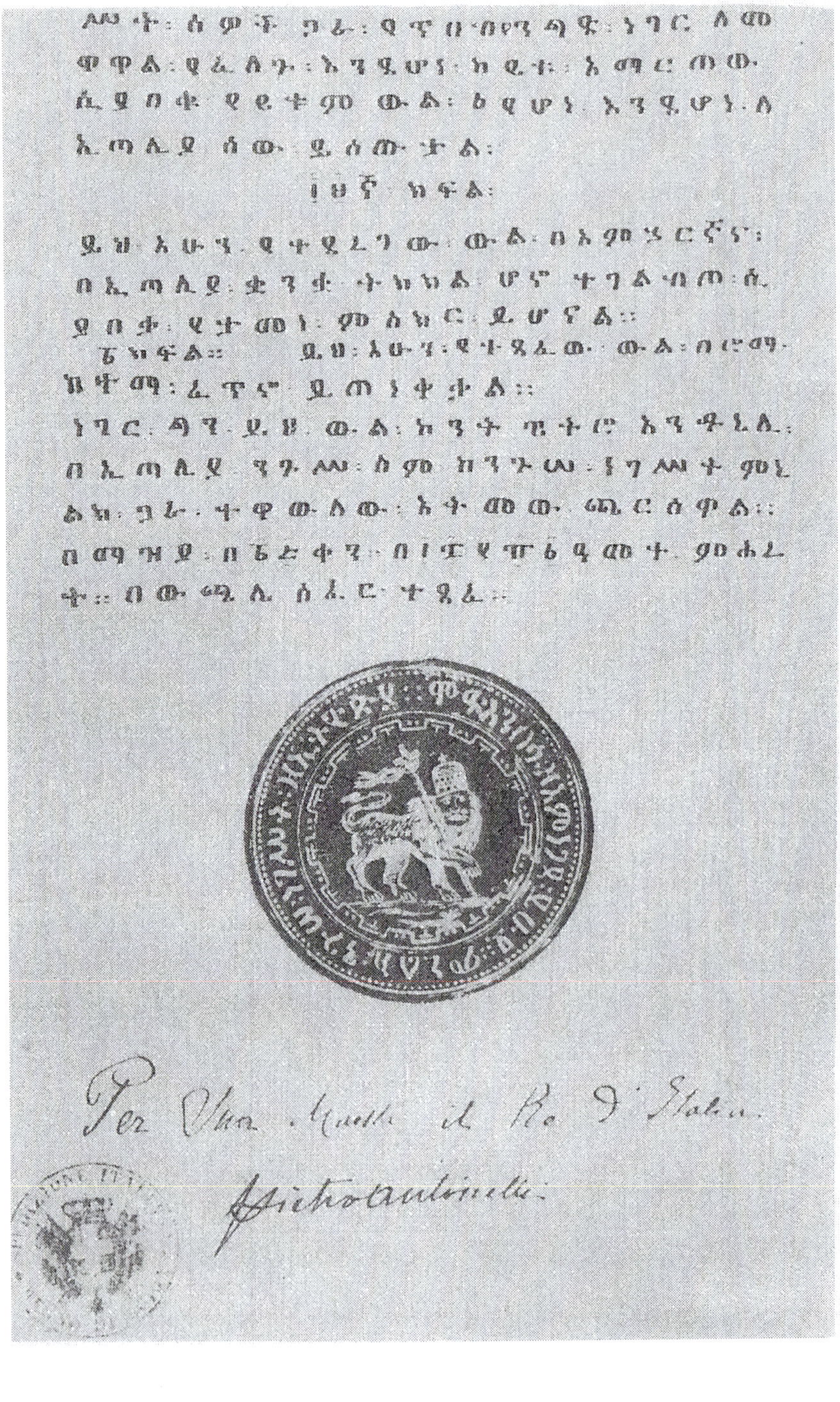

Per Sua Maestà il Re d'Italia

Pietro Antonelli

Contributors

Paulos Milkias, a former Canada Council Doctoral Fellow, is a professor of Humanities and Political Science at Marianopolis College/Concordia University in Montreal, Canada. He is Co-editor of the *Journal of North-East African Studies* [Michigan State University], Associate Editor of *Horn of Africa Journal* [Rutgers University], *International Journal of Ethiopian Development Studies* [Western Michigan University] and *International Journal of Ethiopian Studies* [Hollywood Calif.]. Dr. Milkias's book *Ethiopia: a Comprehensive Bibliography* [G.K. Hall/Macmillan and co.] was cited as an exemplary work by Oxford University Guide to Library Research. Dr. Milkias was a contributing editor of the *World Education Encyclopedia*, and a feature authors of the Politics, Government and Law section of *Encyclopaedia Aethiopica* [Hamburg University, Germany]. His *ABC of Ethiopian Christianity: a Concise Dictionary* was published by University Press of America, 2005.

Getachew Metaferia co-editor, teaches political science and coordinates the graduate program in International Studies at Morgan State University. Dr. Getachew Metaferia is associated with the Political Leadership Institute at Morgan State University, which, in collaboration with the National Association for the Advancement of Colored People (NAACP), provides leadership training. His publications include a book on the exodus of Ethiopia's educated classes and numerous scholarly articles and book chapters. He received his department's "Distinguished Service" award in 2005. Dr. Metaferia was also a recipient of Fulbright-Hayes awards and was assigned to Myanmar and Thailand (2002), and China (2004).

Richard Pankhurst has published 36 books and more than 400 scholarly articles. His seminal works, *The Economic History of Ethiopia*, Cambridge University Press, 1976, and *The Ethiopians: a History*, Oxford University Press, 2001, are classics in the field. He was awarded the prestigious title of Officer of the Order of the British Empire (OBE) for his contribution to Ethiopian studies in 2004.

Zewde Gabra-Selassie, Dejazmach, served as Governor and Mayor of the capital city of Addis Ababa, Minister of Public Works, and in other leadership positions during the reign of Emperor Haile Selassie of Ethiopia. As well as being decorated by the Emperor, he is a recipient among others of the GC of the Orders of Phoenix of Greece (1959) and Cdr. of the Orders of St Olav of Norway (1956). Dr. Dejazmach Zewde is also a distinguished African historian and is the author of many works including *Yohannes IV - Political Biography*, Oxford University Press – 1975; and *Eritrea–Ethiopia, In the context of the Red Sea and Africa*, Washington D.C, Smithsonian Institute, 1976.

Negussay Ayele, a former Ethiopian Ambassador to Scandinavia, is Professor of Political Science and International Relations. A cofounder of the African Association of Political Science, he has been awarded Fulbright, Ford, and Friedrich-Ebert Stiftung Fellowships. His recent books include *Ethiopia and the United States: The Seasons of Courtship* and *In Search of the DNA of the Ethiopia-Eritrea Problem*. He teaches for the Bunche Center for African-American Studies and for the Honors Collegium at the University of California in Los Angeles.

Harold Marcus was Distinguished Professor of History at Michigan State University. He was the founding editor of the refereed journal *Northeast African Studies*; he is perhaps best known for his biographies of Emperors Menelik II and Haile Selassie I, and his textbook *History of Ethiopia* [Oxford University Press]. He also authored numerous articles dealing with Ethiopia, and edited several monographs.

Theodore M. Vestal is professor of political science and international studies at Oklahoma State University. He holds degrees from Yale Law School, Harvard, and Stanford University. In 2005, Professor Vestal was Hiob Ludolf Endowed Professor in Contemporary Ethiopian Affairs at the University of Hamburg in Germany. His books include *Ethiopia: A Post Cold War African State*, Praeger, 1999.

Maimire Mennasemay teaches in the humanities/philosophy department of Dawson College, Montreal, Canada and is a fellow of the Center for Developing-Area Studies (CDAS) of McGill University. Dr. Mennasemay has published many scholarly works and is currently a member of the editorial board of

Labor, Capital and Society published by CDAS, McGill Universtiy, Montreal, Canada, *Horn of Africa Journal*, Rutgers University, and the *International Journal of Ethiopian Studies*, Hollywood, CA.

Mesfin Araya is Associate Professor of African Studies at York College/ City University of New York, where he is Head of African-American Studies. He has produced numerous scholarly works on Ethiopia and Eritrea, from a political science perspective; his next book analyzes Eritrean nationalism.

BIBLIOGRAPHY

Aquarone, A., L. De Courten, et al. (1989). *Dopo Adua : politica e amministrazione coloniale*. Roma: Ministero per i beni culturali e ambientali, Ufficio centrale per i beni archivistici.

Bairu, T., A. Ilg, et al. (2000). *Ethiopian records of the Menilek era : selected Amharic documents from the Nachlass of Alfred Ilg, 1884-1900*. Wiesbaden, Harrassowitz.

Baratieri, Oreste (1899). *Memorie d'Africa* (1892-1896). Paris, Delgrave

Bellavita, E. (1931). *Adua; i precedenti--la battaglia--le conseguenze (1881-1931)*. Genova: "Rivista di Roma".

Berkeley, G. F. H. (1902). *The campaign of Adowa and the rise of Menelik*. Westminster: A. Constable.

Berkeley, G. F. H. (1969). *The Campaign of Adwa and the Rise of Menelik*. New York.

Berkeley, G. F. H. *The Battle of Adwa*. London: Cambridge University Press.

Bulatovich, A. K. and R. Seltzer (2000). *Ethiopia through Russian eyes : country in transition, 1896-1898*. Lawrenceville, N.J.:Red Sea Press.

Caioli, A. and Universitá degli studi di Trieste. Dipartimento di scienze politiche (1998). *L'Italia e la questione etiopica alla vigilia della disfatta di Adua, 1885-1893*. Trieste: Dipartimento di Scienze Politiche Universitáa degli Studi di Trieste.

Cancogni, F. and M. Cancogni (1996). *Adua : Romanzo*. Milano: Longanesi.

Canuti, G. (1897). *L'Italia in Africa e le guerre con l'Abissinia : dall' occupazione di Massaua alla resa dei priogionieri dopo la battaglia d'Adua : narrazione storica*. Firenze: Adriano Salani.

Carlo Zaghi (1941). "L'Italia e l'Etiopia alla vigilia di Adua nei dispacci segreti di Luigi Capucci". *Gli annali dell'Africa Italiana* 4. 2.

Caulk, R. A. (1969). *Menelik II and the diplomacy of commerce; prelude to an imperial foreign policy*. Addis Ababa: Haile Sellassie I University.

Cicognani, L. and C. Zaghi (1935). *Pietro Antonelli e l'ambiente scioano nel diario inedito.* Ferrara: "Nuovi problemi".

Corticelli, (1896) *Inchiesta tecnicomilitare. sul combattimento del I. Marzo.* Roma.

Crispi, F. and L. Rossi (2000). *Sotto il Borbone non soffrii tanto : lettere di Francesco Crispi dopo Adua (1896-1898).* Roma: Carocci.

Crispi, F. and T. Palamenghi-Crispi (1914). *La prima guerra d'Africa.* Milano: Fratelli Treves.

Darkwah, R. H. K. (1972). *Menelik of Ethiopia.* London: Heinemann Educational.

Darkwah, R. H. K. (1975). *Shewa, Menilek, and the Ethiopian Empire, 1813-1889.* London: Heinemann Educational.

De Coppet, M. (1924). *Chronique du regne de Menelik II*, Bibliot: Univ. et revue de Geneve.

De Felice, R. (2000). *Breve storia del fascismo : con i due saggi "Il problema della identitáa nazionale" e "Dall'ereditáa di Adua all'intervento".* Milano: Mondadori.

Decleva, E. (1971). *Da Adua a Sarajevo. La politica estera italiana e la Francia. 1896-1914.* Bari: Laterza.

Del Boca, A. and D. Adorni (1997). *Adua : le ragioni di una sconfitta.* Rom: Laterza.

Del Boca, Angelo, , (1976). *Gli italiani in Africa Orientale.* Milano, vol. 1.

Diouf, S. A. (2000). *Kings and queens of East Africa.* New York: F. Watts.

Erlich, Haggai (1996). *Ras Alula and the Scramble for Africa.* New Jersey: Red Sea Press.

Gabra Selassie, Wolde Aregay. Tsehafe Teizaz. (1960). *Tarik Zemen ze dagmawi Menelik. Niguse Negest ze Etiopia* [Amharic] 'Chronicle of Menelik II. King of Kings of Ethiopia'. Addis Ababa: Berhanenna Selam.

Gaibi, A. and Italy. *Esercito. Corpo di stato maggiore. Ufficio storico.* (1928). Manuale di storia politico-militare delle colonie italiane. Roma: Provveditorato generale dello stato, Libreria.

Gleichen, E. (1898). *With the mission to Menelik, 1897.* London: E. Arnold.

Goglia, L. (1981). *Il colonialismo italiano da Adua all'impero.* Roma: Bari, Laterza.

Labanca, N. (1993). *In marcia verso Adua.* Torino: Giulio Einaudi.

Lombardi, E. (1994). *Il disastro di Adua.* Milano, Mursia.

Mekuria, Tekle Tsadik (1990). *Atse Menelik ena Ye -Ethiopia Andennet.* Addis Ababa: Kuraz Asatami Dirijit.

Mérab (1921). *Impressions d'Ethiopie : l'Abyssinie sous Ménélik II.* Paris: H. Libert.

Marcus, Harold G.(1994). *The Life and Times of Menelik I, 2nd ed.* Lawrenceville: NJ.

Marcus, Harold G. (1975). *The Life and Times of Menelik I: Ethiopia 1844-1913*, Oxford: Clarendon Press.

Marcus, H. G. (1975). *The life and times of Menelik II : Ethiopia 1844-1913.* Oxford: Clarendon Press.

Mersi'e Hazen Wolde Qirqos. G. Prunier, et al. (2004). *Of what I saw and heard : the last years of Emperor Menelik II & the brief rule of Iyassu.* Addis Abeba: Centre français des études ethiopiennes, Zamra Publishers.

Monfreid, H. d. (1954). *Menélik tel qu'il fut*. Paris : B. Grasset.

Morié, L. J. (1908). *L'Ethiopie et l'empereur Menilek*. Paris: Augustin Challamel.

Nadaillac (1898). *Ménélik II négus négusti, roi des rois de l'Ethiopie*. Paris: De Soye et fils, imprimeurs.

Orléans, H. P. M. (1898). *Une visite á l'empereur Ménélick. Notes et impressions de route*. Paris: Librairie Dentu.

Petrides, S. Pierre (1963). *Le Heros d'Adoua. Ras Makonnen. Prince d'Ethiopie*. Paris: Plon

Prather, R. (1981). *The king of kings of Ethiopia, Menelik II*. Nairobi: Kenya Literature Bureau.

Prouty, Chris(1986). *Empress Taytu and Menelik II*. Trenton, NJ.: The Red Sea Press.

Prouty, C. (1976). *A chronology of Menilek II of Ethiopia, 1844-1913, Emperor of Ethiopia, 1889-1913*. East Lansing, Mich.: African Studies Center.

Prouty, C. (1986). *Empress Taytu and Menilek II : Ethiopia, 1883-1910*. Trenton NJ: Red Sea.

Quirico, D. (2004). *Adua : la battaglia che cambiáo la storia d'Italia*. Milano: Mondadori.

Rainero, R. (1971). *L'anticolonialismo italiano da Assab ad Adua. (1869-1896)*. Milano: Edizioni di Comunitá.

Ropponen, R. (1986). *Italien als Verbundeter : die Einstellung der politischen und militarischen Fuhrung Deutschlands und Osterreich-Ungarns zu Italien von der Niederlage von Adua 1896 bis zum Ausbruch des Weltkrieges 1914*. Helsinki: SHS.

Rossetti, C. (1910). *Storia diplomatica dell'Etiopia durante il regno di Menelik II; trattati, accordi, convenzioni, protocolli, atti di concessione, ed altri documenti relativi all'Etiopia, corredati da note esplicative, un indice e due carte*. Torino: Societáa tipografico-editrice nazionale.

Rossini, Conti C. (1935). *Italia ed Etiopia dal trattato d'Uccialli alla battaglia di Adua*. Roma: Istituto per l'Oriente.

Rossini, Conti C. (1939). *La battaglia di Adua*. Roma: Edizioni Universitarie.

Roth-Rosthof, A. v. (1930). *Ba Menelik; erlebnisse mit abessinischen pflanzern, jagern, fursten und goldsuchern*. Leipzig: F. A. Brockhaus.

Rubenson, Sven. (1976). *The Survival of Ethiopian Independence*. London: Heinemann.

Rubenson, Sven (1970). "Adwa 1896: The Resounding Protest" in Robert I. Rotberg and Ali A. Mazrui (eds) *Protest and Power In Black Africa*: Oxford.

Salbucci, S. (1962). *Taitu, Empress of Ethiopia*. New York: Vantage Press.

Salimbeni, A. (1956). *Crispi e Menelich nel diario inedito del conte Augusto Salimbeni*. Torino: Industria libraria tipografica editrice.

Scovazzi, T. (1998). *Assab, Massaua, Uccialli, Adua : gli strumenti giuridici del primo colonialismo italiano*. Torino: G. Giappichelli.

Stella, G. C. (1966). *Adwa, a bibliography*. Addis Ababa: Addis Ababa University, Ye Etiopia Yetinatinna Mirimmir Tequam.

Tugnoli, G. (1978). *Adua*. Milano : Rizzoli.

Vanderheym, J. G. (1897). *Une expédition avec le Négous Ménélik; vingt mois en Abyssinie*. Paris: Librairie Hachette Press.

Veltzé, A. (1935). *Die Schlacht bei Adua am 1. Marz 1896, nach den Memoiren Baratieris*. Berlin: Junker und Dèunnhaupt.

Wellby, M. S. (1901). *'Twixt sirdar & Menelik; an account of a year's expedition from Zeila to Cairo through unknown Abyssinia*. New York: Harper and Brothers.

Welde Aregai, Gabre-Selassie (1966). *Tarike Zemen Ze-Dagmawi Menelik*, Addis Ababa: Berhan ena Selam.

Index

E

F

G

H

I

J

K

L

M